Theodore W. Whitley, Ph.D.
East Carolina University, Greenville

STUDY GUIDE
AND
COMPUTER WORKBOOK

for

STATISTICS
FOR
PSYCHOLOGY

FIFTII EDITION

Arthur Aron
State University of New York at Stony Brook

Elaine N. Aron
State University of New York at Stony Brook

Elliot J. Coups
Fox Chase Cancer Center

PEARSON
Prentice
Hall

Upper Saddle River, New Jersey 07458

© 2009 by PEARSON EDUCATION, INC.
Upper Saddle River, New Jersey 07458

10 9 8 7 6 5 4 3 2 1

ISBN 10: 0-13-604325-9
ISBN 13: 978-0-13-604325-6

Contents

Introduction

This Study Guide is designed to help you learn the material in the text by providing summaries of chapter contents and by providing self-tests at the end of each chapter consisting of the following:

- ∞ Completion items based on the Key Terms defined in the chapter.
- ∞ Multiple choice items to test your knowledge of important terms and concepts presented in the chapter.
- ∞ Practice problems to test your ability to perform the calculations presented in the chapter.

Responses to the practice problems in the Answer Key follow the computational format in the text and are intended to be sufficiently complete to help you identify any mistakes you may make. These responses also follow the five-step hypothesis testing process used throughout the text where appropriate. Chapters presenting analyses that can be conducted using a computer conclude with a section providing additional practice using SPSS.

Please note that no data were collected from any person, and although the studies are based on the author's research experience, no studies like those used as examples, to the author's knowledge, have actually been conducted. All data in the text examples and the practice problems were contrived to illustrate specific points, and the topics of the studies were designed to reflect studies that a psychologist might conduct. I hope you find that the contexts of these hypothetical studies hold your interest and provide additional insight into psychological research. I also hope the data clearly reflects the instructional points made by the authors of the text.

Chapter 1
Displaying the Order in a Group of Numbers

Learning Objectives
After studying this chapter, you should:
- Be able to differentiate descriptive statistics and inferential statistics.
- Be able to use the terms variable, value, and score correctly.
- Be able to explain the concept of levels of measurement and know the different levels at which variables may be measured.
- Be able to construct frequency and grouped frequency tables, and histograms.
- Be able to differentiate unimodal, bimodal, and multimodal frequency distributions.
- Know the differences between symmetrical and skewed frequency distributions.
- Know what floor and ceiling effects are.
- Be able to differentiate normal and kurtotic distributions.
- Know the ways that frequency tables and graphs based on them can misused.
- Know how frequency tables and graphs based on them are reported in research articles.

Statistics and the Two Branches of Statistical Methods
Statistics is the branch of mathematics that focuses on the organization, analysis, and interpretation of groups of numbers, or data.

Descriptive statistics are used to summarize and make groups of numbers more understandable.

Inferential statistics are used to draw conclusions based on the numbers actually collected during a research study, but going beyond these numbers.

Variables, Values, and Scores
A **variable** is a condition or characteristic that can have different values.

A **value** is a number or category that can result from the measurement of a variable.

A **score** is the value obtained by a particular person when a variable is measured.

Levels of Measurement
Numeric variables are also called *quantitative variables*. The three kinds of numeric variable are:

1. **Equal- interval variables** are numeric variables in which the numbers represent equal amounts of the condition or characteristic being measured. The intervals between the numbers are equal so that the distance between scores of 10 and 12 is the same as the distance between 22 and 24 or 43 and 45. When the scale on which a variable is measured has an absolute zero point, meaning that the person does not possess any of the characteristic or condition being measured, the scale is called a **ratio scale**. Equal-interval variables also can be discrete or continuous. **Discrete variables** have specific values and cannot have any values between these values. **Continuous variables** can have an infinite number of values between any two measured values. For example, the number of times a person receives therapy for depression in a year is a discrete variable, but the person's score on a depression inventory is a continuous variable because it is theoretically limited only by the precision of the inventory's measurement scale.

2. **Rank-order variables** are numeric variables in which numbers correspond only to the relative position of the person on the condition or characteristic being measured, i.e., the person's rank as first, second, and so on. Rank-order variables are also called *ordinal variables*. An example of an ordinal scale would be ranking a group of people on a scale using markers like "severely depressed," "moderately depressed," "somewhat depressed," and "not significantly depressed."

3. **Nominal variables** are also called *categorical variables* because the values represent names or categories.A person's gender or diagnoses of anxiety or depression are examples of nominal variables.

Thus, **levels of measurement** reflect the types of underlying numerical information provided by a measure.

Frequency Tables
Frequency tables show the number of individuals having each of the different values of a particular variable and are used to make the pattern of scores clear at a glance.

How to Make a Frequency Table
1. Make a list down the page of each possible value down the left side of a page, starting from the lowest and ending with the highest.
2. Go one by one through the group of scores, making a mark for each next to the corresponding value on the list.
3. Make a table showing how many times each value on the list is used.
4. Figure the percentage of scores for each value.

Frequency tables can also be made for nominal variables, e.g., the numbers of men and women with a diagnosis of depression.

Grouped Frequency Tables
Grouped frequency tables are used when there are so many possible values that a frequency table would be too large to give a simple account of the information. The intent is to create a group of values, called an **interval**, so that after entering all the scores that fall within a certain interval, the pattern is easier to see at a glance.

How to Make a Grouped Frequency Table
The steps for making a grouped frequency table are the same as those for making a frequency table except that intervals replace the listing of possible values in Step 1. for making a frequency table.. When determining the interval size, use a whole number that will result in 5 to 15 intervals. The lower limit of each interval should be a multiple of the interval size. For example, intervals including three values might look like this:

0–2
3–5
6 –8
9–11
12–14

Histograms
A **histogram** is a chart used to display the information in a frequency table graphically. It is like a bar chart except that the bars are placed next to each other with no space between them. The height of each bar corresponds to the frequency of each value in the frequency table or in each interval of a grouped frequency table.

How to Make a Histogram from a Frequency Table
1. Make a frequency table (or a grouped frequency table).
2. Place the scale of values along the bottom of the page from left to right and lowest to highest.
3. Make a scale of frequencies along the left edge of the page that extends from zero at the bottom to the highest frequency observed for any value.
4. Make a bar for each value that is as high as the frequency of the value it represents, making sure the middle of the bar is above its value on the horizontal axis.

Shapes of Frequency Distributions
A frequency table or histogram may be used to describe a **frequency distribution**, which shows the pattern of frequencies over various values, or how the frequencies are spread out or "distributed."

Unimodal and Bimodal Frequency Distributions
- A distribution with a single high peak is a **unimodal distribution.**
- A distribution with two approximately equal peaks is a **bimodal distribution.**
- A distribution with two or more peaks is a **multimodal distribution.**
- A distribution in which all the values have about the same frequency is a **rectangular distribution**.

A *frequency polygon* is a line graph that may also be used to display the information in a frequency table. The line extends from point to point with height at any point corresponding to the frequency of each value in the frequency table or in each interval of a grouped frequency table.

Symmetrical and Skewed Distributions

A distribution with approximately equal numbers of cases on both sides of the middle is a **symmetrical distribution**, the pattern of frequencies on the left and right sides of the distribution are mirror images of each other.

A distribution that clearly is not symmetrical is a **skewed distribution**. The side of the distribution that has fewer scores indicates the direction of the skew. That is, the direction of skew is the side with the long tail. A distribution that is skewed to the right—the positive side of the distribution – is also called *positively skewed*. A distribution skewed to the left—the negative side of the distribution – is also called *negatively skewed*.

In practice, highly skewed distributions in psychology are seen primarily when the variable being measured has an upper or lower limit. The situation in which many scores pile up at the low end because it is impossible to have any lower score is called a **floor effect**. The situation in which many scores pile up at the high end because it is impossible to have any higher score is called a **ceiling effect**.

Normal and Kurtotic Distributions

Distributions also may be described in terms of whether the middle is particularly peaked or flat. The standard of comparison is a bell–shaped curve, called the **normal curve**, that is widely approximated psychological research and in nature generally. (This curve will be described in detail in Chapter 3.) **Kurtosis** describes how much the shape of a distribution differs from a normal curve in terms of whether its middle is more peaked or flat than a normal curve.

Misleading Graphs

Graphs may be misleading when:
- Interval sizes are unequal.
- Proportions are exaggerated. The overall proportion of histograms or bar graphs should be 1 to 1.5 times as wide as it is tall.

Frequency Tables, Histograms, and Frequency Polygons in Research Articles

Researchers mainly use frequency tables, histograms, and frequency polygons as a step in more elaborate statistical analyses, so they are not usually included in research articles. Frequency tables are used to summarize the characteristics of people in studies, especially demographic variables like age or gender. Histograms and frequency polygons rarely appear in research articles (except articles *about* statistics); but researchers may comment on the shape of distributions in the text of articles, particularly if the distribution seems to be far from normal.

Chapter Self–Tests

The practice test items that follow are based on the following scenario. A group of psychologists plans to administer an inventory designed to measure the self-esteem reported by students in a statistics course. The inventory asks students to indicate which of 40 statements about their chances to succeed in the course are true for them. True responses are scored as 1 and false responses as 0, so that scores can range from 0 – 40.

Understanding Key Terms in Chapter 1

Directions: Using the word bank that follows, complete each statement.

Word Bank: bimodal distribution / ceiling effect / continuous variable / descriptive statistics / equal-interval variables / discrete variable / floor effect / frequency distribution / frequency table / grouped frequency table / histogram / inferential statistics / interval / kurtosis / levels of measurement / multimodal distribution / nominal variables / normal curve / numeric variable / rank-order variables / ratio scale / rectangular distribution / score / skewed distribution / statistics / symmetrical distribution / unimodal distribution / values / variable

In order to organize, analyze, and interpret the data they collect, the psychologists will use the branch of science known as **(1)** _____. If the psychologists want to make a statement about the self-esteem reported by students in general, the psychologists will calculate **(2)** _____. If the psychologists compute the percentages of male and female students who report various levels of self-esteem, the psychologists are computing **(3)** _____. Self-esteem is the measured **(4)** _____, and can assume **(5)** _____ between 0 and 40. If the sum of a student's responses is 20, the student's **(6)** _____ is 20.

As the psychologists plan the statistical analyses they will conduct as they collect data, they consider the level at which they will measure the variables in the study. Since numbers will reflect the amount of the construct being measured, the psychologists are using **(7)** _____. If a student who has a score of 20 on the self-esteem inventory is reporting twice as much self-esteem as a student with a score of 10, self-esteem is an **(8)** _____. If the scale has an absolute zero point reflecting the complete absence of self-esteem, self-esteem is being measured on a **(9)** _____. If students are asked how many colds they have had during the past year, the number of colds is a **(10)** _____. If students are asked how many pounds they have gained or lost during the past 6 months, weight change is a **(11)** _____. If the differences between self-esteem scores of 10 and 20 and 20 and 30 are not equal, allowing the psychologists only to say that the three people are reporting different amounts of self-esteem, self-esteem is being measured as a **(12)** _____. If the psychologists say that people in the top half of the distribution have "high" self-esteem and people in the bottom half have "low" self-esteem, self-esteem is being measured as a **(13)** _____. The three types of variables are based on different **(14)** _____.

As a first step in analyzing their data, the psychologists tally the number and percentage of times each self-esteem score occurred. The resulting table is a **(15)** _____. Because they have measured the self-esteem of so many people, the psychologists then decide to combine values into groups of five values and report the number of people whose scores fall in each group. This combined category of values is called an **(16)** _____, and the resulting table is a **(17)** _____. If the psychologists create a graph using their data consisting of bars with no spaces between them, the graph is a **(18)** _____. If the psychologists create a graph that shows the pattern or shape of the spread of self-esteem scores, they have created a **(19)** _____. If this graph shows only one high point in the data, it depicts a **(20)** _____. If the graph shows that the distribution of self-esteem scores has two approximately equal high points, it depicts a **(21)** _____. Any distribution that has two or more high points is a **(22)** _____. If two students have scores of 0, two students have scores of 1, two students have scores of 2, two students have scores of 3, and so on, the graph will depict a **(23)** _____.

If the psychologists examine a graph of the self-esteem scores and find that there are equal numbers of scores on either side of the middle, the scores form a **(24)** _____. If the graph shows that there are more low self-esteem scores than high self-esteem scores, the graph is depicting a **(25)** _____. Since scores on the self-esteem inventory cannot be lower than zero, a **(26)** _____ is present for students with very low self-esteem. If the 40 statements do not permit students to express the true extent of their self-esteem, scores may pile up at the high end of the distribution, demonstrating a **(27)** _____. If the curve of self-esteem scores is bell-shaped, the curve is a **(28)** _____. The extent to which a curve has heavier or lighter tails than this symmetrical curve is **(29)** _____.

Multiple Choice Items

1. If the psychologists use statistics like frequency tables to summarize the numbers collected in their study, they are reporting
    A. inferential statistics.
    B. descriptive statistics.
    C. intuitive statistics.
    D. abstract statistics.

2. If the psychologists use the numbers collected in their study to make generalizations about the self-esteem levels of students throughout the United States, they will calculate
   A. inferential statistics.
   B. descriptive statistics.
   C. intuitive statistics.
   D. abstract statistics.

3. If the psychologists also study the amount of anxiety students experience before a test, anxiety is a
   A. score.
   B. descriptive statistic.
   C. value.
   D. variable.

4. Since a student can make a score between 0 and 40, 0 to 40 are
   A. ranks.
   B. intervals.
   C. variables.
   D. values.

5. A student's score on the self-esteem inventory is an example of a
   A. numeric variable.
   B. qualitative variable.
   C. confounding variable.
   D. independent variable.

6. If a student who has a score of 18 on the self-esteem inventory is reporting two times as much self-esteem as a student who has a score of 9, self-esteem is
   A. a nominal variable.
   B. a rank-order variable.
   C. in equal-interval variable.
   D. an independent variable.

7. If a student who has a score of 28 on the self-esteem inventory is experiencing twice as much self-esteem as a student who has a score of 14, and seven times as much self-esteem as a student who has a score of 6, self-esteem is
   A. a nominal variable.
   B. a rank-order variable.
   C. in equal-interval variable.
   D. an independent variable.

8. If a student who has a score of 0 on the self-esteem inventory can be said to be experiencing no self-esteem, self-esteem is being measured on
   A. a nominal scale.
   B. an ordinal scale.
   C. an interval scale.
   D. a ratio scale.

9. If the psychologists ask students to report the number of times they missed statistics class during the semester, the number of absences is
   A. a continuous variable.
   B. a discrete variable.
   C. a unimodal variable.
   D. a bimodal variable.

10. When compared to the number of absences from statistics, a student's score on the self-esteem inventory is
    A. a continuous variable.
    B. a discrete variable.
    C. a unimodal variable.
    D. a bimodal variable.

11. When the psychologists talk about the level of measurement at which self-esteem is measured, they are discussing
    A. whether floor or ceiling effects are present.
    B. differences between unimodal and multimodal distributions.
    C. differences between rank-order and equal-interval variables.
    D. whether their distributions will be normal or skewed.

12. Since the scores on the self-esteem inventory can have any value between 0 and 40, the psychologists may want to summarize the data using a grouped frequency table instead of an ordinary frequency table because an ordinary frequency table would
    A. include too many values.
    B. not be able to include all cases.
    C. not depict a skewed distribution.
    D. have to start at 0 (or 0%).

13. In general, the largest number of intervals in a grouped frequency table should be
    A. 5.
    B. 10.
    C. 15.
    D. 20.

14. If the graph the psychologists use to display the data in a frequency table consists of adjacent bars, the graph is a
    A. pie chart.
    B. normal curve approximation.
    C. histogram.
    D. frequency polygon.

15. In a frequency distribution, the vertical (up and down) dimension represents the
    A. frequency of values.
    B. possible values a variable can take.
    C. intensity of the variable.
    D. percentage of scores at each value.

16. If 60 students complete self-esteem inventory just before the first statistics test and another 60 students complete it close to the end of the semester, the distribution will probably be
    A. unimodal.
    B. bimodal.
    C. normal.
    D. skewed.

17. If the psychologists examine the distributions of student self-esteem scores and find that most of the scores are low with a few high scores at the positive end of the distribution, the distribution is
    A. unimodal.
    B. bimodal.
    C. normal.
    D. skewed.

18. The psychologists may suspect that a ceiling effect exists if
    A. most of the scores in the distribution are located at the high end.
    B. the curve is skewed to the right.
    C. the distribution is symmetrical, but heavy-tailed.
    D. the distribution describes the spread of a rank-order variable.

19. When the psychologists create distributions of self-esteem scores, the standard of comparison when describing the shape of these distributions is a
    A. rectangular distribution.
    B. flat distribution.
    C. normal curve.
    D. a square curve.

20. A graphic display of a frequency distribution of self-esteem scores may be misleading when the
    A. proportions are 1.5 across to 1 up.
    B. frequencies are obtained from a grouped frequency table.
    C. interval sizes are unequal.
    D. values are indicated on the horizontal axis.

Problems

1. The psychologists administered the self-esteem inventory to 22 students in a statistics class and obtained the following scores:

15 29 26 23 24 21 16 23 20 23 24 18 20 22 23 17 28 19 21 20 28 25

Make a frequency table.
Use the frequency table to make a histogram.
Describe the shape of the distribution.

2. The psychologists then administered the self-esteem to 38 more students in statistics classes and obtained the following scores:

35 24 27 30 26 30 32 20 32 33 24 19 25 18 17 33 31 19 30 28 20 35 16 29 27 21 27 24 31 36 22 26 20 25 28 24 22 29

Add the 38 new scores to the 22 scores obtained earlier and make a frequency table. Make a grouped frequency table and explain why a grouped frequency table might be preferred in this instance. Make a histogram using the grouped frequency data.

3. Using the self-esteem inventory data, explain what a ceiling effect is and contrast it to a floor effect.

Additional Practice: Complete any Practice Problems in Set I that your instructor has not assigned and compare your responses to those provided by the authors. Pay particular attention to the problems that require you to explain your results to someone who has never taken a course in statistics.

SPSS Applications

Note: SPSS is revised frequently. Version 15.0 is the latest version. As a result, students may encounter different versions of the software at their institutions. For the problems prepared for this Study Guide, versions available in most academic computing centers should be adequate. Version 15.0 was used for the computations in this Study Guide. If you are unfamiliar with SPSS, you will want to follow the instructions in the section of the text chapters entitled "Using SPSS" carefully, and you may want to consult the Appendix for this study guide. Consult your instructor about naming variables and removing decimals. Note that decimals are not removed in the text examples.

Application 1
Open SPSS.
Enter the self-esteem inventory scores used in Problem 1in one column of a data window. Again, the scores are

15 29 26 23 24 21 16 23 20 23 24 18 20 22 23 17 28 19 21 20 28 25

To create a frequency table:
✐ Analyze
✐ Descriptive statistics
✐ Frequencies
✐ the name of the variable "esteem" and ✐ the arrow to move the variable to Variable(s) window
The screen should look like the one in Figure 1.

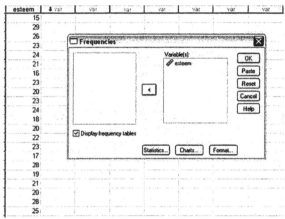

Figure 1
✐ OK
The output should look like the output in Figure 2.

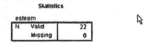

Statistics

esteem

N	Valid	22
	Missing	0

esteem

		Frequency	Percent	Valid Percent	Cumulative Percent
Valid	15	1	4.5	4.5	4.5
	16	1	4.5	4.5	9.1
	17	1	4.5	4.5	13.6
	18	1	4.5	4.5	18.2
	19	1	4.5	4.5	22.7
	20	3	13.6	13.6	36.4
	21	2	9.1	9.1	45.5
	22	1	4.5	4.5	50.0
	23	4	18.2	18.2	68.2
	24	2	9.1	9.1	77.3
	25	1	4.5	4.5	81.8
	26	1	4.5	4.5	86.4
	28	2	9.1	9.1	95.5
	29	1	4.5	4.5	100.0
	Total	22	100.0	100.0	

Figure 2

To create a histogram:
✐ Analyze
✐ Descriptive statistics
✐ Frequencies

the name of the variable and the arrow to move the variable to Variable(s) window
 Charts Histograms Continue
 OK
The output should look like the output in Figure 3.

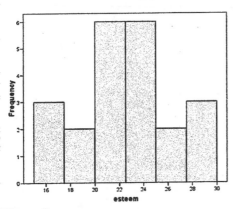

Figure 3

Instructions for saving SPSS datasets and then reopening them are provided in the Appendix. You should consult your instructor about whether he or she wants you to save files and whether personal files can be saved on lab computers. Be aware that some lab computers may be programmed to delete user files automatically, some as often as daily.

Application 2

Open SPSS.

Enter the following motivation scores in one column of a data window. The scores are

1, 4.5, 9, 7.5, 4.5, 8.5, 5.5, 2.5, 4.5, 9, 4.5, 5, 6.5, 7.5, 8, 8.5, 6, 2.5, 7, 3.5, 8, 1.5, 2.5, 6.5, 3.5, 5.5, 9.5, 6.5, 1.5, 7.5

To create a frequency table:
 Analyze
 Descriptive statistics
 Frequencies
 the name of the variable "motivation" and the arrow to move the variable to Variable(s) window
The screen should look like the one in Figure 4.

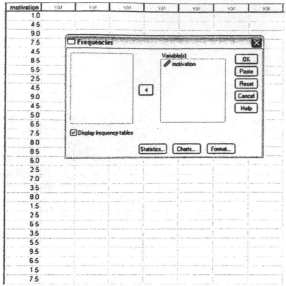

motivation	var	var	var	var	var	var	var
1.0							
4.5							
9.0							
7.5							
4.5							
8.5							
5.5							
2.5							
4.5							
9.0							
4.5							
5.0							
6.5							
7.5							
8.0							
8.5							
6.0							
2.5							
7.0							
3.5							
8.0							
1.5							
2.5							
6.5							
3.5							
5.5							
9.5							
6.5							
1.5							
7.5							

Figure 4

🖑 OK

The output should look like the output in Figure 5.

Statistics

motivation

N	Valid	30
	Missing	0

motivation

		Frequency	Percent	Valid Percent	Cumulative Percent
Valid	1.0	1	3.3	3.3	3.3
	1.5	2	6.7	6.7	10.0
	2.5	3	10.0	10.0	20.0
	3.5	2	6.7	6.7	26.7
	4.5	4	13.3	13.3	40.0
	5.0	1	3.3	3.3	43.3
	5.5	2	6.7	6.7	50.0
	6.0	1	3.3	3.3	53.3
	6.5	3	10.0	10.0	63.3
	7.0	1	3.3	3.3	66.7
	7.5	3	10.0	10.0	76.7
	8.0	2	6.7	6.7	83.3
	8.5	2	6.7	6.7	90.0
	9.0	2	6.7	6.7	96.7
	9.5	1	3.3	3.3	100.0
	Total	30	100.0	100.0	

Figure 5

To create a histogram:

🖑 Analyze

🖑 Descriptive statistics

🖑 Frequencies

🖑 the name of the variable and 🖑 the arrow to move the variable to Variable(s) window

🖑 Charts 🖑 Histograms 🖑 Continue

🖑 OK

The output should look like the output in Figure 6.

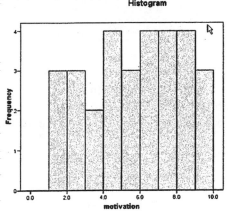

Figure 6

Chapter 2
Central Tendency and Variability

Learning Objectives
After studying this chapter, you should:
- Be able to compute the mean, locate the median, and identify the mode of a distribution of scores.
- Be able to compute the variance and standard deviation of a distribution of scores.
- Know the statistical symbols and formulas used to compute the measures of central tendency and variability of a distribution of scores.
- Know how measures of central tendency and variability are reported in research articles.

Central Tendency
The **central tendency** of a distribution refers to the typical or most representative value of the group of scores. The three measures of central tendency are the mean, mode, and median.

The **mean** is usually the best single number for describing a group of scores. That is, if only the mean of a group of scores is known, the best guess of any person's score is the mean. The mean is the ordinary average, the sum of all the scores divided by the number of scores. The formula for the mean is $M = \Sigma X / N$, where
- M is the symbol for the mean,
- Σ is the symbol for "sum of,"
- X refers to scores in the distribution of the variable X, and
- N is the number of scores in the distribution.

The **mode,** the most common single value in a distribution, is a second measure of central tendency. The mode is the value with the largest frequency in a frequency table, which makes it the high point or peak of a distribution's frequency histogram. In a perfectly symmetrical, unimodal distribution, the mode and the mean are identical. When the mode and the mean are not equal, the mode may not be a good reflection of the central tendency of a distribution. Furthermore, while the mean is affected by a change to any score in a distribution, several scores in a distribution may be changed without affecting the mode. Consequently, the mode is rarely used in psychological research.

The **median** is the third measure of central tendency. The value of the median may vary slightly depending on the number of scores in the distribution and on whether two or more scores in the middle of the distribution have the same value. Steps in determining the median are:
1. Rank all the scores in the distribution from lowest to highest.
2. Figure how many scores there are to the middle score by adding 1 to the number of scores and dividing by 2.
3. Count to the middle score or scores.

If the distribution contains a single middle score, it is the median. If the distribution contains two middle scores, the median is the average of the two middle scores. An advantage of the median is that it is less influenced by an extreme case, called an **outlier**, than the mean.

Variability
In addition to information about scores in the middle of a distribution, researchers need to know about the spread of scores in a distribution.

The **variance** of a group of scores is a measure of how the scores in a distribution are spread around the mean. By definition, the variance is the average of each score's squared difference from the mean. The steps in figuring the variance are:
1. Subtract the mean of the scores from each score in the distribution to obtain a **deviation score**.
2. Square each of these deviation scores to remove the effect of positive and negative deviations, which would cancel each other when summed, obtaining a **squared deviation score**.
3. Add all the squared deviation scores to obtain the **sum of squared deviations**.
4. Divide this sum of squared deviations by the number of scores.

Although the variance plays an important role in many statistical procedures, it is rarely reported as a descriptive statistic because it is based on squared units, which do not give a clear sense of the spread of the distribution of the scores in the units in which they were measured.

The **standard deviation** is the most widely used statistic for describing the spread of scores in a distribution, and it is directly related to the variance in that it is the positive square root of the variance.

The formula for the variance is $SD^2 = \Sigma(X - M)^2 / N$, where
- SD^2 is the symbol for the variance,
- Σ is the symbol for "sum of,"
- X refers to scores in the distribution of the variable X,
- M is the mean of the distribution, and
- N is the number of scores in the distribution.

$\Sigma(X - M)^2$ refers to the sum of squared deviations from the mean and is also symbolized SS, for **sum of squares**, so that SD^2 can be written as SS / N.

The formula for the standard deviation is $SD = \sqrt{SD^2}$ (The formula may also be written $SD = \sqrt{SS / N}$.)

Computational formulas that are mathematically equivalent to the formulas presented in this chapter are available as shortcuts when computing statistics using calculator. However, computers and programmable calculators have largely relegated these formulas to historical notes. Since the formulas in this chapter show the meaning of the procedure directly, they are called **definitional formulas**.

The variance and standard deviation are sometimes figured using the sum of squared deviations divided by $N - 1$. Appropriate uses of this denominator are described beginning in Chapter 7. Be aware that programmable calculators and computer outputs may use $N - 1$ instead of the formula emphasized in this chapter.

Central Tendency and Variability in Research Articles
The mean and standard deviation are commonly reported, and in a variety of ways – either in the text, in tables, or in graphs. The mode, median, and variance rarely appear in research articles.

Chapter Self-Tests

The practice test items that follow are based on the following scenario. A group of psychologists has administered an inventory designed to measure perceived stress to 100 students. The inventory consists of 18 statements about stressful situations. Students use a 5-point scale in which responses are scored 0-4 to indicate the extent to which each statement describes their behavior, so that scores can range from 0-72.

Understanding Key Terms in Chapter 2

Directions: Using the word bank that follows, complete each statement.

Word Bank: central tendency / computational formula / definitional formula / deviation score / mean / median / mode / outlier / squared deviation score / standard deviation / sum of squared deviations / sum of squares / variance / N / X / Σ
Some words or symbols will be used twice.

The psychologists are interested in the scores that describe the most typical or representative values of the distribution of stress scores, so they need to examine the measures of **(1)** _____. If the psychologists find that the arithmetic average of the 100 scores is 29.3, they have calculated the **(2)** _____. The step of computing the sum of the 100 scores is symbolized by **(3)** _____, and each score by

(4) _____. If eight students have a score of 26, but no more than five students obtain any other score, 26 is the **(5)** _____. If the psychologists rank the scores of the 100 students and find that 50 of the scores are greater than 27 and 50 are less than 27, then 27 is the **(6)** _____. If most of the student scores range from 15-55, a score of 68 would be an **(7)** _____.

Now the psychologists want to obtain an index of how the scores are spread about the mean. They begin their calculations by subtracting the mean from each score, which yields a **(8)** _____. This difference is squared, yielding a **(9)** _____, and then summed, yielding the **(10)** _____, which is also known as a **(11)** _____. This last sum is divided by 100, yielding the **(12)** _____. Finally, the square root of the result of the last calculation is the **(13)** _____.

The formula $SD^2 = \sum(X - M)^2 / N$ is an example of a **(14)** _____. Mathematically equivalent formulas designed to simplify hand calculations are **(15)** _____. In this formula, SD^2 stands for the **(16)** _____, the operation of summing the deviations from the mean is indicated by **(17)** _____. The number of subjects in the analysis is designated by **(18)** _____. SD stands for the **(19)** _____.

Multiple-Choice Items

1. If the psychologists want to describe the central tendency of the stress scores, they will report the
   - A. variance.
   - B. kurtosis.
   - C. median.
   - D. standard deviation.

2. If the psychologists compute a statistic using the formula $\sum X / N$, they are computing the
   - A. variance.
   - B. standard deviation.
   - C. mean.
   - D. median.

3. In the formula $\sum X / N$, $\sum$ instructs the psychologists to
   - A. add.
   - B. subtract.
   - C. multiply.
   - D. divide.

4. In the formula $\sum X / N$, N refers to the
   - A. normal curve.
   - B. normative scores.
   - C. natural logarithm.
   - D. number of students.

5. If the psychologists examine a frequency distribution of the 100 stress scores and find that more students had a score of 35 than any other score, they have determined the
   - A. mode.
   - B. median.
   - C. variance.
   - D. standard deviation.

6. If the psychologists examine a frequency distribution of the 100 stress scores and find that a score of 36 divides the distribution in half, they have determined the
   A. mode.
   B. median.
   C. variance.
   D. standard deviation.

7. If the psychologists examine a frequency distribution of the 100 stress scores and find that while most of the scores are between 25 and 45, scores of 11 and 55 would be considered
   A. normal.
   B. outliers.
   C. variant.
   D. deviant.

8. If the psychologists compute a statistic using the formula $\Sigma(X - M)^2 / N$, they are computing the
   A. variance.
   B. standard deviation.
   C. skewness.
   D. kurtosis.

9. In the formula $\Sigma(X - M)^2 / N$, $X - M$ is a
   A. sum of squares.
   B. standard deviation.
   C. deviation score.
   D. range.

10. In the formula $\Sigma(X - M)^2 / N$, $(X - M)^2$ is a
   A. sum of squares.
   B. standard deviation.
   C. squared deviation score.
   D. squared range.

11. In the formula $\Sigma(X - M)^2 / N$, the sum of squared deviations is also known as the
   A. sum of squares.
   B. standard deviation.
   C. squared deviation score.
   D. squared range.

12. If the psychologists determine that the variance of the distribution of 100 stress scores is 49, the standard deviation is
   A. $\sqrt{49}$.
   B. 49^2.
   C. $\sqrt{49}$ / 100.
   D. 49^2 / 100.

13. If the psychologists use a calculator to compute the mean and standard deviation "by hand," they may use a formulas developed for this purpose called
   A. definitional formulas.
   B. computational formulas.
   C. logarithmic formulas.
   D. notational formulas.

14. If the psychologists use a calculator to compute the mean and standard deviation "by hand" following all the steps required by $\Sigma X / N$ and $\Sigma(X - M)^2 / N$, they are using
   A. definitional formulas.
   B. computational formulas.
   C. logarithmic formulas.
   D. notational formulas.

Problems

1. The psychologists administered the stress inventory to 25 students in a freshman orientation session and obtained the following scores:

49 14 35 47 38 24 46 27 41 32 44 15 36 37 22 38 48 31 42 34 26 17 38 49 12

Using the definitional formulas described in the text,
1. What is the mode?
2. What is the median?
3. Compute the mean, the variance, and the standard deviation.
4. Explain your calculations as you would to a person who has never taken statistics.

2. Returning to the data described in Chapter 1, the psychologists administered self-esteem inventory to 22 students in a statistics class and obtained the following scores:

15 29 26 23 24 21 16 23 20 23 24 18 20 22 23 17 28 19 21 20 28 25

Again, using the definitional formulas described in the text,
1. What is the mode?
2. What is the median?
3. Compute the mean, the variance, and the standard deviation.
4. Explain your calculations as you would to a person who has never taken statistics.

Additional Practice: Complete any Practice Problems in Set I that your instructor has not assigned and compare your responses to those provided by the authors. Pay particular attention to the problems that require you to explain your results to someone who has never taken a course in statistics.

SPSS Applications

Application 1
Open SPSS.
Enter the stress inventory scores used in Problem 1 in one column of a data window. Rename the variable "stress" and remove the zeros following the decimal if you wish. Again, the scores are

49 14 35 47 38 24 46 27 41 32 44 15 36 37 22 38 48 31 42 34 26 17 38 49 12

⌐ Analyze
⌐ Descriptive statistics
⌐ Frequencies
⌐ the name of the variable and ⌐ the arrow to move the variable to Variable(s) window
⌐ Statistics
⌐ Mean ⌐ Median ⌐ Mode ⌐ Standard deviation ⌐ Variance ⌐ Continue
Unless you want more practice, ⌐ the box labeled *Display frequency tables*, which will suppress the frequency table that would be constructed for the dataset

√ð OK
The output should look like the output in Figure 1

Statistics

stress

N	Valid	25
	Missing	0
Mean		33.68
Median		36.00
Mode		38
Std. Deviation		11.430
Variance		130.643

Figure 1

Compare the results to those you obtained using your calculator for Problem 1. Remember that the computer calculates the variance and standard deviation using $N-1$ in the denominator so that these statistics should be slightly larger than those you calculated by hand.

Application 2

Open SPSS.
Enter the self-esteem scores in one column of a data window. If you saved the scores after you completed the application in Chapter 1, you may √ð on the SPSS icon for the file to open both the file and SPSS, or you may open SPSS and use the *Open an existing data source* window. If you did not save the file, the scores are

15 29 26 23 24 21 16 23 20 23 24 18 20 22 23 17 28 19 21 20 28 25

√ð Analyze
√ð Descriptive statistics
√ð Frequencies
√ð the name of the variable and √ð the arrow to move the variable to Variable(s) window
√ð Statistics
√ð Mean √ð Median √ð Mode √ð Standard deviation √ð Variance √ð Continue
Unless you want more practice, √ð the box labeled *Display frequency tables*, which will suppress the frequency table that would be constructed for the dataset
√ð OK

The output should look like the output in Figure 2

Statistics

osteem

N	Valid	22
	Missing	0
Mean		22.05
Median		22.50
Mode		23
Std. Deviation		3.823
Variance		14.617

Figure 2

Compare the results to those you obtained using your calculator for Problem 1. Remember that the computer calculates the variance and standard deviation using $N-1$ in the denominator so that these statistics should be slightly larger than those you calculated by hand.
Note: Remember that you can use the SPSS capability to create a new variable to calculate the variance and standard deviation using N instead of $N-1$ in the denominator as is shown on pp. 62-65 in the text. The procedure applied to the stress data follows.
The mean of the stress scores is 33.68.
√ð Transform
√ð Compute variable
The window should look like the one in Figure 3

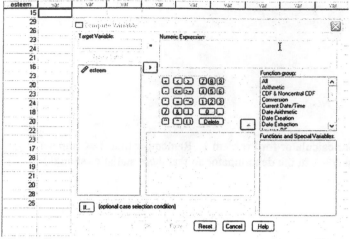

Figure 3

In the Target Variable window, name the new variable "stdev."

⌖ "esteem" in the Type & Label window and ⌖ the arrow to move the variable to the Numeric Expression window. Modify the Numeric Expression window so that it contains the formula ("esteem" – 22.05) * ("esteem" – 22.05), which will calculate the squared deviation score.

The second column in the Data View window now contains the values of the computed variable for each student. Since the mean of the squared deviation scores is the variance ($SD^2 = \Sigma(X - M)^2 / N$), you can use SPSS to calculate the mean of "stdev," which is 13.95. The standard deviation is the square root of the variance, which in this case is 3.73. You can see that these values are smaller than the values computed by SPSS.

Chapter 3
Some Key Ingredients for Inferential Statistics: *Z* Scores, the Normal Curve, Sample versus Population, and Probability

Learning Objectives
After studying this chapter, you should:
- Be able to convert raw scores to *Z* scores.
- Be able to convert *Z* scores to raw scores.
- Be able to describe the normal curve.
- Be able to use the normal curve table.
- Be able to figure the percentage of scores above or below a particular raw score or *Z* score using the normal curve table.
- Be able to figure *Z* scores and raw scores from percentages using the normal curve table.
- Know the difference between a sample and a population and the associated statistical terminology.
- Be able to define probability and explain the long-run relative-frequency interpretation of probability.
- Be able to differentiate random and nonrandom methods of sampling.
- Know how *Z* scores, normal curves, samples and populations, and probabilities are reported in research articles.
- Advanced Topic: Be able to define and apply the addition and multiplication probability rules and know how to calculate conditional probabilities.

Z Scores
A **Z score** is the number of standard deviations an actual score lies above or below the mean; i.e., a *Z* score is a score expressed in standard deviation units. Thus, *Z* scores are units of measure in their own right and will be used in calculations encountered in future chapters. If the actual score, or **raw score**, is greater than the mean, its *Z* score will have a positive value. If the actual score is less than the mean, its *Z* score will have a negative value. *Z* scores are useful in determining where scores fall on the normal curve.

The formula used to compute a *Z* score is $Z = (X - M) / SD$. *Z* scores can also be converted to raw scores using the formula $X = (Z) (SD) + M$.

Looking at the formula for *Z*, if the raw score *X* is equal to the mean, $X - M = 0$, and 0 divided by any number is 0. Therefore, the mean of a distribution of *Z* scores is always 0. Similarly, since computation of a *Z* score involves dividing by the standard deviation, the standard deviation is always 1. For example, suppose that 10,000 students have taken the inventory designed to measure perceived stress, and that the mean stress score is 36 and the standard deviation is 8. If a student obtains a score of 36, the student's *Z* score $= (36 - 36) / 8 = (0) / 8 + 0$. If another student obtains a score of 44, this student's *Z* score $= (44 - 36) / 8 = 8 / 8 = 1.00$, and if a third obtains a score of 28, this student's *Z* score $= (28 - 38) / 8 = (-8) / 8 = -1.00$.

Computing *Z* scores from raw scores
Formula: $Z = (X - M) / SD$
Steps:
1. Figure the deviation score: subtract the mean from the raw score.
2. Figure the *Z* score: divide the deviation score by the standard deviation.

Example 1:
If the mean score for a large number of people on a self-esteem inventory is 66 and the standard deviation is 8, what is the *Z* score for a personwith a score of 66?
$Z = (X - M) / SD$
$= (66 - 66) / 8$
$= 0 / 8$
$= 0.00$
Because the person's score of 66 is equal to the mean, the *Z* score is zero.

With a score of 54?
$Z = (X - M) / SD$
$= (54 - 66) / 8$
$= -12 / 8$
$= -1.50$
Because the person's score of 54 is less than the mean, the Z score is negative.

With a score of 78?
$Z = (X - M) / SD$
$= (78 - 66) / 8$
$= 12 / 8$
$= 1.50$
Because the person's score of 78 is greater than the mean, the Z score is positive.

Based on their Z scores, the self-esteem score of the person whose score is 54 is as far below the mean as the self-esteem score of the person whose score is 78 is above the mean in standard deviation units.

Example 2:
If the mean score of a large number of people on a self-esteem inventory is 66 and the standard deviation is 8, what is the Z score for a person with a score of 56?
$Z = (X - M) / SD$
$= (56 - 66) / 8$
$= -10 / 8$
$= -1.25$

If the mean score of a large number of people on a depression inventory is 16 and the standard deviation is 4, what is the Z score for a person with a score of 11?
$Z = (X - M) / SD$
$= (11 - 16) / 4$
$= -5 / 4$
$= -1.25$

Based on their Z scores, the self-esteem score of the person whose score is 58 is as far below the mean self-esteem score as the depression score of the person whose score is 11 is below the mean depression score. Thus, converting scores on different variables to Z scores places the score on the same scale, permitting comparisons of variables measured on different scales.

Computing raw scores from Z scores
Formula: $X = (Z) (SD) + M$
Steps:
1. Figure the deviation score: multiply the Z score by the standard deviation.
2. Figure the raw score: add the mean to the deviation score.

Example 1:
If the mean score of a large number of people on a self-esteem inventory is 66 and the standard deviation is 8, what is the raw score for a person with a Z of 0.00?
$X = Z (SD) + M$
$= (0.00) (8) + 66$
$= 0 + 66$
$= 66$
Because the Z score for the mean is always zero, the raw score of a person who has a Z score equal to the mean will be the mean.

With a Z score of -1.50?

$X = Z\,(SD) + M$
  $= (-1.50)\,(8) + 66$
  $= -12 + 66$
  $= 54$

Because the person's Z score is negative, the raw score will be lower than the mean.

With a Z score of 1.50?

$X = (Z)\,(SD) + M$
  $= (1.50)\,(8) + 66$
  $= 12 + 66$
  $= 78$

Because the person's Z score is positive, the raw score will be greater than the mean.

Example 2:
If the mean score of a large number of people on a self-esteem inventory is 66 and the standard deviation is 8, what is the raw score for a person with a Z score of -1.25?

$X = (Z)\,(SD) + M$
  $= (-1.25)\,(8) + 66$
  $= -10 + 66$
  $= 56$

If the mean score of a large number of people on a depression inventory is 16 and the standard deviation is 4, what is the raw score for a person with a Z score of 11?

$X = (Z)\,(SD) + M$
  $= (-1.25)\,(4) + 66$
  $= -5 + 16$
  $= 11$

A person whose score on the self-esteem inventory is 58 is as far below the mean self-esteem score as a person whose score on the depression inventory is 11. Again, Z scores place scores on different measuring instruments on the same scale, permitting comparisons of variables measured on different scales.

Characteristics of Z Score Distributions
1. As demonstrated above, the Z score for the mean is always 0.
2. The standard deviation is always 1.0 because converting a raw score to a Z score involves dividing between the raw score and the mean by the standard deviation. From the previous example, if the mean score of a large number of people on a self-esteem inventory is 66 and the standard deviation is 8, a person who has a raw score of 74 will have a Z score of 1.00 because:
    $Z = (X - M) / SD$
      $= (74 - 66) / 8$
      $= 8 / 8$
      $= 1.00$
    Similarly, a person who has a raw score of 58 will have a Z score of -1.00 because:
    $Z = (X - M) / SD$
      $= (58 - 66) / 8$
      $= -8 / 8$
      $= -1.00$
3. The variance is always 1.00 because it is the square of the standard deviation, and both 1.00^2 and $-1.00^2 = 1.00$.
4. Because Z scores have standard values for the mean and standard deviation, they are also called *standard scores* (although this term is sometimes only used when the Z scores are computed for a normal distribution.)

The Normal Distribution

The distributions of many variables measured by psychologists, e.g., the intelligence or reaction times of a large number of people, are unimodal, roughly symmetrical, and bell-shaped. These bell-shaped histograms or frequency polygons approximate a precise and important mathematical distribution called the **normal distribution**, or more simply, the **normal curve**. The normal curve is common in nature because a person's score on any particular variable can be influenced by a large number of essentially random factors that cause most of the scores to cluster around a middle value, with equal, but smaller numbers of scores falling above and below the middle value. Mathematics will show that in the long run, if the influences are truly random, a precise normal curve will result.

The shape of the normal curve is standard, so the percentage of scores above or below any particular point in the curve can be determined. Because normal curves are symmetrical, exactly 50% of the cases fall above the mean and exactly 50% are below the mean. In addition, approximately 34% of the cases fall between the mean and one standard deviation above the mean and approximately 34% fall between the mean and one standard deviation below the mean. Furthermore, approximately 14% of the cases fall between one and two standard deviations above the mean and one and two standard deviations below the mean.

Returning to the example of stress scores, remember that the mean is 36 and the standard deviation is 8. Therefore, 50% of the scores will be greater than 36 and 50% will be less than 36. Considering scores above the mean, approximately 34% of the population will have scores between 36 and 44 (i.e., between the mean and one standard deviation above the mean) and approximately 14% of the population will have scores between 44 and 52 (i.e., between one standard deviation above the mean and two standard deviations above the mean). Since the normal curve is symmetrical, approximately 34% of the population will have scores between 28 and 36 (i.e., between the mean and one standard deviation below the mean) and approximately 14% of the population will have scores between 20 and 28 (i.e., between one standard deviation below the mean and two standard deviations below the mean). Since these percentages are constant for any variable that is normally distributed, the percentage of cases that lie above or below any Z score can be determined, as can the percentage of cases that lie between any two Z scores.

The normal curve table and Z scores

Because the normal curve is mathematically defined, it is also possible to determine the exact percentage of cases between any two Z scores. A **normal curve table** like Table A-1 in the text Appendix provides the percentage of cases between the mean (a Z score of 0) and any other Z score. This table also can be used to determine the percentage of cases between any two Z scores, and if raw scores are converted to Z scores, between any two raw scores. Finally, the table includes the percentage of area in the tail of the distribution for any particular Z score.

Determining the Percentage of Scores above or below a Particular Raw Score or Z Score Using the Normal Curve Table

1. Convert raw scores to Z scores using $Z = (X - M) / SD$.
2. Draw the normal curve, locate the position of the Z score, and shade the area for which the percentage is to be found.
3. Make a rough estimate of the shaded area's percentage based on the 50%–34%–14% percentages.
4. Find the exact percentage using the normal curve table. If the percentage of cases <u>above</u> a particular Z score is to be determined and the Z score is positive, subtract the percentage between the mean and the Z score from 50%. If the Z score is negative, add 50% to the percentage between the Z score and the mean.
5. Check to be sure the exact percentage is within the range of the estimate in Step 2.

Example 1:
If the mean score of a large number of people on a self-esteem inventory is 66 and the standard deviation is 8, what percentage of scores is higher than 72?

$Z = (X - M) / SD$
$= (72 - 66) / 8$
$= 6 / 8$
$= 0.75$

From the table of areas of areas under the normal curve, the percentage from the mean to a Z score of 0.75 is 27.34%. Therefore, the number of scores greater than 72 is 50.00% − 27.34% = 22.66% of the scores. Note that 22.66% is also shown as the area in the tail of the normal curve in Table A-1.

Example 2:
If the mean score of a large number of people on a self-esteem inventory is 66 and the standard deviation is 8, what percentage of scores is higher than 60?
$Z = (X − M) / SD$
  $= (60 − 66) / 8$
  $= -6 / 8$
  $= -0.75$
From the table of areas of areas under the normal curve, the percentage from the mean to a Z score of -0.75 is 27.34%. Therefore, the number of scores greater than 60 is 50.00% + 27.34% = 77.34% of the scores.

6. If the percentage of cases <u>below</u> a particular Z score is to be determined and the Z score is positive, add 50% to the percentage between the Z score and the mean. If the Z score is negative, subtract the percentage between the Z score and the mean from 50%.

Example 3:
If the mean score of a large number of people on a self-esteem inventory is 66 and the standard deviation is 8, what percentage of scores is lower than 72?
$Z = (X − M) / SD$
  $= (72 − 66) / 8$
  $= 6 / 8$
  $= 0.75$
From the table of areas of areas under the normal curve, the percentage from the mean to a Z score of 0.75 is 27.34%. Therefore, the number of scores lower than 72 is 50.00% + 27.34% = 77.34% of the scores.

Example 4:
If the mean score of a large number of people on a self-esteem inventory is 66 and the standard deviation is 8, what percentage of scores is lower than 60?
$Z = (X − M) / SD$
  $= (60 − 66) / 8$
  $= -6 / 8$
  $= -0.75$
From the table of areas of areas under the normal curve, the percentage from the mean to a Z score of -0.75 is 27.34%. Therefore, the number of scores greater than 60 is 50.00% − 27.34% = 22.66% of the scores. Again, note that 22.66% is shown as the area in the tail of the normal curve in Table A-1.

In each case, check to be sure that the exact percentage is similar to the rough estimate in Step 3.

Determining Z Scores and Raw Scores from Percentages of Cases Using the Normal Curve Table
1. Draw a picture of the normal curve and shade in the approximate area for the percentage of area under the curve using the 50% − 34% − 14% percentages.
2. Make a rough estimate of the Z score where the shaded area stops.
3. Find the exact Z score using the normal curve table, subtracting 50% if necessary.
4. Check that the exact Z score is similar to the rough estimate from step 2.
5. Convert the Z score to a raw score: $X = (Z)(SD) + M$.

Sample and Population
A **population** is the entire group of people to be studied, i.e., the larger group about which inferences are to be made on the basis of the scores of a particular group of people (the sample). A **sample** is the scores of the particular group of people studied, which is usually considered representative of the larger population about which experimenters actually have information.

Psychologists study samples instead of populations because studying populations is usually impractical. The general strategy of psychological research is to study a sample of individuals believed to be representative of the general population, or of some particular population of interest. Realistically, researchers try to study people who at least do not differ from the general population in a systematic way that could influence the results of a research study. For example, if researchers were interested in the self-esteem of students who entered college following military service, they would not include students who had no military service in their sample.

Methods of Sampling
Random selection, in which researchers obtain a complete list of members of the population of interest and randomly select some of them for inclusion in the study, is the ideal method for selecting a sample. *Haphazard selection*, which may involve selecting anyone who is available or who happens to be first in a list, may result in a sample that is different from the population.

Statistical Terminology for Samples and Populations
Population parameters include the mean, variance, and standard deviation of populations. Population parameters are usually an unknown and can only be estimated from data collected from a sample drawn from the population. Greek letters symbolize population parameters.

Population mean = μ

Population variance = σ^2

Population standard deviation = σ

Sample statistics include the mean, variance, and standard deviation calculated from scores collected from a sample. Thus, sample statistics are computed from known information. Roman letters symbolize sample statistics.

Sample mean = M

Sample variance = SD^2

Sample standard deviation = SD

Probability
Probability is important in scientific research in general, and in psychological research in particular, because of the role of probability in inferential statistics, which permit researchers to draw conclusions about whether theories or experimental procedures can be applied in other settings. While probability is a broad, controversial topic, only a few key ideas are needed to understand basic inferential statistics.

- **Probability** is the expected relative frequency of a particular outcome.
- An **outcome** is the result of an experiment, or virtually any event for which the outcome is not known in advance.
- Frequency is how many times something happens, and relative frequency is the number of times something happens relative to the number of times it could have happened.
- The **expected relative frequency** is the frequency obtained when an experiment is repeated many times, and interpretation of research results in terms of this frequency is known as the **long-run relative-frequency interpretation of probability**.
- Probability can also be used to describe how certain a researcher is that a particular event will happen, which is known as the **subjective interpretation of probability.**

A probability is equal to the number of possible successful outcomes divided by the number of all possible outcomes. As a formula: Probability = Possible successful outcomes / All possible outcomes

Probabilities can range from 0, when something that has no chance of happening, to 1, when something is certain to happen. Probability is usually symbolized by the letter p and is expressed as being equal to, greater than, or less, than some fraction or percentage.

The normal distribution can also be thought of as a probability distribution because the percentage of scores between any two Z scores is the same as the probability of selecting a case between those two Z scores.

Z Scores, Normal Curves, Samples and Populations and Probabilities in Research Articles

Although important to understanding the statistical procedures that follow, the topics in this chapter are rarely found discussed explicitly in research articles. The normal curve is sometimes mentioned when describing the distribution of scores on a particular variable and the method of selecting the sample from the population may be described, particularly if the study reports the results of a survey. Probability is rarely discussed directly except in the context of statistical significance, which will be discussed in later chapters.

Advanced Topic: Probability Rules and Conditional Probabilities

The probability rules described in this section are used to determine probabilities in more complex situations requiring calculation of probabilities.

- The *addition rule* (also known as the *or rule*) is applied when two or more *mutually exclusive outcomes* are possible. In this situation, the total probability of obtaining either outcome is the sum of the outcomes.
- The *multiplication rule* (also called the *and rule*) is applied when the probability of obtaining both of two or more *independent outcomes* is needed.
- A *conditional probability* is the probability of one event occurring, based on the occurrence of another event.

For example, suppose that 20% of the students in your statistics class earned an A in a particular section of an introduction to psychology course, and 30% earned a B. According to the addition rule, the probability of selecting a student from your section of statistics who earned an A or a B at random is 50% (20% + 30%). Suppose that 25% of the students in your statistics section earn an A. According to the multiplication rule, the probability of earning an A in both sections of both courses is only 5% (.20 * .25 = .05 * 100 = 5%). Applying a conditional probability rule, the probability of randomly selecting a student who earned an A in the introductory course is 20% if the student was enrolled in the section of the course noted above.

Chapter Self-Tests

The practice test items that follow are based on the following scenario. A group of psychologists plans to administer an inventory designed to measure depression in the general population to a sample of college students. The inventory asks students to indicate whether they have experienced any of 20 thoughts or feelings during the past week. Students use a 4-point scale in which responses are scored 0–3, so that scores can range from 0–60.

Understanding Key Terms in Chapter 3

Directions: Using the word bank that follows, complete each statement.

Word Bank: addition rule / conditional probabilities / expected / haphazard selection / long-run relative-frequency / multiplication rule / normal curve / normal curve table / normal distribution / outcome / population / population parameters / probability / random selection / raw score / sample / sample statistics / standard score / subjective interpretation / Z score / σ / σ^2 / μ

The psychologists are now preparing to perform inferential statistical analyses. Although the psychologists have enrolled only 40 students in their **(1)** _____, they are interested in applying what they learn to the **(2)** _____ of all students. The total points obtained by any student comprise the student's **(3)** _____. If the mean and standard deviation of the depression scores of students in the sample are calculated, a student's **(4)** _____ locates the student's actual score as a number of standard deviations above or below the mean. Any score that is transformed so that the mean and standard deviation have set values is called a **(5)** _____. If a graph of the distribution of depression scores is unimodal, approximately symmetrical, and shaped like a bell, the graph reflects the **(6)** _____, or more simply, the **(7)** _____ normal curve. Because this curve is a precise mathematical curve, the percentage of scores between two points on the curve can be found using the **(8)** _____.

If the psychologists created the sample by administering the depression inventory to the 40 students enrolled in one of their classes, they have used **(9)** _____. The ideal method for selecting a sample for a study is **(10)** _____. The psychologists find that the mean on the depression for the 40 students is 12.4 with a standard deviation of 4.6, which are **(11)** _____. If the psychologists could determine the mean depression score and its standard deviation for the population of all students, they would know the **(12)** _____. The symbol for the population mean is **(13)** _____, the symbol for the population variance is **(14)** _____, and the symbol for the population standard deviation is **(15)** _____.

If the psychologists state that the expected relative frequency of depressed students in their sample will be four students out of 40, the have defined a **(16)** _____. The identification of 6 of the 40 students as depressed is an **(17)** _____. If the psychologists were able to repeat their study a large number of times and found that the mean number of depressed students over all the studies was 4, the psychologists would have determined the **(18)** _____ relative frequency. This series of studies would provide data for a **(19)** _____ relative frequency interpretation of probability. If the psychologists indicated that they were 90% certain that at least two depressed students would be identified in any sample of 40 students, they would be using **(20)** _____ interpretation of probability.

Finally, if the psychologists want to determine the probability of selecting only students who are depressed, but who have no other mental disorder in a sample, they would apply the **(21)** _____. On the other hand, if the psychologists want to identify both students who are depressed and who have high levels of perceived stress, they would apply the **(22)** _____. If the psychologists know that 30% of male students who are depressed have requested services from the university counseling center, while 70% of male students who are depressed have requested services, the psychologists would use **(23)** _____ to determine the probability that a male student selected at random who has not requested services from the counseling center.

Multiple Choice Items

1. If the total of a student's responses on the depression inventory is 22, this number is the student's
   A. expected relative frequency.
   B. raw score.
   C. standard score.
   D. Z score.

2. If the total of a student's responses on the depression inventory is converted so that it can be located on a distribution with a mean of 0.00 and a standard deviation of 1.00, the psychologists have calculated a
   A. expected relative frequency.
   B. raw score.
   C. standard score.
   D. Z score.

3. A description of the normal distribution would include a statement that it is
   A. slightly skewed to the left.
   B. slightly skewed to the right.
   C. unimodal.
   D. bimodal.

4. If the psychologists wanted to determine the precise percentage of students whose depression scores were greater than 2 standard deviations above the mean, they would use a
   A. normal curve table.
   B. population parameter.
   C. sample statistic.
   D. long-run relative-frequency interpretation.

5. If depression is normally distributed among students, the psychologists can expect approximately 2/3 of the students to have depression scores that transform to Z scores between
    A. 0.00 and 1.00.
    B. 0.00 and -1.00.
    C. -1.00 and 1.00.
    D. -2.00 and 2.00.

6. If depression is normally distributed among students, the psychologists can expect approximately 1/3 of the students to have depression scores that transform to Z scores between
    A. 0.00 and 1.00.
    B. 0.00 and -2.00.
    C. -1.00 and 1.00.
    D. -2.00 and 2.00.

7. If the psychologists state that 5% of all students are clinically depressed, they are making a statement about
    A. the normal distribution.
    B. a population.
    C. a sample.
    D. skewness.

8. If the psychologists choose 40 students from the 400 students taking statistics during a semester to participate in their survey to assess the number of students experiencing clinical depression, the psychologists have selected a
    A. normal distribution.
    B. population.
    C. sample.
    D. focus group.

9. If the psychologists obtain a numbered list of all 1,000 full-time students enrolled at a school during a semester and a computer identifies students numbered 3, 501, 256, 782, and 650 as the first five subjects to be selected for a sample, the psychologists will be using
    A. relative selection.
    B. haphazard selection.
    C. random selection.
    D. subjective selection

10. If the psychologists select subjects by posting notices asking for volunteers in all the dormitories on campus, they will have a
    A. relative selection.
    B. haphazard selection.
    C. random selection.
    D. subjective selection.

11. If the psychologists state in a report that $\mu = 16$, they are reporting a
    A. population parameter.
    B. random sample.
    C. sample statistic.
    D. Bayesian statistic.

12. If the psychologists state in a report that $\sigma = 4$, they are reporting the
    A. normal standard deviation.
    B. Bayesian standard deviation.
    C. sample standard deviation.
    D. population standard deviation.

13. If the psychologists state in a report that $M = 16$ and $SD = 4$, they are reporting
    A. population parameters.
    B. random samples.
    C. sample statistics.
    D. Bayesian statistics.

14. If the psychologists know that four of every 100 students are clinically depressed, the probability of selecting a depressed student at random from a sample of 100 students can be expressed as
    A. 4.0.
    B. .04.
    C. 40.0.
    D. .004.

15. If the psychologists repeat the study of depression among students and find that 5% of the students in this second study are clinically depressed, the result is
    A. a probability.
    B. a relative frequency.
    C. an outcome.
    D. an expected relative frequency.

16. If the psychologists repeat the study of depression among students several more times and find that approximately 5% of the students in all these studies are clinically depressed, the psychologists can expect that many more replications will yield the same result. In this case, the psychologists can say that a 5% rate of clinical depression is the
    A. probability.
    B. relative frequency.
    C. outcome.
    D. expected relative frequency.

17. If the psychologists state that any investigation of depression among students is likely to yield a 5% rate of clinical depression, the psychologists are
    A. interpreting population parameters.
    B. using normal curve tables.
    C. transforming raw scores to standard scores.
    D. applying the long-run relative-frequency interpretation of probability.

18. If the psychologists state that any student has a 5% chance of being clinically depressed, the psychologists are
    A. interpreting sample statistics.
    B. applying the subjective interpretation of probability.
    C. applying the long-run relative-frequency interpretation of probability.
    D. transforming raw scores to standard scores.

19. The probability rule that applies when two mutually exclusive outcomes are possible is the
    A. addition rule.
    B. subtraction rule.
    C. multiplication rule.
    D. division rule.

20. The probability rule that applies when figuring the probability of obtaining both of two independent outcomes is the
    A. addition rule.
    B. subtraction rule.
    C. multiplication rule.
    D. division rule.

21.   If a Group 1 includes 50% women, Group 2 includes 45% women, and Group 3 includes 55% women, the probability of drawing a woman who is a member of Group 2 is said to be
   A.   additive.
   B.   conditional.
   C.   multiplicative.
   D.   dependent.

Problems:

1. If the mean score on the depression scale is 12 and the standard deviation is 3, what is the Z score for a student whose depression score is 9?

2. If the mean score on the depression scale is 12 and the standard deviation is 3, what is the Z score for a student whose depression score is 18?

3. If the mean score on the depression scale is 12 and the standard deviation is 3, what is the Z score for a student whose depression score is 16?

4. If the mean score on the depression scale is 12 and the standard deviation is 3, what is the Z score for a student whose depression score is 11?

Using the 50%–34%–14% approximation of areas under the normal curve, what percentage of normally distributed scores lie:

5. Between 1 standard deviation below the mean and 1 standard deviation above the mean?

6. Between 2 standard deviations below the mean and 2 standard deviations above the mean?

7. Between 2 standard deviations below the mean and the mean?

8. Between 2 standard deviations above the mean and the mean?

9. Above 1.5 standard deviations above the mean?

10. Below 0.5 standard deviations below the mean?

Calculate the areas under the normal curve between the following pairs of Z scores.

11. $Z = -0.36$ and $Z = 0.88$

12. $Z = 1.74$ and $Z = 2.05$

13. $Z = -1.51$ and $Z = 1.32$

14. $Z = -0.49$ and $Z = -1.89$

15. $Z = 1.31$ and $Z = -1.61$
Determine the areas under the normal curve based on the following Z scores.

16. Above $Z = 0.68$

17. Below $Z = -2.74$

18. Above $Z = 1.33$

19. Below $Z = 1.33$

20. Above $Z = -1.33$

21. Advanced Topic: In a particular university, 400 of the students are freshmen, 200 are sophomores, 200 are juniors, and 200 are seniors. If a polling firm were conducting a survey at this university and telephoned a student at random, (a) what is the probability that this person would be a sophomore or a junior, or (b) either a freshman or a senior?

22. Advanced Topic: At a particular small college, 200 students will be admitted to natural science majors, 300 to social science majors, 250 to humanities majors, and 250 to other majors. If a student wants a double major, (a) what is the probability that a student will be admitted to both the social sciences and humanities, or (b) to both the natural sciences and social sciences?

Additional Practice: Complete any Practice Problems in Set I that your instructor has not assigned and compare your responses to those provided by the authors. Pay particular attention to the problems that require you to explain your results to someone who has never taken a course in statistics.

SPSS Applications

Application 1
Open SPSS.
Enter the following self-esteem scores in one column of a data window. If you saved the scores after you completed the application in Chapter 1, you may ⁓🖰 on the SPSS icon for the file to open both the file and SPSS, of you may open SPSS and use the *Open an existing data source* window. If you did not save the file, the scores are

15 29 26 23 24 21 16 23 20 23 24 18 20 22 23 17 28 19 21 20 28 25

In order to transform raw scores to Z scores, you need the mean and standard deviation for the distribution of scores. From Chapter 2, the mean self-esteem score is 22.05 and the standard deviation is 3.73. Again, you will use the SPSS capability to create a new variable to calculate a standard score called "zesteem."

⁓🖰 Transform
⁓🖰 Compute variable
In the Target Variable window, name the new variable "zesteem."
⁓🖰 "esteem" in the Type & Label window and ⁓🖰 the arrow to move the variable to the Numeric Expression window. Modify the Numeric Expression window so that it contains the formula ("esteem" − 22.05) / 3.73, which will calculate the Z scores.
If you have been saving this dataset, the third column in the Data View window now contains self-esteem Z scores for each student. (If you have not been saving the dataset, the Z scores will be in the second column.)
Compare your Z scores to those in Figure 1.

esteem	stdev	zesteem
-22	49.70	-11.82
29	48.30	1.86
26	15.60	1.06
23	.90	.25
24	3.80	.52
21	1.10	-.28
16	36.60	-1.62
23	.90	.25
20	4.20	-.55
23	.90	.25
24	3.80	.52
18	16.40	-1.09
20	4.20	-.55
22	.00	-.01
23	.90	.25
17	25.50	-1.35
28	35.40	1.60
19	9.30	-.82
21	1.10	-.28
20	4.20	-.55
28	35.40	1.60
25	8.70	.79

Figure 1

Chapter 4
Introduction to Hypothesis Testing

Learning Objectives
After studying this chapter, you should:
- Be able to apply the core logic of hypothesis testing.
- Be able to define the populations involved in hypothesis testing.
- Be able to write research hypotheses and null hypotheses.
- Be able to define the comparison distribution.
- Know how to determine the cutoff score on the comparison distribution.
- Be able to define significance and know the conventional levels of significance.
- Know when to reject the null hypothesis and the implications of this decision.
- Know when not to reject the null hypothesis and the implications of this decision.
- Be able to follow the steps of hypothesis testing.
- Know the difference between directional and nondirectional hypotheses.
- Know the difference between one-tailed and two-tailed tests.
- Know how results of hypothesis tests are reported in research articles.

Research in behavioral or social sciences often begins with a **hypothesis**, which is a prediction about the results of a research study. This hypothesis is often derived from a **theory**, or a set of principles that explain one or more facts, relationships, or events. **Hypothesis testing** is a procedure for deciding whether the outcome of a study conducted with a sample of participants supports a theory or innovation that in turn can be applied to a population.

The Core Logic of Hypothesis Testing
The principle underlying hypothesis testing is that researchers test the idea that an experimental treatment makes no difference, i.e., that it has no effect. If the idea that the experimental treatment makes no difference can be rejected, then researchers can accept the idea the treatment does make a difference, i.e., that it has an effect. In other words, researchers draw conclusions by evaluating the probability of getting the observed research results if the opposite of what they are predicting were true. This double negative, roundabout logic is awkward, but necessary, because researchers use comparison distributions to determine the probability of obtaining the observed results if the opposite of what they are predicting is true.

The Hypothesis Testing Process
Suppose that a group of psychologists have measured the stress perceived by students and want to see if a one-hour counseling session each week for six weeks will reduce stress. Although such a study would most likely involve more than one student, suppose that the psychologists have selected only one student to undergo the six counseling sessions. In order to conduct the study, the psychologists will follow the five steps that follow.

Step 1: Restate the question as a research hypothesis and a null hypothesis about the populations.
Research is conducted using samples to test hypotheses about populations. One population (*Population 1*) includes the people who undergo the experimental treatment. This population is hypothetical, but, in this case, it denotes the group of students to whom the experimental results might be applied. The other population (*Population 2*) includes the people who have not been exposed to the experimental treatment. This population is real and consists of people of the same category as those in the sample, but who were not exposed to the experimental manipulation. In this case, Population 2 would consist of students like those whose stress was measured. Furthermore, the characteristics of the distribution of this population are known, perhaps from previous research. More concisely,
Population 1: Students who undergo one hour of counseling per week for six weeks.
Population 2: Students who do not undergo one hour of counseling per week for six weeks.

The **research hypothesis** is a statement about the predicted difference between populations. Typically, the research hypothesis states that the means of the populations will be different, or perhaps more specifically, that one population mean will be higher or lower than the other population mean. The **null hypothesis** is the crucial opposite of the research hypothesis, and states that the means of the populations will be different, or that if a difference is observed, it will be in the opposite direction from the predicted direction. Thus, the research hypothesis and the null hypothesis are opposites and mutually exclusive. The research hypothesis is sometimes called the *alternative hypothesis* because researchers are interested in rejecting the null hypothesis to make a decision about its alternative. The hypotheses for the hypothetical stress study will be presented later.

Step 2: Determine the characteristics of the comparison distribution.

The question in hypothesis testing is "Given a particular sample result, what is the probability of obtaining this result if the null hypothesis is true?" In order to answer this question, researchers must know the characteristics of the **comparison distribution**. (The comparison distribution may be called a *sampling distribution*, terminology that will be discussed further in Chapter 5.) The comparison distribution is the distribution of the variable being measured if the null hypothesis is true, i.e., in the absence of an experimental treatment, or if an experimental treatment has no effect. Thus, the comparison distribution is the distribution for Population 2 in Step 1. Stated another way, if the null hypothesis is true, the distributions for Population 1 and Population 2 in Step 1 are identical so that any score is equally likely to come from either population. In the example, the comparison distribution is a normal distribution that reflects the scores of students who do not undergo one hour of counseling per week for six weeks.

Step 3: Determine the cutoff sample score on the comparison distribution at which the null hypothesis should be rejected.

Before conducting a study, researchers should determine how extreme a sample score must be to reject the null hypothesis. This score is called the **cutoff sample score** (or the *critical value*). Cutoff sample scores are expressed as Z scores instead of the units in which the experimental variable is measured, in this case, stress inventory scores. These Z scores are selected based on the percentage of area in the one or both tails of the comparison distribution. For example, if the mean stress score for a large number of students is 36 and the standard deviation is 8, a score more extreme than 20 ($Z = -2.00$) would occur fewer than 2% of the time. Therefore, the psychologists might decide to reject the null hypothesis if the student in the study obtains a score on the stress inventory lower than 20 after undergoing one hour of counseling per week for six weeks. If the student's stress score is greater than (or equal to) 36, the psychologists will not reject the null hypothesis.

Psychologists generally select cutoff sample scores that will be observed less than 5% of the time if the null hypothesis is true, or if they want to be more conservative, 1% of the time. These probabilities are written as $p < .05$ and $p < .01$, respectively. Very small percentages (probabilities of getting this extreme a score) are taken as the cutoff. These cutoff percentages are the **conventional levels of significance**, are also called the 5% (or .05) and the 1% (or .01) significance levels. When sample values are so extreme that researchers reject the null hypothesis, the results are said to be **statistically significant**.

Step 4: Determine the sample's score on the comparison distribution.

After conducting a study, the raw score result is converted to a Z score so that it can be compared to the cutoff sample score. For example, if a student in the sample study obtains a stress inventory score of 16 after undergoing one hour of counseling per week for six weeks, the student's Z score will be -2.50. Since a score this extreme will occur if the null hypothesis is true less than 2% of the time, the psychologists will reject the null hypothesis.

Step 5: Decide whether to reject the null hypothesis.

This step involves simply comparing the sample's Z score obtained in Step 4 with the cutoff sample score determined in Step 3. If the sample score is more extreme than the cutoff sample score, the researchers will reject the null hypothesis and accept the research hypothesis. If the sample score is not more extreme than the cutoff sample score, the researchers will fail to reject the null hypothesis. In Step 4 above, the student in the sample study obtained a score a stress inventory score of 16 after undergoing one hour of counseling per week for six weeks, yielding a Z score of -2.50. Since the student's Z score is more extreme than the cutoff sample score of $Z = -2.00$, the psychologists will reject the null hypothesis and accept the research hypothesis.

Implications of Rejecting or Failing to Reject the Null Hypothesis

Since the decision to reject or fail to reject the null hypothesis is based on probabilities, two points should be remembered.

1. Even if the null hypothesis is rejected, the results do not prove the research hypothesis. Experimenters can never prove a research hypothesis because the results of research studies are based on probabilities. They can only demonstrate that the likelihood of obtaining those results due to chance alone is very low *if the null hypothesis is true.*

2. When the results are not sufficiently extreme to reject the null hypothesis, experimenters do not say their results support the null hypothesis. Demonstrating that the null hypothesis is true would require that there be absolutely no difference between the two populations. The experimental treatment may cause a difference between or among the groups, but the difference may be too small to attribute to the treatment. Therefore, when the results are not sufficiently extreme to reject the null hypothesis, they are said to be inconclusive.

One–Tailed and Two–Tailed Hypothesis Tests

As indicated in the example in which the psychologists have measured the stress perceived by students and want to see if a one hour counseling session each week for six weeks will reduce stress, the psychologists expect that the counseling sessions will reduce the level of stress perceived by the student. In this case, the psychologists would state a **directional hypothesis**. Psychologists state directional hypotheses when they are interested in predicting the direction of effect of the experimental treatment; e.g., whether the value of the variable being measured will increase or decrease.

In general, a directional research hypothesis states that the Population 1 mean is higher (or lower, if that is the prediction) than the Population 2 mean. The directional hypothesis for the example study would be that the level of stress perceived by a student who attends a one-hour counseling session each week for six weeks would be lower than the level of stress perceived by students who does not attend such counseling sessions. If the psychologists were interested in increasing the student's self-esteem, the directional hypothesis would be that attending a one-hour counseling session each week for six weeks will increase self-esteem.

In general, the null hypothesis is that the Population 1 mean is the same as, or is in the opposite direction from, the Population 2 mean. The null hypothesis for the example study would be that the level of stress perceived by a student who attends a one hour counseling session each week for six weeks will be the same as, or higher than, the level of stress perceived by students who do not attend such counseling sessions. Again, if the psychologists were interested in increasing the student's self-esteem, the null hypothesis would be that attending a one-hour counseling session each week for six weeks will result in the same level of self-esteem or will lead to a decrease in self-esteem.

Therefore, if the 5% level of significance is being used, the obtained score has to lie in either the upper or the lower 5% of comparison distribution in order to reject the null hypothesis. That is, the score after the experimental treatment must lie in only one tail of the comparison distribution. For this reason, the statistical tests of such hypotheses are called **one-tailed tests**.

However, human behavior is difficult to predict. Despite the psychologists expectation that the counseling sessions will reduce stress, suppose that discussion of the student's problems in one area lead to discussions of problems in other areas. Awareness of these additional problems may lead to increased perceptions of stress. If the psychologists are unsure about the effect of the proposed experimental treatment, they may state a **nondirectional hypothesis**, in which they state that one population will be different from the other, but they do not specify whether Population 1scores will be higher or lower than Population 2 scores.

In general, a nondirectional research hypothesis states that the Population 1 mean is different from the Population 2 mean. The nondirectional hypothesis for the example study would be that the level of stress perceived by a student who attends a one-hour counseling session each week for six weeks would be different from the level of stress perceived by students who do not attend such counseling sessions. If the psychologists were interested in the effect of the experimental treatment on the student's self-esteem, the nondirectional hypothesis would be that attending a one-hour counseling session each week for six weeks will result in a different level of self-esteem.

In general, the null hypothesis is that the Population 1 mean will be no different from the Population 2 mean. The null hypothesis for the example study would be that the level of stress perceived by a student who attends a one-hour counseling session each week for six weeks would be *no* different from the level of stress perceived by students who do not attend such counseling sessions. Again, if the psychologists were interested in increasing the student's self-esteem, the null hypothesis would be that attending a one-hour counseling session each week for six weeks will have no effect on self-esteem.

Therefore, if the 5% level of significance is being used, the null hypothesis can be rejected if the obtained score lies in either the upper 2.5% or the lower 2.5% of comparison distribution. In other words, because the 5% probability that is being used to make the decision about the null hypothesis must be divided to accommodate the possibility of either an increase or decrease in the amount of the variable being measured, the Population 1 score after the experimental treatment can lie in either tail of the comparison distribution. For this reason, the statistical tests of such hypotheses are called **two-tailed tests**.

Note that the cutoff sample scores for two-tailed tests are more extreme than the cutoff sample scores for one-tailed tests. The cutoff sample scores for a two-tailed test at the .05 level are +1.96 and -1.96, while for a one-tailed test the scores are +1.64 and -1.64. At the .01 level, the scores are +2.58 and -2.58, and +2.33 and -2.33, respectively.

When to use one-tailed versus two-tailed tests

In principle, one-tailed tests are used when the hypothesis is clearly directional, and two-tailed tests are used when the hypothesis is clearly nondirectional. In practice, the situation is not so simple. Obtaining a statistically significant result is "easier" using a one-tailed test because the sample value after the experimental treatment does not have to be as extreme as the sample value for a two-tailed test. However, the price is that extreme results in the opposite direction do not permit rejection of the null hypothesis, no matter how extreme, or interesting, the result. For this reason, using one-tailed tests introduces the risk of having to ignore potentially important results. For this reasons, many researchers use two-tailed tests for both types of hypotheses. In most psychology articles, unless the researcher specifically notes that a one-tailed test was used, a two-tailed test is assumed. In most cases, the conclusion is not really affected by the choice of a one-tailed or a two-tailed test. Usually the results of studies are sufficiently extreme to reject the null hypothesis using either test, or *vice versa*. On the other, if the null hypothesis would be rejected by the result of a one-tailed test, but not by the result of a two-tailed test, the results of the study should be interpreted cautiously pending further research.

Hypothesis Tests As Reported in Research Articles

Decisions based on hypothesis tests are typically reported in the context of one of the statistical procedures described in later chapters. Articles usually include the symbol describing the statistic used (e.g., F for analysis of variance), the value of the statistic, and a statement about statistically significant results accompanied by notation like $p < .05$. Results that are not statistically significant are said to be nonsignificant or are indicated by the letters *ns*. Since statistical packages like SPSS provide exact probabilities for statistical procedures, many experimenters report exact p values like $p = .033$ or $p = .333$. Experimenters will usually note if statistical tests are one-tailed. The absence of such descriptions indicates that the tests were most likely two-tailed. In tables, one or more asterisks may indicate statistically significant results. Be aware that the research and null hypotheses are not stated explicitly in many articles, and decision errors are rarely mentioned.

Summary of the Hypothesis Testing Procedure
Step 1. Restate the question as a research hypothesis and a null hypothesis about populations.
Identify the two populations.
- Population 1: people like those who are exposed to the experimental treatment.
- Population 2: people like members of Population 1 who have not been exposed to the experimental treatment, i.e., the population to which the results of the experiment are to be generalized.

State the hypotheses.
- Research hypothesis: how is the experimental treatment expected to affect Population 1, i.e., is the hypothesis directional or nondirectional?
- Null hypothesis: the hypothesis that Population 1 and Population 2 will be the same with respect to the variable being measured after Population 1 has been exposed to the experimental treatment, i.e., the treatment will have no effect.

Step 2. Determine the characteristics of the comparison distribution.
- The comparison distribution is the Population 2 distribution.
- Describe μ, σ^2, and its shape, which will be normal until additional statistical procedures are learned.

Step 3. Determine the cutoff sample score on the comparison distribution at which the null hypothesis should be rejected.
- Select the significance level (.05 or .01).
- Determine the percentage of cases between the mean and Z score that will serve as the cutoff sample score on the normal curve. (For a one-tailed test at the .05 level, the Z score is +1.64 or -1.64, depending on the expected effect of the experimental treatment. For a two-tailed test at the .05 level, the Z scores are +1.96 and -1.96.)

Step 4. Determine the sample's score on the comparison distribution.
- Observe the raw score of the individual exposed to the experimental treatment.
- Convert the raw score to a Z score and locate the Z score on the comparison distribution.

Step 5. Decide whether to reject the null hypothesis.
- If the Z score of the individual exposed to the experimental treatment (Step 4) is more extreme than the cutoff Z score (Step 3), reject the null hypothesis and accept the research hypothesis.
- If the Z score of the individual exposed to the experimental treatment (Step 4) is not more extreme than the cutoff Z score (Step 3), do not reject the null hypothesis and state that the results of the experiment are inconclusive.

Chapter Self–Tests

The practice test items that follow are based on the following scenario. A group of psychologists has decided to conduct the study used as an example in this chapter. A student has been asked to attend a one-hour counseling session each week for six weeks. At the end of the six weeks, the student's level of perceived stress will be measured using an 18-statement inventory, each statement describing a possible response to stress. The student will use a 5-point scale on which responses are scored 0–4, so that scores can range from 0–72.

Understanding Key Terms in Chapter 4

Directions: Using the word bank that follows, complete each statement. **Some words maybe used more than once.**

Word Bank: comparison / conventional / cutoff sample / directional / hypothesis / hypothesis testing / nondirectional / null / one-tailed / research / statistically significant / theory / two-tailed

After reviewing previous research about the effect of counseling on stress, the behavioral scientists develop a set of principles that will guide their study. This set of principles is called a **(1)** _____. Based on these principles, the behavioral scientists make the prediction that counseling will reduce stress among students. This prediction is called a **(2)** _____. The general procedure the behavioral scientists will use to determine whether six weekly counseling sessions are effective in reducing the student's level of perceived stress is **(3)** _____. If the behavioral scientists believe that the counseling sessions will reduce stress, they have stated their **(4)** _____ hypothesis. If they make a formal statement to this effect as they plan their statistical analysis, the behavioral scientists will be stating a **(5)** _____ hypothesis, and they will analyze their data using a **(6)** _____ test. If the behavioral scientists are not sure what effect the counseling sessions will have on the student's stress, they may state a **(7)** _____ hypothesis and analyze their data using a **(8)** _____ test. The statement that the student's level of stress after the six counseling sessions will be no different from the levels of students who have not experienced counseling is a **(9)** _____ hypothesis.

In order to make a decision about the effectiveness of the counseling sessions, the behavioral scientists will locate the student's score after the six sessions on the distribution for Population 2. This distribution is called the (10) _____ distribution. If the student's score is more extreme than the (11) _____ score, the behavioral scientists will reject the (12) _____ hypothesis and accept the (13) _____ hypothesis. The behavioral scientists may decide that the student's score must be so extreme that it will occur fewer than either 5% of the time or 1% of the time if the counseling sessions have no effect. These values are known as the (14) _____ levels of significance. If the student's score is so extreme that the behavioral scientists conclude that the sessions were effective in reducing stress, the results are said to be (15) _____.

Multiple Choice Items

Items 1-3 are based on the hypothesis that a student's level of stress after attending one counseling session per week for six weeks will be no different than the student's level of stress before the counseling sessions.

1. This hypothesis is an example of
    A. a comparison hypothesis.
    B. a conventional hypothesis.
    C. a null hypothesis.
    D. a research hypothesis.

2. This hypothesis is also an example of
    A. a directional hypothesis.
    B. a nondirectional hypothesis.
    C. a Type I hypothesis.
    D. a Type II hypothesis.

3. The statistical analysis of this hypothesis will be
    A. Type I.
    B. Type II.
    C. one-tailed.
    D. two-tailed.

Items 4-6 are based on the hypothesis that a student's level of stress after attending one counseling session per week for six weeks will be the same as, or higher than, the student's level of stress before the counseling sessions.

4. This hypothesis is an example of
    A. a comparison hypothesis.
    B. a conventional hypothesis.
    C. a null hypothesis.
    D. a research hypothesis.

5. This hypothesis is also an example of
    A. a directional hypothesis.
    B. a nondirectional hypothesis.
    C. a Type I hypothesis.
    D. a Type II hypothesis.

6. The statistical analysis of this hypothesis will be
    A. Type I.
    B. Type II.
    C. one-tailed.
    D. two-tailed.

7. The overall procedure reflected in Items 1-6 is
   A. alpha testing.
   B. beta testing.
   C. conventional testing.
   D. hypothesis testing.

8. The research hypothesis may also be called the
   A. alternative hypothesis.
   B. cutoff hypothesis.
   C. decision hypothesis.
   D. significant hypothesis.

9. The comparison distribution is the distribution that describes
   A. population 1.
   B. population 2.
   C. decision errors.
   D. conventional levels of significance.

10. Comparison distributions may also be called
    A. conventional distributions.
    B. cutoff distributions.
    C. sampling distributions.
    D. Type I distributions.

11. The target score against which researchers will compare their experimental result is called
    A. beta.
    B. the cutoff sample score.
    C. significance.
    D. the type error score.

12. The conventional levels of statistical significance include
    A. .10 and .20.
    B. .05 and .10.
    C. .05 and .20.
    D. .05 and .01.

13. An experimental result is said to be statistically significant when the
    A. research hypothesis is rejected.
    B. Type II errors are identified.
    C. null hypothesis is rejected.
    D. alpha level is set prior to the analysis.

14. If the psychologists are using the .05 level of significance and find that the observed reduction in the student's level of stress would fewer than 2 times in 100, they
    A. can accept the research hypothesis.
    B. have proved the null hypothesis.
    C. should report that the results are inconclusive.
    D. must use a more conservative alpha.

15. If the psychologists report a difference between the student's stress level after counseling and the stress level of students in general and include the notation "$p < .05$" to describe this difference, they are indicating that
    A. the result is not statistically significant at the .05 level.
    B. the sample score falls in either the upper 5% or the lower 5% of the comparison distribution.
    C. there is a 95% chance that the research hypothesis is true.
    D. the chance of obtaining this result is less than 5% if the null hypothesis is true.

Problems

1. Describe the difference between the null hypothesis and the research hypothesis of a study. Describe the difference between directional and nondirectional research hypotheses and describe how the corresponding null hypotheses are different.

2. A group of psychologists wants to see if a 10-week self-defense training program will increase the self-esteem of an adolescent student being bullied by classmates. Describe the two populations of interest and write both directional and nondirectional research hypotheses with the corresponding null hypotheses for this study.

3. If the normal curve is the comparison distribution, what are the cutoff sample scores for both conventional levels of significance?

4. Why are psychologists reluctant to use directional hypotheses and the corresponding one-tailed tests?

5. Suppose the psychologists interested in the effect of a 10-week self-defense program on the self-esteem of bullied adolescent students know that the population distribution of self-esteem scores is normally distributed with $\mu = 66$ and $\sigma = 12$. Calculate the Z score for each of the following students, enter the cutoff sample score, and indicate the appropriate decision about the null hypothesis.

Student	Student Score	p	Tails of Test
1	90	.05	2
2	84	.05	1
3	94	.01	2
4	94	.01	1

6. Suppose the psychologists interested in the effect of a 10-week self-defense program on the self-esteem of bullied adolescent students also want to see if the program reduces the students' anxiety. They know that the population distribution of anxiety scores is normally distributed with $\mu = 32$ and $\sigma = 8$. Calculate the Z score for each of the following students, enter the cutoff sample score, and indicate the appropriate decision about the null hypothesis.

Student	Student Score	p	Tails of Test
1	20	.05	2
2	14	.05	1
3	10	.01	2
4	18	.01	1

7. Using the five steps of hypothesis testing, describe how a group of psychologists would determine the effect of the 12-week exercise program on the life satisfaction of a person whose score on a satisfaction with life scale after the program score after the program is 75. The population distribution of life satisfaction scores is normal with $\mu = 50$ and $\sigma = 10$. Just for practice, write both directional and nondirectional hypotheses and test each hypothesis at both the .05 and .01 levels. Using your decision about the null hypothesis based on the one-tailed test at the .05 significance level, explain your response to someone who has not had a statistics course, but who is familiar with the mean, standard deviation, and Z scores.

8. Now the psychologists want to determine the effect of the 12-week exercise program on the depression of a person whose depression score after the program is 9. The population distribution of depression scores is normal with $\mu = 15$ and $\sigma = 3$. Using the five steps of hypothesis testing, describe how the psychologists would conduct the study. Just for practice, write both directional and nondirectional hypotheses and test each hypothesis at both the .05 and .01 levels. Using your decision about the null hypothesis based on the two-tailed test at the .05 significance level, explain your response to someone who has not had a statistics course, but who is familiar with the mean, standard deviation, and Z scores.

Additional Practice: Complete any Practice Problems in Set I that your instructor has not assigned and compare your responses to those provided by the authors. Pay particular attention to the problems that require you to explain your results to someone who has never taken a course in statistics.

SPSS Applications
There are no SPSS applications for this chapter.

Chapter 5
Hypothesis Tests with Means of Samples

Learning Objectives
After studying this chapter, you should:
- Be able to explain the use of a distribution of means as a comparison distribution for experimental samples that include more than one person.
- Be able to describe the hypothetical method for constructing a distribution of means.
- Know how to calculate the mean of a distribution of means and explain its relationship to the mean of the population of individual cases.
- Know how to calculate the variance of a distribution of means and explain why it is smaller than the variance of the population of individual cases.
- Know how to calculate the standard deviation of a distribution of means.
- Be able to explain why a distribution of means tends to be unimodal and symmetrical.
- Be able to describe the conditions under which a distribution of means is identical to, or closely approximates, the normal curve.
- Know how to apply the five steps of hypothesis testing using samples that include more than one person and a known population distribution.
- Advanced Topic: Know how to calculate and interpret confidence intervals.
- Advanced Topic: Know how confidence intervals are reported in research results.

The Distribution of Means as a Comparison Distribution
When testing hypotheses with a sample of more than one person, the comparison distribution defined in Step 2 of the hypothesis testing procedure changes. Specifically, the comparison distribution is no longer the distribution of Population 2, the general population of individuals who are not exposed to the experimental treatment. Instead, when a sample of two or more individuals experiences the treatment, the score of interest is the mean of the group of scores. Therefore, the appropriate comparison distribution becomes a **distribution of means**, which is a distribution of all possible means of samples of the same size as the sample in the experiment.

Suppose that a group of psychologists is interested in reducing the stress perceived by college freshmen and has enrolled a group of 40 freshmen in a self-help discussion group. Since this group of freshmen comprises Population 1, the psychologists need to describe the distribution for Population 2, the comparison distribution. The intuitive approach to the problem of describing the comparison distribution is to select a random sample of 40 freshmen who are not receiving the experimental treatment from the population of all freshmen, measure their perceived stress, calculate the sample mean, and plot it as the first value in a frequency distribution. Then repeat the process for a second sample of 40 untreated freshmen and plot the mean for this sample. After repeating this process many times, the mean and standard deviation of this frequency distribution means can be calculated, and the distribution can be used as a comparison distribution just like a normal distribution of scores of individuals. [Note that the characteristics of a distribution of means can be determined without this process of repeated sampling, as will be shown in the next section.]

Characteristics of a Distribution of Means
The three characteristics of a comparison distribution that must be determined are its mean, variation (variance and then standard deviation), and shape. Due to the relationships between distributions of means and the populations of individual cases from which samples are drawn, the characteristics of the distribution of means can be determined directly from knowledge of the characteristics of the population and from the size of the samples involved by applying three rules.

Rule1: The **mean of the distribution of means** is the same as the mean of the population of individuals. Expressed as a formula, this rule states that $\mu_M = \mu.$, where μ_M represents the mean of the distribution of means and μ represents the mean of the population of individual scores.
The rationale for this rule is that as random samples of a given size are drawn, the effect of extremely low scores in a sample on the mean of the sample are cancelled by the effects of extremely high scores and *vice versa*. For this

reason, sample means will tend to cluster about the mean of the population of individual scores, and if an infinite number of samples are drawn, the mean of all the sample means will be equal to the population mean.

Rule2a: The **variance of a distribution of means** is the variance of the distribution of the population of individuals divided by the number of individuals in each sample.

The distribution of means will have less variation than the population of individual cases from which the samples are drawn because the probability is low that all the scores in a sample will be extremely high or extremely low. In other words, in any sample, extreme scores tend to be balanced out by scores in the middle of the distribution, or by extreme scores in the opposite direction. With fewer extreme means, the variance of the distribution of means is smaller.

Expressed as a formula, this rule states that $\sigma_M{}^2 = \sigma^2 / N$, where $\sigma_M{}^2$ is the variance of the distribution of means, σ^2 is the variance of the distribution of individual scores, and N is the number of cases in each sample.

Rule2b: The **standard deviation of a distribution of means** is the square root of the variance of the distribution of means.

Expressed as a formula, this rule states that $\sigma_M = \sqrt{\sigma_M{}^2} = \sqrt{(\sigma^2/N)}$, where $\sigma_M{}^2$ is the variance of the distribution of means, σ^2 is the variance of the distribution of individual scores, and N is the number of cases in each sample. The standard deviation of the distribution of means is also called the **standard error of the mean (_SEM_)**, or simply the **standard error (_SE_)**.

Rule 3: The shape of a distribution of means is approximately normal if either (a) each sample includes 30 or more individuals or (b) the distribution of the population of individuals is normal.
Distributions of means tend to be unimodal due to the process of extreme scores balancing each other described in the discussion of the variance of distributions of means. Distributions of means tend to be symmetrical for the same reason – since skew is caused by extreme scores, the presence of fewer extreme scores results in distributions that are more symmetrical, or less skewed.

As the number of subjects in a sample increases, the distribution of means for samples of that size becomes an increasingly closer approximation to the normal curve. When samples include 30 or more individuals, even if the population of individual cases is quite skewed, the distribution of means will closely resemble a normal curve, and the percentages of area under the normal curve table will be accurate. If the population distribution of individual cases is normal, any distribution of means obtained from samples drawn from the population will be normal, regardless of sample size.

All the rules described are based on the _central limit theorem_.

Determining the Characteristics of a Distribution of Means
Example 1: The distribution of scores of large numbers of individuals on certain widely used intelligence tests is approximately normal with a mean of 100 and a standard deviation of 15. What would be the characteristics of the distribution of means for a sample of 25 individuals?

Rule1: The mean of the distribution of means is the same as the mean of the population of individuals. Since the mean of the population is 100, the mean of the distribution of means will be 100, as well.

Rule2a: The variance of a distribution of means is the variance of the distribution of the population of individuals divided by the number of individuals in each sample. The standard deviation of the population is 15, so the variance of the population is 15^2, or 225. The variance of the distribution if means is 225/25 = 9 $[\sigma_M{}^2 = \sigma^2 / N]$.

Rule2b: The standard deviation of a distribution of means is the square root of the variance of the distribution of means. The standard deviation of the distribution of means is square root of 9, or 3 $[\sigma_M = \sqrt{\sigma_M{}^2} = \sqrt{(\sigma^2/N)}]$.

Rule 3: The shape of a distribution of means is approximately normal if either (a) each sample includes 30 or more individuals or (b) the distribution of the population of individuals is normal. Although the sample only includes 25 individuals, the distribution of individual scores is described as normal.

Example 2: A widely used achievement test is also has a mean of 100 and a standard deviation of 15, but the population distribution is slightly skewed. What would be the characteristics of the distribution of means for a sample of 60 individuals?
Rule1: The mean of the distribution of means is the same as the mean of the population of individuals. Since the mean of the population is 100, the mean of the distribution of means will be 100, as well.

Rule2a: The variance of a distribution of means is the variance of the distribution of the population of individuals divided by the number of individuals in each sample. The standard deviation of the population is 15, so the variance of the population is 15^2, or 225. The variance of the distribution if means is $225 / 60 = 3.75$ $[\sigma_M^2 = \sigma^2 / N]$.

Rule2b: The standard deviation of a distribution of means is the square root of the variance of the distribution of means. The standard deviation of the distribution of means is square root of 3.75, or 1.94 $[\sigma_M = \sqrt{\sigma_M^2} = \sqrt{(\sigma^2/N)}\,]$.

Rule 3: The shape of a distribution of means is approximately normal if either (a) each sample includes 30 or more individuals or (b) the distribution of the population of individuals is normal. Although the distribution of individual scores is slightly skewed, the sample includes 60 individuals. Therefore, the distribution of means will be normally distributed.

Hypothesis Testing with a Distribution of Means: The Z Test
The *Z test* is the hypothesis-testing procedure used to compare a single sample mean with a population mean when the population variance is known. Again, the distribution of means is the comparison distribution described in Step 2 of the hypothesis testing procedure, and it is used to determine the likelihood that a sample mean the size of the one obtained could have been selected if the null hypothesis is true. Remember that sample means are now being treated like the scores of individuals, so the formula for Z changes from $Z = (X - M) / SD$ to $Z = (M - \mu) / \sigma_M$. In addition, the sample will be located on the distribution of means in Step 4. Otherwise, the hypothesis testing process is identical to the process described in Chapter 4, when the sample consisted of a single individual.

Example 1: Suppose that the psychologists interested in reducing the stress perceived by college freshmen have enrolled 40 freshmen in a semester-long self-help discussion group based on the idea that discussions will let participants know that others are dealing with the same stressful issues, and that participants may help each other by suggesting solutions to problems causing stress. The mean score on a widely used stress inventory is 36 and the standard deviation is 8. The mean stress score of the 40 freshmen at the end of the semester is 32. Conduct a Z test following the five steps of hypothesis testing and using the .05 level of significance.

Step 1: Restate the question as a research hypothesis and a null hypothesis about the populations.
Population 1: Freshmen who participate in a self-help discussion group.
Population 2: Freshmen who do not participate in a self-help discussion group.
Research hypothesis: The perceived stress of freshmen who participate in a self-help discussion group will be different than the perceived stress of freshmen who do not participate in a self-help discussion group.
Null hypothesis: The perceived stress of freshmen who participate in a self-help discussion group will be no different from the perceived stress of freshmen who do not participate in a self-help discussion group.

Step 2: Determine the characteristics of the comparison distribution.
Distribution of means with
Mean = 36 $[\mu_M = \mu = 36$: Rule 1]
Variance = $8^2 / 40 = 64 / 40 = 1.60$ $[\sigma_M^2 = \sigma^2 / N$: Rule 2a]
Standard deviation = 1.26 $[\sigma_M = \sqrt{\sigma_M^2} = \sqrt{(\sigma^2/N)}$: Rule 2b]

Shape = normal [$N > 30$: Rule 3]

Step 3: Determine the cutoff sample score on the comparison distribution at which the null hypothesis should be rejected.
Using the .05 level of significance for a two-tailed test, the cutoff sample score is ±1.96.

Step 4: Determine the sample's score on the comparison distribution.
$Z = (M - \mu) / \sigma_M = (32 - 36) / 1.26 = -3.17$

Step 5: Decide whether to reject the null hypothesis.
The psychologists would reject the null hypothesis because a Z score of -3.17 is more extreme than the cutoff sample score of -1.96 and conclude that the self-help discussion group did reduce the perceived stress of the participants.

Example 2: Suppose that the psychologists interested in reducing the stress perceived by college freshmen decide to replicate their study during the following semester and have enrolled 25 freshmen in the semester-long self-help discussion group. Again, scores on the stress inventory are normally distributed with a mean of 36 and a standard deviation of 8. The mean stress score of the 25 freshmen at the end of the semester is again 32. Conduct a Z test following the five steps of hypothesis testing using the .01 level of significance.

Step 1: Restate the question as a research hypothesis and a null hypothesis about the populations.
Population 1: Freshmen who participate in a self-help discussion group.
Population 2: Freshmen who do not participate in a self-help discussion group.
Research hypothesis: Freshmen who participate in a self-help discussion group will report lower levels of perceived stress than freshmen who do not participate in a self-help discussion group.
Null hypothesis: The perceived stress of freshmen who participate in a self-help discussion group will be the same as, or higher than, the perceived stress of freshmen who do not participate in a self-help discussion group.

Step 2: Determine the characteristics of the comparison distribution.
Distribution of means with
Mean = 36 [$\mu_M = \mu = 36$: Rule 1]
Variance = $8^2 / 25 = 64 / 25 = 2.56$ [$\sigma_M^2 = \sigma^2 / N$: Rule 2a]

Standard deviation = 1.60 [$\sigma_M = \sqrt{\sigma_M^2} = \sqrt{(\sigma^2/N)}$: Rule 2b]
Shape = normal [Population of individual scores is normally distributed: Rule 3]

Step 3: Determine the cutoff sample score on the comparison distribution at which the null hypothesis should be rejected.
Using the .01 level of significance for a one-tailed test, the cutoff sample score is -2.33.

Step 4: Determine the sample's score on the comparison distribution.
$Z = (M - \mu) / \sigma_M = (32 - 36) / 1.60 = -2.50$

Step 5: Decide whether to reject the null hypothesis.
The psychologists would reject the null hypothesis because a Z score of -2.50 is more extreme than the cutoff sample score of -2.33, and conclude that the self-help discussion group did reduce the perceived stress of the participants.

Hypothesis Tests about Means of Samples (Z Tests) and Standard Errors in Research Articles
Research measuring variables with known population means and standard deviations is rare in psychology. Consequently, Z tests are seldom encountered. However, the standard deviation of the distribution of means, which provides an indication of the amount of variation that might be expected among means of samples of a given size from a particular population may be reported as the standard error or standard error of the mean. Standard errors are

often used in graphs to indicate the extent that scores on the measured variable varied around a mean. When used in this manner, the lines reflecting the standard errors are called *error bars*.

Advanced Topic: Estimation, Standard Errors, and Confidence Intervals

If researchers want to estimate an unknown population mean from scores in a sample, the best estimate of the population mean is the sample mean. One way to determine the accuracy of a sample mean as an estimate of the population mean is to determine how much the means vary in a distribution of means, which can be done by calculating the standard deviation of a distribution of means. Remember that the standard deviation of a distribution is also called the standard error of the mean.

Assuming that the distribution of means is normally distributed, which it typically is, areas under the normal curve can be used to define intervals with a known probability of including the population mean. For example, since 34% of a normally distributed population lies between the mean and one standard deviation above the mean, and the same percentage lies between the mean and one standard deviation below the mean, the area under the curve between these two points includes 68% of the area under the curve. Since there is a 68% chance that this area includes the population mean, the area extending from one standard deviation below the mean to one standard deviation above is an example of a **confidence interval**, specifically the 68% confidence interval. The values of the variable being measured that lie one standard deviation above the mean and one standard deviation below the mean are the **confidence limits**. Thus, a confidence interval is the range of values calculated from sample data (statistics) that has specified probability of containing a parameter, and the confidence limits are the upper and lower values of the confidence interval.

Most experimenters want to be more than 68% confident about their estimates, so the **95% confidence interval** and the **99% confidence interval** are usually calculated. A 95% confidence interval includes the middle 95% of a normal distribution, leaving 2.5% in each tail. Since the normal curve is symmetrical, 47.5% of the confidence interval is above the mean and 47.5% is below the mean. Using the normal curve table, the Z scores that define this area above and below the mean are +1.96 and -1.96, respectively. To calculate the 99% confidence interval, the Z scores are +2.57 and -2.57, respectively. These Z scores include the middle 99% of a normal curve, leaving 0.5% in each tail.

Example: Using the results of the study in which 40 freshmen participated in a self-help discussion group to help them cope with stress, sample mean was 32 and the standard deviation of the distribution of means was 1.26.

$M = 32$

$\sigma_M^2 = SD^2 / N = 64 / 40 = 1.60$

$\sigma_M = \sqrt{1.60} = 1.26$ [This value is also the standard error of the mean.]

Formula: 95% confidence interval $= M + (\pm 1.96) \, (SEM)$

Applying the formula for calculating the 95% confidence interval,
the lower limit $= 32 + (-1.96) \, (1.26) = 29.53$,
the upper limit $= 32 + (1.96) \, (1.26) = 34.47$, so that
the 95% confidence interval $= 29.53 - 34.47$

Applying the formula for calculating the 99% confidence interval,
the lower limit $= 32 + (-2.57) \, (1.26) = 28.76$,
the upper limit $= 32 + (2.57) \, (1.26) = 35.24$, so that
the 99% confidence interval $= 28.76 - 35.24$

Confidence Intervals and Hypothesis Testing

Confidence intervals can be used to test hypotheses. If a confidence interval does not include the mean of the comparison distribution (i.e., the null hypothesis distribution), then the result of the hypothesis test is statistically significant. Considering the 95% confidence interval in Example 1, the population mean of 36 is not included in the interval, so the results are statistically significant at the .05 level, which confirms the result of the Z test. In addition, the population mean of 36 is not included in the 99% confidence interval, which means that the result is statistically significant at the .01 level, as well.

Advanced Topic: Confidence Intervals in Research Articles
Confidence intervals are reported in research articles. Remembering that the 95% and 99% confidence intervals extend approximately two standard errors and approximately 2.5 standard errors to either side of the mean, respectively, will help in the interpretation of such results.

Chapter Self-Tests

The practice test items and problems that follow are based on the following scenario. In the last chapter, a group of psychologists conducted a study in which a student attended a one hour counseling session each week for six weeks that was designed to help the student reduce stress. Based on the results of this study, the psychologists have conducted a larger study in which 30 freshmen attended the counseling sessions. At the end of the six weeks, the mean score on a stress inventory was 28. Examination of the responses to the inventory by a large number of freshmen collected over several years reveals that the scores of freshmen are normally distributed with a mean of 36 and a standard deviation of 8.

Understanding Key Terms in Chapter 5

Directions: Using the word bank that follows, complete each statement.

Word Bank: confidence interval / confidence limits / distribution of means / means / standard deviation / standard error / standard error of the mean / variance / Z test / 95% confidence interval / 99% confidence interval / μ_M / σ_M^2 / σ_M

When the study involved only a single student, the comparison distribution was the distribution of scores of freshmen who did not participate in counseling sessions. Now that the psychologists have expanded the study to involve a group of freshmen, the appropriate comparison distribution is a distribution of **(1)** _____. Knowing that the mean stress score for a large number of freshmen who had taken the inventory previously was 36 informed the psychologists that 36 would be the mean of the **(2)** _____, The symbol for this parameter is **(3)** _____. Dividing the square of the standard deviation of the distribution of scores of previous respondents by 30 yields the **(4)** _____ of the comparison distribution, which is symbolized by **(5)** _____. and the square root of this quotient is the **(6)** _____ of the comparison distribution, which is symbolized by **(7)** _____.. At the conclusion of the six weeks, the psychologists can use a **(8)** _____ to compare the sample mean and the population mean.

The psychologists are also interested in estimating the range of possible values the mean of groups of 30 freshmen might take. These estimates are bases on the standard deviation of the distribution of means, which is also called the **(9)** _____, or simply the **(10)** _____. When such ranges are calculated, they are called **(11)** _____, and the upper and lower values are called **(12)** _____. If the range extends approximately 2 standard errors from the mean of the distribution of means, the **(13)** _____ has been calculated. If the range extends approximately 2.5 standard errors from the mean of the distribution of means, the **(14)** _____ has been calculated.

Multiple-Choice Items

1. Since the psychologists are now comparing the mean of an experimental group with a known population mean, the appropriate comparison distribution is the distribution of
    A. all possible means of 30 freshmen.
    B. freshmen from which the sample was drawn.
    C. freshmen on whom the counseling sessions had no effect.
    D. the distribution of means with a standard error of 2.13.

2. Since the mean for the population of freshmen who have taken the stress inventory is 36 and the standard deviation is 8, the mean of the distribution of means is
   A. 8.
   B. 26.
   C. 36.
   D. 64.

3. The psychologists will calculate the variance of their distribution of means by
   A. multiplying the variance of the population of individual cases by the number of subjects in the sample.
   B. subtracting the sample's variance from the population variance.
   C. taking the square root of the variance of the distribution of means.
   D. dividing the variance of the population of individual cases by the number of subjects in the sample.

4. The symbol for the variance of the distribution of means is
   A. μ_M
   B. σ_M^2
   C. σ_M
   D. σ^2

5. The psychologists will calculate the standard deviation of their distribution of means by
   A. multiplying the variance of the population of individual cases by the number of subjects in the sample.
   B. subtracting the sample's variance from the population variance.
   C. taking the square root of the variance of the distribution of means.
   D. dividing the variance of the population of individual cases by the number of subjects in the sample.

6. The standard deviation of the distribution of means calculated by the psychologists is also known as
   A. the standard error.
   B. the confidence limit.
   C. a point estimate.
   D. an interval estimate.

7. In comparison to the distribution of scores of all freshmen who have ever taken the inventory, the shape of the distribution of means will
   A. have more spread.
   B. have less spread.
   C. be skewed.
   D. be rectangular.

8. By using a sample of 30 freshmen, the psychologists can assume that the distribution of means will be
   A. bimodal.
   B. generally rectangular.
   C. seriously skewed.
   D. approximately normal.

9. To determine whether the difference between the sample mean and the population mean is statistically significant, the psychologists will calculate
   A. Σ.
   B. N.
   C. Z.
   D. μ.

Items 10–11 are related.

10. If the psychologists make a statement about the probability that the true population mean lies between 25.61 and 30.39, the values 25.61 and 30.39 define
    A. a confidence interval.
    B. a statistically significant Z.
    C. the standard error of the mean.
    D. the population mean.

11. The values 25.61 and 30.39 are called
    A. confidence intervals.
    B. confidence limits.
    C. point estimates.
    D. standard errors.

12. Which of the following formulas would be used in calculating the 95% confidence interval?
    A. $M + (\pm 1.64) (SEM)$.
    B. $M + (\pm 2.33) (SEM)$.
    C. $M + (\pm 1.96) (SEM)$.
    D. $M + (\pm 2.57) (SEM)$.

13. Which of the following formulas would be used in calculating the 99% confidence interval?
    A. $M + (\pm 1.64) (SEM)$.
    B. $M + (\pm 2.33) (SEM)$.
    C. $M + (\pm 1.96) (SEM)$.
    D. $M + (\pm 2.57) (SEM)$.

Problems

1. The standard deviation for the population of freshmen who have taken the stress inventory is 8. Calculate the standard deviation of the distribution of means for samples comprised of (a) 4, (b) 8, (c) 12, and (d) 20 freshmen.

2. Advanced Topic: Use the sample mean of 28 obtained by the 30 freshmen in the psychologists sample to calculate the 95% confidence interval and the 99% confidence interval for the 4 samples in Problem 1.

3. If the psychologists replicate the study with a sample of 25 freshmen and obtain a mean of 33 on the stress inventory, is the sample mean significantly different from the population mean of 36? Remember that the scores of freshmen who have previously taken the inventory are normally distributed. Use the five steps of hypothesis testing to describe how the psychologists would conduct the study. State a nondirectional research hypothesis and use the .05 level of significance to determine the cutoff sample score. Advanced Topic: Calculate the 95% confidence interval.

4. Based on the results of the studies they have conducted, the psychologists are confident that the counseling sessions are an effective means of reducing stress. In a final replication, they again use a sample of 25 freshmen and obtain a mean of 30 on the stress inventory. Is the sample mean significantly different from the population mean of 36? Use the five steps of hypothesis testing to describe how the psychologists would conduct the study. State a directional research hypothesis and use the .01 level of significance to determine the cutoff sample score. Advanced Topic: Calculate the 99% confidence interval.

Problems 5–6. are based on the following scenario. Having observed the effect of the counseling sessions on student stress, the psychologists have decided to see if the sessions have an effect on other variables. Therefore, in their final replication, they have also measured self-esteem and coping skills. The self-esteem inventory has been used in a number of studies and the resulting scores are normally distributed with a mean of 65 and a standard deviation of 11. Scores on the measure of coping skills have also been shown to be normally distributed and have a mean of 72 and a standard deviation 14.

5. After participating in the counseling sessions, the mean self-esteem score of the 25 freshmen was 70. Use the five steps of hypothesis testing to describe this portion of the final replication. State a nondirectional research hypothesis and use the .05 level of significance to determine the cutoff sample score. Advanced Topic: Calculate the 95% confidence interval. Explain your results to someone who is familiar with the logic of hypothesis testing, the normal curve, Z scores, and probability, but not with a distribution of means.

6. After participating in the counseling sessions, the mean coping skills score of the 25 freshmen was 76. Use the five steps of hypothesis testing to describe this portion of the final replication. State a directional research hypothesis and use the .05 level of significance to determine the cutoff sample score. Advanced Topic: Calculate the 95% confidence interval. Explain your results to someone who is familiar with the logic of hypothesis testing, the normal curve, Z scores, and probability, but not with a distribution of means.

Additional Practice: Complete any Practice Problems in Set I that your instructor has not assigned and compare your responses to those provided by the authors. Pay particular attention to the problems that require you to explain your results to someone who has never taken a course in statistics.

SPSS Applications
There are no SPSS applications for this chapter.

Chapter 6
Making Sense of Statistical Significance: Effect Size and Statistical Power

Learning Objectives
After studying this chapter, you should:

- Be able to describe the two types of decision errors that can be made during hypothesis testing.
- Be able to describe effect size.
- Be able to compute effect size.
- Know the conventional effect sizes.
- Be able to describe meta-analysis and list its advantages and disadvantages.
- Be able to define statistical power and apply the concept while conducting research and reading research reports.
- Know the resources available to determine power and know how to use power tables.
- Be able to list factors that determine power and describe how each functions to determine power.
- Be able to determine power from effect size.
- Know how to use sample size tables.
- Be able to list the six influences on statistical power and describe each.
- Be able to explain the relationship between effect size and statistical significance in interpreting research results.
- Be able to explain the role of power in evaluating significant and nonsignificant research results.
- Know how decision errors, effect size, and power are described in research reports.

Decision Errors
In statistics, **decision errors** are NOT due to making mistakes in calculations or using an inappropriate procedure. Instead, decision errors are made when experimenters make the wrong decision about the null hypothesis based on their experimental data.

Remember:
1. The hypothesis testing involves studying samples to draw inferences about populations of interest. For example, suppose a psychologist wanted to determine the effect of a one-hour counseling session each week for six weeks on the stress perceived by college students. The ultimate purpose of the study would be to see whether the results could be generalized to all students like those in the study.
2. This inference would be based on the probability that any observed difference in perceived stress would have occurred even if the counseling sessions were ineffective. For example, suppose the students received unanticipated financial aid that removed an important source of stress.
3. The hypothesis testing procedure is designed to make the probability of errors as small as possible, but the possibility of error is always present.

One error is rejecting the null hypothesis when it is true; i.e., concluding that the experimental treatment has an effect when it does not. This error is a **Type I error**, and the probability of making a Type I error is called **alpha (α)**, which is the same as the level of significance chosen, usually either .05 or .01. A second error is failing to reject the null hypothesis when it is false; i.e., concluding that the experimental treatment is ineffective when it does have an effect. This error is a **Type II error**, and the probability of making a Type II error is called **beta (ß)**.

The problem posed by these errors is that experimenters never know when they are making either of these errors. In the case of Type I errors, ineffective treatments may be presented as effective. For example, a one-hour counseling session each week for six weeks may appear to reduce stress when it actually does not. On the other hand, the effectiveness of a one-hour counseling session each week for six weeks will be missed if a Type II error is made. Type I and Type II errors are related. The probability of making a Type I error is determined by the level of significance. Therefore, using larger significance levels like .20 decreases the chance of making a Type II error, i.e., of failing to identify a potentially effective treatment. However, using a larger significance level increases the chance of making a Type I error, i.e., of deciding that a treatment that is actually ineffective is effective. Using a more conservative significance level like .001 has the opposite effect. In this situation, the probability of making a Type I error is reduced, but the probability if making a Type II error is increased. Therefore, the resolution of this difficulty is the use of the conventional levels of significance, the .05 and .01 levels.

Effect Size
Statistical significance indicates that the experimental treatment had an effect, e.g., counseling sessions reduced the amount of stress perceived by students. However, statistical significance does not indicate the size of the experimental effect, e.g., whether the reduction in perceived stress was large or small. **Effect size**, a measure of the difference between population means, does indicate the amount of change in the variable being measured after an experimental treatment.

One way to conceptualize effect size is to think about the distributions, including their means, of the two populations used in the hypothesis testing examples in previous chapters being drawn on transparencies. If the experimental treatment has no effect, the overlap of the two distributions will be perfect – the transparencies will appear to depict only one distribution. If the experimental treatment is designed to increase the variable being measured, think about sliding the transparency for Population 1 to the right. The more the transparency moves to the right, the less the distributions overlap and the greater the difference between the means becomes, indicating a greater effect of the experimental treatment. If the experimental treatment is designed to decrease the variable being measured, the transparency for Population 1 is simply moved to the left.

The difference between the Population 1 and Population 2 means is a *raw score effect size*, which is useful in interpreting the effect of the experimental treatment in one study, but does not permit comparison with the results of similar studies. However, in a manner analogous to the computation of Z scores, the difference between means can be divided by its population standard deviation, yielding a *standardized effect size*. The formula is $d = (\mu_1 - \mu_2)/\sigma$, where d (or Cohen's d) is a symbol for effect size. Note that the denominator is the standard deviation of the population of individuals, not the standard deviation of the distribution of means. Also, d can be positive or negative depending on whether the experimental treatment is designed increase or decrease the variable being measured.

Based on psychology research results, Cohen developed **effect size conventions**.

Effect Size	Value of d	Overlap between distributions
Small	.20 (difference = .2 standard deviations)	85%
Medium	.50 (difference = .5 standard deviations)	67%
Large	.80 (difference = .8 standard deviations)	53%

Meta-analysis
Calculation of standardized effect sizes provides a statistical method for combining the results of studies in a particular area of research called **meta-analysis**. This technique can be useful in making sense of the results of many studies in applied areas of psychology like treatment for clinical disorders such as depression or anxiety, either of which can be measured using any of a number of inventories. Since standardized effect sizes can be averaged, a hypothetical meta-analysis might reveal that self-help discussion groups have a mean effect = -.20 (a small effect) on depression, group therapy has a mean effect = -.50 (a medium effect) on depression, and individual therapy has a mean = -.80 (a large effect) on depression. Thus, all three types of therapy reduce depression, but individual therapy is the most effective, self-help discussion groups are the least effective, and group therapy falls between the other two.

Statistical Power
Statistical power, or simply power, is the probability that a study will yield a significant result if the research hypothesis is true. Two points to remember about power are that:
1. If the research hypothesis is not true, experimenters do not want to obtain significant results. Significant results in this situation are Type I errors.
2. Even if the research hypothesis is true, a study may not yield significant results if the sample drawn from the population studied is not sufficiently extreme to reject the null hypothesis. For example, in a study involving a treatment to reduce depression, the experimenters may draw a sample of individuals whose depression scores are so low that even if the treatment is successful, the sample scores may not demonstrate the improvement in relation to the comparison population. Depending on the goal of the study, such nonsignificant results could be a Type II error.

Remember that the probability of making a Type II error is beta, the probability of not obtaining a significant result even though the research hypothesis is true. Since power is the probability of obtaining a significant result when the research hypothesis is true, power and beta are opposites. Therefore, power + beta = 100%, and power = 100%-beta.

Determining Power
Three methods are available for determining power include computer software, Internet power calculators, and *power tables*. [Some power calculations will be presented in the Advanced Topics section of this chapter.]

What Determines Power
The two main influences on power are:
1. Effect size
2. Sample size

Additional influences include:
1. Level of statistical significance
2. Use of a one-tailed or a one-tailed test
3. Type of hypothesis-testing procedure used

Effect Size
Examination of the formula for calculating the effect size, $d = (\mu_1 - \mu_2) / \sigma$ shows that the greater the difference an experimenter expects to observe between two populations, as indicated in numerator of the formula, the greater the effect size will be. In other words, the larger the effect size, the greater the power. However, the population standard deviation affects effect size. The smaller the standard deviation, as reflected in the denominator of the formula, the greater the effect size. Another way to view these concepts is that the greater the difference between means, the less the Population 1 and Population 2 distributions will overlap. Likewise, the smaller the standard deviations of the two distributions, the less they will overlap.

Considering the statistical procedures presented to this point in the text, when experimenters calculate power prior to conducting a study, the mean for Population 2 is known. Experimenters can also use the known Population 2 mean and standard deviation in conjunction with Cohen's conventions to predict a Population 1 mean. All that is required is solving the formula for d for μ_1 so that $\mu_1 = \mu_2 + (d)(\sigma)$. For example, suppose the psychologists measuring stress wanted to know the amount of reduction in stress required to demonstrate a medium effect size. Remembering that the Population 2 mean for the stress inventory is 36 with a standard deviation of 8, the psychologists would simply substitute these values and .50 as the value for a medium effect size according to Cohen's conventions into the formula $\mu_1 = \mu_2 + (-d)(\sigma)$, which would yield
$\mu_1 = 36 + (-.50)(8)$
$\mu_1 = 36 - 4$
$\mu_1 = 32$.
[Note that the effect size is entered as -.50 because the psychologists are interested in reducing stress.]

Sample Size
In addition to effect size, the other major influence on power is sample size. Simply stated, the larger the sample size, the greater the power. This influence of sample size on power is due the fact that the variance of a distribution of means is calculated by dividing the variance of the population of individual scores (the Population 2 variance) by the sample size. Therefore, the larger the sample used in a study, the smaller the variance of the distribution of means, and the smaller the variance, the less the overlap between distributions of means. Remember that sample size and effect size are separate influences on power.

Sample Sizes Required for Given Levels of Power
The main reason experimenters consider power when planning an experiment is that the desired power determines the number of participants who must be enrolled in an experiment. Consideration of the number of participants is important because too few participants may result in low power, which may result in a Type II error, i.e., failing to reject the null hypothesis when the research hypothesis is true.

Determining the number of participants needed for a given level of power is done by reversing the steps for computing power, beginning with a desired level of power, say 80%, and calculating the number of participants needed to obtain the desired level of power. [This topic will be covered in more detail in the Advanced Topic section at the end of this chapter.]

Other Influences on Power

1. The significance level (alpha) used for an experiment affects power because using less stringent significance level like .05 instead of .01 means that the cutoff sample score will not be as extreme. For example, the cutoff sample score for a two-tailed test at the .05 level is ±1.96, while the cutoff sample for the same test at the .01 level is ±2.58. Since power is the probability of obtaining a significant result when the research is true, testing a hypothesis at the .05 level will increase power.

2. Using a two-tailed test increases the difficulty of obtaining a significant result in any one tail. Therefore, if all other factors are the same, one-tailed tests have more power (for results in the predicted direction) than two-tailed tests. For example, the cutoff sample score for a one-tailed test at the .05 level is + or -1.64, while the cutoff sample for a two-tailed test at the .0 level is ±1.96.

3. Sometimes the data collected in an experiment can be analyzed appropriately by two or more statistical procedures to apply to a given set of results, each of which has its own power. [This possibility will be discussed in Chapter 14.]

Power in Study Planning

If the power of a planned experiment is low, this study is unlikely to yield significant results, even if the research hypothesis is true. Since conducting the study as planned would be a waste of time and resources, experimenters can look for practical ways to increase the power to an acceptable level. One widely cited rule is that if a power of 80% cannot be obtained, the study may not be worth conducting.

Increasing the Power of a Planned Study

1. Although experimenters cannot arbitrarily increase the predicted difference between population means, if there is a logical basis for such an increase, the increase will increase power. In the absence of increasing the effect size, changing the way the experiment is conducted, e.g., by increasing the intensity of the experimental manipulation, may permit the experimenter to expect a larger difference between means. However, such changes may be difficult or costly to implement or change the experimental treatment so much that the results cannot be generalized to the intended population.

2. The population standard deviation can be decreased by using a population that is less diverse than the one originally planned. However, this approach also limits the scope of the population to which the results can be generalized. A second, and recommended, method for reducing the population standard deviation is to use more standardized conditions (e.g., laboratory settings) or measures that are more precise.

3. Increasing the sample size is the most straightforward way to increase power, but the number of available participants may be a limiting factor. In addition, increasing the number of participants may increase the cost of an experiment in both time and money.

4. Using a less stringent significance level, e.g., .10 instead of .05 will increase power; however, the less stringent level will also increase the risk of a Type I error. The .05 level of significance is conventional in psychology research, so careful justification for the use of a less stringent level will be expected.

5. Using a one-tailed test will increase power. However, the type of test used depends on the logic of the hypothesis being tested, so experimenters usually have little opportunity to influence power in this way.

6. Using a more sensitive hypothesis-testing procedure will increase the probability of detecting the effects of the experimental treatment, but experimenters typically start with the most powerful procedure available. Again, experimenters usually have little opportunity to influence power in this way.

The Role of Power When Interpreting the Results of a Study
Considerations when a result is statistically significant.
Statistical significance indicates that an experiment has had an effect. However, statistical significance does not indicate that the results of an experiment are either theoretically or practically important. While simply knowing that a statistically significant effect (i.e., real effect) is present may be theoretically important, the size of an effect may determine the practical importance of an experimental result. For example, a small effect having little practical importance may be statistically significant if the study has power due to other factors, particularly large sample size.

However, if the sample size for an experiment was small, a statistically significant result is probably practically important, as well. Therefore, when comparing two studies, the effect sizes, not the significance levels, should be compared. In other words, a statistically significant result indicates a real effect – the participants changed as a result of the experimental treatment.

The practical importance of the result must be interpreted, however. For example, the stress inventory described earlier has a mean of 36, a standard deviation of 8, and scores can range from 0-72. Suppose 100 students had participated in one counseling session per week for six weeks, and their mean stress score at the end of the experiment was 34. The decrease is statistically significant $[Z = (34 - 36) / .64 = -3.13]$ at any of the conventional levels of significance for either a one-tailed or a two-tailed test. Is the result practically significant? Was the time spent by the 100 students, as well as by the psychologists, worth the two-point reduction in perceived stress? If the answer to these questions is "No," what amount of change in a sample of what size would have produced a practically significant result?

Considerations when a result is not statistically significant.
If the power of an experiment is low, nonsignificant results of an experiment are probably inconclusive. Conversely, nonsignificant results from an experiment with high power suggest that
1. The research hypothesis is false
2. The effect size is smaller than predicted when the power of the study was calculated.

Effect Size and Power in Research Articles
Decision errors are rarely mentioned in research articles, However, discussions of effect size are increasingly common, most frequently in reports of meta-analyses. Power is most often considered during the planning phase of an experiment. When power is mentioned, the context is often the interpretation of other articles or as a possible explanation for nonsignificant results.

Advanced Topic: Figuring Statistical Power

Example 1: A group of psychologists are planning a study of the effect of a teaching method designed to increase the probability of successful completion of a statistics course on the self-esteem of students in the course. The mean score for a large group of individuals who have responded to the inventory previously is 63 and the standard deviation is 12. The predicted mean for the 40 students enrolled in the course is 69. Calculate the power (and beta) of the study. The null hypothesis will be tested at the .05 level of significance using a one-tailed test.

1. Gather the needed information.
Population 2 Mean = 63
Mean of the distribution of means (μ_M) = 63
Population 2 Standard Deviation = 12

Standard Deviation of the distribution of means (μ_2) = $\sqrt{12^2 / N}$ = $\sqrt{144/40}$ = $\sqrt{3.60}$ = 1.90
Predicted Population 1 Mean = 69

2. Figure the raw-score cutoff point on the comparison distribution to reject the null hypothesis.
The cutoff sample score for a one-tailed test at the .05 level of significance = +1.64.
The formula to convert this Z-score to a raw score is $(Z) (\sigma_M) + (\mu_M) = (+1.64) (1.90) + 63 = 66.12$.
The alpha area of the comparison distribution is the area to the right of a raw score of 66.12.

3. Figure the Z score for this point, but on the distribution of means for the population that receives the experimental manipulation (Population 1).
Z = (mean of predicted distribution – cutoff sample score in raw score units) / σ_M
  = (66.12 – 69.00) / 1.90
  = -1.52

4. Using the normal curve table, figure the probability of getting a score more extreme than that Z score. The normal curve shows that 43.57% of the curve lies between a Z score of -1.52 and the mean. That percentage of area added to the 50% of the curve that lies above the mean is equal to 93.57%. Therefore, the power of this study is 94%, and beta = 100% − 94% = 6%.

Chapter Self-Tests

The practice test items that follow are based on the following scenario. In the last two chapters, a group of psychologists has conducted a study in which one student attended a one-hour counseling session each week for six weeks designed to help the student reduce stress. The psychologists have also conducted a larger study in which 30 freshmen attended the counseling sessions, and now they are planning studies in which they will use sample data to estimate population values.

Understanding Key Terms in Chapter 6

Directions: Using the word bank that follows, complete each statement. **You may need to use some terms more than once.**

Word Bank: alpha / beta / *d* / decision / decreasing / effect size / effect size conventions / increasing / liberal /meta-analysis / power tables / statistical power / stringent / .20 / .50 / .80 / practically / statistically / one-tailed / two-tailed / Type I / Type II

Although the psychologists performed a well-planned statistical analysis and double-checked their calculations before concluding that six weekly counseling sessions can be expected to reduce stress, several replications of the study have not demonstrated significant reductions in stress. These replications suggest that the psychologists may have made a **(1)** _____ error. If the null hypothesis stated that the level of stress would be the same as, or higher than, the level before the counseling sessions, and the psychologists have erroneously concluded that the sessions effectively reduced stress, they have made a **(2)** _____ error. Had the psychologists concluded that the sessions were ineffective, but replications indicated that they were effective, the psychologists may have made a **(3)** _____ error. The probability of making the first error is called **(4)** _____, and the probability of making the second error is called **(5)** _____.

As an initial step in their planning, the psychologists have referred to a study that combines the results of many other studies of activity levels among depressed people. This study is an example of a **(6)** _____, and its primary data are obtained by calculating the **(7)** _____ of each study reviewed. As they continue planning, the psychologists discuss their desire to conduct a study that will yield a statistically significant result when the research hypothesis is true. These discussions are about **(8)** _____. As guidelines for planning this aspect of their studies, the psychologists can use Cohen's **(9)** _____, which are based on the calculation of **(10)** _____. Different studies may have different effects on their participants, and may include different numbers of participants. Therefore, the psychologists may obtain more precise estimates of this aspect of their studies by using **(11)** _____.

According to Cohen's conventions for assessing the power of a study, a small effect size is **(12)** _____, a medium effect size is **(13)** _____, and a large effect size is **(14)** _____. Cohen has also expressed the opinion that investigators should plan studies to have a power of **(15)** _____. In order to increase the power of their statistical analysis, the psychologists might consider **(16)** _____ the size of their sample, using a less **(17)** _____ level of significance, or using a **(18)** _____ test. If the psychologists use a very large sample that results in a small, but **(19)** _____ significant, increase in the average number of activities of daily living performed after a treatment like group therapy, their results may not be **(20)** _____ significant.

Multiple-Choice Items

1. The psychologists are said to have made a decision error when they
   A. miscalculate the student's Z score after the counseling sessions.
   B. use the normal curve table incorrectly and obtain an incorrect cutoff sample score.
   C. use a significance level of .10 instead one of the conventional levels of significance.
   D. reject the null hypothesis when the counseling sessions had no effect on the student's stress.

2. The psychologists have committed a Type I error when they
   A. reject the null hypothesis when it is true.
   B. fail to prove the research hypothesis.
   C. incorrectly estimate beta.
   D. use a one-tailed test.

3. The psychologists have committed a Type II error when they
   A. fail to prove the research hypothesis.
   B. incorrectly estimate beta.
   C. use a conventional level of alpha.
   D. fail to reject the null hypothesis when it is false.

4. If the psychologists could know that they were making a Type II error, their concern would be that
   A. the experiment must be repeated to confirm their results.
   B. they had incorrectly rejected the null hypothesis.
   C. a potentially useful practice would not be implemented.
   D. their results would not be statistically significant.

5. When the psychologists set beta for their study, they are
   A. setting the level of significance.
   B. establishing the probability of making a Type II error.
   C. acknowledging the appropriateness of a two-tailed test.
   D. determining the appropriate comparison distribution.

6. The degree to which the stress scores of students who participate in the counseling sessions differ from the scores of students who do not is an indication of
   A. experimental effectiveness.
   B. power.
   C. the effect size.
   D. the significance level.

7. If the psychologists noted that in one of the experiments they conducted, the distribution of the population expected under the research hypothesis had little overlap with the distribution of the known population, the psychologists had observed
   A. the use of a liberal alpha.
   B. the effect of low power.
   C. a large effect size.
   D. a practically significant result.

8. $(\mu_1 - \mu_2)/\sigma$ is a formula for calculating
   A. power.
   B. sample size.
   C. raw effect size.
   D. standardized effect size.

9. The calculation in <u>Item 8</u> is also known as
   A. d.
   B. σ_M.
   C. μ_M.
   D. α.

10. According to Cohen's conventions for research that compares means, a small effect size would be
    A. .20.
    B. .50.
    C. .80.
    D. .90.

11. According to Cohen's conventions, for research that compares means, a large effect size would be
    A. .20.
    B. .50.
    C. .80.
    D. .90.

12. If the psychologists calculate the average effect size from a number of the studies they review, they will have
    A. conducted a meta-analysis.
    B. set a stringent alpha.
    C. specified the desired level of power.
    D. determined the number of participants they will need.

13. Statistical power can be defined as the probability
    A. that the results of a study will result in advances in applied psychology.
    B. of rejecting the null hypothesis if the null hypothesis is true.
    C. of obtaining an effect size that will always be significant.
    D. that the study will yield a significant result if the research hypothesis is true.

14. The majority of previous studies the psychologists have reviewed have shown that counseling has significantly reduced the stress perceived by a variety of groups. If the psychologists fail to demonstrate a statistically significant reduction in one of their studies, they might
    A. have used a liberal alpha.
    B. suspect that the power of the study was low.
    C. need to conduct another meta-analysis.
    D. have made a Type I error.

Items 15–16 are related.

15. As the psychologists review previous studies, they will expect to find that the studies having the highest power are those with
    A. smaller samples.
    B. more stringent alphas.
    C. larger population standard deviations.
    D. larger effect sizes.

16. They will expect to find that the studies having the highest power are those with
    A. smaller samples.
    B. more stringent alphas.
    C. smaller population standard deviations.
    D. greater overlap between populations.

17. Sample size affects power because the size of the sample determines the
    A. effect size.
    B. standard deviation of the distribution of means.
    C. choice of an alpha level.
    D. size of beta.

Items 18–19 are related.

18. Based on previous studies, the psychologists know that the reduction in stress is likely to be small. However, if they believe that uncovering even a small reduction will be useful, they can increase the power of their studies by
    A. increasing the variance of the known population.
    B. selecting students with very different levels of stress.
    C. using an alpha of .01 instead of .05.
    D. increasing the size of the study samples.

19. Power will be greatest if the psychologists if the psychologists use an alpha level of
    A. .10.
    B. .05.
    C. .01.
    D. .025.

20. The psychologists may also increase power by
    A. stating a directional hypothesis.
    B. basing effect sizes on the smallest difference reported in prior studies.
    C. enrolling a small number of very diverse students in the study.
    D. using an alpha of .001.

21. The effect size conventions proposed by Cohen are useful to researchers for
    A. predicting the value of the dependent variable to use for the experimental condition.
    B. determining the power of a planned experiment.
    C. evaluating research results to determine if they are statistically significant.
    D. predicting the effect their independent variable will have on various populations.

22. According to Cohen, for an experiment to be worth conducting, it should have a level of power of about
    A. 1%.
    B. 5%.
    C. 50%.
    D. 80%.

23. If the psychologists want to decrease the standard deviation of the distribution of means in one of the studies they are planning study to increase power, they can
    A. use a more stringent alpha level.
    B. use the sample variance in place of the variance of the population.
    C. use a less diverse population.
    D. decrease the predicted difference between population means.

24. The primary change the psychologists can make in their experiments to increase power is to
    A. increase sample size.
    B. increase beta.
    C. use a two-tailed test.
    D. predict a smaller effect.

25. The psychologists' belief that even a relatively small reduction in stress resulting from attending the counseling sessions will cause other therapists to change their practice refers to the study's
  A. effect size.
  B. statistical significance.
  C. power.
  D. practical significance.

Problems

1. Consider the study of the effect of a teaching method designed to increase the probability of successful completion of a statistics course on the self-esteem of students in the course. Again, for the normally distributed known population, $\mu = 63$ and $\sigma = 12$. What is the estimated effect size for samples that have completed the treatment and have means of (a) 54, (b) 57, (c) 60, (d) 71, and (e) 78? For each sample mean, indicate whether the effect is approximately small, medium, or large.

2. What will be the predicted effect size of the following studies of student test anxiety if the means are (a) 35, (b) 42, (c) 50, (d) 56, and (e) 60? The known population of students experiencing test anxiety is normally distributed with $\mu = 44$ and $\sigma = 8$. For each sample mean, indicate whether the effect is approximately small, medium, or large.

3. A group of psychologists are planning a study to assess the effect of television viewing on reading achievement. The known population distribution of reading achievement scores is normal with $\mu = 36$ and $\sigma = 8$. What will the predicted mean achievement test score be if the psychologists predict (a) a small positive effect size, (b) a medium negative effect size, (c) a large negative effect size, (d) an effect size of .10, and (e) an effect size of -1.25?

4. A group of psychologists wants to see if discussion groups about the coping skills will help freshmen make a better adjustment to college. If coping skills are normally distributed in the population, what are the effect sizes and power for each of the possible versions of the study described in the table that follows? Sketch the necessary distributions following the examples in the text.

Study Version	Pop. μ	Pop. σ	Predicted Mean	N	alpha	1- or 2-tailed test
(a)	75	5	76	50	.05	1
(b)	75	10	77	50	.05	2
(c)	75	10	77	50	.05	1
(d)	75	10	76	100	.05	1
(e)	75	5	77	100	.01	2

5. The psychologists have conducted one of the studies of the effect of a teaching method designed to increase the probability of successful completion of a statistics course on the self-esteem of students in the course. The study revealed a statistically significant difference between the Population 1 and Population 2 means ($p < .5$) with $N = 100$ students. How would you interpret this result to a person who understands hypothesis testing, but who has never learned about effect size and power?

6. The psychologists have replicated the study described in Problem 5 and obtained a statistically significant difference between the Population 1 and Population 2 means ($p < .5$), but with $N = 15$. How would this result change your interpretation of this result to a person who understands hypothesis testing, but who has never learned about effect size and power

7. Use your responses to Problem 5. and Problem 6. as the basis for summarizing the relationship between statistical significance and effect size as concisely as possible.

8. A group of psychologists predict that depressed people who participate in group therapy will perform a greater number of activities of daily living than depressed people in general. The number of activities of daily living performed by depressed people in general is normally distributed with a mean of 14 and a standard deviation of 4. The psychologists expect that on average, a group of 30 depressed people will increase the number of activities performed to 16. The hypothesis will be tested at the .05 level of significance. What is the power of the study?

Additional Practice: Complete any Practice Problems in Set I that your instructor has not assigned and compare your responses to those provided by the authors. Pay particular attention to the problems that require you to explain your results to someone who has never taken a course in statistics.

SPSS Applications
There are no SPSS applications for this chapter.

Chapter 7
Introduction to *t* Tests: Single Sample and Dependent Means

Learning Objectives
After studying this chapter, you should:
Be able to estimate population variances based on sample scores.
Know when and how to conduct a *t* test for a single sample.
Be able to describe the differences between *t* distributions and the normal curve.
Be able to use the *t* table.
Know when and how to conduct a *t* test for dependent means.
Be able to define the normality assumption for the *t* test for dependent means and describe its implications.
Be able to calculate effect sizes for studies requiring a *t* test for dependent means and interpret these effect sizes using Cohen's conventions.
Be able to use tables to estimate power for *t* tests for dependent means.
Be able to use tables to estimate sample size for *t* tests for dependent means.
Be able to describe the limitations of pretest-posttest designs.
Be able to interpret results for *t* tests for dependent means as reported in research articles.

The *t* **tests** are used to compare:
1. A sample mean with a known population mean.
2. The changes in a variable measured in a sample of people before and after a treatment.
3. The means of two groups of people (Chapter 8).

The *t* Test for a Single Sample (One-Sample *t* Test)
The *t* **test for a single sample** is the hypothesis testing procedure used to compare a sample mean and a known population mean. This test is like the *Z* test introduced in Chapter 5 with two important exceptions:
1. The population variance required to define the comparison distribution in Step 2 of the hypothesis testing procedure must be estimated, and
2. One of a theoretically infinite number of *t* distributions is used to determine the cutoff sample score in Step 3 of the hypothesis testing procedure.

Estimating the Population Variance from Sample Scores
Estimating the population variance from the sample data is based on the premise that since a sample represents its population, the sample variance is representative of the population variance. However, the variance of a random sample is, on the average, slightly smaller than the variance of the population from which the sample is drawn. Such an estimate of the sample variance is said to be a **biased estimate** of the population's variance. An **unbiased estimate of the population variance (S^2)**, which means that the estimate is equally likely to be too high or too low, is obtained by modifying the formula for the variance by subtracting 1 from the number of people in the sample. Thus, the formula is $S^2 = \sum(X - M)^2 / (N - 1) = SS / (N - 1)$. Note that S^2 is the symbol used to represent the estimated population variance.

Degrees of Freedom
The denominator in the formula for estimating the population variance from sample data, $\sum(X - M)^2 / (N - 1)$, is also called the **degrees of freedom (*df*)**. The term refers to the number of scores that are "free to vary" when computing a mean. Thus, the formula for computing the estimated population variance can be written $S^2 = SS / df$. In order to understand the concept of degrees of freedom, the sum of the numbers 1-5 is 15 and the mean is 3. If any four numbers are known, the fifth score can have only one value that will yield a sum of 15 and a mean of 3, e.g., if four numbers are 1, 2, 3, and 4, the fifth value must be 5. Thus, one degree of freedom *to vary* has been lost and is subtracted from the number of scores accordingly.

The Standard Deviation of the Distribution of Means
Once S^2 has been calculated, calculate the variance of the comparison distribution as before, i.e., by dividing the variance by *N*, NOT by $N-1$. The new symbol is S^2_M. As before, the standard deviation of the comparison distribution is the square root of the variance, $\sqrt{S^2_M}$, or S_M.

The Shape of the Comparison Distribution When Using an Estimated Population Variance: The *t* Distribution

Hypothesis testing using estimated population variances means experimenters have less true information, leaving more room for error. Specifically, samples are more likely to include extreme means than would be expected in a normal curve, and the smaller the N, the higher the probability that extreme means will be obtained. Therefore, the appropriate comparison distribution in Step 2 of the hypothesis testing procedure changes from the normal distribution to a *t* **distribution**.

One *t* distribution exists for every possible number of degrees of freedom. The *t* distributions have heavier tails than the normal distribution, which means that sample means must be slightly more extreme to be significantly different from population means when experimenters are using a *t* distribution instead of the normal distribution as the comparison distribution. For example, the cutoff sample score for a two-tailed test at the .05 significance level using the normal distribution is ±1.96, regardless of the size of the sample. With a sample of 11 ($df = 10$), the cutoff sample score for the same test at the same level of significance is ±2.228, and for a sample of 31($df = 30$), the cutoff sample score is ±2.043. Note that as the sample size increases, the cutoff sample score for a *t* distribution is closer to that of the normal curve. In fact, when sample size is infinite, the *t* distribution and normal distribution coincide. The two types of distribution yield very similar cutoff sample scores when N is ≥ 30.

The Cutoff Sample Score for Rejecting the Null Hypothesis: Using the *t* Table

Determining the cutoff sample score in Step 3 of the hypothesis testing process now requires a *t* **table** that lists the cutoff sample *t* scores for any number of degrees of freedom. Table A-2 in the text Appendix is a table of *t* distributions that includes crucial cutoff scores.

Using the *t* table requires specification of the number of degrees of freedom, the chosen significance level, and a decision about whether a one- or two-tailed test will be conducted. As is the case with the table of areas under the normal curve, the values in *t* tables are positive numbers. However, *t* distributions are symmetrical, so the same cutoff sample score can be used for either a positive or a negative experimental effect. For example, if the experimental treatment is designed to increase the self-esteem of a sample of 26 students ($df = 25$), the cutoff sample score for a one-tailed test at the .05 level of significance will be +1.708. If the experimental treatment is designed to reduce the perceived stress of a sample of 26 students (again, $df = 25$), the cutoff sample score for a one-tailed test at the .05 level of significance will be -1.708.

When the exact number of degrees of freedom required by a study is not given in the *t* table, the nearest number that is lower than the required number should be used to minimize the risk of a Type I error. For example, if a two-tailed test at the .05 level of significance is planned, and the actual number $df = 37$, the cutoff sample score for 35 df should be used instead of the cutoff sample score for 40 df. The cutoff sample scores for these two df are 2.030 and 2.021, respectively, making the former more conservative, i.e., making the criterion for statistical significance more conservative.

Determining the Score Sample's Mean on the Comparison Distribution: The *t* Score

Step 4 of the hypothesis testing process, locating the sample mean on the comparison distribution, is identical to the procedure for a Z test. However, due to the estimation of the population variance, the resulting score is called a *t* **score**. The formula is $t = (M - \mu) / S_M$. [Remember that μ now refers to the mean of a distribution of means.]

Deciding Whether to Reject the Null Hypothesis

Step 5 of the hypothesis testing procedure involves the decision about the null hypothesis and is conducted exactly as it was for the Z test.

Example of a *t* Test for a Single Sample

A psychologist is consulting with a national chain of bookstores to monitor customer complaints. The national average for all bookstores is 6.5 complaints per month. Seven stores in the chain have been selected to determine whether the chain has a different average number of complaints than bookstores in general. The numbers of complaints are 4, 8, 9, 0, 3, 5, and 6. Using the .05 level of significance, what should the psychologist conclude?

Step 1: Restate the question as a research hypothesis and a null hypothesis about the populations.
Population 1: Bookstores in the chain
Population 2: Bookstores in general

Research Hypothesis: There will be a difference in the average number of complaints received by bookstores in the chain and the average number received by bookstores in general.
Null hypothesis: There will be no difference in the number average number of complaints received by bookstores in the chain and average number received by bookstores in general.

Step 2: Determine the characteristics of the comparison distribution.
$M = 4 + 8 + 9 + 0 + 3 + 5 + 6 / 7 = 35 / 7 = 5$
$\Sigma(X - M)^2 = 56$
$S^2 = \Sigma (X - M)^2 / N - 1 = 56 / 6 = 9.33$
$S^2{}_M = S^2 / N = 9.33 / 7 = 1.33$
$S_M = \sqrt{S^2{}_M} = \sqrt{1.33} = 1.15$
The comparison distribution will be a t distribution with 6 df.

Step 3: Determine the cutoff sample score on the comparison distribution at which the null hypothesis should be rejected.
The cutoff sample score for a t distribution with 6 df using a two-tailed test at the .05 level of significance $= \pm 2.447$

Step 4: Determine the sample score on the comparison distribution.
$t = (M - \mu) / S_M$
$\quad = (5 - 6.5) / 1.15$
$\quad = -1.30$

Step 5: Decide whether to reject the null hypothesis.
Since -1.30 is not as extreme as -2.447, the psychologist would fail to reject the null hypothesis and state that the results of the study are inconclusive, i.e., the mean number of complaints received by bookstores in the chain is not significantly different from the mean number of complaints received by bookstores in general.

The t Test for Dependent Means

In most research situations, experimenters do not have a population mean against which to compare the mean of the sample exposed to the experimental treatment. Instead, experimenters have two sets of scores. One such situation occurs when experimenters use a **repeated-measures design** (or within subjects design). In this design, each participant has two scores on the variable being measured, one collected before, and the second collected after, the experimental treatment. The hypothesis testing procedure when this design is used is called the ***t* test for dependent means**.

The differences between the t test for a single sample and the t test for dependent means are
1. The use of difference scores and
2. The assumption that the population mean of the difference scores is zero.

Difference Scores

Difference scores (change scores) are computed by subtracting one of each participant's scores from the other. Experimenters often subtract the score obtained at the conclusion of the treatment from the score obtained before the treatment to reflect the direction of the change resulting from the treatment. For example, if the experimental treatment is designed to enhance student self-esteem, a positive difference score in which the post-treatment score is greater than the pre-treatment score, would indicate that the treatment had the expected effect. On the other hand, if the treatment is intended to reduce anxiety, a negative difference score would indicate that the treatment had the expected effect. Although the t score will be the same numerically no matter which mean is subtracted from which, interpretation of the results may be simplified if the sign of the t score indicates the direction of the experimental effect. Computing difference scores combines the two sets of scores for each participant into a single score. Once difference scores have been computed, the hypothesis testing procedure is conducted using difference scores.

Population of Difference Scores with a Mean of Zero

The population of difference scores (Population 2) to which the population represented by the sample (Population 1) will be compared is ordinarily assumed to have a mean of zero. This assumption makes sense because the experimenter's are comparing their sample's population to a population in which there is, on the average, no difference, or change.

Example of a *t* Test for Dependent Means

A psychologist is interested in the effect of a volunteer tutoring program on the reading achievement of a group of students. The reading achievement scores of eight students before and after the tutoring program are listed in the table that follows. Using the .05 level of significance, did the tutoring program increase reading achievement?

Student	Before Score	After Score	Difference Score	Deviation Score	Squared Deviation Score
A	24	31	7	3.37	11.36
B	20	29	9	5.37	28.84
C	22	25	3	-0.63	0.40
D	26	25	-1	-4.63	21.44
E	30	29	-1	-4.63	21.44
F	31	35	4	0.37	0.14
G	27	32	5	1.37	1.88
H	25	28	3	-0.63	0.40
Σ	205	234	29		85.88

Step 1: Restate the question as a research hypothesis and a null hypothesis about the populations.
Population 1: Students in the volunteer tutoring program
Population 2: Students whose reading achievement scores do not change

Research Hypothesis: The reading achievement scores of students in the volunteer tutoring program will be higher after the program than before the program.
Null hypothesis: The reading achievement scores of students in the volunteer tutoring program will be the same as, or lower than, their scores before the program.

Step 2: Determine the characteristics of the comparison distribution.
For the difference scores:
$M = 29 / 8 = 3.63$
$\mu = 0$ (The basis of comparison is no change.)
$S^2 = SS / df = 85.88 / 7 = 12.27$
$S^2_M = S^2 / N = 12.27 / 8 = 1.53$

$S_M = \sqrt{S^2_M} = \sqrt{1.53} = 1.24$
The comparison distribution will be a *t* distribution with 7 *df*.

Step 3: Determine the cutoff sample score on the comparison distribution at which the null hypothesis should be rejected.
The cutoff sample score for a *t* distribution with 7 *df* using a one-tailed test at the .05 level of significance = +1.895 because the experimenters are interested in an increase in reading achievement scores.

Step 4: Determine the sample score on the comparison distribution.
$t = (M - \mu) / S_M$
$= (3.63 - 0) / 1.24$
$= 2.931$

Step 5: Decide whether to reject the null hypothesis.
Since 2.931 is more extreme than +1.895, the psychologist would reject the null hypothesis and conclude that the volunteer tutoring program did increase reading achievement.

_t_ Test for Dependent Means with Scores from Pairs of Research Participants

Some experiments are conducted with participants who have been selected because they are equivalent or related in some way. For example, participants may be selected so that there are equal numbers of men and women or equal numbers of people in various age groups. Although the participants are different people, the _t_ test for dependent means is appropriate for analyzing data collected in such experiments. For this reason, the _t_ test for dependent means is also called the _t test for paired samples_, the _t test for correlated means_, the _t test for matched samples_, or the _t test for matched pairs_.

Assumptions of the _t_ Test for a Single Sample and the _t_ Test for Dependent Means

When sample data are used to estimate the population variance, the comparison distribution will be a _t_ distribution only if the distribution of individuals from which the sample is drawn is normally distributed. Otherwise, the shape of the appropriate comparison distribution will have a different shape that is usually unknown. Thus, a normal population distribution is an **assumption,** a logical and mathematical requirement, of the _t_ test.

Determination of the actual shape of the population of individual scores is rarely possible based on information provided by sample data. However, the results of t tests are reasonably accurate even when population distributions are skewed, even very skewed. This accuracy is attributable to the **robustness** of the _t_ test, which means that it is insensitive to violations of the normality assumption, and the _t_ test is said to be _robust_ over moderate violations of this assumption. For this reason, psychologists use the _t_ test unless

1. There is reason to expect a very large discrepancy from normal, and
2. The population is highly skewed and a one-tailed test is being used.

Effect Size and Power for the _t_ Test for Dependent Means

The effect size for the _t_ test for dependent means is computed using the same formula presented in Chapter 6, $d = (\mu_1 - \mu_2) / \sigma$. Since the mean of Population 2 is nearly always zero and the standard deviation (σ) is the standard deviation of populations of difference scores, the formula reduces to $d = \mu_1 / \sigma$, with both terms relating to difference scores. Remember that the denominator of the effect size formula is the standard deviation of the distribution of individual scores (σ), not the standard deviation of the distribution of means (σ_M or S_M). To figure effect size you divide by σ (or its estimate S), and not by σ_M (or S_M).

In the reading achievement example above, the mean for the difference scores of the eight students is 3.63, and the variance of their difference scores is 12.27. The square root of the variance is 3.50. Solving the equation, $d = (\mu_1 - \mu_2) / \sigma$, results in $d = (3.63 - 0) / 3.50 = 1.04$. Cohen's conventions for effect sizes are also the same for the _t_ test for dependent means: a small effect size is .20, a medium effect size is .50, and a large effect size is .80. Thus, the effect size for the reading achievement study is large

A table is provided in the text that indicates the approximate power for small, medium, and large effect sizes and one- and two-tailed tests the .05 significance level. This power table is useful for interpreting the practical importance of nonsignificant results presented in research articles. A second table that indicates the approximate number of participants needed to achieve 80% power for estimated small, medium, and large effect sizes using one- and two-tailed tests at the .05 significance level is provided, also.

_t_ Tests for a Single Sample t for Dependent Means in Research Articles

The results of _t_ tests for single samples are seen rarely, but the results of _t_ tests for dependent are seen more frequently. The format for reporting the results _t_ tests in research articles is fairly standard. For example, the results of the reading achievement study could be reported as $t(7) = 2.931$, $p < .05$ with $t(7)$ indicating that the comparison distribution was a _t_ distribution with 7 _df_, the _t_ value was 2.931, and the result was statistically significant at the .05 level. Since the results are from a one-tailed test, the experimenters should note this fact. Otherwise, two-tailed tests are usually assumed. The effect size might also be reported.

Chapter Self-Tests

Understanding Key Concepts in Chapter 7

The test items that follow are based on the following scenario. A group of psychologists has conducted a study to determine the effects of group therapy on the number of activities of daily living performed by depressed people. During this investigation, they measured the number of activities of daily living performed by a sample of depressed clients before and after 6 weeks of group therapy.

Directions: Complete each statement using the word bank that follows. **You may use terms more than once.**

Word Bank: assumption / biased estimate / change scores / degrees of freedom / difference scores / repeated-measures design / robustness / *t* distribution / *t* score / *t* table / *t* test for dependent means / *t* test for a single sample / *t* tests / unbiased estimate

The plan for the study is known as a **(1)** _____. Since the psychologists do not know the population variance for the distribution of activities of daily lining, they will estimate the variance of the distribution of activities for the population of depressed people, which means they will use $N - 1$ as the denominator in the formula for computing the variance. Using this denominator will provide an **(2)** _____ estimate of the population variance, and it also indicates the number of **(3)** _____. This adjustment is necessary because using sample data to compute the population variance yields a value that is too small, which is a **(4)** _____. This adjustment means that the psychologists will analyze their data using one of several **(5)** _____.

If the psychologists knew that the mean number of activities of daily living performed by the population of depressed people was 14 activities per day, but they did not know the variance for the population, the appropriate statistical test would be a **(6)** _____. However, to analyze the data from the design they are using, the psychologists will analyze their data using a **(7)** _____.

As an initial step in performing the analysis, the psychologists subtract the number of activities each client performs before therapy from the number performed after therapy. This arithmetic yields **(8)** _____, which are also known as **(9)** _____, for each client. The result of the analysis is a **(10)** _____. In order to interpret this result, the psychologists will consult a **(11)** _____ and use the number of **(12)** _____ to select one of an infinite number of **(13)** _____. In order to interpret the results of their analysis correctly, the psychologists need to recognize that activities of daily living should be normally distributed in the population of depressed people. This logical and mathematical requirement of a statistical test is an **(14)** _____. Tests that yield reasonably accurate results despite violations of such requirements are said to possess **(15)** _____.

Multiple Choice Items

1. The *t*-tests were developed for situations in which
   A. the population variance is unknown.
   B. the population mean is unknown.
   C. the sample distribution is seriously skewed.
   D. the normal curve is too narrow.

2. The psychologists have conducted the study and found that following therapy, the 30 depressed clients performed an average of 18 activities each day. From their review of earlier studies, the psychologists know that most depressed people perform an average of 14 activities. The appropriate statistical test in this situation is a
   A. *t* test for dependent means.
   B. *t* test for a single sample.
   C. *Z* test.
   D. repeated-measures test.

3. If the psychologists used the same formula to calculate the variance for the sample of depressed clients that they would use to calculate the variance from a population, the result would
    A. skewed.
    B. kurtotic.
    C. too large.
    D. too small.

4. An unbiased estimate of the population variance based on sample data is
    A. more like the normal curve variance.
    B. equal to the population variance.
    C. equally likely to be too high or too low.
    D. a robust estimate of the population variance.

5. The degrees of freedom for the statistical test performed by the psychologists on the data collected from the sample of clients would be
    A. $30 + 1$.
    B. 30^2.
    C. $30 - 1$.
    D. $30 / \sigma$.

6. The symbol for the variance estimated from sample data is
    A. S^2.
    B. SS.
    C. SD^2.
    D. SD.

7. The numerator of the formula for estimating the variance from sample data, $\Sigma(X - M)^2$, is also symbolized by
    A. S^2.
    B. SS.
    C. SD^2.
    D. SD.

8. The denominator for the formula for estimating the population variance from sample data is also called
    A. an unbiased estimator.
    B. the sum of squares.
    C. a t distribution.
    D. degrees of freedom.

9. In the formula for estimating the population variance from sample data, the substitution of $N - 1$ in the denominator alters the interpretation of the test statistic
    A. by making a t distribution the appropriate comparison distribution.
    B. because the normal curve becomes skewed.
    C. due to the use of a repeated-measures design.
    D. by making the test statistic too robust to use the normal curve as the comparison distribution.

10. After calculating a t score, the psychologists will determine whether it is statistically significant by comparing it to
    A. the t distribution.
    B. the appropriate t distribution.
    C. any of an infinite number of t distributions.
    D. the more appropriate of an infinite number of t distributions or the normal distribution.

11. Which of the following statements is true about the comparison of a normal distribution and a t distribution?
   A. A t distribution may be bimodal
   B. The distributions will be identical when $df=1$
   C. The distributions are approximately identical when $N \geq 30$
   D. A t distribution is more light-tailed when $N \leq 30$

12. The appropriate cutoff sample score in a t table is located by
   A. squaring the variance used to calculate the test statistic.
   B. converting a Z score to a t score.
   C. transforming t scores to Z scores.
   D. using the degrees of freedom used to determine the test statistic.

13. If the psychologists use a two-tailed t test to test the hypothesis that therapy will increase the number of activities performed at the .05 level, which t score will permit them to reject the null hypothesis? (No table should be necessary to respond to this item.)
   A. +1.699.
   B. +1.960.
   C. ±1.960.
   D. +2.045.

Items 14–18 are related.

14. The psychologists plan to determine the effectiveness of the experimental treatment by comparing the number of activities performed before therapy with the number performed after therapy. This research design is a
   A. zero effect design.
   B. repeated-measures design.
   C. robust design.
   D. two-sample design.

15. If the psychologists use a repeated-measures design, the appropriate analysis will be a
   A. t test for dependent means.
   B. t test for a single sample.
   C. Z test.
   D. normal deviate test.

16. The psychologists will create a single score for each client by computing
   A. standard scores.
   B. t scores.
   C. difference scores.
   D. robust scores.

17. The scores described in Item 16 are also called
   A. dependent scores.
   B. independent scores.
   C. unbiased scores.
   D. change scores.

18. The population mean in the analysis will be
   A. 0.
   B. 1.
   C. 29.
   D. 30.

19. If the psychologists justify calculating a *t* score on their belief that activities are normally distributed in the population of depressed people, they are concerned about
    A. meeting an assumption.
    B. making a biased estimate.
    C. making an unbiased estimate.
    D. using difference scores.

20. If the psychologists decide to use the *t* test for dependent samples instead of some other test because the *t*-test is insensitive to violations of its assumptions, they are basing their decision on the test's
    A. power.
    B. effectiveness.
    C. robustness.
    D. sensitivity.

Problems

1. The psychologists are interested in whether depressed people undergoing group therapy will perform a different number of activities of daily living after group therapy. Therefore, the psychologists have randomly selected 12 depressed clients to undergo a 6-week group therapy program. Use the five steps of hypothesis testing to determine whether the average number of activities of daily living (shown below) obtained after therapy is significantly different than a mean number of activities of 14 that is typical for similar depressed people. Test the difference at the .05 level of significance (and, for practice, at the .01 level). In Step 2, show all calculations. As part of Step 5, indicate whether the psychologists should recommend group therapy for all depressed people based on evaluation of the null hypothesis at both levels of significance and calculate the effect size.

Client	After therapy
A	17
B	15
C	12
D	21
E	16
F	18
G	17
H	14
I	13
J	15
K	12
L	19

2. The psychologists are interested in whether depressed people undergoing group therapy will perform a different number of activities of daily living before and after group therapy. Therefore, the psychologists have randomly selected 8 depressed clients participating in a 6-week group therapy program. Use the five steps of hypothesis testing to determine whether the observed differences in numbers of activities of daily living (shown below) obtained before and after therapy are statistically significant at the .05 level of significance (and, for practice, at the .01 level). In Step 2, show all calculations. As part of Step 5, indicate whether the psychologists should recommend group therapy for all depressed people based on evaluation of the null hypothesis at both levels of significance and calculate the effect size.

Client	Before therapy	After therapy
A	12	17
B	7	15
C	10	12
D	13	21
E	9	16
F	8	18
G	14	17
H	11	8

3. A psychologist is interested in whether a standard anxiety-reduction program will be effective for reducing test anxiety. The average test anxiety level for a university population is 40, but the variance is unknown. Nine students experiencing test anxiety have enrolled in a 4-week program designed to reduce test anxiety. The students' scores on an anxiety inventory administered the day before a test are listed in the table that follows. Use the five steps of hypothesis testing to determine whether the observed differences in anxiety obtained after therapy are statistically significant at the .05 level of significance (and, for practice, at the .01 level). In Step 2, show all calculations. As part of Step 5, indicate whether the psychologists should recommend the therapy for students experiencing test anxiety based on evaluation of the null hypothesis at both levels of significance. Explain your answer to a person who familiar with the Z test, but not with the t test.

Student	After therapy
A	37
B	35
C	42
D	31
E	46
F	48
G	37
H	44
I	43

4. Based on the results obtained with the nine students enrolled in the 4-week anxiety-reduction program, the psychologist expanded the program to six weeks and enrolled 10 students. The psychologist also measured anxiety before and after the program. The students' scores on the two administrations of the anxiety are presented in the table that follows. Use the five steps of hypothesis testing to determine whether the observed differences in anxiety obtained after therapy are statistically significant at the .05 level of significance (and, for practice, at the .01 level). In Step 2, show all calculations. As part of Step 5, indicate whether the psychologists should recommend the therapy for students experiencing test anxiety based on evaluation of the null hypothesis at both levels of significance and calculate the effect size. Explain your answer to a person who familiar with the Z test, but not with the t test.

Student	Before therapy	After therapy
A	48	40
B	46	38
C	44	42
D	48	41
E	43	46
F	47	43
G	47	37
H	41	44
I	44	43
J	45	40

5. Determine the power of each of the following studies that is to be analyzed using a *t* test for dependent means at the .05 level of significance.

Study	Effect Size	N	Tails
(a)	Small	50	One
(b)	Medium	40	One
(c)	Small	40	Two
(d)	Small	100	Two
(e)	Medium	40	Two
(f)	Large	20	Two

6. Determine the approximate number of subjects that will be needed for the following studies if a *t* test for dependent means will be used to analyze data at the .05 level of significance

Study	Predicted Effect Size	Tails
(a)	Medium	One
(b)	Small	Two
(c)	Large	Two

Additional Practice: Complete any Practice Problems in Set I that your instructor has not assigned and compare your responses to those provided by the authors. Pay particular attention to the problems that require you to explain your results to someone who has never taken a course in statistics.

SPSS Applications

Application 1: *t* Test for a Single Sample
Open SPSS.
Enter the number of activities of daily living performed by the depressed clients studied in Problem 1 in the Data View window.
In the Variable View window, change the variable name to "activities" and set the decimals to zero if you wish.
✧ Analyze
✧ Compare means
✧ One-Sample T Test
✧ the name of the variable (activities) and ✧ the arrow to move the variable to the Variable(s) window
Enter the population mean (14) in the "Test Value" box
The SPSS window should look like Figure 1

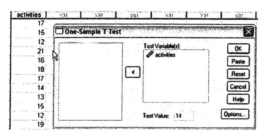

Figure 1
✧ OK
The output should look like the output in Figures 2 and 3.

One-Sample Statistics

	N	Mean	Std. Deviation	Std. Error Mean
activities	12	15.75	2.800	.808

Figure 2

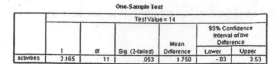

One-Sample Test

	Test Value = 14					
					95% Confidence Interval of the Difference	
	t	df	Sig. (2-tailed)	Mean Difference	Lower	Upper
activities	2.165	11	.053	1.750	-.03	3.53

Figure 3

Compare these results to those you obtained when you calculated the test "by hand." Note that the 95% confidence interval includes zero, so the possibility that there is no difference between the sample mean and the population mean cannot be eliminated, which confirms the result of the hypothesis test that the difference is not statistically significant at the .05 level of significance.

Application 2: *t* Test for Dependent Means

Open SPSS.

Enter the number of activities of daily living performed by the depressed clients studied in Problem 2 in the Data View window. Be sure to enter the "before therapy" score in the first column and the "after therapy" scores in the second column.

In the Variable View window, change the variable name for the first variable to "adlpre" and the variable name for the second variable to "adlpost." Set the decimals for both variables to zero if you wish.

⫟ Analyze

⫟ Compare means

⫟ Paired-Samples T Test

⫟ the first variable (adlpre) and ⫟ the second variable (adlpost) to highlight both variables. Then ⫟ the arrow to move both variables to the Paired Variable(s) window

The SPSS window should look like Figure 4

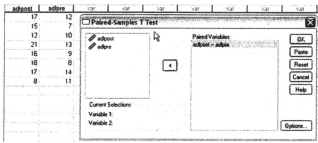

Figure 4

⫟ OK

The output should look like the output in Figures 5, 6, and 7.

Paired Samples Statistics

		Mean	N	Std. Deviation	Std. Error Mean
Pair 1	adlpost	15.50	8	3.964	1.402
	adlpre	10.50	8	2.449	.866

Figure 5

Paired Samples Correlations

| | | N | Correlation | Sig. |
| Pair 1 | adlpost & adlpre | 8 | .206 | .625 |

Figure 6

Paired Samples Test

		Paired Differences					t	df	Sig. (2-tailed)
		Mean	Std. Deviation	Std. Error Mean	95% Confidence Interval of the Difference				
					Lower	Upper			
Pair 1	adlpost - adlpre	5.000	4.209	1.488	1.481	8.519	3.360	7	.012

Figure 7

Compare these results to those you obtained when you calculated the test "by hand." Your *t* score would have been negative if you subtracted the "after" score from the "before" score. However, examining the means in Figure 5 shows that therapy had the desired effect of increasing the number of activities performed by the clients. Note that the 95% confidence interval does not include zero, which confirms the result of the hypothesis test that the difference is statistically significant at the .05 level of significance.

If you would like additional practice, use SPSS to analyze the data for Problem 3 and Problem 4 and compare the results to your calculations and those in the Answer Key.

Chapter 8
The *t* Test for Independent Means

Learning Objectives
After studying this chapter, you should:
- Be able to describe the logical construction of, and use of, distributions of differences between means.
- Know how to calculate the mean and variance for a distribution of differences between means.
- Know how to identify the appropriate *t* distribution for a *t* test for independent means.
- Know when and how to conduct a *t* test for independent means.
- Be able to define the normality and equality of variances assumptions for the *t* test for independent means and describe their implications.
- Be able to calculate effect sizes for studies requiring a *t* test for independent means and interpret these effect sizes using Cohen's conventions.
- Be able to use tables to estimate power for *t* tests for independent means.
- Be able to use tables to estimate sample size for *t* tests for independent means.
- Be able to interpret results of *t* tests for independent means as reported in research articles.
- Be able to use the harmonic mean to estimate the power of a study for which a *t* test for independent means is the appropriate statistical test, but in which the sample sizes are unequal.

The ***t* test for independent means** is an appropriate statistical test when an experiment involves two samples comprised of different individuals, e.g., when an experiment involves an experimental group and a control group, but the population variances are not known. Thus, each person has only one score on the variable being measured, not two scores, as was the case with the *t* for dependent means. Since the population variances must be estimated from sample data, a *t* distribution will serve as the comparison distribution. The numerator of the *t* formula will involve subtracting the mean of one group from the mean of the other group so that the comparison distribution will be a distribution of <u>differences</u> between means, not a distribution of means.

The Distribution of Differences between Means

The **distribution of differences between means** is two steps removed from the distribution of the population of individuals. The logic of constructing a distribution of differences between means is as follows. First, imagine two populations of individuals like those to be included in a study. The actual characteristics of the populations are unknown, but if the null hypothesis is true, $\mu_1 = \mu_2$ and the variances (S^2_1 and S^2_2) can be estimated. Using the estimated population variances and the size of the samples to be drawn from each population, the variances of each distribution of means can be computed as usual (S^2_1 / N and S^2_2 / N). A distribution of differences between means can be conceptualized by imagining that a mean is randomly selected from each distribution of means for each of the two populations, one mean is subtracted from the other, and the difference is plotted. If this process is repeated a large number of times, a distribution of differences between means will result. Since the variance of this distribution is ultimately based on the estimated variances of the two populations of individuals, the distribution can be viewed as a *t* distribution.

KEY DETAILS

1. The *t* test for independent means compares the means of two samples drawn from populations having unknown means. However, if the null hypothesis is true, the two population means are equal. Therefore, $\mu_1 - \mu_2 = 0$, and so the mean of the distribution of differences between means is zero.

2. In order for a *t* test for independent means to provide valid results, the assumption that the variances of the two populations of individual scores are equal must be reasonable. Although the two variances are rarely equal, the best solution for identifying a single variance for the distribution of differences between means is to average the two estimates to obtain the best single estimate of this distribution. The resulting average is the **pooled estimate of the population variance** (S^2_{Pooled}). If sample sizes are equal, the pooled estimate of the population variance is the average of the estimates for the two populations ($S^2_1 + S^2_2 / 2$). However, if the sample sizes are unequal, the pooled estimate of the population variance estimate is calculated as a **weighted average** that adjusts the estimate for each

sample by giving more weight to the larger sample. This weighted average is not based on the size of each sample, but rather on the number of degrees of freedom for each sample. Thus, the formula becomes

$$S^2_{Pooled} = [(df_1 / df_{Total}) (S^2_1)] + [(df_2 / df_{Total}) (S^2_2)].$$

Example: Suppose that an experimenter enrolls 40 participants in a study, equally divided between the experimental and control groups. At the conclusion of the study, the estimated variance for the experimental group is 20 and the estimated variance for the control group is 50. If all 40 participants complete the study, the pooled estimate of the population variance is

$$S^2_{Pooled} = S^2_1 + S^2_2 / 2 = (20 + 50) / 2 = 70 / 2 = 35.$$

3. However, suppose the experimenter had enrolled 41 participants in the experimental group and 21 participants in the control group. The estimated variances remain the same. In this situation, the total number of degrees of freedom for the experimental group is $41 - 1 = 40$, and for the control group, $21 - 1 = 20$. The total number of degrees of freedom is 60. Now the pooled estimate of the population variance is

$$S^2_{Pooled} = [(df_1 / df_{Total}) (S^2_1)] + [(df_2 / df_{Total}) (S^2_2)] = [(40 / 60) (20) + (20 / 60) (50)] = [(2 / 3) (20) + (1 / 3) (50)]$$
$$= (13.33 + 16.67) = 30.$$ Note that S^2_{Pooled} is between the group variances of 20 and 50, and it is closer to the variance of the larger group.

Remember that the variance for a distribution of means is the variance of the population of individual scores divided by the sample size. However, although the two populations involved when t test for independent means is being conducted are assumed to have equal variances, the distributions of means will not have the equal variances if the sample sizes are different. Therefore, the variance for each distribution of means must be calculated using the formulas $S^2_{M1} = S^2_{Pooled} / N_1$ and $S^2_{M2} = S^2_{Pooled} / N_2$.

Returning to the example with 41 participants in the experimental group and 21 in the control group, the variance for the distribution of means for the experimental group is $S^2_{M1} = S^2_{Pooled} / N_1 = 30 / 41 = 0.73$, and the variance for the distribution of means for the control group is and $S^2_{M2} = S^2_{Pooled} / N_2 = 30 / 21 = 1.43$.

4. The **variance of the distribution of differences between means** ($S^2_{Difference}$) is simply the sum of the variances of the distributions of means for the two populations, i.e., $S^2_{Difference} = S^2_{M1} + S^2_{M2}$. The **standard deviation of the distribution of differences between means** ($S_{Difference}$) is the square root of the variance, i.e., $S_{Difference}$

$$= \sqrt{S^2_{Difference}}.$$ Returning to the example, $S^2_{Difference} = S^2_{M1} + S^2_{M2} = 0.73 + 1.43 = 2.16$, and $S_{Difference} = \sqrt{S^2_{Difference}} = \sqrt{2.16} = 1.47.$

5. Again, since the distribution of differences between means is based on estimated population variances, the distribution of differences between means for a study follows a specific t distribution. The number of degrees of freedom for this t distribution is the sum of the degrees of freedom for the two samples. Therefore, the formula is $df_{Total} = df_1 + df_2$. Using the data from the example, $df_{Total} = 40 + 20 = 60$. Reference to the t table in the text indicates that the cutoff sample t score for a one-tailed test with 60 degrees of freedom at the .05 level of significance is $+ 1.671$ or -1.671. For a two-tailed test, the cutoff sample score would be ± 2.001.

6. The t score for a t test for independent means is the difference between the two sample means divided by the standard deviation of the distribution of differences between means. The formula is $t = M_1 - M_2 / S_{Difference}$. Suppose that in the example, the mean for the first sample is 14 and the mean for the second sample is 10. In this example, $t = 14 - 10 / 1.43 = 4 / 1.43 = 2.80.$

Hypothesis Testing with a t Test for Independent Means
The hypothesis testing procedure for a t test for independent means is changed for Steps 2-4. In Step 2, the comparison distribution is a distribution of differences between means. In Step 3, the number of degrees of freedom used to find the cutoff sample score is based on the degrees of freedom for two samples. In Step 4, the sample score on the comparison distribution is based on the difference between the means of two samples.

An Example of a *t* Test for Independent Means (Equal Sample Sizes)

A psychologist is interested in determining the effect of self-defense training on the self-confidence of employees who have been transferred from a small city to a large metropolitan city. A group of 10 employees willing to be trained in self-defense is identified, and 5 are randomly assigned to a training program. The other 5 receive no special training. At the end of training, all 10 employees complete a questionnaire to assess their levels of self-confidence. The data are presented in the table included in Step 2 of the hypothesis testing procedure. Using the .05 level of significance, did the program make a difference in the levels of self-confidence of the two groups?

Step 1: Restate the question as a research hypothesis and a null hypothesis about the populations.
Population 1: Employees who receive self-defense training
Population 2: Employees who do not receive self-defense training

Research hypothesis: The self-confidence of employees who receive self-defense training will be different from the self-confidence of employees who do not receive self-defense training.
Null hypothesis: The self-confidence of employees who receive self-defense training will be no different from the self-confidence of employees who do not receive self-defense training.

Step 2: Determine the characteristics of the comparison distribution.

Training Group	Deviation from M	(Deviation from the $M)^2$	No Training Group	Deviation from M	(Deviation from $M)^2$
45	3.2	10.24	24	-5.20	27.04
48	6.2	38.44	34	4.80	23.04
44	2.2	4.84	29	-0.20	0.04
37	-4.8	23.04	27	-2.20	4.84
35	-6.8	46.24	32	2.80	7.84
$\sum = 209$	$\sum = 0.00$	$\sum = 122.80$	$\sum = 146.00$	$\sum = 0.00$	$\sum = 62.80$

$M_1 = 41.80$; $S^2_1 = 122.80 / 4 = 30.70$;
$M_2 = 29.20$; $S^2_2 = 62.80 / 4 = 15.70$
$N_1 = 5$; $df_1 = N_1 - 1 = 5 - 1 = 4$
$N_2 = 5$; $df_2 = N_2 - 1 = 5 - 1 = 4$
$df_{total} = df_1 + df_2 = 4 + 4 = 8$

$S^2_{pooled} = df_1 / df_{total} (S^2_1) + df_2 / df_{total} (S^2_2)$
$= 4 / 8 (30.70) + 4 / 8 (15.70) = .5 (30.70) + .5 (15.70) = 15.35 + 7.85 = 23.20$

$S^2_{M1} = S^2_{pooled} / N_1 = 23.20 / 5 = 4.64$
$S^2_{M2} = S^2_{pooled} / N_2 = 23.20 / 5 = 4.64$

$S^2_{Difference} = S^2_{M1} + S^2_{M2} = 4.64 + 4.64 = 9.28$

$S_{Difference} = \sqrt{S^2_{Difference}} = \sqrt{9.28} = 3.05$

The comparison distribution is a *t* distribution with 8 *df*.

Step 3: Determine the cutoff sample score on the comparison distribution at which the null hypothesis should be rejected.
For a *t* distribution with 8 *df*, the cutoff sample score at the .05 level of significance is ±2.306

Step 4: Determine the sample score on the comparison distribution.

$t = (M_1 - M_2) / S_{\text{Diff}}$
$= (41.80 - 29.20) / 3.05$
$= 12.60 / 3.05$
$= 4.13$

Step 5: Decide whether to reject the null hypothesis.
Since 4.13 is more extreme than 2.306, the psychologist will reject the null hypothesis at the .05 level of significance and accept the research hypothesis that self-defense training improves the self-confidence of employees.

An Example of a *t* Test for Independent Means (Unequal Sample Sizes)

Based on the success of the initial study on the effect of self-defense training on self-confidence, the psychologist decided to replicate the study with a larger number of employees. The results of the second study are again presented in Step 2 of the hypothesis testing procedure. Note that 10 participants were included in each group at the beginning of the study, but two participants in the group that did not receive training did not complete the study.

Step 1: Restate the question as a research hypothesis and a null hypothesis about the populations.
Population 1: Employees who receive self-defense training
Population 2: Employees who do not receive self-defense training

Research hypothesis: The self-confidence of employees who receive self-defense training will be different from the self-confidence of employees who do not receive self-defense training.
Null hypothesis: The self-confidence of employees who receive self-defense training will be no different from the self-confidence of employees who do not receive self-defense training.

Step 2: Determine the characteristics of the comparison distribution.

Training Group	Deviation from M	(Deviation from $M)^2$	No Training Group	Deviation from M	(Deviation From $M)^2$
45	3.4	11.56	38	7.75	60.06
43	1.4	1.96	27	-3.25	10.56
44	2.4	5.76	17	-13.25	175.56
32	-9.6	92.16	28	-2.25	5.06
38	-3.6	12.96	42	11.75	138.06
48	6.4	40.96	31	0.75	0.56
36	-5.6	31.36	22	-8.25	68.06
45	3.4	11.56	37	6.75	45.56
39	-2.6	6.76			
46	4.4	19.36			
$\sum = 416$	$\sum = 0.00$	$\sum = 234.40$	$\sum = 242$	$\sum = 0.00$	$\sum = 503.50$

$M_1 = 41.60; S^2_1 = 234.40 / 9 = 26.04$
$M_2 = 30.25; S^2_2 = 503.50 / 7 = 71.93$
$N_1 = 10; df_1 = N_1 - 1 = 10 - 1 = 9$
$N_2 = 8; df_2 = N_2 - 1 = 8 - 1 = 7$
$df_{\text{total}} = df_1 + df_2 = 9 + 7 = 16$

$S^2_{\text{pooled}} = df_1 / df_{\text{total}} (S^2_1) + df_2 / df_{\text{total}} (S^2_2)$
$= 9 / 16 (26.04) + 7 / 16 (71.93) = .56 (26.04) + .44 (71.93) = 46.23$

$S^2_{M1} = S^2_{\text{pooled}} / N_1 = 46.23 / 10 = 4.62$
$S^2_{M2} = S^2_{\text{pooled}} / N_2 = 46.23 / 8 = 5.78$

$S^2{}_{\text{Difference}} = S^2{}_{M1} + S^2{}_{M2} = 4.62 + 5.78 = 10.40$

$S_{\text{Difference}} = \sqrt{S^2{}_{\text{Difference}}} = \sqrt{10.40} = 3.22$

The comparison distribution is a t distribution with 16 df.

Step 3: Determine the cutoff sample score on the comparison distribution at which the null hypothesis should be rejected.
For a t distribution with 16 df, the cutoff sample score at the .05 level of significance is ± 2.120

Step 4: Determine the sample score on the comparison distribution.
$t = (M_1 - M_2) / S_{\text{Diff}}$
$\quad = (41.60 - 30.25) / 3.22$
$\quad = 11.35 / 3.22$
$\quad = 3.52$

Step 5: Decide whether to reject the null hypothesis.
Since 3.52 is more extreme than 2.120, the psychologist will reject the null hypothesis at the .05 level of significance and accept the research hypothesis that self-defense training improves the self-confidence of employees.

Assumptions of the t Test for Independent Means
The t test for independent means has two assumptions:
1. Each of the populations of individual scores for the two groups is normally distributed. Violations of this assumption pose problems if the two population distributions are seriously skewed, and are skewed in opposite directions. Even if the population distributions are skewed, the test is robust when two-tailed tests are used and the sample sizes are not extremely small.
2. As has been indicated, the variances of the two populations of individual scores are assumed to be equal. The test is robust even if the differences in the population variances are large when the sample sizes equal.

If the population distributions are very skewed, or the variances are quite different, or both conditions are present, the t test for independent means can yield misleading results. Alternative tests (described in Chapter 14) may provide results that are more valid. In addition, computer programs like SPSS provide two types of output for the t test for independent means, one assuming that the variances are equal, and one assuming that they are not. The latter approach does result in lower power.

Effect Size and Power for the t Test for Independent Means
The effect size is calculated as usual with $d = \mu_1 - \mu_2 / \sigma$, and Cohen's conventions are the same as they have been: $d = .20$ indicates a small effect; $d = .50$ indicates a medium effect; and $d = .80$ indicates a large effect. For a completed study, effect size is estimated by dividing the difference between the sample means by the pooled estimate of the population standard deviation; estimated $d = M_1 - M_2 / \sigma$.

In the first of the two studies investigating the effect of self-defense training on employee self-confidence, the mean for the group that received training was 41.80, the mean for the control group was 29.20 and $S^2{}_{\text{pooled}}$ was 23.20. S_{pooled} is equal to the square root of 23.20, which is 4.82. Therefore, $d = (41.80 - 29.20) / 4.82 = 12.6 / 4.82 = 2.60$, a very large effect size. In the second of the two studies, the mean for the group that received training was 41.60, the mean for the control group was 30.25 and $S^2{}_{\text{pooled}}$ was 46.23. S_{pooled} is equal to the square root of 46.23, which is 6.80. Therefore, $d = (41.60 - 30.25) / 6.80 = 11.35 / 6.80 = 1.67$, a very large effect size, as well.

Power tables for t tests for independent means are available. As the power table in the text indicates, one-tailed tests are more powerful than two-tailed tests, and power increases as sample size increases or as effect size increases. For example, suppose a study is being designed to compare differences between two means reflecting a medium effect size. If each group includes 20 participants, a one-tailed test at the .05 level of significance will have a power of .46. A two-tailed test at the .05 level of significance will have a power of .33. Thus, the chances that the results of the t tests will be statistically significant, even if the research hypothesis is true, are only 46% and 33%, respectively.

Power can also be used to evaluate the results of completed studies. Neither of the two studies described in the preceding paragraph had even a 50% chance of detecting a medium effect. In fact, the sample sizes would need to be increased to 50 participants per group in order the have the 80% power suggested as a guideline for designing a study that will be worth conducing if a one-tailed test is used. If a two-tailed test is used, the number of participants will need to be greater than 50, but less than 100, in order to achieve 80% power.

Planning Sample Size
As indicated in the preceding section, sample size determination involves effect size and power considerations, as well as consideration of the type of test to be conducted and the significance level at which the result will be evaluated. The suggested guideline of 80% power can be reached with only 20 participants per group is a large effect size is expected and the experimenters plan to use a one-tailed test and the .05 level of significance. If the experimenters plan to use a two-tailed test and the .05 level of significance, 30 participants per group are required to achieve 80% power. Note that even with 100 participants per group, 80% power cannot be obtained if a small effect size is to be detected. In this situation, the power is 41% for a one-tailed test at the .05 level and 29% for a two-tailed test at the same level.

In this chapter and the preceding one, three different t tests have been described. The common factor is that the population variances must be estimated from the scores of the individuals that comprise the experimental samples, which means that the comparison distribution is a t distribution. The three t tests are:
1. The t test for one sample, in which a sample mean is compared to a known population mean,
2. The t for dependent means, in which each participant has two scores (or the participants are matched in some way), and
3. The t test for independent means, in which the participants in each sample are different (independent).

The t Test for Independent Means in Research Articles
The t test for independent means is usually reported in research articles by listing the two sample means (and sometimes the standard deviations) followed by the t test results in the usual format. For example, the results for the first study describing the effects of self-defense training on employee self-confidence could be reported as follows: The mean score on the self-confidence inventory for the employees who received self-defense training was 41.80 ($SD = 5.54$), while the mean score for the employees who did not receive training was 29.20 ($SD = 3.96$); $t(8) = 4.13, p < .05$.

Advanced Topic: Power for the t Test for Independent Means when Sample Sizes are Not Equal
Power for the t test for independent means is greatest when the number of participants in each group is equal. When sample sizes are not equal, the **harmonic mean** is used to estimate the sample size for the t test for independent means. The formula for the harmonic mean is

Harmonic mean $= [(2) (N_1) (N_2)] / [N_1 + N_2]$.

The harmonic mean is equal to the size of the sample that would exist if the unequal samples were divided into samples of equal size. For example, calculating the harmonic mean for the study that included 41 participants in the experimental group and 21 in the control group would yield:

$(2) (41) (21) / (41 + 21) = 1722 / 62 = 27.77$

Although the study included 62 participants, the study had a power equal to that of a study with approximately 56 participants if they were divided into equal groups.

Chapter Self Tests

Understanding Key Concepts in Chapter 8

The test items that follow are based on the following scenario. The group of psychologists that has been studying the effect of depression on the number of activities of daily living performed by depressed people is now interested in whether depressed people undergoing group therapy will perform a different number of activities than depressed people undergoing individual therapy. Therefore, the psychologists have randomly selected two groups of depressed clients, one of which has undergone a 6-week group therapy program and the other a 6-week individual therapy program. The psychologists have measured the number of activities of daily living performed by both samples of depressed clients at the completion of the therapy sessions.

Directions: Complete each statement using the word bank that follows.

Word Bank: dependent / differences between means / equal / harmonic mean / independent / normal / pooled estimate / single-sample / $S^2_{Difference}$ / $S_{Difference}$ / weighted average

In order to conduct the comparison between the effects of group and individual therapy, the appropriate test is a t test for (1) _____ means. If the psychologists had matched the participants in each group on variables including age, duration of symptoms, and score on a depression inventory, the appropriate tests would be a t test for (2) _____ means. Finally, if the psychologists wanted to compare the scores of their clients to a score on a depression inventory that divides people into clinically depressed or not clinically depressed categories based on a known population mean, the appropriate test would be a t test for a (3) _____. Returning to the intended comparison between the means of groups undergoing group and individual therapy, the comparison distribution for their analysis will be a sampling distribution of (4) _____. In order to create this distribution, the psychologists will have to estimate the variances of the populations of individual scores and use them to create distributions of means for each of the populations. Next, the psychologists will have to combine the two distributions of means to create a single variance estimate. This combined estimate is the (5) _____ of the population variance. Since this estimate is adjusted to take the influence of possibly different sample sizes into account, it is a (6) _____. The new concepts for this distribution are (7) _____ and (8) _____. This t test assumes that the distributions of depression scores for both the population of depressed people undergoing group therapy and the population of depressed people undergoing individual therapy are (9) _____, and have (10) _____ variances. The power of their statistical test will be highest if the sizes of the two groups are equal. When group sizes are unequal, the (11) _____ provides an estimate of the power if the participants were divided into groups of equal size.

Multiple-Choice Items

1. If the psychologists plan to conduct a two-tailed t test for independent means, the null hypothesis will be that
    A. the mean of Population 1 will be equal to the mean of Population 2.
    B. the mean of Population 1 will be different from the mean of Population 2.
    C. the mean of Population 1 will be less than the mean of Population 2.
    D. the mean of Population 1 will be greater than the mean of Population 2.

Items 2–6 are related.

The psychologists are explaining the conceptual basis for the analysis they plan to conduct to an intern who understands descriptive statistics and hypothesis testing, but who has never been taught about the *t* test. They begin the explanation by stating that they will be making inferences about two hypothetical populations, depressed people who undergo group therapy and depressed people who undergo individual therapy.

2. Next, they explain that to conduct a *t* test for independent means
    A. two scores are obtained from each participant in the experimental groups.
    B. the comparison distribution is a distribution of means.
    C. only two-tailed tests are possible.
    D. the variance of the populations of individual scores must be estimated.

3. The next conceptual step is that once they have determined the characteristics of the two distributions of individual scores, this information, along with the number of clients in each sample, will be used to determine
    A. the relationship between the sample distributions and the normal distribution.
    B. the characteristics of the distributions of means of the samples.
    C. the characteristics of the distribution of differences between means.
    D. the shape of the comparison distribution when the samples include infinite numbers of participants.

4. Since the calculated *t* is a single score, the final conceptual step is to imagine the comparison distribution as a distribution of
    A. paired variances.
    B. means.
    C. random *t* scores.
    D. differences between means.

5. Based on the numerator of the *t* formula, $(M_1 - M_2)$, the mean of the comparison distribution is
    A. $df + 2$.
    B. $df / 2$.
    C. 0.
    D. 1.

6. Conceptually, the standard deviation of this comparison distribution is the average of the variances of the distributions of means of individual depression scores of the two experimental groups. Consequently, this average is called the
    A. mean estimate of the population variance.
    B. pooled estimate of the population variance.
    C. harmonic estimate of the population variance.
    D. weighted estimate of the population variance.

Items 7–12 are related.

The psychologists have conducted their analysis and report that they obtained the mean number of activities performed by clients undergoing group therapy was 15.87 ($SD = 3.07$) and the mean number of activities performed by clients undergoing individual therapy was 18.35 ($SD = 3.04$); $t(30) = -2.30$, $p < .05$.

7. The description of the analysis indicates that the number of participants in the study was
    A. 28.
    B. 30.
    C. 32.
    D. 34.

8. If M_1 was the mean number of activities performed by clients who underwent group therapy and M_2 was the mean number of activities performed by clients who underwent individual therapy, the t score indicates that
    A. clients who underwent individual therapy performed more activities.
    B. clients who underwent group therapy performed more activities.
    C. the means of the groups were nearly identical.
    D. the variances of the two groups were nearly identical.

9. The p value means that the psychologists
    A. were measuring a large treatment effect on the number of activities performed.
    B. identified a practically significant difference in the two types of treatment.
    C. could accept a research hypothesis that treatment had an effect on the number of activities performed.
    D. could also reject the null hypothesis at the .01 level.

10. The standard deviations of the two experimental groups indicate that
    A. the effect size was large.
    B. the variances were approximately equal.
    C. the populations of individual scores were normally distributed.
    D. the study had adequate power to identify a practically significant difference between therapies.

11. If the psychologists decide to replicate their study with 50 participants, they will have the most power if they divide the participants so that
    A. 25 participants receive group therapy and 25 receive individual therapy.
    B. 30 participants receive group therapy and 20 receive individual therapy.
    C. 20 participants receive group therapy and 30 receive individual therapy.
    D. 10 participants receive group therapy and 40 receive individual therapy.

12. If different numbers of participants drop out of each experimental group so that the numbers in each group are different, the psychologists can estimate the power of a study that divides the remaining participants into two groups of equal size by calculating
    A. the pooled variance estimate.
    B. $S^2_{\text{Difference}}$.
    C. $S_{\text{Difference}}$.
    D. the harmonic mean.

Problems

1. The psychologists have randomly selected 2 groups of depressed clients, one of which has undergone a 6-week group therapy program and the other a 6-week individual therapy program. Use the five steps of hypothesis testing to determine whether the observed differences in activities of daily living (shown in the table that follows) performed by the two groups are statistically significant at the .05 (and, for practice, the .01) level of significance. In Step 2, show all calculations. As part of Step 5, indicate which type of therapy the psychologists should recommend for depressed people based on evaluation of the null hypothesis at both levels of significance and calculate the effect size. Explain what you have done to someone who is familiar with the t test for a single sample, but not with the t test for independent means.

Group Therapy	Individual Therapy
15	17
15	15
19	20
17	20
14	15
14	15
16	18
18	20

2. The results of the study described in Problem 1 were not statistically significant, but seven of the eight depressed clients who underwent individual therapy increased the number of activities of daily living performed, and the power of the study was low. Therefore, the psychologists have decided to replicate the study using a larger number of participants. They enrolled 20 participants in each group. However, as indicated in the table that follows, some participants did not complete the study. Use the five steps of hypothesis testing to determine whether the participants who undergo individual therapy perform more activities of daily living than participants who undergo group therapy and whether the differences are statistically significant at the .05 (and, for practice, the .01) level of significance. In Step 2, show all calculations. As part of Step 5, indicate which type of therapy the psychologists should recommend for depressed people based on evaluation of the null hypothesis at both levels of significance and calculate the effect size. Explain what you have done to someone who is familiar with the t test for a single sample, but not with the t test for independent means.

Group Therapy	Individual Therapy
15	17
17	14
20	22
18	21
15	16
18	17
14	12
11	18
10	16
15	20
13	19
17	24
18	18
21	17
16	22
	20
	19

3. Six months after an industrial accident, a psychologist has been asked to compare the job satisfaction of employees who participated counseling sessions with the satisfaction of employees who chose not to participate. The scores on a job satisfaction inventory for both groups are listed in the table that follows. Use the five steps of hypothesis testing to determine whether the job satisfaction scores of the group that participated in counseling are statistically higher than the scores of employees who did not participate in counseling at the .01 level of significance. In Step 2, show all calculations. As part of Step 5, indicate whether the psychologist should recommend counseling as a method to improve job satisfaction following industrial accidents based on evaluation of the null hypothesis and calculate the effect size. Explain what you have done to someone who is familiar with the t test for a single sample, but not with the t test for independent means.

Participated in Counseling	Did not Participate in Counseling
36	37
39	35
40	36
36	33
38	30
35	38
37	39
39	35
42	32

4. Based on the results of the study in Problem 3, what justification might the psychologist give for reinterpreting the results of the study?

5. A psychologist interested in the effect of exercise on perceptions of well-being among the elderly identified 30 residents of a retirement community and divided them into two groups of 15 residents. Both groups were encouraged to walk at least 20 minutes per day. One group, however, also participated in structured exercise program that emphasized flexibility. After six weeks, the psychologist mailed questionnaires to the 30 residents. Responses to an item asking residents to rate their perceptions of their health on a 10-point scale on which 1 indicated "very unhealthy" and 10 indicated "very healthy" are presented in the table that follows. Use the five steps of hypothesis testing to determine whether the observed differences in health ratings of the two groups are statistically significant at the .05 level of significance. In Step 2, show all calculations. As part of Step 5, indicate whether the psychologist should recommend exercise as a method to improve perceptions of health among the elderly based on evaluation of the null hypothesis and calculate the effect size. Explain what you have done to someone who is familiar with the t test for a single sample, but not with the t test for independent means.

Walking & Flexibility	Walking Only
5	2
6	3
6	4
4	3
9	6
4	7
7	7
9	6
6	7
7	4
9	6
7	
4	
9	
8	

6. Determine the power of each of the following studies that is to be analyzed using a t test for independent means at the .05 level of significance.

Study	Effect Size	N	Tails
(a)	Small	10	One
(b)	Medium	30	One
(c)	Small	20	Two
(d)	Small	100	Two
(e)	Medium	40	Two
(f)	Large	20	Two

7. Determine the approximate number of subjects that will be needed for the following studies if a t test for independent means will be used to analyze data at the .05 level of significance. First list the total number of participants that will need to be included in the study. Then list the number that will be assigned to each group.

Study	μ_1	μ_2	σ	Tails
(a)	36	58	44	2
(b)	152	120	40	2
(c)	50	52	10	1
(d)	12	9	6	1

8. Which t test is appropriate in the following studies?
   A. Comparing the depression scores of men and women
   B. Comparing the reading achievement scores of students who have been tutored with a mean of 100
   C. Comparing the depression scores of disaster victims with a score that distinguishes normal depression from clinically significant depression
   D. Comparing the depression scores of people before and after an exercise program
   E. Comparing the reading achievement scores of students before and after a tutoring program
   F. Comparing the reading achievement scores of boys and girls after a tutoring program

Additional Practice: Complete any Practice Problems in Set I that your instructor has not assigned and compare your responses to those provided by the authors. Pay particular attention to the problems that require you to explain your results to someone who has never taken a course in statistics.

SPSS Applications

Application 1: t Test for Independent Means
Open SPSS.
Analyze the data for Problem 1. Remember that SPSS assumes that all the scores in a row are from the same participant. In this study, there are 16 participants divided into two groups of eight. Therefore, each of the 16 participants will be described by two variables, type of therapy and the number of activities of daily living performed. Using "1" to represent group therapy and "2" to represent the individual therapy, the first participant can be described by entering "1" in the top cell of the first column in the Data View window and "15" in the top cell of the second column, indicating that the participant underwent group therapy and performed 15 activities of daily living. The second participant can be described by "1" and "15," and so on. When the two variables have been entered for the eight participants who underwent group therapy, repeat the process for participants who underwent individual therapy using "2" to describe their therapy group. Name the variables "therapy" and "activities" and set the decimals for both to zero if you wish. The Data View should look like Figure 1.

therapy	activities
1	15
1	16
1	19
1	17
1	14
1	14
1	16
1	18
2	17
2	15
2	20
2	20
2	15
2	15
2	18
2	20

Figure 1
✒ Analyze
✒ Compare means
✒ Independent-Samples T Test
✒ "activities" and ✒ the arrow to move the variable to the Test Variable(s) window
✒ "therapy" and ✒ the arrow to move the variable to the Grouping Variable(s) window

"Define Groups" and enter "1' in the box for Group 1 and "2" in the box for Group 2
The "Independent Samples T-Test" and"Define Groups" window2 should look like Figure 2.

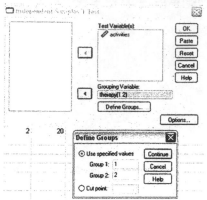

Figure 2

Continue

OK

The SPSS output should look like Figure 3 and Figure 4

Group Statistics

	therapy	N	Mean	Std Deviation	Std. Error Mean
activibes	1	8	16.00	1.852	.655
	2	8	17.50	2.330	.824

Figure 3

Independent Samples Test

		Levene's Test for Equality of Variances		t-test for Equality of Means						95% Confidence Interval of the Difference	
		F	Sig.	t	df	Sig. (2-tailed)	Mean Difference	Std Error Difference	Lower	Upper
activibes	Equal variances assumed	1.167	.298	-1.426	14	.176	-1.500	1.052	-3.757	.757
	Equal variances not assumed			-1.426	13.321	.177	-1.500	1.052	-3.768	.768

Figure 4

The table in Figure 3 summarizes the data obtained during the study including the number of participants in each therapy group, the mean and standard deviation for each group, and the standard error of the mean. This last value is the standard deviation of the distribution of means, S_M, for each group, but they are not based on the pooled variance estimate. Instead, they are based on each population variance and are not equal to the square root of S^2_M as calculated in the solution to the problem.

Figure 4 contains the results of the *t* test and includes some additional information, the first being the results of *Levene's Test for Equality of Variances*, which is exactly what its title indicates it is. If the test is statistically significant, i.e., if "Sig." is less than .05, the variances of the two groups cannot be assumed to be equal, and the results of the *t* test in the row labeled "Equal variances not assumed" will be interpreted. Note that the number of degrees of freedom has been reduced. This reduction means that the cutoff sample score will be slightly larger, making statistical significance more difficult to obtain, reducing the probability of a Type I error. In this instance, Levene's test is not significant, so the assumption of equal variances is reasonable, and the results in this row can be interpreted. With small differences due to rounding at various stages of the "hand" calculations presented in the solution to the Problem in the Answer Key, the results are quite similar, and their interpretation will be the same. Although the 95% confidence interval was not calculated, note that it includes zero, which indicates that the mean numbers of activities performed by participants in the two groups may well be equal, confirming the failure to reject the null hypothesis at the .05 level of significance.

Application 2: *t* Test for Independent Means

Open SPSS.

Enter the data from Problem 2 just as you did in Application 1. The purpose of this application is to reinforce the fact that the *t* test for independent means does not require that the group sizes be equal. Because the directional research hypothesis predicts that clients who undergo individual therapy will perform more activities of daily living, you may want to reverse the group numbers so that the results of the *t* test will be positive, as has been done in the results that follow. Quantitatively, the results will be identical if you do not reverse the group numbers, but the sign of *t* will be negative if the prediction is accurate.

⤳ Analyze

⤳ Compare means

⤳ Independent-Samples T Test

⤳ "activities" and ⤳ the arrow to move the variable to the Test Variable(s) window

⤳ "therapy" and ⤳ the arrow to move the variable to the Grouping Variable(s) window

⤳ "Define Groups" and enter "1' in the box for Group 1 and "2" in the box for Group 2

The "Define Groups" window should look like Figure 2

⤳ Continue

The "Independent-Samples T Test" window should look like Figure 2

⤳ OK

The SPSS output should look like Figure 5 and Figure 6

Group Statistics

	therapy	N	Mean	Std. Deviation	Std. Error Mean
activities	1	17	18.35	3.040	.737
	2	15	15.87	3.057	.792

Figure 5

Independent Samples Test

		Levene's Test for Equality of Variances		t-test for Equality of Means						
									95% Confidence Interval of the Difference	
		F	Sig.	t	df	Sig. (2-tailed)	Mean Difference	Std. Error Difference	Lower	Upper
activities	Equal variances assumed	.003	.956	2.299	30	.029	2.486	1.081	.278	4.695
	Equal variances not assumed			2.298	29.436	.029	2.486	1.082	.275	4.698

Figure 6

Again, the table in Figure 5 summarizes the data obtained during the study including the number of participants in each therapy group, the mean and standard deviation for each group, and the standard error of the mean. Again, this last value is the standard deviation of the distribution of means, S_M, for each group, but they are not based on the pooled variance estimate. Instead, they are based on each population variance and are not equal to the square root of S^2_M as calculated in the solution to the problem.

Figure 6 contains the results of the *t* test, which indicates that the results of Levene's Test are not statistically significant. Since the assumption of equal variances is reasonable, the results in this row can be interpreted. However, SPSS only provides "Sig. (2-tailed)," and the psychologists stated a directional research hypothesis, which calls for a one-tailed test. The solution is to divide the two-tailed significance provided by SPSS to obtain the one-tailed significance. In this case, dividing .029 by 2 yields .015. Again, with small differences due to rounding at various stages of the "hand" calculations presented in the solution to the Problem in the Answer Key, the results are quite similar, and their interpretation will be the same.

If you would like additional practice, use SPSS to analyze the data for Problem 3 and Problem 4 and compare the results to your calculations and those in the Answer Key.

Chapter 9
Introduction to the Analysis of Variance

Learning Objectives
After studying this chapter, you should:

- Know when and how to conduct an analysis of variance.
- Be able to calculate the within-groups estimate of the population variance, the between-groups estimate of the population variance, and the F ratio.
- Be able to describe the F distribution and use an F table.
- Be able to define the normality and equality of variances assumptions underlying the analysis of variance and describe their implications.
- Be able to describe and calculate planned contrasts, and know the function of the Bonferroni procedure.
- Know the distinction between planned contrasts and post hoc tests.
- Know how to calculate the Scheffé test.
- Be able to calculate effect sizes for studies requiring an analysis of variance and interpret these effect sizes using Cohen's conventions.
- Be able to use tables to estimate power for analyses of variance.
- Be able to use tables to estimate sample size for analyses of variance.
- Be able to interpret the results of analyses of variance as reported in research articles.
- Advanced Topic: Know how to calculate an analysis of variance using the structural model.

Basic Logic of the Analysis of Variance
Analysis of variance (ANOVA) may be used to compare the means of more than two groups. [Analysis of variance can be used to compare the means of two groups, but t is simpler and more straightforward.] The null hypothesis is that the means of three or more populations are equal, and the research hypothesis is that the means are unequal. Since the data being analyzed are collected from samples, the question is whether the observed differences are greater than would be expected by chance if the null hypothesis is true. While using variances to compare may seem confusing, think about the fact that a question about the way means differ can be conceptualized as a question about how the means vary. Also, bear in mind that population variances can be estimated in two different ways, which will be described next.

Estimating the Population Variance from Variance within Each Sample
As was the case with the t test, population variances are estimated from sample data. Like t, analysis of variance assumes that the population variances are equal, which permits averaging estimates from each sample into a single poled estimate called the **within-groups estimate of the population variance** (S^2_{Within} or MS_{Within}). Remember that the within-groups variance is not influenced by whether the null hypothesis is true or false because it is the variance within separate populations. Thus, this variance can be attributed to chance factors like differences in the ways individuals respond to an experimental treatment or measurement error.

Estimating the Population Variance from Variation between the Means of the Samples
Since each sample mean is a number, the sample means of an experiment can be treated like the scores of individuals, i.e., the mean of the means can be computed, and this mean can be used to estimate the variance of this distribution of means. The variance of this distribution of means provides another way to estimate the variance in the populations from which samples are drawn.

When the null hypothesis is true, all the populations from which samples are drawn have same mean. However, samples drawn from identical populations will still have somewhat different means depending on the variation in the population. In addition, the greater the variation in a population, the greater the variation will be in samples drawn from the population, and the more likely the means of the samples are to be different. These expected differences between the means of samples permit calculation of the **between-groups estimate of the population variance** ($S^2_{Between}$ or $MS_{Between}$).

When the null hypothesis is not true, the populations have different means. The within-groups variation is still present, but since the research hypothesis is also true, the population means are different. Now variation among the means is not only due to the sources of variation that affect the within-groups estimates of the population variances, but also to the effects of the experimental treatment that have caused the population means to differ.

Comparing the Within-Groups and Between Groups Estimates of Population Variance
Stated another way, when the null hypothesis is true, any variation among the experimental groups is attributable to variation within the groups. Therefore, the variation between groups and the variation within groups are, within the limits of sampling error, identical. Accordingly, the ratio between the two types of variance should be close to 1. However, when the research hypothesis is true, the observed variation between groups reflects both variation among individual scores and variation among means. In this situation, the between-groups variance should be larger than the within-groups variance, and their ratio should be greater than 1.

Considering the information just presented, examine the two datasets that follow.

Dataset 1: Weight loss in pounds

Exercise	Diet	Both Diet & Exercise
5	2	4
33	32	32
19	22	26
27	12	10
11	17	18
$\Sigma X = 95$	$\Sigma X = 85$	$\Sigma X = 90$
$M = 19$	$M = 17$	$M = 18$

Grand Mean = 18

Dataset 2: Weight loss in pounds

Exercise	Diet	Both Diet & Exercise
7	19	26
9	16	29
8	18	28
7	20	29
9	17	28
$\Sigma X = 40$	$\Sigma X = 90$	$\Sigma X = 140$
$M = 8$	$M = 18$	$M = 28$

Grand Mean = 18

Although the grand means of the two datasets are equal, the scores in each group in Dataset 1 are quite variable compared to the scores in each group in Dataset 2. In addition, comparable losses are present in each group, e.g., the participants whose data are entered in the first row of Dataset 1 lost 4, 2, and 5 pounds, while the participants listed in the second row lost 32, 32, and 33 pounds, respectively. On the other hand, the weight losses of participants in each group in Dataset 2 are within 2-3 pounds. Also, the group means in Dataset 1 reflect weight loss differences of 1 pound; the group means in Dataset 2 reflect weight differences of 10 pounds. Thus, the ratio of the between-groups variance to the within-groups variance for Dataset 1 will be close to 1, but the ratio for Dataset 2 will be much larger. Concisely stated, the treatment had little effect on weight loss in the first instance, but a substantial effect in the second.

The ratio described in the preceding paragraph is called the **F ratio**, and the question is how much larger than 1 an F ratio has to be in order to reject the null hypothesis. As was the case with the t test, an **F distribution** can be described mathematically, and an **F table** can be consulted to determine how extreme an F ratio must be to reject the null hypothesis.

Conducting an Analysis of Variance
In order to conduct an analysis of variance, three values must be calculated:
1. The within-groups variance is calculated using the usual method of estimating a population variance from sample data. If the sample sizes are equal, the variance estimates for the experimental groups (the samples) can be pooled

by averaging. The formula is

S^2_{Within} or $MS_{\text{Within}} = (S_1^2 + S_2^2 + \dots + S_{\text{Last}}^2) / N_{\text{Groups}}$, where

S_1^2 is the unbiased estimate of the variance of Population 1 based on the scores in the first experimental group,

S_2^2 is the unbiased estimate of the variance of Population 2 based on the scores in the second experimental group, and

S_{Last}^2 is the unbiased estimate of the variance of the population based on scores in the last experimental group.

Remember that the value of each $S^2 = \Sigma(X - M)^2 / df$ or SS / df.

Also remember that MS_{Within} is "mean squares within."

2. Calculating the between-groups variance requires two steps.

The first step involves treating each mean as an individual number and calculating the mean of the group of means, which is called the **grand mean (GM)**, and then applying the usual formula for estimating a population variance. The formula is

$S_M^2 = \Sigma(M - GM)^2 / df_{\text{Between}}$, where

M is the mean of each sample,

When sample sizes are equal, $GM = \Sigma M / N_{\text{Groups}}$, and

df_{Between} is the degrees of freedom in the between-group estimate, i.e., the number of groups minus 1 ($N_{\text{Groups}} - 1$).

The second step involves converting the estimated variance of the distribution of means to an estimate of the variance of individual scores by multiplying variance of the distribution of means by the size of each sample. [This computation is the reverse of the earlier division of the variance of a population of individual cases by the size of the sample to obtain the variance of a distribution of means.] The between-group variance is also called the "mean-squares between." The formula is S^2_{Between} or $MS_{\text{Between}} = (S_M^2)(n)$.

3. The F ratio is the ratio of the between-groups estimate of the population variance to the within-groups estimate of the population variance. The formula is $F = S_{\text{Between}}^2 / S^2_{\text{Within}}$ or $F = MS_{\text{Between}} / MS_{\text{Within}}$.

When the F ratio has been calculated, it is compared to an F distribution to determine the probability that an F as large as the one obtained will occur if the null hypothesis is true. Since variances are squared numbers, they are always positive, and the ratio of two positive numbers cannot be less than 0. Most F ratios clustered around 1, but since the possibility of very large numbers cannot be eliminated, F distributions are skewed to the right.

Two degrees of freedom must be known to enter an F table.

The **between-groups degrees of freedom**, or **numerator degrees of freedom (df_{Between})**, are equal to the number of groups minus 1. [$df_{\text{Between}} = N_{\text{Groups}} - 1$.]

The **within-groups degrees of freedom**, or **denominator degrees of freedom (df_{Within})**, are equal to the sum of the degrees of freedom for all of the groups. [$df_{\text{Within}} = df_1 + df_2 + \dots + df_{\text{Last}}$.]

Hypothesis Testing with Analysis of Variance

Suppose a health psychologist conducted a weight loss program for morbidly obese people and obtained the data presented in the table in Step 4 of the hypothesis testing procedure. (The table is placed in Step 4 so it will be easier to follow the calculations.) Use the five steps of hypothesis testing to determine whether there is a difference in the three weight loss methods and whether the differences are statistically significant at the .05 (and, for practice, the .01) level of significance. In Step 4, show all calculations.

Steps of Hypothesis Testing

Step 1: Restate the question as a research hypothesis and a null hypothesis about the populations.

Population 1: People attempting to lose weight using diet alone

Population 2: People attempting to lose weight using exercise alone

Population 3: People attempting to lose weight using diet and exercise

Research hypothesis: There will be a difference in the mean number of pounds lost by the three groups.

Null hypothesis: There will be no difference in the mean number of pounds lost by the three groups.

Step 2: Determine the characteristics of the comparison distribution.

The study involves three groups of 10 participants each.

$df_{Between} = N_{Groups} - 1 = (3 - 1) = 2$

$df_{Within} = df_1 + df_2 + df_3 = (9 + 9 + 9) = 27$

The comparison distribution will be an F distribution with 2 and 27 df.

Step 3: Determine the cutoff sample score on the comparison distribution at which the null hypothesis should be rejected.

$F_{2,27}$ at the .05 level of significance = 3.36

$F_{2,27}$ at the .01 level of significance = 5.49

Step 4: Determine the sample's score on the comparison distribution.

Participant	Exercise	Diet	Diet & Exercise
1	21	67	78
2	54	62	50
3	26	57	55
4	21	68	62
5	28	58	56
6	57	70	77
7	52	58	71
8	37	59	53
9	26	68	79
10	47	50	69

$M_E = 36.9$

$M_D = 61.7$

$M_{D\&E} = 65.0$

$M_{Means} (GM) = 54.53$

$\Sigma(M - GM)^2 = 471.85$

$S^2_M = \Sigma(M - GM)^2 / df_{Between} = 471.85 / 2 = 235.92$

$S^2_{Between} = (S^2_M)(n) = (235.92)(10) = 2359.23$

$\Sigma(X - M)^2_D = 1848.90$

$S^2_D = \Sigma(X - M)^2_D / df_D = 1848.90 / 9 = 205.43$

$\Sigma(X - M)^2_E = 370.10$

$S^2_E = \Sigma(X - M)^2_E / df_E = 370.10 / 9 = 41.12$

$\Sigma(X - M)^2_{D\&E} = 1120$

$S^2_{D\&E} = \Sigma(X - M)^2_{D\&E} / df_{D\&E} = 1120 / 9 = 124.44$

$S^2_{Within} = (124.44 + 41.12 + 205.43) / 3 = 123.67$

$F = S^2_{Between} / S^2_{Within} = 2359.23 / 123.67 = 19.08$

Step 5: Decide whether to reject the null hypothesis.

Since $F = 19.08$ is more extreme than 3.36, the psychologist will reject the null hypothesis that there is no difference among the three weight loss methods at the .05 level of significance and conclude that the mean number of pounds lost by people using each of the three methods is different. Since $F = 19.08$ is more extreme than 5.49, the psychologist will make the same decision at the .01 level of significance.

Assumptions in the Analysis of Variance

As with the t test, analysis of variance assumes that scores in the populations are normally distributed and that the populations have equal variances. However, analysis of variance results are robust when violations of its assumptions are moderate. A rule-of-thumb is that analysis of variance results are reasonably accurate when group sizes are equal and the largest variance estimate is no more than 4-5 times greater than the smallest. In the weight-loss example, the largest variance was calculated for the Diet group (205.43) and the smallest for the Exercise group (41.12). Applying the rule-of-thumb (205.43 / 41.12 = 4.9958) indicates that while the ratio of the two variances is just within the limit, the psychologist may want to interpret the results cautiously, e.g., mention this ratio in the discussion or verify the result with one of the tests described in Chapter 14.

Planned Contrasts

Analysis of variance is an omnibus test in that the results indicate that the population means are, or are not, significantly different. The test does not indicate which specific population means are significantly different from each other. Considering the weight-loss example, on average the Exercise group lost 36.9 pounds, the Diet group lost 61.7 pounds, and the Diet & Exercise group lost 65.0 pounds. The analysis of variance has indicated that there is a difference among the three means, and the most probable statistically significant difference is between the means of the Exercise and Diet & Exercise groups. The remaining questions are whether the difference between the Diet group and the Exercise group is statistically significant, which seems likely, and whether the difference between the Diet group and the Diet & Exercise group is statistically significant, which seems less likely. **Planned contrasts** are procedures used to compare pairs of population means to detect those that are significantly different. [Planned contrasts are usually determined during the design stage of a study, so they are also called *a priori* comparisons, planned comparisons, and, more generally, linear contrasts.]

Calculation of planned contrasts is a direct extension of analysis of variance calculations in that between-groups and within-groups estimates of population variance are calculated and used to compute an F ratio. The within-groups estimate is the same as the estimate for the overall analysis of variance, the between-groups estimate is calculated using only the two groups being compared, and F is computed as usual.

In the weight-loss example, the within-groups variance is $S^2_{Within} = 123.67$. To compare the difference between the means of the Diet & Exercise and Exercise groups, the next step is to estimate the variance of the distribution of means for these two groups, which involves summing the deviations of the group means from the grand mean. The grand mean for the two means is 50.95 [(65.0+36.9) / 2 = 101.9 / 2 = 50.95]. Since two means are being compared, the number of degrees of freedom is 1 ($df = 2 - 1 = 1$). The variance of the distribution of means is 394.80 $\{S^2_M = \Sigma(M - GM)^2_{Means} / df_{Between} = [(65.0 - 50.95)^2 + (36.9 - 50.95)^2] / 1 = (197.40 + 197.40) / 1 = 394.80\}$. The next step is to compute the estimated variance of the population of individual scores, and $S^2_{Between} = (S^2_M)(n) = (394.80)(10) = 3948.00$. $F = S^2_{Between} / S^2_{Within} = 3948.00 / 123.67 = 31.92$. The cutoff sample score is $F_{1,27} = 4.21$ at the .05 level of significance. Since 31.92 is more extreme than 4.21, the psychologist will reject the null hypothesis that the Exercise group and the Diet & Exercise group means are the same and conclude that the latter group lost significantly more weight than the former.

The Bonferroni Procedure

A problem arises when several planned contrasts are conducted because the actual level of significance increases with each contrast. If the level of significance is set at .05, the probability of a Type I error for the first contrast is 5%. However, if two contrasts are made, the probability of making a Type I error rises to 10%, and the third contrast increases the probability to 15%. One method for dealing with this problem is called the **Bonferroni procedure**. This procedure creates a more stringent significance level for each contrast by dividing the original level by the number of contrasts to be made. Suppose the psychologist in the weight-loss example set the significance level at .05 and planned to compare all possible pairs of groups. With three groups, three paired contrasts are possible. Therefore, the psychologist would compute .05 / 3 = .017, and compare each contrast to this probability. This procedure is simplified by computer analysis because the output will include the exact probability of a Type I error. When tables are used, experimenters may simply use the .01 level of significance to be safe. When only two, or perhaps three, contrasts are planned, no correction may be made.

Post Hoc Comparisons

Although they serve the same purpose as planned contrasts, i.e., determining which pairs of means are significantly different following an analysis of variance, **post hoc comparisons** are not planned in advance. (These comparisons are also called *a posteriori* comparisons for this reason, and they are also called *pairwise comparisons* because all possible pairs of means are compared.) Using the Bonferroni procedure is a possibility, but sometimes so many comparisons are possible that the power for any single comparison is very low. For example, if five groups are used in an experiment, 15 paired comparisons are possible (1-2, 1-3, 1-4, 1-5, 1-6, 2-3, 2-4, 2-5, 2-6, 3-4, 3-5, 3-6, 4-5, 4-6, 5-6), and dividing an alpha of .05 by 15 = .003, making statistical significance quite difficult to obtain. Therefore, statisticians have developed a number of procedures for comparing means following analysis of variance that keep the overall risk of making a Type I error at a level like .05 while maintaining a reasonable level of power. Two of the most common tests are the **Scheffé test** and *Tukey test*. The *Newman-Keuls* and *Duncan* procedures are used frequently, as well.

The Scheffé Test

The advantage of the Scheffé test is that it can be used to make simple comparisons (e.g., between two means) and complex comparisons (e.g., comparing the mean of two groups to the mean of a third group). Its disadvantage is that it is the most conservative of the post hoc tests. The Scheffé test requires calculation of the F for the comparison and dividing F by the between-groups degrees of freedom. In the weight-loss example, the F for the comparison of the Diet & Exercise and Exercise groups calculated previously was 31.92 and $df_{Between} = (N_{Groups} - 1)$ $= (3 - 1) = 2$. Dividing 31.92 by 2 yields $F = 15.96$, which is more extreme than the cutoff sample F of 3.36 at the .05 level of significance. Again, the psychologist will reject the null hypothesis that the Exercise group and the Diet & Exercise group means are the same and conclude that the latter group lost significantly more weight than the former.

Effect Size and Power for the Analysis of Variance

The **proportion of variance accounted for (R^2)** is the measure of effect size for analysis of variance. R^2 is the proportion of the total variation of scores from the grand mean accounted for by variation between the means of groups. For example, how much of the variance in weight loss is accounted for (explained by) the different weight-loss programs? The formula is $R^2 = (S^2_{Between})(df_{Between}) / (S^2_{Between})(df_{Between}) + (S^2_{Within})(df_{Within})$. For the weight-loss example, $R^2 = (2359.23)(2) / (2359.23)(2) + (123.67)(27) = 4718.46 / 4718.46 + 3339.09 = 4718.46 / 8057.55 = 0.59$.

R^2 can also be calculated directly from F and the number of degrees of freedom using the formula $R^2 = (F)(df_{Between}) / (F)(df_{Between}) + df_{Within}$. For the weight-loss example, $R^2 = (19.08)(2) / (19.08)(2) + 27 = 38.16 / 38.16 + 27 = 38.16 / 65.16 = 0.59$.

R^2 is also known as **eta squared (η^2)**, and as the *correlation ratio*. R^2 can have a minimum value of 0 and a maximum value of 1, but values like the .59 obtained following the analysis of variance for the weight-loss data are rare. Therefore, Cohen's conventions for R^2 are .01 for a small effect size, .06 for a medium effect size, and .14 for a large effect size.

Tables are available for determining the power and effect size of studies in which the results are analyzed using analysis of variance. Practice using tables like those provided in the text will be provided later.

Analyses of Variance in Research Articles

The format for reporting analysis of variance results is relatively standard and includes the F ratio, the df, and the significance level. For example, the results of the analysis of variance for the weight-loss example would be $F(2,27) = 19.08$, $p < .05$. Group means, and perhaps standard deviations, may be reported in the text of the article or in tables. Experimenters may report planned contrasts using t tests, but they are special tests that control the overall level of significance. Experimenters often report post hoc comparisons of all pairs of means.

Advanced Topic: The Structural Model in the Analysis of Variance

The **structural model** is an alternative way to view and conduct analyses of variance that is particularly useful when sample sizes are unequal.

93

Principles of the Structural Model

Understanding the structural model requires understanding the deviations that must be calculated to conduct an analysis of variance. For example, each score deviates from the grand mean, and each deviation has two parts:

1. The deviation of the score from the mean of its group, and
2. The deviation of the mean of the group including the score from the grand mean.

For example, think about a participant in Diet group of the weight-loss study who lost 62 pounds. The grand mean of the study was 54.53 pounds, so this participant's deviation from the grand mean, or total deviation, was 7.47 pounds ($62 - 54.53 = 7.47$). The mean of the Diet group was 61.7 pounds, so the deviation of the participant's score from the group mean is 0.3 pounds ($62 - 61.7 = .3$), and the deviation of the group mean from the grand mean is 7.17 pounds ($61.7 - 54.53 = 7.17$). Note that $.3 + 7.17 = 7.47$, which is the amount of the participant's score from the grand mean, i.e., the participant's total deviation.

Summing the Squared Deviations

The next step in using the structural model is to square each deviation described in the previous section and add the squared deviations of both types for all participants to obtain a sum of squared deviations for each type for all participants. Note that the sum of squared deviations of each score from the grand mean is equal to

1. The sum of the squared deviations of each score from its group's mean plus
2. The sum of the squared deviations of each score's group's mean from the grand mean.

Stated as a formula, $\Sigma(X - GM)^2 = \Sigma(X - M)^2 + \Sigma(M - GM)^2$ or $SS_{Total} = SS_{Within} + SS_{Between}$, where
SS_{Total} = the sum of squared deviations of each score from the grand mean,
SS_{Within} = the sum of squared deviations of each score from its group's mean summed across all participants, and
$SS_{Between}$ = the sum of squared deviations of each score's group's mean from the grand mean summed across all participants.

From the Sums of Squared Deviations to the Population Variance Estimates

The population variance estimates required to conduct an analysis of variance can be obtained by dividing each sum of squared deviations by the appropriate number of degrees of freedom.

The between-groups population variance estimate ($S^2_{Between}$ or $MS_{Between}$) is the sum of squared deviations of each score's group mean from the grand mean ($SS_{Between}$) divided by the number of degrees of freedom on which it is based. As usual, $df_{Between}$ = the number of groups minus 1. Stated as a formula, $S^2_{Between} = \Sigma(M - GM)^2 / df_{Between}$ or $MS_{Between} = SS_{Between} / df_{Between}$. The within-groups population variance estimate (S^2_{Within} or MS_{Within}) is the sum of squared deviations of each score from its group mean (SS_{Within}) divided by the total degrees of freedom on which this is based (df_{Within}), which is the sum of the degrees of freedom for all the groups. Stated as a formula, $S^2_{Within} = \Sigma(X - M)^2 / df_{Within}$ or $S^2_{Within} = SS_{Within} / df_{Within}$. Since $SS_{Total} = SS_{Within} + SS_{Between}$, this formula can be used to check the calculation of the within-groups and between-groups variances.

Relation of the Structural Model to the Earlier Method

Both methods yield the same result, but the method presented earlier in the chapter emphasizes groups, while the structural model emphasizes individual scores.

Applying the Structural Model

The computations for applying the structural model to the weight-loss study follow and demonstrate that the two methods yield the same results. The only difference in the steps of hypothesis testing involves the calculations in Step 4. Remember that the grand mean = 54.53 pounds.

Exercise Group

X	X − GM		X − M		M − GM	
	Deviation	Deviation^2	Deviation	Deviation^2	Deviation	Deviation^2
21	-33.53	1124.26	-15.90	252.81	-17.63	310.82
54	-0.53	0.28	17.10	292.41	-17.63	310.82
26	-28.53	813.96	-10.90	118.81	-17.63	310.82
21	-33.53	1124.26	-15.90	252.81	-17.63	310.82
28	-26.53	703.84	-8.90	79.21	-17.63	310.82
57	2.47	6.10	20.10	404.01	-17.63	310.82
52	-2.53	6.40	15.10	228.01	-17.63	310.82
37	-17.53	307.30	0.10	0.01	-17.63	310.82
26	-28.53	813.96	-10.90	118.81	-17.63	310.82
47	-7.53	56.70	10.10	102.01	-17.63	310.82
Σ = 369		Σ = 4957.07		Σ =1848.90		Σ = 3108.17
M = 36.90						

Diet Group

X	X − GM		X − M		M − GM	
	Deviation	Deviation^2	Deviation	Deviation^2	Deviation	Deviation^2
67	12.47	155.50	5.30	28.09	7.17	51.41
62	7.47	55.80	0.30	0.09	7.17	51.41
57	2.47	6.10	-4.70	22.09	7.17	51.41
68	13.47	181.44	6.30	39.69	7.17	51.41
58	3.47	12.04	-3.70	13.69	7.17	51.41
70	15.47	239.32	8.30	68.89	7.17	51.41
58	3.47	12.04	-3.70	13.69	7.17	51.41
59	4.47	19.98	-2.70	7.29	7.17	51.41
68	13.47	181.44	6.30	39.69	7.17	51.41
50	-4.53	20.52	-11.70	136.89	7.17	51.41
Σ = 617		Σ = 884.19		Σ = 370.10		Σ = 514.09
M = 61.7						

Exercise & Diet Group

X	X − GM		X − M		M − GM	
	Deviation	Deviation^2	Deviation	Deviation^2	Deviation	Deviation^2
78	23.47	550.84	13.00	169.00	10.47	109.62
50	-4.53	20.52	-15.00	225.00	10.47	109.62
55	0.47	0.22	-10.00	100.00	10.47	109.62
62	7.47	55.80	-3.00	9.00	10.47	109.62
56	1.47	2.16	-9.00	81.00	10.47	109.62
77	22.47	504.90	12.00	144.00	10.47	109.62
71	16.47	271.26	6.00	36.00	10.47	109.62
53	-1.53	2.34	-12.00	144.00	10.47	109.62
79	24.47	598.78	14.00	196.00	10.47	109.62
69	14.47	209.38	4.00	16.00	10.47	109.62
Σ = 650		Σ = 2216.21		Σ = 1120.00		Σ = 1096.21
M = 65.0						

Sums of squared deviations:

$\Sigma (X - GM)^2$ or SS_{Total} = 4957.07 + 884.19 + 2216.21 = 8057.47

$\Sigma (X - M)^2$ or SS_{Within} = 1848.90 + 370.10 + 1120.00 = 3339.00

$\Sigma (M - GM)^2$ or $SS_{Between}$ = 3108.17 + 514.09 + 1096.21 = 4718.47

Check ($SS_{Total} = SS_{Within} + SS_{Between}$); SS_{Total} = 8057.47 and 3339.00 + 4718.47 = 8057.47

Degrees of freedom:

$df_{Total} = N - 1 = 30 - 1 = 29$

$df_{Within} = df_1 = df_2 = df_3 = (10 - 1) + (10 - 1) + (10 - 1) = 9 + 9 + 9 = 27$

$df_{Between} = N_{Groups} - 1 = 3 - 1 = 2$

Check $(df_{Total} = df_{Within} + df_{Between})$ $29 = 27 + 2$

Population variance estimates:

S^2_{Within} or $MS_{Within} = SS_{Within} / df_{Within} = 3339.00 / 27 = 123.67$

$S^2_{Between}$ or $MS_{Between} = SS_{Between} / df_{Between} = 4718.47 / 2 = 2359.35$ (slight difference due to rounding)

$F = S^2_{Between} / S^2_{Within}$ or $MS_{Between} / MS_{Within} = 2359.35 / 123.67 = 19.08$

Analysis of Variance Tables

An **analysis of variance table** automatically produced by computer packages like SPSS presents analysis of variance results based on the structural model approach. The five columns that are standard report the

1. Source (type of variance estimate / deviation score),
2. SS (sum of squared deviations),
3. df (degrees of freedom),
4. MS (mean squares – SS divided by the df), and
5. F ratio.

The three standard rows refer to one of the variance estimates and present the estimates in the following order: between groups, within groups, and the total.

Most analysis of variance tables look like the one that follows.

Source	SS	df	MS	F
Between	$SS_{Between}$	$df_{Between}$	$MS_{Between}$	F_{Ratio}
Within	SS_{Within}	df_{Within}	MS_{Within}	
Total	SS_{Total}	df_{Total}		

Chapter Self-Tests

Understanding Key Concepts in Chapter 9

The test items that follow are based on the following scenario. The psychologists studying the effects of different types of therapy on the number of activities of daily living performed by depressed people have concluded that individual therapy is more effective than group therapy in increasing the number of activities performed by their clients. Now the psychologists are interested in learning how the number of hours of individual therapy affects the number of activities. Consequently, the psychologists have formed three groups comprised of six clients each. Clients in Group 1 will receive one hour of therapy every two weeks, clients in Group 2 will receive one hour of therapy each week, and Group 3 will receive two hours of therapy each week.

Complete each statement using the word bank that follows.

Word Bank: analysis of variance / analysis of variance table / Bonferroni procedure / $df_{Between}$ / df_{Within} / η^2 / F disribution / F ratio / F table / grand / $MS_{Between}$ / MS_{Within} / planned contrasts / post hoc comparisons / R^2 / $S^2_{Between}$ / S^2_{Within} / $SS_{Between}$ / SS_{Total} / SS_{Within} / Scheffé / structural model

If the psychologists want to compare the mean numbers of activities performed by the clients in the three groups, they will use an ANOVA, which stands for **(1)** _____. In order to calculate this statistic, the psychologists will have to calculate the mean of a distribution of means that is called the **(2)** _____ mean. Using this mean of a distribution of means, the psychologists will estimate the population variance between groups, which is called **(3)** _____. Next, they will estimate the population variance within each group and the average of these variances, which is called (4) _____. The test statistic, called an (5) _____, is equal to (6) _____ divided by (7) _____. In order to determine the statistical significance of the statistic, the psychologists will use the (8) _____ as the basis for comparison and locate the cutoff sample score in an (9) _____. The psychologists would locate the cutoff sample using 2 and 15 degrees of freedom, which are (10) _____ and (11) _____, respectively.

If the psychologists find a statistically significant difference among the three group means, they will want to identify pairs of means that are statistically different. If they indicate the pairs of means that they will compare before they conduct the study, they are using (12) _____. Since multiple comparisons increase the probability of Type I errors, the psychologists may divide their chosen level of significance by the number of comparisons they plan to make. This method of adjustment is called the (13) _____. Another approach the psychologists might take is to compare all the different pairs of means following the overall analysis. Such comparisons are called (14) _____ The most general of these tests is the (15) _____. Effect size in analysis is measured as the proportion of variance accounted for, symbolized (16) _____. This measure is also called eta squared, symbolized (17) _____.

If one or more clients do not complete the study, the psychologists will have unequal numbers of participants in each group. In this case, they will analyze their data using the (18) _____. In this type of analysis, $S^2_{Between}$ is replaced by (19) _____ and S^2_{Within} by (20) _____, both of which sum to (21) _____. The abbreviations used in this type of analysis are more like those that will be found in a computer-generated (22) _____.

Multiple-Choice Items

1. If the psychologists want to compare the mean number of activities performed by clients in the three groups, they will use the
    A. t test for independent means.
    B. t test for dependent means.
    C. analysis of variance.
    D. Z test.

2. If the null hypothesis is true, the psychologists can expect the
    A. the within-groups variances to be large.
    B. the between-group variance to be large.
    C. the ratio of the between- and within-groups variances to be approximately 10.
    D. the within-groups variances to be small.

3. Since the sample sizes are equal, the psychologists will be able to convert the estimated variance of the distribution of means to an estimate of the variance of the population of individual scores by
    A. dividing the estimated variance of the distribution of means by the number of clients in each sample.
    B. dividing the estimated variance of the distribution of means by the degrees of freedom in each sample.
    C. multiplying the estimated variance of the distribution of means by the number of clients in each sample.
    D. multiplying the estimated variance of the distribution of means by the number of degrees of freedom in each sample.

4. If the F ratio yielded by the variance in analysis of variance is statistically significant,
    A. S^2_{Within} is larger than S^2_{Total}.
    B. $S^2_{Between}$ is larger than S^2_{Total}.
    C. S^2_{Within} is larger than $S^2_{Between}$.
    D. $S^2_{Between}$ is larger than S^2_{Within}.

5. If an *F* ratio is not statistically significant, its value will be close to
   A. -1
   B. 0
   C. 1
   D. $\sqrt{1}$

6. In order to calculate this statistic, the psychologists will have to calculate the mean of a distribution of means that is called the
   A. harmonic mean.
   B. grand mean.
   C. ordinary mean.
   D. pooled mean.

7. In order to determine the statistical significance of the statistic, the number of degrees of freedom the psychologists would use to locate the critical value of the statistic in a table would be
   A. 2, 15.
   B. 3, 15.
   C. 2, 18.
   D. 3, 18.

Items 8–9 are related.

Remember that clients in Group 1 will receive one hour of therapy every two weeks, clients in Group 2 will receive one hour of therapy each week, and Group 3 will receive two hours of therapy each week.

8. If the psychologists decide before the study is conducted to compare the mean of Group 3 with the mean of Group 1 and the mean of Group 2, respectively, they will be making
   A. Bonferroni comparisons.
   B. complex contrasts.
   C. planned contrasts.
   D. post hoc comparisons.

9. If the psychologists are concerned about the effect of the number of comparisons on the overall level of significance, they can use
   A. Bonferroni comparisons.
   B. complex contrasts.
   C. planned contrasts.
   D. post hoc comparisons.

Items 10–11 are related.

Since the psychologists believe that any statistically significant differences may have practical implications, they plan to compare all possible pairs of means following analysis of variance.

10. The most conservative test the psychologists could use for this purpose is the
    A. Tukey test.
    B. Neuman-Keuls test.
    C. Duncan test.
    D. Scheffé test.

11. Collectively, such tests are known as
    A. Bonferroni comparisons.
    B. complex contrasts.
    C. planned contrasts.
    D. post hoc comparisons.

Items 12–15 are related.

12. Effect size in analysis of variance is calculated as the
    A. average difference between all possible pairs of means.
    B. proportion of variance accounted for.
    C. between-groups variance estimate divided by the within-groups standard deviation.
    D. estimated power of the study divided by the total number of degrees of freedom.

13. The effect size is also designated by
    A. R^2.
    B. F^2.
    C. N^2.
    D. Σ^2.

14. Yet another name for the effect size is
    A. alpha squared.
    B. beta squared.
    C. delta squared.
    D. eta squared.

15. The structural model is particularly useful when
    A. population variances cannot be estimated.
    B. sample sizes are unequal.
    C. F will approach 0.
    D. within-groups variances are very unequal.

16. In the structural model, S^2_{Within} is likely to be replaced by
    A. MS_{Within}.
    B. SS_{Within}.
    C. df_{Within}.
    D. R^2_{Within}.

17. If the term is used in an analysis of variance table, "error" is a substitute for the
    A. total term.
    B. between-groups term.
    C. within-groups term.
    D. comparison term.

Problems

1. Remember that clients in Group 1 will receive one hour of therapy every two weeks, clients in Group 2 will receive one hour of therapy each week, and Group 3 will receive two hours of therapy each week. Use the five steps of hypothesis testing to determine whether the observed differences in the number of activities in the following table performed by the three groups are statistically significant at the .05 level of significance. Calculate the effect size and perform planned contrasts of all possible pairs of groups without applying the Bonferroni procedure. Then calculate the Scheffé test for the pair of groups with the largest difference between means to see if the results lead to the same conclusion as the planned contrast. Discuss these comparisons as part of Step 5 using the observed differences between the three means to indicate which category of therapy the psychologists should recommend for depressed people based on the test of the null hypothesis.

Client	Group 1	Group 2	Group 3
1	16	21	24
2	15	20	21
3	18	17	25
4	21	23	20
5	19	19	22

2. A psychologist interested in the relationship between student perception of the probability of success in a statistics course and student motivation has administered an inventory designed to assess motivation to 18 students. The students have been divided into groups as follows: students in Group 1 believe they are highly likely to succeed in the course, students in Group 2 believe they have an intermediate probability of success, and students in Group 3 do not believe they have much chance of success. Use the five steps of hypothesis testing to determine whether the observed differences in level of motivation in the following table are statistically significant at the .05 level of significance. Calculate the effect size and perform planned contrasts of all possible pairs of groups without applying the Bonferroni procedure. Then calculate the Scheffé test for the pair of groups with the largest difference between means to see if the results lead to the same conclusion as the planned contrast. Explain your results to someone who is familiar with the *t* test for independent means, but not with analysis of variance and methods for determining which pairs of means are statistically different.

Student	Group 1 (High)	Group 2 (Intermediate)	Group 3 (Low)
1	9.0	3.5	4.5
2	8.5	5.5	5.5
3	6.5	6.5	6.5
4	7.0	3.5	8.0
5	8.0	4.5	5.5
6	5.5	7.0	6.0

3. Due to the increasing number of trials involving testimony by psychologists, a professional organization of psychologists asked judges, attorneys, jurors, and law enforcement officials to use a 10-point scale to rate the effectiveness of such testimony in trial outcomes. The results are presented in the table that follows. Use the five steps of hypothesis testing to determine whether the observed differences in effectiveness ratings are statistically significant at the .01 level of significance. Calculate the effect size and perform planned contrasts of all possible pairs of groups at the .05 level of significance, applying the Bonferroni procedure for all comparisons except the comparison of judges and jurors. Explain your results to someone who understands analysis of variance, but who is unfamiliar with paired comparisons and the Bonferroni procedure.

Category	Judges	Attorneys	Jurors	Law Enforcement
	6	7	8	1
	7	4	9	5
	5	6	7	1
	8	5	6	5
	7	7	8	4
	9	6	9	2

4. Reanalyze the data presented in Problem 1 using the structural model and compare the two *F* ratios.

5. What level of significance would applying the Bonferroni procedure yield in the following situations?

Situation	(a)	(b)	(c)	(d)	(e)
Overall Significance Level	.05	.05	.01	.01	.01
# of Planned Comparisons	3	6	2	4	6

6. Which of the following post hoc comparisons made using the Scheffé test would be statistically significant if the experimenter obtained an $F = 9.66$?

Comparison	# of Groups	Participants per Group	Significance Level
(a)	3	9	.05
(b)	4	8	.05
(c)	4	11	.01
(d)	5	10	.01
(e)	6	11	.05

7. What would be the power of the following planned studies if the experimenters plan to use analysis of variance and the .05 level of significance?

Predicted Effect Size	# of Groups	# of Participants in Each Group
Small	5	30
Medium	4	20
Medium	5	30
Large	3	30
Large	4	20

8. How many participants would need to be included in each group to have 80% power in each of the following planned studies if the experimenters plan to use analysis of variance and the .05 level of significance?

Predicted Effect Size	# of Groups
Small	5
Medium	4
Medium	5
Large	4
Large	5

Additional Practice: Complete any Practice Problems in Set I that your instructor has not assigned and compare your responses to those provided by the authors. Pay particular attention to the problems that require you to explain your results to someone who has never taken a course in statistics.

SPSS Applications

Application 1: Analysis of Variance
Open SPSS.
Analyze the data for Problem 1. Remember that SPSS assumes that all the scores in a row are from the same participant. In this study, there are 15 participants divided into three groups of five. Therefore, each of the 15 participants will be described by two variables, type of therapy and the number of activities of daily living performed. Use "1" to represent the group receiving individual therapy for one hour every two weeks, "2" to represent the group receiving one hour of individual therapy each week, and "3" to represent the group receiving two hours of individual therapy each week. In this case, the first participant will be described by entering "1" in the top cell of the first column in the Data View window and "16" in the top cell of the second column to indicate that the participant underwent one hour of therapy every two weeks and performed 16 activities of daily living. The second participant will be described by "1" and "15," and the third by "1" and "18." When the two variables have been entered for the five participants in this group, repeat the process for participants who underwent one hour of individual therapy each week using "2" to describe their therapy group. When the two variables for the five participants this group have been entered, repeat the process for Group 3, entering "3" in the first column. In the Variable View window, change the first variable name to "therapy" and the second to "activities" and set the decimals for both to zero if you wish. The Data View window should look like Figure 1.

therapy	activities
1	16
1	15
1	18
1	21
1	19
2	21
2	20
2	17
2	23
2	19
3	24
3	21
3	25
3	20
3	22

Figure 1

✐ Analyze

✐ Compare means

✐ One-Way ANOVA

✐ "activities and ✐ the arrow to move the variable to the Dependent List window, which instructs SPSS to conduct the analysis of variance on the number of activities performed

✐ "therapy" and ✐ the arrow to move the variable to the Factor window

The "One-Way ANOVA" window should look like Figure 2

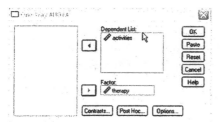

Figure 2

✐ "Options" and click the box labeled "Descriptive" to obtain descriptive statistics

The "Options" window should look like Figure 3

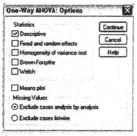

Figure 3

✐ Continue

Planned comparisons and post hoc comparisons can be obtained using the "Contrasts" and "Post Hoc" buttons in the "One-Way ANOVA" window. ✐ "Post Hoc" and click "Scheffe"

The "One-Way ANOVA Post Hoc Multiple Comparisons" window should look like Figure 4

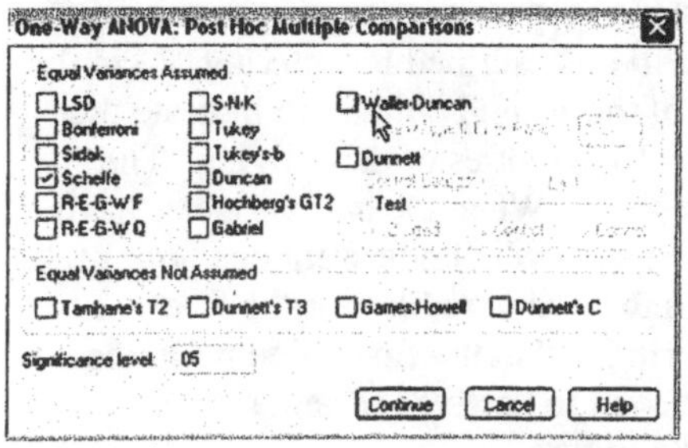

Figure 4

✐ Continue

🖰 OK

The SPSS output should look like Figure 5 and Figure 6

Descriptives

activities

	N	Mean	Std Deviation	Std Error	95% Confidence Interval for Mean		Minimum	Maximum
					Lower Bound	Upper Bound		
1	5	17.80	2.387	1.068	14.84	20.76	15	21
2	5	20.00	2.236	1.000	17.22	22.78	17	23
3	5	22.40	2.074	.927	19.83	24.97	20	25
Total	15	20.07	2.840	.733	18.49	21.64	15	25

Figure 5

ANOVA

activities

	Sum of Squares	df	Mean Square	F	Sig.
Between Groups	52.933	2	26.467	5.293	.022
Within Groups	60.000	12	5.000		
Total	112.933	14			

Figure 6

Comparing the descriptive statistics in Figure 5 with the means calculated in order to solve Problem 1 shows that the means are the same, and using the within-groups variances you calculated, you can verify the standard deviations. The first column in the ANOVA table in Figure 5 lists the types of population variance estimates needed for the calculation of F. If you studied the Advanced Topic section in this chapter, the second column of the ANOVA table includes the between-groups and within-groups sums of squares. Notice that the former value is slightly different from the value calculated "by hand." The third column contains the degrees of freedom for this analysis. The "Mean Square" column contains the population variance estimates $S^2_{Between}$ and S^2_{Within}, used to calculate the F ratio presented in the next column. Again, the between-groups mean square is slightly different, but the F ratio is the same. Note that the mean squares are calculated by dividing a sum of squares by its degrees of freedom. As you found when you solved problem 1, the F ratio is statistically significant.

The SPSS results for the Scheffé test are presented in Figure 7. The * indicates pairs of means that are statistically different. As you found earlier, the group of clients receiving two hours of therapy each week performed significantly more activities than the group that received one hour of therapy every two weeks, and the group that received one hour of therapy each week did not differ significantly from either group.

Multiple Comparisons

Dependent Variable: activities

Scheffe

(I) therapy	(J) therapy	Mean Difference (I-J)	Std. Error	Sig.	95% Confidence Interval	
					Lower Bound	Upper Bound
1	2	-2.200	1.414	.332	-6.14	1.74
	3	-4.600*	1.414	.023	-8.54	-.66
2	1	2.200	1.414	.332	-1.74	6.14
	3	-2.400	1.414	.275	-6.34	1.54
3	1	4.600*	1.414	.023	.66	8.54
	2	2.400	1.414	.275	-1.54	6.34

* The mean difference is significant at the .05 level.

Figure 7

Application 2: Analysis of Variance with Unequal Sample Sizes

Again, if you studied the Advanced Topic section in this chapter, you will remember that the structural model is useful when the groups contain unequal number of participants. The ANOVA table that follows was created by conducting an analysis of variance on the data for Problem 2 after eliminating the data for students 2 and 3 in Group1 and student 5 in Group 3. See if you obtain the results shown in Figure 7 and Figure 8.

Descriptives

motivation

	N	Mean	Std. Deviation	Std. Error	95% Confidence Interval for Mean		Minimum	Maximum
					Lower Bound	Upper Bound		
1	4	7.375	1.4930	.7465	4.999	9.751	5.5	9.0
2	6	5.083	1.4972	.6112	3.512	6.655	3.5	7.0
3	5	6.100	1.2942	.5788	4.493	7.707	4.5	8.0
Total	15	6.033	1.6308	.4211	5.130	6.936	3.5	9.0

Figure 7

ANOVA

motivation

	Sum of Squares	df	Mean Square	F	Sig.
Between Groups	12.638	2	6.319	3.083	.083
Within Groups	24.596	12	2.050		
Total	37.233	14			

Figure 8

If you would like additional practice, use SPSS to analyze the data for Problem 2 and Problem 3 and compare the results to your calculations and those in the Answer Key.

Chapter 10
Factorial Analysis of Variance

Learning Objectives
After studying this chapter, you should:
- Be able to describe the logic and advantages of factorial designs.
- Be able to interpret interaction effects using tables of means and graphs.
- Be able to conduct and interpret two-way analysis of variance.
- Know the assumptions underlying factorial analysis of variance.
- Be able to describe the extensions of factorial analysis of variance.
- Be able to interpret the results of factorial analyses of variance as reported in research articles.
- Advanced Topic: Know how to calculate a two-way analysis of variance.
- Advanced Topic: Know how to calculate the effect size following a factorial analysis of variance using either of two methods.
- Advanced Topic: Be able to use tables to estimate power for factorial analyses of variance.
- Advanced Topic: Be able to use tables to estimate sample sizes for factorial analyses of variance.

Factorial analysis of variance is an extension of the analysis of variance procedures learned previously that permits flexible, efficient analyses by examining of the effects of every possible combination of two or more variables on an outcome variable.

Basic Logic of Factorial Designs and Interaction Effects
As an example, suppose that an industrial / organizational psychologist has been hired to evaluate the effectiveness of an orientation program for new employees of a large corporation with supervisory ratings after six weeks on the job being the measure of effectiveness. A secondary question is whether the program will be effective for employees who have held at least one full-time job, as opposed to employees for whom the current job is their first full-time job. Therefore, the psychologist decides to randomly assign new employees to one of four groups as shown in the table that follows:
1. Employees who attend the orientation program who have held a full-time job
2. Employees who attend the orientation program who have never held a full-time job
3. Employees who do not attend the orientation program who have held a full-time job
4. Employees who do not attend the orientation program who have held a full-time job

		Previous Full-time Job	
		Yes	No
Attend Orientation	Yes	Group 1	Group 2
	No	Group 3	Group 4

This **factorial research design** will enable the psychologist to examine the effects of two or more variables simultaneously by creating groups that reflect every possible combination of levels of the variables. One advantage of factorial designs is the efficiency that results from being able to examine the two variables at one time using the same participant pool, i.e., without having to double the number of participants.

A second advantage is that factorial designs permit examination of the effects of combining two or more variables. For example, the psychologist will learn that employees in Groups 1 and 3 had the highest ratings, employees in Group 4 had the lowest ratings, and employees in Group 2 had intermediate ratings. In this case, the combination attending the orientation session and work experience appears to have had a special effect called an **interaction effect**, which occurs when the influence of one of the variables used to classify participants on the measured variable differs across the levels of the other classification variable.

The analysis of variance procedure learned in the previous chapter is called **one-way analysis of variance** because the effect of only one variable, e.g., method of weight reduction, is used to explain differences in weight loss. Since the design described in the preceding paragraph involves two potential explanatory variables, i.e., attending the orientation program and previous work experience, it is a **two-way factorial research design**, and the results will be analyzed with a **two-way analysis of variance**. Had a third possible explanatory variable like gender (a very common factorial variable) or motivation categorized as high or low been added, the design would have been a *three-way factorial design*, and the results would have been analyzed using *three-way analysis of variance*.

In a two-way analysis of variance, each possible explanatory variable, or **grouping**, **variable** is a possible **main effect**. In the example, the possible main effects are participation in the orientation program and prior full-time employment. Using these two variables, one interaction effect is possible. Thus, in any two-way design, experimenters can test for two possible main effects and one possible interaction effect.

Each grouping combination in a factorial design is called a **cell**, and each cell has a **cell mean**. The table that follows shows the hypothetical cell means for the orientation study.

		Previous Full-time Job		Marginal means
		Yes	No	
Attend Orientation	Yes	$M = 4.00$	$M = 3.33$	3.67
	No	$M = 4.00$	$M = 1.83$	2.92
Marginal means		4.00	2.58	

Marginal means are the means for each of the grouping variables. The four marginal means for the orientation example are shown in the preceding table.

Recognizing and Interpreting Interaction Effects

Detecting interaction effects may be the primary purpose of a study. For example, the corporation may be interested in determining the usefulness of the orientation program for new employees who have prior full-time work experience. Statistically significant interaction effects can be described verbally, numerically, or graphically.

- Verbal descriptions of interaction effects can be made in terms of either variable, i.e., the effect of participating in the orientation program depends on employment history, or the effect of employment history depends on participating in the orientation program.
- Numerical descriptions of interaction effects are determined by examining the pattern of differences in cell means. An interaction effect is present if the pattern of differences in one row is not the same as the difference in the other row. Equivalently, an interaction arises when the pattern of differences in one column is not the same as the difference in the other column. As will be shown later, the interaction effect between attending the orientation program and having had a full-time job is statistically significant. Employees without previous full-time work experience who attended the orientation program received higher supervisory ratings than those who did not attend, while the supervisory ratings for employees who had previous full-time work experience were the same for employees who did and did not attend the orientation program. Such dissimilar patterns of cell means across rows or columns suggest the possibility of statistically significant interaction effects.
- Bar graphs are replacing line graphs as the preferred method for depicting statistically significant interaction effects. An interaction effect is indicated when the pattern of the bars in one section of the graph differs from the pattern in the other section. Main effects also may be detected from graphs in which the patterns of bars are dissimilar. For example, the statistically significant difference in supervisory ratings for employees with no previous full-time work experience can be seen in the figure that follows.

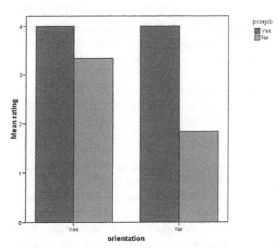

Remember that any combination of main and interaction effects can be statistically significant. As will be shown later, both the main effects for participation in the orientation program and for having prior full-time work experience are statistically significant, as is the interaction between these two variables. However, both main effects could have been statistically significant and the interaction effect nonsignificant, or only one of the main effects and the interaction effect could have been significant.

Basic Logic of the Two-Way Analysis of Variance

Remember that two-way analysis of variance is used to test hypotheses about main and interaction effects in studies conducted according to a two-way factorial research design. Every two-way analysis of variance yields three F ratios, one for each main effect, i.e., each row effect and each column effect, and one for the interaction effect. As before, each F ratio is obtained by dividing a between-groups variance estimate by a within-groups variance estimate. The between-groups population variance estimates are based on the groupings compared for the two main effects and the interaction effect. The within-groups variance estimate is the average of the population variance estimates calculated from each cell, and is the same for all three F ratios.

The main effect for the columns grouping variable is based on the variation among the column marginal means, and the main effect for the rows grouping variable is based on the variation among the row marginal means. In the example, the between-groups variance for the rows grouping variable is based on the variation between the mean supervisory ratings for employees who did and did not attend the orientation program. Likewise, the between-groups variance for the columns grouping variable is based on the variation between the mean supervisory ratings for employees who had prior full-timework experience and employees who did not have prior experience. Both between-groups variance estimates are divided by the within-groups variance estimate.

Interaction effects are like the cell combinations remaining after the main effects have been examined. More specifically, the between-groups variance estimate for interaction effect is based on the variation among combinations of cells other than those in the same columns or rows. In a 2 X 2 design, these combinations include the combination of the two cells on one diagonal of a 2 X 2 table and the combination of the two cells on the other diagonal. In the orientation example, the left diagonal includes: a) employees who attended the orientation program and who had had a full-time job [Group 1] and b) employees who did not attend the orientation program and who had not had a full-time job [Group 4]. The right diagonal includes: a) employees who attended the orientation program and who had not had a full-time job [Group 2] and b) employees who did not attend the orientation program but who had had a full-time job [Group 3]. In designs with three or more levels on either grouping variable (e.g., 2 X 3 or 2 X 4 designs), more than one combination of cells must be considered, so that calculating the between-groups variance estimate for the interaction effect is more complicated.

Assumptions in the Factorial Analysis of Variance

The factorial analysis of variance assumes that the populations reflected in each cell are normally distributed and have equal variances.

107

Extensions and Special Cases of the Analysis of Variance

Three-way and higher factorial designs are straightforward extensions of two-way analysis of variance except that additional main effects and interaction effects are calculated. In the orientation example, the psychologists might add educational level, e.g., completed high school vs. more education, as a third variable in the design.

In repeated-measures designs, participants are measured more than once, and the results are analyzed using **repeated-measures analysis of variance.** For example, supervisory ratings might be obtained after one month, three months, six months, and one year.

Dichotomizing Numeric Variables

Sometimes experimenters administer a test or inventory and then create groups to be included in a factorial design by **dichotomizing** participants (i.e., dividing them into two groups) based on their scores on the test or inventory. In the example, the psychologist might have administered a measure of achievement motivation to the employees and then categorized them as having high or low motivation. Such dichotomization is often based on being above or below the median, which may be called a *median split*. The advantage of this procedure is that the resulting variable can be used in a factorial analysis of variance. The disadvantage is that information is lost when a range of scores is reduced to two scores. Experimenters should have a sound theoretical basis for using this procedure and be sure that the split produces two groups that differ on the characteristic being measured. Procedures like regression avoid the necessity for dichotomizing and may be more appropriate for analyzing such data.

Factorial Analysis of Variance Results as Described in Research Articles

Descriptions of the results of a factorial analysis of variance usually include a description in the text and a table. The F ratios and information accompanying them for each main effect and the interaction effect are presented in the text, while the cell means and sometimes the marginal means are presented in a table. Statistically significant interaction effects may be depicted in graphs.

The results of the orientation example might be described as follows.
A 2 X 2 analysis of variance on supervisory ratings showed main effects both for participating in the orientation program, $F(1,20) = 5.548$, $p = .029$ and for having had a prior full-time job, $F(1,20) = 19.795$, $p = .000$. In addition, the analysis revealed a statistically significant interaction effect between the two grouping variables, $F(1,20) = 5.548$, $p = .029$. The cell means and standard deviations are shown in the table that follows. Inspection of the means reveals that employees who had held a full-time job previously received very similar supervisory ratings, regardless of whether they attended the orientation program. However, in the case of employees who had not held a full-time job, the mean supervisory rating for those who attended the orientation program was higher than that of employees who did not attend.

		Previous Full-time Job		Marginal means
		Yes	No	
Attend Orientation	Yes	$M = 4.00$ $SD = 0.63$	$M = 3.33$ $SD = 1.03$	3.67
	No	$M = 4.00$ $SD = 0.63$	$M = 1.83$ $SD = 0.75$	2.92
Marginal means		4.00	2.58	

Advanced Topic: Figuring a Two-Way Analysis of Variance

The Structural Model for the Two-Way Analysis of Variance

When data obtained from a factorial research design are analyzed, each score's deviation from the grand mean can be divided into four components:

1. The score's deviation from the mean of its cell, which is used for computing the within-groups variance estimate.
2. The deviation of the score's row's mean from the grand mean, which is used for computing the between-groups population variance estimate for the grouping variable that divides the rows.
3. The deviation of the score's column's mean from the grand mean, which is used for computing between-groups population variance estimate for the grouping variable that divides the columns.

4. The remainder after subtracting the three deviations above from the total of the overall deviations from the grand mean, which is used for computing the between-groups population variance estimate for the interaction effect.

A two-way analysis of variance can be calculated using the six steps that follow:
1. Compute each cell mean, row mean, column mean, and the grand mean.
2. Compute the deviation scores for each mean in Step 1.
3. Square each deviation score in Step 2.
4. Add the squared deviation scores in Step 3.
5. Obtain the variance estimates by dividing each sum of squared deviations in Step 4 by the appropriate number of degrees of freedom.
6. Divide the between-groups variance estimates by the within-groups variance estimate.

The formulas for the sums of squares computed to conduct a two-analysis of variance are as follows. Remember that in formulas for SS_{Rows}, $SS_{Columns}$, $SS_{Interaction}$, and SS_{Within}, Σ indicates summing over all scores – not just over all rows, columns, or cells.

- The sum of squared deviations for rows = $SS_{Rows} = \Sigma(M_{Row} - GM)^2$
- The sum of squared deviations for columns = $SS_{Columns} = \Sigma(M_{Column} - GM)^2$
- The sum of squared deviations for the interaction = $SS_{Interaction} = \Sigma[(X - GM) - (X - M) - (M_{Row} - GM) - (M_{Column} - GM)]^2$
- The sum of squares within groups (within cells) = $SS_{Within} = \Sigma(X - M)^2$
- The total sum of squares = $SS_{Total} = \Sigma(X - GM)^2$

As before, $SS_{Total} = SS_{Rows} + SS_{Columns} + SS_{Interaction} + SS_{Within}$.

As usual, population variance estimates are obtained by dividing the sums of squares by their associated degrees of freedom so that:

- S^2_{Rows} or $MS_{Rows} = SS_{Rows} / df_{Rows}$
- $S^2_{Columns}$ or $MS_{Columns} = SS_{Columns} / df_{Columns}$
- $S^2_{Interaction}$ or $MS_{Interaction} = SS_{Interaction} / df_{Interaction}$
- S^2_{Within} or $MS_{Within} = SS_{Within} / df_{Within}$

The F ratios are computed by dividing the population variance estimate for each effect by the within-groups population variance estimate so that:

- $F_{Rows} = S^2_{Rows} / S^2_{Within}$ or MS_{Rows} / MS_{Within}
- $F_{Columns} = S^2_{Columns} / S^2_{Within}$ or $MS_{Columns} / MS_{Within}$
- $F_{Interaction} = S^2_{Interaction} / S^2_{Within}$ or $MS_{Interaction} / MS_{Within}$

The number of degrees of freedom for each main effect is one less than the number of levels of each variable. Thus, the number of degrees of freedom for the interaction effect is the number of cells minus the number of degrees of freedom for both main effects minus 1 so that:

$$df_{Interaction} = N_{Cells} - df_{Rows} - df_{Columns} - 1$$

The number of degrees of freedom for the within-groups estimate of the population variance estimate is the sum of the degrees of freedom for all groups in a study, or all the cells in a factorial design, so that:

$$df_{Within} = df_1 + df_2 + \dots df_{Last}$$

The total number of degrees of freedom can be computed in two ways:

$$df_{Total} = N - 1 \text{ or } df_{Total} = df_{Rows} + df_{Columns} + df_{Interaction} + df_{Within}$$

Two-way analysis of variance tables include the following information:

Source	SS	df	MS	F
Between:				
Columns	$SS_{Columns}$	$df_{Columns}$	$MS_{Columns}$	$F_{Columns}$
Rows	SS_{Rows}	df_{Rows}	MS_{Rows}	F_{Rows}
Interaction	$SS_{Interaction}$	$df_{Interaction}$	$MS_{Interaction}$	$F_{Interaction}$
Within	SS_{Within}	df_{Within}	MS_{Within}	
Total	SS_{Total}	df_{Total}		

Hypothesis Testing Using Factorial Analysis of Variance

Application of the steps of hypothesis testing to the orientation example follows. As the steps are presented, referring to the formulas in the preceding section will help ensure understanding of all the calculations involved in conducting a factorial analysis of variance. The data are presented in the table that follows.

Employee	Orientation	Work Experience	Rating
1	Yes	Yes	4
2	Yes	Yes	5
3	Yes	Yes	4
4	Yes	Yes	3
5	Yes	Yes	4
6	Yes	Yes	4
7	Yes	No	5
8	Yes	No	4
9	Yes	No	3
10	Yes	No	2
11	Yes	No	3
12	Yes	No	3
13	No	Yes	4
14	No	Yes	3
15	No	Yes	4
16	No	Yes	4
17	No	Yes	5
18	No	Yes	4
19	No	No	1
20	No	No	2
21	No	No	1
22	No	No	3
23	No	No	2
24	No	No	2

Steps of Hypothesis Testing

Step 1: Restate the question as a research hypothesis and a null hypothesis about the populations.

Population 1,1: Employees who attend the orientation program and who have had a full-time job
Population 1,2: Employees who attend the orientation program and who have not had a full-time job
Population 2,1: Employees who do not attend the orientation program and who have had a full-time job
Population 2,2: Employees who do not attend the orientation program and who have not had a full-time job

Research hypothesis 1: The supervisory ratings received by the combined populations of employees who attend the orientation program will be different from the supervisory ratings received by the combined populations of employees who do not attend the orientation program.

Null hypothesis 1: The supervisory ratings received by the combined populations of employees who attend the orientation program will be the same as the supervisory ratings received by the combined populations of employees who do not attend the orientation program.

Research hypothesis 2: The supervisory ratings received by the combined populations of employees who have had a full-time job will be different from the supervisory ratings received by the combined populations of employees who have not had a full-time job.
Null hypothesis 2: The supervisory ratings received by the combined populations of employees who have had a full-time job will be the same as the supervisory ratings received by the combined populations of employees who have not had a full-time job.

Research hypothesis 3: The difference between the mean supervisory ratings of the two populations of employees who attend the orientation program will be different from the difference between the mean supervisory ratings of the two populations who do not attend the orientation program.
Null hypothesis 3: The difference between the mean supervisory ratings of the two populations of employees who attend the orientation program will be the same as the difference between the mean supervisory ratings of the two populations who do not attend the orientation program.

Step 2: Determine the characteristics of the comparison distribution.
The three comparison distributions will be F distributions. Since $df_{\text{Within}} = df_1 + df_2 + \ldots df_{\text{Last}}$, $df_{\text{Within}} = (6-1) + (6--1) + (6-1) + (6-1) = 5 + 5 + 5 + 5 = 20$. Since there are two rows, the numerator for the comparison distribution for the orientation main effect $= df_{\text{Rows}} = Nf_{\text{Rows}} - 1 = 1$. Likewise, since there are two columns, the numerator for the comparison distribution for the previous full-time employment main effect $= df_{\text{Columns}} = N_{\text{Columnss}} - 1 = 1$. Finally, since $df_{\text{Interaction}} = N_{\text{Cells}} - df_{\text{Rows}} - df_{\text{Columns}} - 1$, $df_{\text{Interaction}} = 4 - 1 - 1 - 1 = 1$.

As a check, the sum of the between-groups, within groups, and interaction degrees of freedom is $1 + 1 + 1 + 20 = 23$, which is equal to the total number of degrees of freedom computed as the number of participants minus 1, or $24 - 1 = 23$.

Step 3: Determine the cutoff sample score on the comparison distribution at which the null hypothesis should be rejected.
Using numerator degrees of freedom $= 1$ and denominator degrees of freedom $= 20$ and the .05 level of significance, the cutoff sample score for both main effects and the interaction effect is $F = 4.35$.

Step 4: Determine the sample's score on the comparison distribution.
Follow the steps for calculating a two-way analysis of variance listed previously.
1. Compute each cell mean, row mean, column mean, and the grand mean.

		Previous Full-time Job		Marginal means
		Yes	No	
Attend Orientation	Yes	$M = 4.00$	$M = 3.33$	3.67
	No	$M = 4.00$	$M = 1.83$	2.92
Marginal means		4.00	2.58	$GM = 3.29$

2. Compute the deviation scores for each mean in Step 1. **Note that all values are rounded, so some discrepancies may be present.**

Orientation & Job	$(X - GM)$	$(X - M)$	$(M_{\text{Row}} - GM)$	$(M_{\text{Column}} - GM)$	Intercept
4	0.71	0	0.38	0.71	-0.38
5	1.71	1	0.38	0.71	-0.38
4	0.71	0	0.38	0.71	-0.38
3	-0.29	-1	0.38	0.71	-0.38
4	0.71	0	0.38	0.71	-0.38
4	0.71	0	0.38	0.71	-0.38

Orientation & No Job	$(X-GM)$	$(X-M)$	$(M_{Row}-GM)$	$(M_{Column}-GM)$	Intercept
5	1.71	1.67	0.38	-0.71	0.37
4	0.71	0.67	0.38	-0.71	0.37
3	-0.29	-0.33	0.38	-0.71	0.37
2	-1.29	-1.33	0.38	-0.71	0.37
3	-0.29	-0.33	0.38	-0.71	0.37
3	-0.29	-0.33	0.38	-0.71	0.37

No Orientation & Job	$(X-GM)$	$(X-M)$	$(M_{Row}-GM)$	$(M_{Column}-GM)$	Intercept
4	0.71	0	-0.37	0.71	0.37
3	-0.29	-1	-0.37	0.71	0.37
4	0.71	0	-0.37	0.71	0.37
4	0.71	0	-0.37	0.71	0.37
5	1.71	1	-0.37	0.71	0.37
4	0.71	0	-0.37	0.71	0.37

No Orientation & No Job	$(X-GM)$	$(X-M)$	$(M_{Row}-GM)$	$(M_{Column}-GM)$	Intercept
1	-2.29	-0.83	-0.37	-0.71	-0.38
2	-1.29	0.17	-0.37	-0.71	-0.38
1	-2.29	-0.83	-0.37	-0.71	-0.38
3	-0.29	1.17	-0.37	-0.71	-0.38
2	-1.29	0.17	-0.37	-0.71	-0.38
2	-1.29	0.17	-0.37	-0.71	-0.38

3. Square each deviation score in Step 2.

Orientation & Job	$(X-GM)^2$	$(X-M)^2$	$(M_{Row}-GM)^2$	$(M_{Column}-GM)^2$	$(Intercept)^2$
4	0.50	0	0.144	0.504	0.14
5	2.92	1	0.144	0.504	0.14
4	0.50	0	0.144	0.504	0.14
3	0.08	1	0.144	0.504	0.14
4	0.50	0	0.144	0.504	0.14
4	0.50	0	0.144	0.504	0.14
$\Sigma = 24$	5.02	2	0.87	3.02	0.87
$M = 4.00$					

Orientation & No Job	$(X-GM)^2$	$(X-M)^2$	$(M_{Row}-GM)^2$	$(M_{Column}-GM)^2$	$(Intercept)^2$
5	2.92	2.79	0.144	0.504	0.14
4	0.50	0.45	0.144	0.504	0.14
3	0.08	0.11	0.144	0.504	0.14
2	1.66	1.77	0.144	0.504	0.14
3	0.08	0.11	0.144	0.504	0.14
3	0.08	0.11	0.144	0.504	0.14
$\Sigma = 20$	5.34	5.33	0.87	3.02	0.87
$M = 3.33$					

No Orientation & Job	$(X-GM)^2$	$(X-M)^2$	$(M_{Row}-GM)^2$	$(M_{Column}-GM)^2$	$(Intercept)^2$
4	0.50	0	0.14	0.504	0.137
3	0.08	1	0.14	0.504	0.137
4	0.50	0	0.14	0.504	0.137
4	0.50	0	0.14	0.504	0.137
5	2.92	1	0.14	0.504	0.137
4	0.50	0	0.14	0.504	0.137
$\Sigma = 24$	5.02	2	0.82	3.02	0.82
$M = 4.00$					

No Orientation & No Job	$(X-GM)^2$	$(X-M)^2$	$(M_{Row}-GM)^2$	$(M_{Column}-GM)^2$	$(Intercept)^2$
1	5.24	0.69	0.14	0.504	0.144
2	1.66	0.03	0.14	0.504	0.144
1	5.24	0.69	0.14	0.504	0.144
3	0.08	1.37	0.14	0.504	0.144
2	1.66	0.03	0.14	0.504	0.144
2	1.66	0.03	0.14	0.504	0.144
$\Sigma = 11$	15.56	2.83	0.82	3.02	0.87
$M = 1.83$					

4. Add the squared deviation scores in Step 3.

$SS_{Rows} = \Sigma(M_{Row} - GM)^2 = 0.87 + 0.87 + 0.82 + 0.82 = 3.38$

$SS_{Columns} = \Sigma(M_{Column} - GM)^2 = 3.02 + 3.02 + 3.02 + 3.02 = 12.08$

$SS_{Interaction} = \Sigma[(X - GM) - (X-M) - (M_{Row} - GM) - (M_{Column} - GM)]^2 = 0.87 + 0.87 + 0.82 + 0.87 = 3.43$

$SS_{Within} = \Sigma(X - M)^2 = 2.00 + 5.33 + 2.00 + 2.83 = 12.16$

$SS_{Total} = \Sigma(X - GM)^2 = 5.02 + 5.34 + 5.02 + 15.56 = 30.94$, or

$SS_{Total} = SS_{Rows} + SS_{Columns} + SS_{Interaction} + SS_{Within} = 3.38 + 12.08 + 3.43 + 12.16 = 31.05$ [**Small rounding difference**]

5. Obtain the variance estimates by dividing each sum of squared deviations in Step 4 by the appropriate number of degrees of freedom.

S^2_{Rows} or $MS_{Rows} = SS_{Rows} / df_{Rows} = 3.38 / 1 = 3.38$

$S^2_{Columns}$ or $MS_{Columns} = SS_{Columns} / df_{Columns} = 12.08 / 1 = 12.08$

$S^2_{Interaction}$ or $MS_{Interaction} = SS_{Interaction} / df_{Interaction} = 3.43 / 1 = 3.43$

S^2_{Within} or $MS_{Within} = SS_{Within} / df_{Within} = 12.16 / 20 = 0.61$

6. Divide the between-groups variance estimates by the within-groups variance estimate.

$F_{Rows} = S^2_{Rows} / S^2_{Within}$ or $MS_{Rows} / MS_{Within} = 3.38 / 0.61 = 5.54$

$F_{Columns} = S^2_{Columns} / S^2_{Within}$ or $MS_{Columns} / MS_{Within} = 12.08 / 0.61 = 19.80$

$F_{Interaction} = S^2_{Interaction} / S^2_{Within}$ or $MS_{Interaction} / MS_{Within} = 3.43 / 0.61 = 5.62$

Step 5: Decide whether to reject the null hypothesis.

Analysis of Variance Table

Source	SS	df	MS	F
Between:				
Rows	3.38	1	3.38	5.54
Columns	12.08	1	12.08	19.80
Interaction	3.43	1	3.43	5.62
Within	12.16	20	0.61	
Total	30.94 (31.05)	23		

Since all three F ratios are more extreme than the cutoff sample score of 4.35, the psychologist will reject all three null hypotheses and accept the research hypotheses. As inspection of the means in the table presented in **Step 4** indicates, employees who attended the orientation program received higher supervisory ratings than employees who did not attend, and employees who had had a full-time job received higher supervisory ratings than employees who had not had a full-time job. The mean supervisory ratings for employees who had had a full-time job were identical, regardless of whether they attended the orientation program. Therefore, the interaction effect is due to the fact that the supervisory ratings for employees holding their first time job who attended the orientation program were higher than the ratings for similar employees who did not attend the orientation program. Graphs of the significant interaction effect follow.

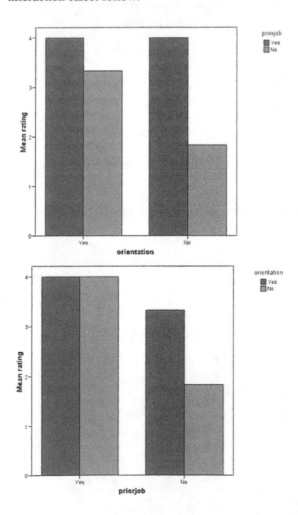

114

Advanced Topic: Power and Effect Size in the Factorial Analysis of Variance

The rationale for calculating effect size and power in a factorial analysis of variance is the same as for a one-way analysis of variance except that separate calculations are made for each main effect and for the interaction effect. Remember that the effect size is indicated by R^2, which is also called eta^2 (η^2), and is the proportion of variance accounted for by the effect. The formula for one-way analysis of variance is $R^2 = (S^2_{Between})\,(df_{Between})\,/\,(S^2_{Between})\,(df_{Between}) + (S^2_{Within})\,(df_{Within})$. Modifying this formula for factorial analysis of variance involves substituting the variance estimate for the effect of interest for $S^2_{Between}$, so that

- the formula for the main effect for rows becomes $R^2 = (S^2_{Rows})\,(df_{Rows})\,/\,(S^2_{Rows})\,(df_{Rows}) + (S^2_{Within})\,(df_{Within})$,
- the formula for the main effect for columns becomes $R^2 = (S^2_{Columns})\,(df_{Columns})\,/\,(S^2_{Columns})\,(df_{Columns}) + (S^2_{Within})\,(df_{Within})$, and
- the formula for the interaction effect becomes $R^2 = (S^2_{Interaction})\,(df_{Interaction})\,/\,(S^2_{Interaction})\,(df_{Interaction}) + (S^2_{Within})\,(df_{Within})$.

Remember also that these R^2 values are partial effect sizes because the proportion of variance accounted for by an effect is the variance that remains after the variance accounted for by the other effects has been "partialed out." Calculating the sizes of the effects in the orientation study yields the following partial R^2 values.

Effect of attending the orientation program:
$R^2 = (S^2_{Rows})\,(df_{Rows})\,/\,(S^2_{Rows})\,(df_{Rows}) + (S^2_{Within})\,(df_{Within})$
  $= (3.38)\,(1)\,/\,(3.38)\,(1) + (0.61)\,(20)$
  $= 3.38\,/\,3.38 + 12.20$
  $= 3.38\,/\,15.58$
  $= 0.22$

Effect of having had a full-time job:
$R^2 = (S^2_{Columns})\,(df_{Columns})\,/\,(S^2_{Columns})\,(df_{Columns}) + (S^2_{Within})\,(df_{Within})$
  $= (12.08)\,(1)\,/\,(12.08)\,(1) + (0.61)\,(20)$
  $= 12.08\,/\,12.08 + 12.20$
  $= 12.08\,/\,24.28$
  $= 0.50$

Effect of the interaction between attending the orientation program and having had a full-time job:
$R^2 = (S^2_{Interaction})\,(df_{Interaction})\,/\,(S^2_{Interaction})\,(df_{Interaction}) + (S^2_{Within})\,(df_{Within})$
  $= (3.43)\,(1)\,/\,(3.43)\,(1) + (0.61)\,(20)$
  $= 3.43\,/\,3.43 + 12.20$
  $= 3.43\,/\,15.63$
  $= 0.22$

Remember that Cohen's conventions for interpreting R^2 following analysis of variance are:
- .01 = a small effect
- .06 = a medium effect
- .14 = a large effect

Therefore, all the effects in the orientation study are large, and the effect of having held a full-time job is extremely large.

As was also the case for one-way analysis of variance, effect sizes can be calculated F ratios and degrees of freedom. Calculating the sizes of the effects in the orientation using this information yields the following partial R^2 values.

Effect of attending the orientation program:
$R^2 = (F_{Rows}\,(df_{Rows})\,/\,(F_{Rows})\,(df_{Rows}) + (df_{Within})$
  $= (5.54)(1)\,/\,(5.54)(1) + (20)$
  $= 5.54\,/\,5.54 + 20$
  $= 5.54\,/\,25.54$
  $= 0.22$

Effect of having had a full-time job:

$R^2 = (F_{Columns}) (df_{Columns}) / (F_{Columns}) (df_{Columns}) + (df_{Within})$

$= (19.80) (1) / (19.80) (1) + (20)$

$= 19.80 / 19.80 + 20$

$= 19.80 / 39.80$

$= 0.50$

Effect of the interaction between attending the orientation program and having had a full-time job:

$R^2 = (F_{Interaction}) (df_{Interaction}) / (F_{Interaction}) (df_{Interaction}) + (df_{Within})$

$= (5.62) (1) / (5.62) (1) + (20)$

$= 5.62 / 5.62 + 20$

$= 5.62 / 25.62$

$= 0.22$

The **power** of each effect in a factorial analysis of variance is determined by the overall design. The table in the text indicates the power of studies using both 2 X 2 and 2 X 3 analyses of variance. This table indicates that a study based on a 2 X 2 factorial design with 10 participants in each cell ($N = 40$) will have a 9% chance of detecting a small effect, a 33% chance of detecting a medium effect, and a 68% chance of detecting a large effect if all effects are tested.

The text also includes a table that indicates the approximate number of participants needed in each cell to obtain 80% power at the .05 level of significance. This table indicates that if only the two-level main effect in a 2 X 3 design is tested, 132 participants will be needed in each cell ($N = 528$) to detect a small effect.

Chapter Self-Tests

Understanding Key Concepts in Chapter 10

The test items that follow are based on the following scenario. The psychologists studying the effects of different types of therapy on the number of activities of daily living performed by depressed people have concluded that more frequent therapy sessions are likely to increase the number of activities performed by their clients. Now the psychologists are interested in determining the effect matching the gender of the therapist with the gender of the client on the number of activities performed. Consequently, the psychologists have formed four groups comprised of five clients each. Group 1 will include women in sessions conducted by a female therapist, Group 2 will include women in sessions conducted by a male therapist, Group 3 will include men in sessions conducted by a male therapist, and Group 4 will include men in sessions conducted by a female therapist.

Complete each statement using the word bank that follows. **You will use some words more than once.**

Word Bank: cell / cell mean / dichotomizing / factorial / interaction effect / main / marginal / one-way / repeated-measures analysis of variance / two-way / two-way factorial

In the previous study, the psychologists compared the mean numbers of activities performed by the clients in the three groups based on the number of therapy sessions. Since the number of therapy sessions was the only effect, they will use a **(1)** _____ analysis of variance. In the current study, the psychologists may be interested in differences in the number of activities performed by depressed men and women, as well as whether the gender of the therapist has an effect on the number of activities performed. Therefore, the psychologists are using a **(2)** _____ research design, and they will analyze their data with a **(3)** _____ analysis of variance. The effect of client gender on the number of activities is a **(4)** _____ effect, as is the effect of therapist gender. However, the psychologists primary interest may be in whether men or women respond differently to male or female therapists, which will be determined by examining the **(5)** _____. Since two variables divide the groups, the design is also called a **(6)** _____ research design, and the appropriate analysis is a **(7)** _____ analysis of variance. When the number of activities for each group are presented in a table, each group occupies a **(8)** _____, each of which has its own **(9)** _____. The means for male and female clients and for clients who have male therapists or female therapists called **(10)** _____ means.

If the psychologists modify the study by measuring the number of activities performed every two weeks for the six-month duration of the study, the appropriate analysis will be a **(11)** _____ analysis of variance. If they add a third variable by dividing clients into those having high anxiety and those having lower anxiety on the basis of scores on an anxiety inventory they are **(12)** _____ clients.

Multiple-Choice Items

1. If the psychologists want to compare the mean numbers of activities performed by clients in three groups defined as having high, moderate, and low motivation, they will use a
   A. repeated-measures analysis of variance.
   B. 2 X 3 analysis of variance.
   C. one-way analysis of variance.
   D. factorial analysis of variance.

2. By examining the effects of client gender and therapist gender in the same study, the psychologists are using a
   A. two-group randomized design.
   B. dichotomized design.
   C. repeated-measures design.
   D. factorial design.

3. The appropriate analysis for this study is a
   A. 1 X 2 analysis of variance.
   B. 2 X 2 analysis of variance.
   C. 2 X 3 analysis of variance.
   D. 2 X 4 analysis of variance.

4. The number of *F* ratios calculated in this analysis will be
   A. 1.
   B. 2.
   C. 3.
   D. 4.

5. If the clients perform more activities when a therapist of the same gender conducts their therapy, the psychologists have detected
   A. an interaction effect.
   B. an omnibus effect.
   C. an effect of therapy.
   D. an effect of gender.

6. A statistically significant difference between the mean number of activities performed by clients who have a male therapist and clients who have a female therapist is evidence of a
   A. an interaction effect.
   B. an omnibus effect.
   C. a main effect of therapy.
   D. a main effect of gender.

Use the table that follows to respond to Items 7–12

		Therapist		
		Male	Female	
Client	Male	$M = 11.0$	$M = 14.0$	$M = 12.5$
	Female	$M = 18.0$	$M = 21.0$	$M = 19.5$
		$M = 14.5$	$M = 17.5$	$M = 16.0$

7. Which of the following numbers is a cell mean?
    A. 11.0
    B. 12.5
    C. 16.0
    D. 17.5

8. Which of the following numbers is a marginal mean?
    A. 11.0
    B. 14.0
    C. 14.5
    D. 21.0

9. Which of the following numbers is the grand mean?
    A. 11.0
    B. 16.0
    C. 17.5
    D. 19.5

10. Which two means would contribute to calculation of an interaction effect?
    A. 11.0 and 18.0
    B. 12.5 and 19.5
    C. 14.0 and 21.0
    D. 14.0 and 18.0

11. The number of degrees of freedom for the effect of client gender is
    A. 1.
    B. 2.
    C. 3.
    D. 4.

12. The number of degrees of freedom for the effect of therapist gender is
    A. 1.
    B. 2.
    C. 3.
    D. 4.

13. The psychologists are want to see if the number of activities increases consistently during therapy or if there are some periods of decline, so they record the number of activities performed the day after the therapy session each week for six weeks. To determine whether the observed differences between depressed men and women were statistically significant, the psychologists would use
    A. factorial analysis of variance.
    B. 2 X 3 analysis of variance.
    C. one-way analysis of variance.
    D. repeated-measures analysis of variance.

14. The psychologists also believe that the length of time a client has been depressed may be an important factor in response to therapy. If they divide clients into "younger" and "older" groups to be included in their analysis, they will be

    A. planning for repeated-measures analysis of variance.
    B. planning for one-way analysis of variance.
    C. dichotomizing their clients.
    D. testing for an interaction effect.

Problems

1. The table of means that follows reflects the hypothetical results of a study using a factorial design to compare the level of stress reported by younger and older nontraditional students in lecture-based and computer-based courses. Assuming that any differences are statistically significant, create two bar graphs, one with bars for course format and one with bars for student age, indicate which effects are present, and describe these effects.

		Student Age	
		Younger	Older
Course Format	Lecture-based	$M = 38$	$M = 28$
	Computer-based	$M = 28$	$M = 38$

2. The table of means that follows reflects the hypothetical results of a study using a factorial design to compare the new words learned by girls and boys in two reading programs, one using the phonics method and the other the whole-word method. Again, assuming that any differences are statistically significant, create two bar graphs, one with bars for method and one with bars for student gender, indicate which effects are present, and describe these effects.

		Method	
		Phonics	Whole-word
Gender	Girls	$M = 19$	$M = 15$
	Boys	$M = 16$	$M = 12$

3. The table of means that follows reflects the hypothetical results of a study using a factorial design to compare the level of anxiety reported by college students based on whether they attended a large or small high school and whether they attended a summer orientation program for incoming students. Again, assuming that any differences are statistically significant, create two bar graphs, one with bars for method and one with bars for student gender, indicate which effects are present, and describe these effects.

		Orientation	
		Yes	No
High school	Large	$M = 15$	$M = 30$
	Small	$M = 20$	$M = 60$

4. The table of means that follows reflects the hypothetical results of a study that expands the study in Problem 1 by adding a category of mixed courses that include both lecture and computer-based components. The purpose of the study is to compare the satisfaction with the three types of courses expressed by older and younger nontraditional students. Assuming that any differences are statistically significant, create two bar graphs, one with bars for course format and one with bars for student age, indicate which effects are present, and describe these effects.

		Student Age	
		Younger	Older
Course Format	Lecture-based	$M = 36$	$M = 30$
	Mixed	$M = 30$	$M = 36$
	Computer-based	$M = 24$	$M = 42$

5. Advanced Topic: The psychologists have identified 20 clients, 10 women and 10 men, and divided them into groups of five as indicated in the table that follows.

Client	Client	Therapist	# of Activities
1	Woman	Woman	19
2	Woman	Woman	17
3	Woman	Woman	18
4	Woman	Woman	20
5	Woman	Woman	21
6	Woman	Man	16
7	Woman	Man	16
8	Woman	Man	17
9	Woman	Man	15
10	Woman	Man	16
11	Man	Woman	15
12	Man	Woman	14
13	Man	Woman	13
14	Man	Woman	14
15	Man	Woman	14
16	Man	Man	16
17	Man	Man	15
18	Man	Man	15
19	Man	Man	15
20	Man	Man	14

Use the five steps of hypothesis testing to determine the effect of matching the gender of the client and the gender of the therapist has an effect on the number of activities of daily living performed by depressed clients. Follow the structural model to test all main and interaction effects at the .05 level of significance, plot the interaction effect, and calculate the effect size for each effect. As part of **Step 4**, create a table including the cell means and marginal means. As part of **Step 5**, create an analysis of variance table like the example in the text. Explain the process and results to someone familiar with one-way analysis of variance including the structural model, but not with factorial analysis of variance.

6. A developmental psychologist interested in the attachment between full-term and pre-term infants and their mothers conducted a study to measure infant willingness to explore a strange environment by counting the number of toys infants handled during a five-minute interval. Four groups of infants, two comprised of full-term infants and two of pre-term infants, were observed both when their mothers were present and when their mothers were absent. The data are presented in the table that follows.

Baby	Birth Condition	Mother	# of Toys
1	Full-term	Present	7
2	Full-term	Present	6
3	Full-term	Present	5
4	Full-term	Present	8
5	Full-term	Absent	6
6	Full-term	Absent	4
7	Full-term	Absent	5
8	Full-term	Absent	4
9	Pre-term	Present	6
10	Pre-term	Present	7
11	Pre-term	Present	5
12	Pre-term	Present	4
13	Pre-term	Absent	3
14	Pre-term	Absent	4
15	Pre-term	Absent	4
16	Pre-term	Absent	2

Use the five steps of hypothesis testing to determine the effect of matching the gender of the client and the gender of the therapist has an effect on the number of activities of daily living performed by depressed clients. Follow the structural model to test all main and interaction effects at the .05 level of significance, plot the interaction effect, and calculate the effect size for each effect. As part of **Step 4**, create a table including the cell means and marginal means. As part of **Step 5**, create an analysis of variance table like the example in the text.

7. Advanced Topic: What is the power of the effect in the following planned studies using analysis of variance at the .05 level of significance?

Study	Predicted Effect Size	Overall Design	#of Levels of the Effect	Participants per Cell
(a)	Medium	2 X 2	2	20
(b)	Medium	2 X 3	3	20
(c)	Medium	2 X 2	2	40
(d)	Large	2 X 2	2	10
(e)	Large	2 X 3	3	20

8. How many participants will be needed in each cell to have 80% power using the .05 level of significance in each of the following planned studies?

Study	Predicted Effect Size	Design	Effect
(a)	Medium	2 X 2	Main
(b)	Large	2 X 2	Interaction
(c)	Medium	2 X 3	Two level main
(d)	Large	2 X 3	Two level main
(e)	Medium	2 X 3	Three level main
(f)	Large	2 X 3	Three level interaction

Additional Practice: Complete any Practice Problems in Set I that your instructor has not assigned and compare your responses to those provided by the authors. Pay particular attention to the problems that require you to explain your results to someone who has never taken a course in statistics.

SPSS Applications

Application 1: Factorial Analysis of Variance
Open SPSS.
Analyze the data for Problem 5. Remember that SPSS assumes that all the scores in a row are from the same clients. In this study, there are 20 clients divided into four groups of five clients. Therefore, three variables: 1) whether the participant is male or female, 2) whether the therapist is male or female, and 3) the number of activities of daily living performed will describe each of the 20 clients. If "1" represents both female clients and female therapists, and "2" represents both male clients and therapists, the first client will be described by entering "1" in the top cell of the first column in the Data View window, a "1" in the top cell of the second column, and "19" in the top cell of the third column. These entries will indicate that the client was a woman whose therapy was conducted by a female therapist and that the client performed 19 activities. The sixth client will be described by "1" in the first column, "2" in the second column, and "16" in the third column. When you have entered the data for all 20 clients, move to the Variable View window, change the first variable name to "client," the second to "therapist," and the third to "activities" and set the decimals for both to zero if you wish. The Data View window should look like Figure 1.

client	therapist	activities
1	1	19
1	1	17
1	1	18
1	1	20
1	1	21
1	2	16
1	2	16
1	2	17
1	2	15
1	2	16
2	1	15
2	1	14
2	1	13
2	1	14
2	1	14
2	2	16
2	2	15
2	2	15
2	2	15
2	2	14

Figure 1

✍ Analyze
✍ General Linear Model
✍ Univariate

The window should look like Figure 2.

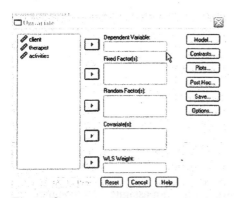

Figure 2

✍ "activities" and ✍ the arrow to move the variable to the Dependent Variable window, which instructs SPSS to conduct the analysis of variance on the number of activities performed
✍ "client" and ✍ the arrow to move the variable to the Fixed Factors window
✍ "therapist" and ✍ the arrow to move the variable to the Fixed Factors window
These actions tell SPSS that the clients were either male or female, as were the therapists.
The "Univariate" window should look like Figure 3

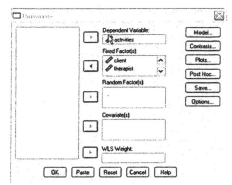

Figure 3

🖱 Options, and then 🖱 the arrow box for Descriptive Statistics, which will provide descriptive statistics for each cell and the marginal means

🖱 Continue

🖱 OK

The three tables in the "Univariate Analysis of Variance" window should look like the three that follow.

Between-Subjects Factors

		Value Label	N
client	1	Female	10
	2	Male	10
therapist	1	Female	10
	2	Male	10

Descriptive Statistics

Dependent Variable: activities

client	therapist	Mean	Std. Deviation	N
Female	Female	19.00	1.581	5
	Male	16.00	.707	5
	Total	17.50	1.958	10
Male	Female	14.00	.707	5
	Male	15.00	.707	5
	Total	14.50	.850	10
Total	Female	16.50	2.877	10
	Male	15.50	.850	10
	Total	16.00	2.128	20

Tests of Between-Subjects Effects

Dependent Variable: activities

Source	Type III Sum of Squares	df	Mean Square	F	Sig.
Corrected Model	70.000ª	3	23.333	23.333	.000
Intercept	5120.000	1	5120.000	5120.000	.000
client	45.000	1	45.000	45.000	.000
therapist	5.000	1	5.000	5.000	.040
client * therapist	20.000	1	20.000	20.000	.000
Error	16.000	16	1.000		
Total	5206.000	20			
Corrected Total	86.000	19			

a. R Squared = .814 (Adjusted R Squared = .779)

The first table, labeled "Between-Subjects Factors," indicates the number of participants in each cell, which is useful as you check to be sure that you have used the correct participants and variables and that you have entered the data for all participants. The second table, labeled, "Descriptive Statistics," includes the descriptive statistics for the number of activities performed by clients in each cell. If you examine the "Total" values in this table, you can also determine the marginal means, which you should do by comparing the table you created as you solved Problem 5.

The third table, labeled "Tests of Between-Subjects Effects," includes the results of the two-way analysis of variance. (Ignore the columns labeled Corrected Model, Intercept, and Corrected Total.) The "Source" column lists the population variance estimates included in the analysis, i.e., the main effects for client and therapist gender, the interaction effect between these two variables, the within-groups estimate, which is labeled "Error," and the Total. The second column lists the sums of squares calculated in the Advanced Topic section, followed by the degrees of freedom in the third column. The fourth column, labeled "Mean Square," lists the population variance estimate for the main effects, the interaction effect, and the within-groups term. The fifth column lists the F ratios for the main

123

effects and the interaction effect, and the sixth column lists the exact significance level for each effect. As you can see, the F ratios are identical to those you obtained when you performed the calculations yourself.

SPSS can also be used to create a bar graph like those in the text and this study guide using the following steps. First, enter value labels in the "Variable View" window to make interpretation of the graphs easier. In this application, the value labels for both "client" and "therapist" are 1 = "Women" and 2 = Men.
⊸ Graphs
⊸ Legacy Dialogs
⊸ Bar
⊸ "the graph next to "Clustered" and ⊸ Define
⊸ the circle labeled Other statistic
⊸ "adl" and ⊸ the arrow to move the variable to the box labeled "Variable," which tells SPSS to plot the mean numbers of activities on the vertical axis
⊸ "therapist" and ⊸ the arrow to move the variable to the box labeled "Category Axis," which tells SPSS to plot separate bars for the two types of therapists on the horizontal axis
⊸ "client" and ⊸ the arrow to move the variable to the box labeled "Define Clusters by," which tells SPSS to plot separate bars for the two types of clients
⊸ OK
The output should look like graph in Figure 4, and should look like the graph you created as you solved Problem 5 above.

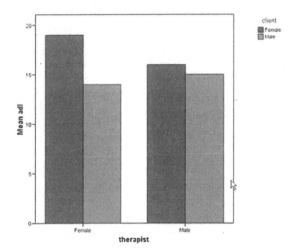

Figure 4

Application 2: Factorial Analysis of Variance
Open SPSS.
Analyze the data for Problem 6. In this study, there are 16 participants divided into four groups of four. Again, each of the 16 participants will be described by three variables, whether the baby is full-term or pre-term, whether the mother is present or absent, and the number of toys handled. If "1" represents both full-term babies and present mothers, and "2" represents both pre-term babies and absent mothers, the first baby will be described by entering "1" in the top cell of the first column in the Data View window, a "1" in the top cell of the second column, and "7" in the top cell of the third column. These entries will indicate that the client was a full-term baby whose mother was present and that the baby handled seven toys. The fifth baby will be described by entering "1" in the fifth cell of the first column in the Data View window, a "2" in the fifth cell of the second column, and "6" in the fifth cell of the third column to indicate a full-term baby whose mother was absent and who handled 6 toys. When you have entered the data for all 16 babies, move to the Variable View window, change the first variable name to "baby," the second to "mother," and the third to "toys." Set the decimals for both to zero if you wish.

⊸ Analyze
⊸ General Linear Model

꒐ Univariate

꒐ "toys" and ꒐ the arrow to move the variable to the Dependent Variable window, which instructs SPSS to conduct the analysis of variance on the number of toys handled

꒐ "baby" and ꒐ the arrow to move the variable to the Fixed Factors window

꒐ "mother" and ꒐ the arrow to move the variable to the Fixed Factors window

These actions tell SPSS that the babies were either full-term or pre-term, and mothers were either present or absent. The "Univariate" window should look like Figure 5

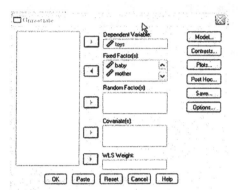

Figure 5

꒐ Options, and then ꒐ the arrow box for Descriptive Statistics, which will provide descriptive statistics for each cell and the marginal means

꒐ Continue

꒐ OK

The three tables in the "Univariate Analysis of Variance" window should look like the three that follow.

Between-Subjects Factors

		Value Label	N
baby	1	full-term	8
	2	preterm	8
mother	1	present	8
	2	absent	8

Descriptive Statistics

Dependent Variable: toys

baby	mother	Mean	Std. Deviation	N
full-term	present	6.50	1.291	4
	absent	4.75	.957	4
	Total	5.63	1.408	8
preterm	present	5.50	1.291	4
	absent	3.25	.957	4
	Total	4.38	1.598	8
Total	present	6.00	1.309	8
	absent	4.00	1.195	8
	Total	5.00	1.592	16

Tests of Between-Subjects Effects

Dependent Variable: toys

Source	Type III Sum of Squares	df	Mean Square	F	Sig.
Corrected Model	22.500[a]	3	7.500	5.806	.011
Intercept	400.000	1	400.000	309.677	.000
baby	6.250	1	6.250	4.839	.048
mother	16.000	1	16.000	12.387	.004
baby * mother	.250	1	.250	.194	.668
Error	15.500	12	1.292		
Total	438.000	16			
Corrected Total	38.000	15			

a. R Squared = .592 (Adjusted R Squared = .490)

Interpretation follows the same process described for **Application 1**. The first table, labeled "Between-Subjects Factors," indicates the number of participants in each cell, which is useful as you check to be sure that you have used the correct participants and variables and that you have entered the data for all participants. The second table, labeled, "Descriptive Statistics," includes the descriptive statistics for the number of toys handled by babies in each cell. If you examine the "Total" values in this table, you can also determine the marginal means, which you should do by comparing the table you created as you solved Problem 6.

The third table, labeled "Tests of Between-Subjects Effects," includes the results of the two-way analysis of variance. (Ignore the columns labeled Corrected Model, Intercept, and Corrected Total.) The "Source" column lists the population variance estimates included in the analysis, i.e., the main effects for "baby" and "mother," the interaction effect between these two variables, the within-groups estimate, which is labeled "Error," and the Total. The second column lists the sums of squares calculated in the Advanced Topic section, followed by the degrees of freedom in the third column. The fourth column, labeled "Mean Square," lists the population variance estimate for the main effects, the interaction effect, and the within-groups term. The fifth column lists the F ratios for the main effects and the interaction effect, and the sixth column lists the exact significance level for each effect. As you can see, the F ratios are quite similar to those you obtained when you performed the calculations yourself.

Again, SPSS can be used to create a bar graph to assist in interpreting an interaction effect. In this application, the value labels for both "full-term babies" and "present mothers" is = 1 and for "preterm babies" and "absent mothers" = 2.
- ⥁ Graphs
- ⥁ Legacy Dialogs
- ⥁ Bar
- ⥁ "the graph next to "Clustered" and ⥁ Define
- ⥁ the circle labeled Other statistic
- ⥁ "toys" and ⥁ the arrow to move the variable to the box labeled "Variable," which tells SPSS to plot the mean numbers of handled toys on the vertical axis
- ⥁ "baby" and ⥁ the arrow to move the variable to the box labeled "Category Axis," which tells SPSS to plot separate bars for the two types of babies on the horizontal axis
- ⥁ "mother" and ⥁ the arrow to move the variable to the box labeled "Define Clusters by," which tells SPSS to plot separate bars for the two types of mothers
- ⥁ OK

The output should look like graph in Figure 6, and should look like the graph you created as you solved Problem 5 above.

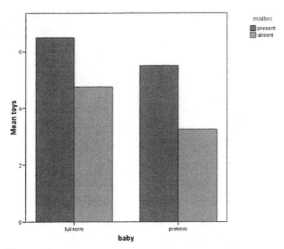

Figure 6

If you would like additional practice, use SPSS to analyze the data for Problem about the effects of attending an orientation program and having held a full-time job on supervisory ratings used as an example in this chapter and compare the results to the calculations presented.

Chapter 11
Correlation

Learning Objectives
After studying this chapter, you should:
- Be able to create and interpret scatter diagrams.
- Be able to interpret the patterns of correlation.
- Know how to calculate a correlation coefficient and determine whether it is statistically significant.
- Be able to explain the relationship between correlation and causality.
- Be able to describe the issues encountered in interpreting correlation coefficients.
- Be able to use tables to estimate power for correlations.
- Know how to use tables to estimate sample sizes for correlations.
- Be able to interpret the results of correlations as reported in research articles.

Correlation is the extent to which two equal-interval numeric variables are related. Conceptually, correlation can be understood by considering whether the pattern of scores is such that high scores on one variable are associated with high scores on the other variable, low scores with low scores, and moderate scores with moderate scores. For example, do people with higher levels of intellectual ability demonstrate higher levels of educational achievement?

Graphing Correlations
One way to examine the relationship between two variables is to create a graph called a **scatter diagram** (also called a *scatterplot*), which displays the degree and pattern of relation of the two variables. Creating a scatter diagram involves three steps:
1. Draw the axes and determine which variable will be placed on which axis. In many studies, either variable can be placed on either axis. However, in some studies, one variable is thought of as predicting the other. In these studies, the predictor variable is placed on the horizontal axis, and the predicted variable is placed on the vertical axis.
2. Determine the range of values to use for each variable and mark them on the axes. The values should increase on each axis, starting from point at which the axes meet. Typically, the low value on each axis is zero. However, if zero is not a reasonable value, the values on an axis can begin with a higher number. The values then continue to the highest value the measure can have, or, if no obvious or reasonable lowest or highest possible value can be identified, the values should extend to the highest score that a participant in a study is likely to achieve. The horizontal and vertical axes should be approximately the same length so that the scatter diagram appears to be square.
3. Mark a dot for the pair of scores for each case. This process involves first locating the place on the horizontal axis for a participant's score on the horizontal-axis variable. Next, move up to the height for the score for the first pair of scores on the vertical axis. Then make a dot at the point defined by the pair of scores. If two individuals have identical scores on both variables, put the number "2" in that place, or locate a second dot as close as possible to the first dot, preferably touching it. Whichever method is used, the presence of two dots in the same place should be evident.

As an example, consider the 10 pairs of stress and depression scores obtained from emergency health care providers that follow.

Stress: 39, 29, 43, 18, 26, 45, 32, 26, 22, 33
Depression: 26, 16, 33, 22, 15, 23, 18, 18, 12, 15

1. Draw the axes and determine which variable will be placed on which axis. Although either variable could be placed on either axis, stress is often used as a predictor of depression in many studies. Therefore, stress can logically be placed on the horizontal axis, and depression can be placed on the vertical axis.
2. Determine the range of values to use for each variable and mark them on the axes. Instead of zero, the scatter diagram that follows begins with a score of 15 on the horizontal axis and 10 on the vertical axis. The horizontal and vertical axes are the same length so that the scatter diagram appears to be square.
3. Mark a dot for the pair of scores for each case, which has been done. Note that all the dots are separate.

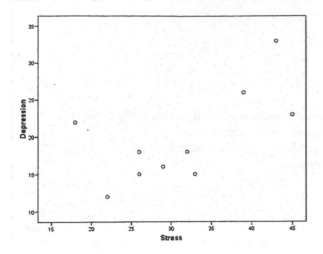

Patterns of Correlation

Patterns of correlation can be identified by the general pattern of dots in a scatter diagram.

1. A **linear correlation** is present when the pattern of dots follows a straight line. In the scatter diagram of stress and depression scores, the pattern of the scores can be described by a straight line extending from the lower left area of the diagram to the upper right area. The previous scatter diagram shows a linear correlation.

2. A **curvilinear correlation** is present when the relationship between two variables does not follow a straight line, but instead follows a curving or more complex pattern. Modification of the stress and depression scores in the example resulted in the scatter diagram that follows. This diagram indicates that both low and high levels of stress are associated with low levels of depression, while moderate levels of stress are associated with high levels of depression.

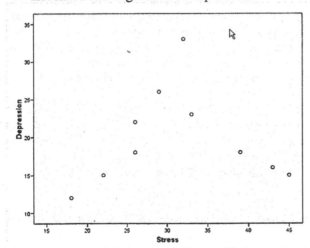

In this case, calculating a correlation coefficient using the method presented later in the chapter will show little or no correlation.

3. When the two variables are essentially unrelated, they are said to be uncorrelated, i.e., **no correlation** is present. Such a relationship is indicated by the scatter diagram that follows. No line describes the relationship.

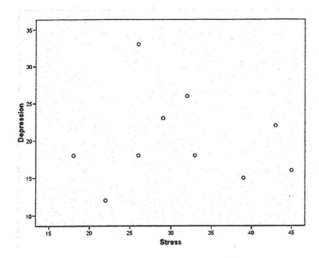

Correlations can also be categorized in another way.

1. A **positive correlation** is present when, as noted previously, low scores on one variable are associated with low scores on the other variable, moderate scores are associated with moderate scores, and high scores are associated with high scores.

2. On the other hand, **negative correlation** is present when low scores on one variable are associated with high scores on the other variable, moderate scores are associated with moderate scores, and high scores are associated with low scores. In a scatter diagram, the dots follow a line that slopes the upper left area of the graph to the lower right area of the graph. The scatter diagram that follows shows a negative correlation between stress and job satisfaction for a group of emergency health care workers.

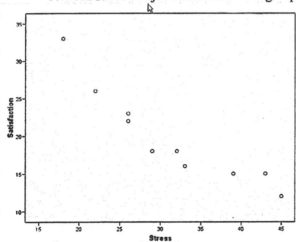

The strength of a correlation is often described by the clarity of the relationship between two variables. If the dots in a scatter diagram all fall close to a straight line, the correlation is said to be large, or strong. If the pattern of dots is unclear, the correlation is said to be small, or weak. Moderate correlations fall somewhere between large and small correlations. One way to think about the strength of correlations is that in a perfect linear correlation, positive or negative, all the dots fall on a straight line. If no correlation is present, the pattern of dots might be described as a circle, and an infinite number of lines can be drawn to represent the dots in a circle. Again, identifying the pattern of a correlation is important because different procedures are used for calculating linear and curvilinear correlations.

The Correlation Coefficient

Scatter diagrams only provide a general idea of the relationship between two variables. Therefore, a number that provides an exact index of the direction and strength of the relationship is useful. Remember that the logic of correlation is that the scores on each variable are related in a certain way. Specifically, if two variables are positively correlated, high scores on one variable are associated with high scores on the other variable, moderate scores with moderate scores, and low scores with low scores. If two variables are negatively correlated, high scores on one variable are associated with low scores on the other variable, with moderate scores being associated with moderate scores. Thus, the calculation of the number that summarizes the relationship between two variables must consistently identify high and low scores. This summarization of the relationship between two variables can be quantified by computing *deviation scores* because any score that is greater than the mean of the distribution of scores for a variable will be positive and any score that is below the mean will be negative. The **product of deviation scores** obtained by multiplying a positive deviation score by another positive deviation score will be positive, as will the product of deviation scores obtained by multiplying a negative deviation score by another negative deviation score. Thus, if the high scores on one variable are associated with high scores on the other variable, and if the low scores on one variable are associated with low score on the other variable, the product of deviation scores will be positive, and when these products are summed, the result will be a large positive number.

On the other hand, obtaining the product of deviation scores obtained by multiplying a positive deviation score by negative deviation score will be negative. Therefore, if the high scores on one variable are associated with low scores on the other variable, the product of deviation scores will be negative, and when these products are summed, the result will be a large negative number.

Obtaining the product of deviation scores when no relationship exists between two variables will mean that while some pairs of scores will consist of high scores on both variables, and some come pairs will consist of low scores on both variables, other pairs will consist of high scores on one variable and low scores on the other. In these latter cases, the product of deviation scores will be negative. If the positive and negative products of deviation scores cancel each other, their sum will be around zero.

Adding the products of deviation scores only indicates the direction of the relationship. Determining the degree of the relationship requires dividing the sum of the products of deviation scores by a number that corrects for
1.   the number of people in the study, and
2.   the variation of the scores for each variable.
This number is based on the sum of the squared deviations for each variable, and it serves as a correction because it increases as
1.   the number of participants in a study increases, and
2.   as the variation of the scores for each variable increases.

The specific number is the square root of product of the sums of squares for each variable, or

$$\sqrt{[(SS_X)(SS_Y)]}$$

Dividing the sum of products of deviation scores divided by this correction number yields a quotient that can never be greater than +1.00, a perfect positive correlation, or less than -1.00, a perfect negative correlation. When no linear correlation is present, the quotient is 0.00. Thus, correlations can range from -1.00 through 0.00 to +1.00.

This quotient is called a **correlation coefficient**, (or the Pearson correlation coefficient or the Pearson product-moment correlation coefficient) and is symbolized by r. The sign indicates the direction of the correlation and the value indicates the strength of the correlation.

The formula for a correlation coefficient is

$$r = \Sigma[(X - M_X)(Y - M_Y)] / \sqrt{[(SS_X) * (SS_Y)]}$$

An Example
The steps for calculating the correlation coefficient for the initial dataset comprised of stress and depression scores of emergency health care providers follow.

The scores are:
Stress: 39, 29, 43, 18, 26, 45, 32, 26, 22, 33
Depression: 26, 16, 33, 22, 15, 23, 18, 18, 12, 15

Calculation Table

$(X - M_X)$	$(X - M_X)^2$	$(Y - M_Y)$	$(Y - M_Y)^2$	$(X - M_X)(Y - M_Y)$
7.70	59.29	6.20	38.44	47.74
-2.30	5.29	-3.80	14.44	8.74
11.70	136.89	13.20	174.24	154.44
-13.30	176.89	2.20	4.84	-29.26
-5.30	28.09	-4.80	23.04	25.44
13.70	187.69	3.20	10.24	43.84
0.70	0.49	-1.80	3.24	-1.26
-5.30	28.09	-1.80	3.24	9.54
-9.30	86.49	-7.80	60.84	72.54
1.70	2.89	-4.80	23.04	-8.16
	$\Sigma = 712.10$		$\Sigma = 355.60$	$\Sigma = 323.60$

Stress = X and $M_X = 31.3$
Depression = Y and $M_Y = 19.8$

1. **Change the scores for each variable to deviation scores.** These scores are in the columns of the Calculation Table headed $(X - M_X)$ and $(Y - M_Y)$.
2. **Figure the product of the deviation scores for each pair of scores.** These products are in the column of the Calculation Table headed $(X - M_X)(Y - M_Y)$.
3. **Add up all the products of the deviation scores.** This sum is in the summation cell of the column in the Calculation Table headed $(X - M_X)(Y - M_Y)$. The sum is 323.60.
4. **For each variable, square each deviation score.** These squared deviation scores are in the columns of the Calculation Table headed $(X - M_X)^2$ and $(Y - M_Y)^2$.
5. **Add up the squared deviation scores for each variable.** These sums are in the summation cells of the columns in the Calculation Table headed $(X - M_X)^2$ and $(Y - M_Y)^2$.
6. **Multiply the two sums of squared deviations and take the square root of the result.** The two sums of squared deviations are 712.10 and 355.60, and their product is 253,222.76. The square root of this product is 503.21.
7. **Divide the sum of the products of deviation scores from Step 3 by the correction number from Step 6.** 323.60 divided by 503.21 is .64.

Substituting these values into the formula yields

$$r = \Sigma[(X - M_X)(Y - M_Y)] / \sqrt{[(SS_X) * (SS_Y)]} = 323.60 / \sqrt{(712.10) * (355.60)} = 323.60 / 503.21 = .64$$

Significance of a Correlation Coefficient
The correlation coefficient by itself is a descriptive statistic that describes the degree and direction of a linear relationship. However, experimenters are often more interested in the relationship between two variables is representative of a population that has not been studied. In these situations, the null hypothesis is that the correlation in the population is zero. As was the case for t tests and analysis of variance, a hypothetical sampling distribution for correlation could be constructed by drawing a very large number of samples, calculating the coefficients, and plotting them. This hypothetical procedure is unnecessary because the correlation coefficient can be used to calculate a t value, which permits use to t tables to determine the statistical significance or r. The formula is

$$t = (r) / \sqrt{(1 - r^2)/(N - 2)}.$$ [Note that if $r = .00$, $t = 0.00$ because the numerator reduces to 0 and the denominator to 1, and 0 divided by 1 (or any other number) is 0. Also, note that as r increases, t increases.] As usual, the number of degrees of freedom is required to use a t table, and the degrees of freedom for the t test for correlation is the number of participants in the sample minus 2 (because two means are calculated when calculating a correlation coefficient). [Note that this number corresponds to the number under the radical in the numerator of the formula.]

Therefore, the number of degrees of freedom for the example calculation is $10 - 2 = 8$, and with 8 df, the cutoff sample score is $t = 2.306$ at the .05 level of significance.   Remember that t will be positive or negative depending on the direction of the relationship between the two variables and that that experimenters can specify directional or nondirectional hypotheses, but the significance test for a correlation coefficient is usually two-tailed.

Applying the formula for t using the correlation coefficient obtained in the example yields

$$t = r / \sqrt{(1 - r^2)/(N - 2)} = .64 / \sqrt{(1 - .64^2)/(10 - 2)} = .64 / \sqrt{.59/8} = .64 / .27 = 2.37.$$

Since the t value of 2.37 is more extreme than the cutoff sample t value of 2.306, the null hypothesis can be rejected and the research hypothesis can be accepted.

Assumptions for the Significance Test of a Correlation Coefficient

The assumptions for testing the significance of a correlation are similar to the assumptions previously defined for t tests for independent means and analysis of variance, i.e., that the populations of each variable are normally distributed and that the variances of the two populations are equal. However, since two variables are involved, the considerations are somewhat different. In addition to the assumption that the populations from which each variable is drawn are normal, the relationship between the two variables is assumed to be *bivariate normal*, meaning that the relationship follows a normal curve. This assumption is usually tested, however, by examining the distribution of each variable. The distribution of each variable is assumed to be equivalent at each point of the other variable, i.e., the variances of one variable are consistent across all values of the other variable and *vice versa*. Unless the violations of the assumptions are extreme, the t test for the significance of a correlation coefficient is robust.

Correlation and Causality

Remember that when constructing scatter diagrams, if justification exists, the convention is to place the predictor variable on the horizontal axis and the variable being predicted on the vertical axis. However, the presence of a statistically significant correlation does not permit a statement about which variable is causing variation in the other variable. That is, the **direction of causality** cannot be identified from a correlation coefficient, even if it is statistically significant. .For any particular correlation between variables X and Y, there are three possible directions of causality:
1. X is causing Y,
2. Y is causing X, or
3.   Some third factor is causing both X and Y.

In the example,
1.   Stress could be causing depression,
2.   Depression could be causing stress, or
3.   Some other factor like job satisfaction could be causing both stress and depression.

Sometimes a possible direction of causality can be logically eliminated, e.g., when one of the variables cannot logically cause the other, as would be the case if age were one of the variables. Age may be correlated with depression, and growing older may lead to depression. However, depression does not cause age (chronologically, at least). Another way to determine causality is to conduct a true experiment, holding all variables constant except the variable of interest. For example, a psychologist interested in the relationship between frequency of supervisory ratings and job satisfaction might randomly assign employees to two groups, one group receiving more frequent ratings and the other group less frequent ratings. In this situation, the frequency of ratings cannot cause job satisfaction because the frequency has been determined and comes before job satisfaction. The influence of a third variable is eliminated because the frequency of ratings for any employee was determined randomly, e.g., the intent of randomization is to balance initial levels of job satisfaction prior to introducing the ratings. The issue may be confused by the fact that correlation may refer to the statistical procedure described in this chapter or to a **correlational research design**. A correlational research design is any design other than a true expedriment. The statistical analysis of these designs may include calculating a correlation, or other statistical analyses may be appropriate. [Correlation may also be appropriate for analyzing data collected in true experiments.]

Issues in Interpreting the Correlation Coefficient

1. Larger values of r, i.e., values farther from zero, indicate greater degrees of correlation. However, differences between correlation coefficients are not proportional. For example, $r = .40$ is not twice as large as $r = .20$. Most experimenters use r^2 to compare correlations, which is called the **proportionate reduction in error**, or the *proportion of variance accounted for*, which was introduced in Chapter 9. Squaring $.40 = .16$ and squaring $.20 = .04$, which means that $r = .40$ is four times larger than $r = .20$.

2. **Restriction in range** refers to the calculation of a correlation coefficient using scores from a limited range of the possible values on one or both variables. Restriction in range typically results in a low correlation when the actual correlation across the entire range of values is large. Suppose that in the example, only people who had been diagnosed as clinically depressed were included in the correlation. Since the restriction in range would apply to depression, the correlation coefficient obtained in this analysis might well be smaller than .64.

3. If a measure is accurate, it is said to be reliable. If one or both variables in a correlation are unreliable, the correlation is lower than it would be with perfect measures of the two variables. This reduction in the size of a correlation coefficient due to unreliable measures is *attenuation*, and coefficients can be corrected for attenuation using formulas that adjust for the underestimation of a correlation.

4. **Outliers**, defined in Chapter 2, are extreme scores that result in an unusual combination of pairs of scores that can have an influence on the correlation. Examination of the scatter diagram of the dataset used in the example shows a pairs of scores toward the left side of the diagram that reflects a relatively low level of stress and a moderate level of depression. This dot represents the fourth observation, and removing this observation makes the linear nature of the relationship more apparent and increases the correlation coefficient to .84.

5. If the relationship is somewhat curvilinear, the scores can be ranked and an alternate correlation called **Spearman's rho** can be calculated. Although this analysis will be discussed in more detail in Chapter 14, note that some experimenters prefer rho because it does not assume that the variables have been measured on an equal-interval scale, and outliers affect it less.

Effect Size and Power for the Correlation Coefficient

Correlation coefficients are measures of effect size, so that the effect size in the example is .64. Cohen's conventions for correlation coefficients are

- .10 = small
- .30 = medium
- .50 = large

Thus, the effect size for the example is large.

The approximate power of studies using correlation coefficients for testing hypotheses can be estimated using tables like Table 11-7 and sample size can be planned using tables like Table 11-8.

How Correlation Coefficients Are Described in Research Articles

Scatter diagrams are sometimes included in research articles, and correlation coefficients are often described in the text and in tables. The correlation coefficient obtained in the example could be reported as: $r = .64$, $p < .05$. When several variables are included in a study, a table of all the correlations called a **correlation matrix** is included.

Chapter Self–Tests

The test items that follow are based on the following scenario. The psychologists studying depression have administered an inventory to assess the level of anxiety experienced by their clients so that they can examine the relationship between these two variables.

Understanding Key Terms in Chapter 11

Directions: Using the word bank that follows, complete each statement.

Word Bank: correlation / correlation coefficient / correlation matrix / correlational / curvilinear / direction of causality / linear / negative / no / outliers / positive / product of deviation scores / proportion of variance accounted for / proportionate reduction in error / reliable / restriction in range / scatter diagram / Spearman's rho

Since the psychologists are interested in the relationship between depression and anxiety, they are interested in a **(1)** _____. As a first step in examining their data, the psychologists will make a graph of each client's depression scores and anxiety scores. This graph is called a **(2)** _____. If the psychologists find that higher depression scores are associated with higher anxiety scores, lower depression scores are associated with lower anxiety scores, and moderate depression scores are associated with moderate anxiety scores, the relationship is called a **(3)** _____ correlation. However, if higher depression scores are associated with lower anxiety scores, lower depression scores are associated with higher anxiety scores, and moderate depression scores are associated with moderate anxiety scores, the relationship is called a **(4)** _____ correlation. If the pattern of pairs of depression scores and anxiety scores approximates a straight line, the psychologists are observing a **(5)** _____ correlation. However, if higher depression scores are associated with higher anxiety scores, lower depression scores are associated with lower anxiety scores, and some moderate depression scores are associated with higher anxiety scores and some with lower anxiety scores, the relationship is called a **(6)** _____ correlation. If the dots representing the pairing of depression scores and anxiety scores have no apparent pattern, the data reflect **(7)** _____ correlation.

In order to identify high scores and low scores, the psychologists subtract the mean depression score from each client's depression score, subtract the mean anxiety score from the each client's anxiety score, and multiply the two results to obtain the **(8)** _____. Dividing the sum of the results of these multiplications by a correction number based on the sum of the squared deviations of each variable yields a **(9)** _____. Although the psychologists anticipate that higher levels of depression will be associated with higher levels of anxiety, the single number they have calculated to summarize the relationship does not allow them to say whether depression causes anxiety or whether anxiety causes depression because the **(10)** _____ cannot be determined from this analysis. If the research design that the psychologists have used to collect the depression and anxiety data is not a true experimental design, it is a **(11)** _____ research design.

The psychologists base a statement about the strength of the relationship between depression and anxiety on r^2, which is called the **(12)** _____, or the **(13)** _____. If scores on the depression inventory can range from 0 to 60, and the psychologists include only clients whose scores are greater than 45, another analysis including clients whose scores extended over the entire range of possible scores might yield very different results. This difference is due to **(14)** _____. The results of similar studies also may vary because the measurement of depression is not perfectly accurate, or **(15)** _____. Suppose that the psychologists compare their results to the results of similar studies and find unexpectedly large differences. When they reexamine their initial graph, they find two clients who have combinations of depression and anxiety scores that are quite different than the scores obtained by other clients. The two clients are **(16)** _____. If the psychologists observe some curvilinearity in their initial graph, they may rank the depression and anxiety scores an use a procedure called **(17)** _____ to analyze the relationship. If the psychologists also correlate the number of activities of daily living with both depression and anxiety, they will report the results of all these correlations in a **(18)** _____.

Multiple Choice Items

1. If the dots in a scatter diagram containing depression and anxiety scores lie close to a straight line extending from the lower left side of the graph to the upper right side, the psychologists will report that the correlation is
   A. positive.
   B. negative.
   C. curvilinear.
   D. rectangular.

2. If the dots in a scatter diagram containing depression and anxiety scores resemble an inverted U, the psychologists will report that the correlation is
   A. positive.
   B. negative.
   C. curvilinear.
   D. rectangular.

3. If the dots in a scatter diagram containing depression and anxiety scores spread evenly across all areas of the graph, the psychologists will report that
   A. the two variables are positively correlated.
   B. no correlation is present.
   C. an error has been made during data collection.
   D. the correlation is perfect.

4. If the dots in a scatter diagram containing depression and anxiety scores lie close to a straight line extending from the upper left side of the graph to the lower right side, the psychologists will report that the correlation is
   A. positive.
   B. negative.
   C. curvilinear.
   D. rectangular.

5. If the dots in a scatter diagram containing depression and anxiety scores lie on a straight line extending from the lower left side of the graph to the upper right side, the psychologists will obtain a correlation coefficient of
   A. +1.00.
   B. ±.50.
   C. 0.00.
   D. -1.00.

6. If the dots in a scatter diagram containing depression and anxiety scores lie on a straight line extending from the upper left side of the graph to the lower right side, the psychologists will obtain a correlation coefficient of
   A. +1.00.
   B. +.75.
   C. -.75.
   D. -1.00.

7. Once the psychologists have determined the deviation scores of each client's depression score from the mean depression score and the deviation scores of each client's anxiety score from the mean, they will calculate the numerator of the formula for a correlation coefficient by computing a
   A. sum.
   B. difference.
   C. product.
   D. quotient.

Items 8–12 are based on the following information.
Based on prior studies, the psychologists know that the relationship between depression and anxiety is positive and the relationship between depression and the number of activities of daily living performed is negative.

8. Which of the following correlation coefficients indicates the strongest correlation between depression and anxiety?
   A. +.75
   B. +.60
   C. .00
   D. -.60

9. Which of the following correlation coefficients indicates the strongest correlation between depression and number of activities of daily living performed?
   A. +.55
   B. +.45
   C. .00
   D. -.60

10. If the psychologists obtain a correlation coefficient of +.50 between depression and anxiety, they can state that
    A. depression causes anxiety.
    B. anxiety causes depression 50% of the time.
    C. low levels of depression are associated with low levels of anxiety.
    D. low levels of anxiety are associated with high levels of depression.

11. On the other hand, if the psychologists obtain a correlation coefficient of -.50 between depression and the number of activities of daily living performed, they can state that
    A. The number of activities causes depression.
    B. 50% of depression is related to the number of activities performed.
    C. low levels of depression are associated with performing fewer activities.
    D. performing fewer activities is associated with high levels of depression.

12. If the psychologists obtain a correlation coefficient between depression and number of activities of daily lining performed of -0.90, they would interpret this coefficient as evidence of a
    A. weak positive linear correlation.
    B. weak negative linear correlation.
    C. strong positive linear correlation.
    D. strong negative linear correlation.

13. The psychologists have calculated a correlation coefficient of +1.05, which indicates
    A. a strong positive correlation.
    B. a calculation error.
    C. no correlation.
    D. a curvilinear correlation.

14. If the psychologists want to test the statistical significance of the correlation between depression and anxiety, they will test the hypothesis that the correlation in the population is
    A. .00.
    B. .05.
    C. .01.
    D. 1.00.

Items 15–16 are related.

The psychologists have obtained a correlation coefficient of .60 between depression and anxiety, which means that $r^2 = .36$.

15. This value of r^2 is called
    A. Pearson product-moment correlation.
    B. Spearman's rho.
    C. the proportionate reduction in error.
    D. the unreliability coefficient.

16. The valid interpretation of this r^2 value is that
    A. depression causes anxiety 36% of the time.
    B. the combined unreliability of the depression and anxiety scores is .36.
    C. restriction of range has reduced the explanatory power of the correlation by 36%.
    D. 36% of the variation in depression and anxiety can be explained by the correlation between them.

17. The depression experienced by the psychologists' clients is not so severe that residential treatment is required. However, if the psychologists generalize their results to the population of depressed people for whom residential treatment is required, problems with application of the results may arise because of
    A. restriction in range.
    B. outliers.
    C. unreliability.
    D. curvilinearity.

18. The psychologists have observed that the correlation between depression and number of activities of daily living performed obtained from their clients and some of the correlations reported in other studies are surprisingly different, which they attribute primarily to inaccurate recording of activities. If the psychologists' interpretation is correct, the problem is
    A. restriction in range.
    B. the presence of outliers.
    C. low reliability.
    D. a curvilinear relationship.

19. Since correlation coefficients are measures of effect size, a large effect is defined by a correlation coefficient of
    A. .10.
    B. .20.
    C. .30.
    D. .50.

20. If the psychologists have calculated correlation coefficients between all possible pairings of depression, anxiety, number of activities of daily living performed, health status, and perceived quality of life, they will present these coefficients in a research article
    A. in a correlation matrix.
    B. as products of deviation scores.
    C. as the proportion of variance accounted for.
    D. in a series of scatter diagrams.

Problems

1. The psychologists conducted their study of depression and anxiety using a sample of 12 depressed clients and obtained the following scores.

Depression: 44, 47, 39, 43, 45, 57, 56, 48, 52, 48, 44, 48
Anxiety: 39, 50, 44, 49, 51, 65, 47, 49, 60, 59, 40, 58

Construct a scatter diagram and describe the general pattern of the relationship. Calculate the correlation coefficient and determine whether it is statistically significant using a two-tailed test at the .05 level. Explain the procedure to someone who is unfamiliar with correlation but who does understand the mean, deviation scores, and hypothesis testing. Describe the three possible directions of causality.

2. The psychologists also examined the relationship between depression and the number of activities of daily living performed by the sample of 12 depressed clients and obtained the following scores.

Depression: 44, 47, 39, 43, 45, 57, 56, 48, 52, 48, 44, 48
Activities: 17, 14, 16, 14, 15, 12, 16, 15, 10, 12, 15, 14

Construct a scatter diagram and describe the general pattern of the relationship. Calculate the correlation coefficient and determine whether it is statistically significant using a two-tailed test at the .05 level.

3. What is the most likely explanation for a distorted estimate of the true correlation in each of the following situations?
A. One person has the lowest possible score on one of the variables being correlated and the highest possible score on the other variable.
B. The correlation between the number of days employees are absent and a rating of their job performance on a 5-point rating scale.
C. The correlation between a general personality inventory and an inventory designed to measure motivation.

4. What is the power of the following studies in which the statistical significance of a correlation coefficient is tested at the .05 level of significance using a two-tailed test?

Study	Effect Size	N
(a)	Small	40
(b)	Small	100
(c)	Medium	40
(d)	Medium	100
(e)	Large	40
(f)	Large	100

5. How many participants are needed to have 80% power in the following studies in which the statistical significance of a correlation coefficient will be tested at the .05 level of significance using a two-tailed test?

Study	Effect Size
(a)	Medium
(b)	Large

Additional Practice: Complete any Practice Problems in Set I that your instructor has not assigned and compare your responses to those provided by the authors. Pay particular attention to the problems that require you to explain your results to someone who has never taken a course in statistics.

SPSS Applications

Application 1: Scatter Diagram and Correlation Coefficient for Problem 1
Open SPSS.
Analyze the data for Problem 1. Remember that SPSS assumes that all the scores in a row are from the same participant. In this study, there are 12 participants, each having both a depression score and an anxiety score. When you have entered the data for all 12 clients, you may move to the Variable View window, and change the first variable name to "depression" and the second to "anxiety," and set the number of decimals for both variables to zero if you wish.

↱ Graphs
↱ Legacy Dialogs and select ↱ Scatter/Dot
The default is a "Simple Scatter" diagram, which is the graph you want.
↱ Define

✓❂ the variable "depression" ✓❂ the arrow next to the box labeled "Y axis" to indicate that the scores for the depression variable should be placed on the Y (vertical) axis

✓❂ the variable "anxiety" and ✓❂ the arrow next to the box labeled "X axis" to indicate that the anxiety variable should be placed on the X (horizontal) axis

The window should look like Figure 1.

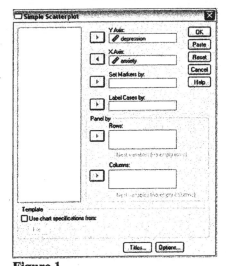

Figure 1

✓❂ OK

The scatter diagram should look like Figure 2.

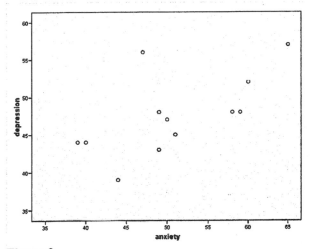

Figure 2

To calculate the correlation coefficient,

✓❂ Analyze

✓❂ Correlate

✓❂ Bivariate

✓❂ the variable "depression" ✓❂ the arrow next to the box labeled "Variables" and then ✓❂ the variable "anxiety" ✓❂ the arrow next to the box labeled "Variables," which indicates that the correlation between depression and anxiety is to be calculated

The window should look like Figure 3.

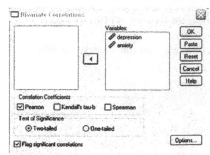

Figure 3

⌐ OK

The output window should look like Figure 4.

Correlations

		depression	anxiety
depression	Pearson Correlation	1	.625*
	Sig. (2-tailed)		.030
	N	12	12
anxiety	Pearson Correlation	.625*	1
	Sig. (2-tailed)	.030	
	N	12	12

*. Correlation is significant at the 0.05 level (2-tailed).

Figure 4

The table in Figure 4 shows that the correlation between depression and anxiety is .625, which would be rounded to .63, and that the probability of obtaining a coefficient this large is .030 if the correlation in the population is zero. [The coefficient is the same size as the one you calculated by hand.] The note indicates that the correlation is significant at the .05 level using a two-tailed test. The table also includes the number of people in the analysis. Note that the two cells indicating that the correlation coefficient is 1.00 define the diagonal of the table and indicate the correlation of each variable with itself. Therefore, these cells can be ignored. Also, note that the information in the upper right cell and the lower left cell is identical. Since only one coefficient has been obtained, this information would probably be reported in the text of a research article instead of in a table.

Application 2: Scatter Diagram and Correlation Coefficient for Problem 2
Open SPSS.
Analyze the data for Problem 2. In this study, the 12 participants each have a depression score and a number of activities of daily living. When you have entered the data for all 12 clients, move to the Variable View window, change the first variable name to "depression" and the second to "activities." When you have entered the data for all 12 clients, you may move to the Variable View window, and change the first variable name to "depression" and the second to "activities," and set the number of decimals for both variables to zero if you wish.

⌐ Graphs
⌐ Legacy Dialogs and select ⌐ Scatter/Dot
The default is a "Simple Scatter" diagram, which is the graph you want.
⌐ Define
⌐ the variable "activities" ⌐ the arrow next to the box labeled "Y axis" to indicate that the scores for the activities of daily living variable should be placed on the Y (vertical) axis
⌐ the variable "depression" and ⌐ the arrow next to the box labeled "X axis" to indicate that the depression variable should be placed on the X (horizontal) axis

The window should look like Figure 5.

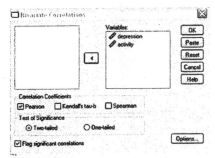

Figure 5
🖰 OK
The scatter diagram should look like Figure 6.

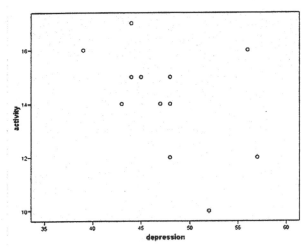

Figure 6

To calculate the correlation coefficient,
🖰 Analyze
🖰 Correlate
🖰 Bivariate
🖰 the variable "depress" 🖰 the arrow next to the box labeled "Variables" and then 🖰 the variable "activ" 🖰 the arrow next to the box labeled "Variables," which indicates that the correlation between depression and activities of daily living is to be calculated

The window should look like Figure 7.

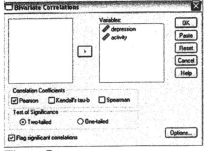

Figure 7
🖰 OK
The output window should look like Figure 8.

Correlations

		depression	activity
depression	Pearson Correlation	1	-.468
	Sig. (2-tailed)		.125
	N	12	12
activity	Pearson Correlation	-.468	1
	Sig. (2-tailed)	.125	
	N	12	12

Figure 8

The table in Figure 8 shows that the correlation between depression and anxiety is -.468, which would be rounded to -.47, and that the probability of obtaining a coefficient this large is .125 if the correlation in the population is zero. [Again, the coefficient is the same size as the one you calculated by hand.] Since the coefficient is not statistically significant at the .05 level, there is no asterisk beside the coefficient and there is no note beneath the table. Again, the table includes the number of people in the analysis, the two cells indicating that the correlation coefficient is 1.00 that define the diagonal of the table, and identical information in the upper right cell and the lower left cell, and this information would probably be reported in the text of a research article instead of in a table.

Chapter 12
Prediction

Learning Objectives

After studying this chapter, you should:

- Know the difference between predictor and criterion variables.
- Know how to calculate linear prediction rules and interpret the results obtained by applying them.
- Know how to draw regression lines.
- Know how to determine the best linear prediction rule.
- Be able to explain why prediction is also called regression.
- Know to calculate standardized regression coefficients and explain their uses.
- Be able to describe the general nature of multiple regression.
- Be able to describe the limitations of prediction.
- Be able to interpret the results of prediction studies as reported in research articles.
- Advanced Topic: Know how to calculate the proportionate reduction in error in bivariate prediction and interpret the results.

Regression differs from correlation in that in the former, one variable is considered to be the **predictor variable** and the other is the variable being predicted, or **criterion variable**. The predictor variable is usually labeled X, and the criterion variable is labeled Y. In other words, X is said to predict Y.

The **linear prediction rule**, also called the *linear prediction model*, can be summarized by the following formula:
$\hat{Y} = a + (b)(X)$ where
$\hat{Y}$ is the predicted score on the criterion variable,
a is the **regression constant**,
b is the **regression coefficient**, and
X is the score on the predictor variable.

Following the example from Chapter 11 and using stress to predict depression, suppose that the regression constant is 5.71 and the regression coefficient is .45. (As will be shown, these are the actual values for the initial dataset in Chapter 11.) Substituting these values in the formula for the linear prediction rule to predict the depression score for an emergency health care provider with a stress score of 26 yields Predicted Depression = 5.71 + (.45) (26) = 5.71 + 11.70 = 17.41. Remember that predictions should not be made from scores on the predictor variable that are much larger or smaller than the scores used to calculate the correlation coefficient on which a particular prediction rule is based.

The Regression Line

The linear prediction rule can be viewed as a line on a scatter diagram like the one that follows with the predictor variable plotted on the horizontal axis and the criterion variable on the vertical axis. The line that would be closest to all the in the scatter diagram that follows is called a **regression line**.

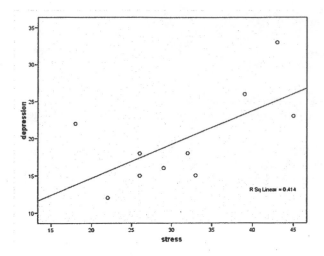

The **slope** of a regression line is the amount the regression line increases on the vertical axis for every unit it moves across on the horizontal axis, and it is equal to b, the regression coefficient. The **intercept** of the regression line, also called the Y intercept, is the point at which the regression line crosses the vertical axis. Therefore, the intercept is the point at which $X = 0$, which means it is equal to a, the regression constant. Following the example, an emergency health care provider's depression score increases by .45 points for each increase of one point on the stress scale, and the regression will intersect the vertical axis at 5.71 units on the depression scale. (Again, these calculations will be shown later.)

Since regression lines are straight lines, they can be drawn from a scatter diagram by following four steps.
1. Draw and label the axes for a scatter diagram.
2. Use the linear prediction rule to calculate the value of the criterion variable for a low value of the predictor variable and mark the point on the graph.
3. Repeat Step 2 using a high value of the predictor variable.
4. Draw a line (the regression line) that passes through the two points.

Identifying the best linear prediction rule involves "the least squared error principle." First, remember that the difference between a predicted score on the criterion variable resulting from applying a linear prediction rule and a person's actual score on the criterion variable is considered **error**. Since positive and negative errors will sum to zero, the differences between predicted and actual values are squared (just as is done to calculate the variance). Once these squared errors have been calculated, a prediction rule is evaluated by calculating the **sum of squared errors**, and the best prediction rule for any dataset is the one with the smallest sum of squared errors, which is called the *least squares criterion*. The formula for calculating b is
$b = \Sigma[(X - M_X)(Y - M_Y)] / SS_X$ where
b is the regression coefficient
$X - M_X$ is the deviation score for each person on the X variable,
$Y - M_Y$ is the deviation score for each person on the Y variable,
$(X - M_X)(Y - M_Y)$ is the product of the deviation scores for each person, and
SS_X is the sum of squared deviations for the X variable.

The formula for calculating a is $a = M_Y - (b)(M_X)$.

The calculations for the example using stress to predict depression among emergency health care workers would be as follows.

Calculation table

$[(X-M_X)]$	$[(X-M_X)^2]$	$(Y-M_Y)$	$(Y-M_Y)^2$	$[(X-M_X)(Y-M_Y)]$
7.70	59.29	6.20	38.44	47.74
-2.30	5.29	-3.80	14.44	8.74
11.70	136.89	13.20	174.24	154.44
-13.30	176.89	2.20	4.84	-29.26
-5.30	28.09	-4.80	23.04	25.44
13.70	187.69	3.20	10.24	43.84
0.70	0.49	-1.80	3.24	-1.26
-5.30	28.09	-1.80	3.24	9.54
-9.30	86.49	-7.80	60.84	72.54
1.70	2.89	-4.80	23.04	-8.16
	$\Sigma = 712.10$		$\Sigma = 355.60$	$\Sigma = 323.60$

Stress = X and M_X = 31.30
Depression = Y and M_Y = 19.80

The steps for calculating b are:
1. **The scores for each variable are changed to deviation scores** in the 1st and 3rd columns of the calculation table.
2. **The products of the deviation scores for each pair of scores** are in the 5th column of the calculation table.
3. **The sum of the products of the deviation scores is 323.60.**
4. **The squared deviation scores for the predictor variable (X) are in the 2nd column.**
5. **The sum of the squared deviation scores for the predictor variable (X) is 712.10.**
6. **Dividing the sum of the deviation scores from Step 3 by the sum of the squared deviation for the predictor variable (X) from Step 5 yields b, which is** = 323.60 / 712.10 = .45.

The steps for calculating a are:
1. **Multiply the regression coefficient (b) by the mean of the X variable, which is** (.45) (31.30) = 14.09.
2. **Subtract the result of Step 1 from the mean of the Y variable, which is** 19.80 – 14.09 = 5.71.

Issues in Prediction
1. Prediction is also called regression because, when two variables are less than perfectly correlated, the predicted score on the criterion variable, in standard deviation units, is closer to the mean of the criterion variable than the value of the predictor variable is to the mean of the predictor variable. As a result, the predicted value of the criterion variable *regresses* toward its mean.
2. Since experimenters may use different measures of the same variable, or change the scales of measures, comparison of linear prediction rules for the effect can be difficult. The reason for the difficulty caused by these changes is that the scales used to measure both the predictor and criterion variables affect the value of the regression coefficient. Using a method similar to calculating Z scores, a regression coefficient can be converted into a **standardized regression coefficient**. Such coefficients are symbolized by the upper case Greek letter beta (β) and indicate the amount of change in standard deviation units of the criterion variable for each change of one standard deviation in the predictor variable. The formula for the standardized regression coefficient is $\beta = (b) \sqrt{SS_X} / \sqrt{SS_Y}$. From the stress and depression example,

$\beta = (.45) \sqrt{712.10} / \sqrt{355.60}$ = (.45) (26.69) / 18.86 = 12.01 / 18.86 = .64.

3. When a linear prediction rule includes only one predictor variable, the standardized regression coefficient is equal to the correlation coefficient. However, the standardized regression coefficient is not equal to the correlation coefficient when more than one predictor variable is used.
4. Since the standardized regression coefficient is equal to the correlation coefficient, the t test for the significance of a correlation can be used to test the significance of a variable as a predictor of a criterion variable, and tests whether the regression coefficient is significantly different from zero. If a regression coefficient is zero, it provides no useful information for predicting a score on the

criterion variable. If a coefficient is not equal to zero, it does provide useful information for predicting a score on the criterion variable.

Bivariate prediction involves one predictor variable and one criterion variable. However, the association between two or more predictor variables and a criterion variable is called **multiple correlation**, and prediction involving or more predictor variables and a criterion variable is called **multiple regression**. The linear prediction rule for a multiple regression involving four predictor variables would be $\hat{Y} = a + (b_1)(X_1) + (b_2)(X_2) + (b_3)(X_3) + (b_4)(X_4)$. Note that in multiple linear prediction rules, none of the standardized regression coefficients is equal to the correlation coefficient, but each is closer to zero than r, in part because of overlap between variables regarding what makes the variables useful in predicting the criterion variable. The correlation between the criterion variable and the combined predictor variables is called the **multiple correlation coefficient**, which is represented by R. R^2, which will be discussed as an Advanced Topic, indicates the proportionate reduction in error in the criterion variable attributable to the combination of predictor variables. Hypothesis testing in multiple regression include:

1. Testing the significance of the multiple correlation,
2. Testing the significance of the predictor variables, and
3. Testing whether the regression constant is significantly different from zero.

(The latter test is rarely of interest in psychological research.)
The limitations of prediction include:

1. Curvilinearity,
2. Restriction in range,
3. Unreliability, and
4. Outliers.

In addition, prediction procedures alone do not indicate causality.

Prediction in Research Articles

Simple correlations instead of bivariate linear prediction rules are usually reported in psychology research articles. On the other hand, multiple regression models are frequently reported, often in tables that may include the unstandardized regression coefficients (b), the standardized regression coefficients (ß), or both, and R or R^2.

Advanced Topic: Error and Proportionate Reduction of Error

The accuracy of a prediction rule can be estimated by comparing the squared error using the rule with the squared error that would be present without the rule. Errors refer to the difference between the actual value of the criterion variable and the predicted value, i.e., $Y - \hat{Y}$. Squared error using a prediction rule is the **sum of squared errors** and is abbreviated SS_{Error}. The calculations needed to determine this value for the example problem are shown in the table that follows. Remember that stress is the predictor variable and depression is the criterion variable. Column 3 includes values obtained by applying the prediction rule $\hat{Y} = a + (b)(X)$ where $\hat{Y}$ is the predicted depression score, $a = 5.72$, $b = .45$, and X is the stress score. Column 4 contains the error scores ($Y - \hat{Y}$ for depression), and Column 5 contains the squared errors ($(Y - \hat{Y})^2$ for depression). As indicated, $SS_{Error} = 208.56$.

Stress	Depression	$\hat{Y}$ (Depression)	$Y - \hat{Y}$ (Depression)	$(Y - \hat{Y})^2$
39	26	23.27	2.73	7.45
29	16	18.77	-2.77	7.67
43	33	25.07	7.93	62.88
18	22	13.82	8.18	66.91
26	15	17.42	-2.42	5.86
45	23	25.97	-2.97	8.82
32	18	20.12	-2.12	4.49
26	18	17.42	0.58	0.34
22	12	15.62	-3.62	13.10
33	15	20.57	-5.57	31.02
				$\Sigma = 208.56$

In the absence of a prediction rule, predictions are predictions of the mean, i.e., $Y - M$. When these differences are squared and summed, the result is the **total squared error when predicting from the mean** and is abbreviated SS_{Total}. The calculation table presented earlier indicates that this value is 355.60. Thus, a prediction rule may be evaluated by determining the reduction in error using the rule (SS_{Error}) compared to the error resulting from using the mean (SS_{Total}). This comparison is called the proportionate reduction in error, and the formula is $SS_{Total} - SS_{Error} / SS_{Total}$. For the example, the proportionate reduction in error is 355.60 − 208.56 / 355.60 = .41. Also, remember that the proportionate reduction in error is equal to r^2, the correlation coefficient squared.

Chapter Self–Tests

The test items that follow are based on the following scenario. The psychologists studying depression have administered an inventory to assess the level of anxiety experienced by their clients so that they can examine the relationship between these two variables.

Understanding Key Terms in Chapter 12

Directions: Using the word bank that follows, complete each statement.

Word Bank: bivariate prediction / criterion / error / intercept / linear prediction rule / multiple correlation / multiple correlation coefficient / multiple regression / predictor / regression coefficient / regression constant regression line / slope / sum of squared errors / standardized regression coefficient

Based on their review of previous studies, the psychologists have decided to analyze their data using the following formula $\hat{Y} = a + (b)(X)$ in which X represents anxiety, which means the psychologists are designating anxiety as the **(1)** _____ variable and depression as the **(2)** _____ variable. The letter b represents the **(3)** _____, and the letter a represents the **(4)** _____. The letter b is also known as the **(5)** _____ of the **(6)** _____, and the letter a is also known as the **(7)** _____. The entire formula is known as a **(8)** _____.

After the psychologists apply the prediction, they will be able to compare each client's predicted score on the criterion variable with the client's actual score on the criterion variable. Any difference between these two scores is **(9)** _____. After obtaining these differences, the psychologists will be able to evaluate the effectiveness of the prediction rule by calculating the **(10)** _____. Since the scales used to measure the predictor and criterion variables will affect the value of b, the psychologists can calculate a value that shows the predicted amount of change in standard deviation units of the criterion variable if the value of the predicted variable increases by one standard deviation. This new value is called the **(11)** _____.

The analysis used by the psychologists to this point is an example of **(12)** _____. If they were to include age and a rating of general health made on a 10-point scale as additional predictor variables, they would examine the association between the criterion variable and the predictor variables using **(13)** _____. Making predictions in this situation would be called **(14)** _____. The correlation between the criterion variable and the predictor variables taken together is called the **(15)** _____.

Multiple Choice Items

Items 1–5 are related.
Remember that the psychologists a examining the relationship between depression and anxiety using the formula $\hat{Y} = a + (b)(X)$.

1. In this formula, the criterion variable is represented by the letter
    A. a.
    B. b.
    C. X.
    D. Y.

2. In this formula, the predictor variable is represented by the letter
    A. a.
    B. b.
    C. X.
    D. Y.

3. In this formula, the regression constant is represented by the letter
    A. a.
    B. b.
    C. X.
    D. Y.

4. In this formula, the regression coefficient is represented by the letter
    A. a.
    B. b.
    C. X.
    D. Y.

5. The formula itself is called a
    A. regression line.
    B. multiple correlation.
    C. linear prediction rule.
    D. sum of squared error.

Items 6–7 are related.

As a first step in analyzing the relationship between anxiety and depression, the psychologists have created a scatter diagram. The visual representation of the linear prediction rule for the relationship between the two variables is the regression line.

6. The amount the line moves up for every unit it moves across is the
    A. correlation.
    B. error.
    C. intercept.
    D. slope.
7. The point at which the line crosses the vertical axis is the
    A. constant.
    B. error.
    C. intercept.
    D. slope.

8. If a client's actual score on the depression inventory is 26 and the client's predicted score is 28, the difference is the
   A. constant.
   B. error.
   C. intercept.
   D. slope.

9. When the psychologists apply the formula to find the prediction rule, the best rule will be the one that has the smallest
   A. sum of the squared errors.
   B. regression coefficient.
   C. multiple correlation coefficient.
   D. standardized regression coefficient.

10. Standardized regression coefficients are represented by the symbol
   A. Σ.
   B. β.
   C. X.
   D. $\hat{Y}$.

11. If the psychologists devise a prediction rule using stress to predict depression, they are
   A. applying multiple regression.
   B. setting the intercept to zero.
   C. incorporating a standardized regression coefficient.
   D. making a bivariate prediction.

12. If the psychologists devise a prediction rule using stress and anxiety to predict depression, they are
   A. applying multiple regression.
   B. setting the intercept to zero.
   C. incorporating a standardized regression coefficient.
   D. making a bivariate prediction.

13. If the psychologists are primarily interested in the association between stress, anxiety, and depression, they are interested in
   A. controlling for outliers.
   B. adjusting for restriction in range.
   C. the multiple correlation.
   D. the standardized regression coefficient.

14. The symbol for a multiple correlation coefficient is
   A. R.
   B. β.
   C. R^2.
   D. $\hat{Y}$.

15. The symbol for the proportionate reduction in error in multiple regression is
   A. R.
   B. β.
   C. R^2.
   D. $\hat{Y}$.

Problems

1. In the text example, the regression constant is 5.71 and the regression coefficient is .45. (a) What is the prediction rule for the example? What are the predicted depression scores for emergency health care workers whose stress scores are (b) 18, (c) 26, (d) 32, (e) 39, (f) 45? If the actual depression scores for these emergency health care workers are (g) 22, (h) 15, (i) 18, (j) 26, and (k) 23, what are the squared errors?

2. In Chapter 11, the psychologists calculated the correlation coefficient for depression and anxiety from a sample of 12 depressed clients who had the following depression and anxiety scores.

Depression: 44, 47, 39, 43, 45, 57, 56, 48, 52, 48, 44, 48
Anxiety: 39, 50, 44, 49, 51, 65, 47, 49, 60, 59, 40, 58

(a) Determine the linear prediction rule for predicting depression from anxiety and draw the regression line. Use the linear prediction rule to determine the predicted depression scores of clients who have anxiety scores of (b) 40, 50, 60, and 65. (c) Determine the standardized regression coefficient. What is the sum of squared errors in depression scores for the four clients with anxiety scores of (d) 40, 50, 60, 65? (e) If the regression constant is changed to 31.70 and the regression coefficient to .46, what are the squared errors for the same four clients, and which prediction rule, the original rule or this rule, is better and why? (f) What is the proportionate reduction in error for the first prediction rule?

3. The psychologists have also collected data on the number of days of work their clients have missed during the past six months.

Depression: 44, 47, 39, 43, 45, 57, 56, 48, 52, 48, 44, 48
Days of work missed: 19, 10, 14, 17, 18, 25, 21, 19, 17, 14, 10, 18

(a) Determine the linear prediction rule for predicting the number of days of work missed from depression and draw the regression line. Use the linear prediction rule to determine the predicted number of days missed by clients who have depression scores of (b) 39, 45, 52, and 57. (c) Determine the standardized regression coefficient. What is the sum of squared errors in numbers of days missed for the four clients with depression scores of (d) 39, 45, 52, and 57? (e) If the regression constant is changed to -5.75 and the regression coefficient to .60, what are the squared errors for the same four clients, and which prediction rule, the original rule or this rule, is better and why? (f) What is the proportionate reduction in error for the first prediction rule?

Additional Practice: Complete any Practice Problems in Set I that your instructor has not assigned and compare your responses to those provided by the authors. Pay particular attention to the problems that require you to explain your results to someone who has never taken a course in statistics.

SPSS Applications

Application 1: Determining the Bivariate Linear Prediction Rule for Problem 2
Open SPSS.
Analyze the data for Problem 2. Remember that SPSS assumes that all the scores in a row are from the same participant. In this study, there are 12 participants, each having both a depression score and an anxiety score. When you have entered the data for all 12 clients, move to the Variable View window, change the first variable name to "depression" and the second to "anxiety and set the number of decimals for both variables to zero if you wish.

↨ Analyze
↨ Regression and ↨ Linear

🖱 the variable "depression" 🖱 the arrow next to the box labeled "Dependent" to indicate that depression is the criterion variable, which is also called the dependent variable in prediction studies

🖱 the variable "anxiety" and 🖱 the arrow next to the box labeled "Independent" to indicate that anxiety is the predictor variable, which is also called the independent variable in prediction studies

· The Linear Regression window should look like Figure 1.

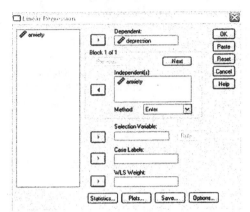

Figure 1

🖱 Statistics and 🖱 Descriptives to obtain the means and standard deviations of the two variables and the correlation coefficient

🖱 OK

The six tables provided by SPSS follow. (Remember that requesting descriptive statistics adds two tables to the four tables provided by the regression procedure.)

Descriptive Statistics

	Mean	Std. Deviation	N
depression	47.58	5.282	12
anxiety	50.92	8.140	12

Correlations

		depression	anxiety
Pearson Correlation	depression	1.000	.625
	anxiety	.625	1.000
Sig. (1-tailed)	depression		.015
	anxiety	.015	
N	depression	12	12
	anxiety	12	12

Variables Entered/Removed[b]

Model	Variables Entered	Variables Removed	Method
1	anxiety[a]	.	Enter

a. All requested variables entered.
b. Dependent Variable: depression

Model Summary

Model	R	R Square	Adjusted R Square	Std. Error of the Estimate	Change Statistics				
					R Square Change	F Change	df1	df2	Sig. F Change
1	.625[a]	.391	.330	4.325	.391	6.408	1	10	.030

a. Predictors: (Constant), anxiety

ANOVA[b]

Model		Sum of Squares	df	Mean Square	F	Sig.
1	Regression	119.862	1	119.862	6.408	.030[a]
	Residual	187.055	10	18.705		
	Total	306.917	11			

a. Predictors: (Constant), anxiety
b. Dependent Variable: depression

| | Coefficients[a] | | | | |
| | Unstandardized Coefficients | | Standardized Coefficients | | |
Model	B	Std. Error	Beta	t	Sig.
1 (Constant)	26.936	8.252		3.264	.009
anxiety	.406	.160	.625	2.531	.030

a. Dependent Variable: depression

Note that the first two tables show results obtained in the analysis of the data for Chapter 11. With slight differences due to rounding differences, the results should be like those you obtained when you solved Problem 2 earlier. Since depression is labeled as the dependent (criterion) variable in the third table, anxiety must be the predictor (independent) variable, even though it is not specifically labeled. The fourth table, labeled Model Summary, includes both R and R^2, the latter being the proportionate reduction in error calculated earlier. Ignore the last columns of this table and the ANOVA table, except to note that the Sum of Squares for Regression is equal to SS_{Error}, the Sum of Squares Total is equal SS_{Total}, and the Residual Sum of Squares is the difference between SS_{Total} and S_{Error}. The final table, labeled Coefficients, includes the components of the linear prediction rule you calculated earlier, the standardized regression coefficient, and t tests indicating whether the regression constant and the regression coefficient are significantly different from zero. In the case of the regression coefficient, the significance level of .030 indicates that anxiety is a significant predictor of depression.

Application 2: Determining the Bivariate Linear Prediction Rule for Problem 3
Open SPSS.
Analyze the data for Problem 3. Remember that SPSS assumes that all the scores in a row are from the same participant. In this study, there are 12 participants, each having both a depression score and a number of days of work missed. When you have entered the data for all 12 clients, move to the Variable View window, change the first variable name to "depression" and the second to "daysabsent" and set the number of decimals for both variables to zero if you wish.

🖱 Analyze
🖱 Regression and 🖱 Linear
🖱 the variable "daysabsent" 🖱 the arrow next to the box labeled "Dependent" to indicate that the number of days absent from work is the criterion variable, which is also called the dependent variable in prediction studies
🖱 the variable "depression" and 🖱 the arrow next to the box labeled "Independent" to indicate that depression is the predictor variable, which is also called the independent variable in prediction studies
The Linear Regression window should look like Figure 2.

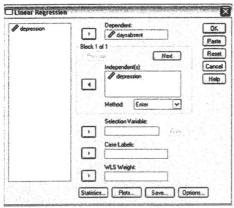

Figure 2
🖱 Statistics and 🖱 Descriptives to obtain the means and standard deviations of the two variables and the correlation coefficient
🖱 OK

The six tables provided by SPSS follow. (Again, requesting descriptive statistics adds two tables to the four tables provided by the regression procedure.)

Descriptive Statistics

	Mean	Std. Deviation	N
daysabsent	16.83	4.324	12
depression	47.58	5.282	12

Correlations

		daysabsent	depression
Pearson Correlation	daysabsent	1.000	.614
	depression	.614	1.000
Sig. (1-tailed)	daysabsent	.	.017
	depression	.017	.
N	daysabsent	12	12
	depression	12	12

Model Summary

Model	R	R Square	Adjusted R Square	Std. Error of the Estimate
1	.614[a]	.377	.314	3.581

a. Predictors: (Constant), depression

ANOVA[b]

Model		Sum of Squares	df	Mean Square	F	Sig.
1	Regression	77.439	1	77.439	6.039	.034[a]
	Residual	128.228	10	12.823		
	Total	205.667	11			

a. Predictors: (Constant), depression
b. Dependent Variable: daysabsent

Coefficients[a]

Model		Unstandardized Coefficients		Standardized Coefficients	t	Sig.
		B	Std. Error	Beta		
1	(Constant)	-7.068	9.781		-.723	.486
	depression	.502	.204	.614	2.457	.034

a. Dependent Variable: daysabsent

The output differs from the output obtained in **Application 1** only because of the different variables, and with slight differences due to rounding, the results should be like those you obtained when you solved Problem 3 earlier.

Chapter 13
Chi-Square Tests

Learning Objectives
After studying this chapter, you should:
- Know how to conduct a chi-square test for goodness of fit and interpret the results.
- Know how to conduct a chi-square test for independence and interpret the results.
- Be able to define the assumptions underlying the chi-square tests.
- Know how to calculate the effect size for chi-square tests for independence.
- Be able to use tables to estimate power for chi-square tests for independence.
- Be able to use tables to estimate sample sizes for chi-square tests for independence.
- Be able to interpret the results of chi-square tests for independence as reported in research articles.

Types of Chi-square Tests
Chi-square tests are appropriate when analyzing nominal variables, i.e., variables in which the values represent categories. The purpose of the chi-square tests is to determine whether the observed frequencies of people falling into particular categories are significantly different from the numbers of people who would be expected to fall into these categories based on the null hypothesis or on some theoretical basis. A **chi-square test for goodness of fit** is conducted when the observed frequencies of a single nominal variable are being compared to a known or theoretical distribution. A **chi-square test for independence** is conducted when the observed frequencies of two (or more) nominal variables, each with two or more categories, are being compared to the frequencies that would be expected based on chance.

The Logic of Chi-square Tests
In chi-square tests, the **observed frequency** is the number of people actually in a particular category, while the **expected frequency** is the number of people expected in a category if the null hypothesis is true. Thus, hypothesis testing using chi-square tests involves determining whether the differences between the observed frequencies and the expected frequencies are greater than would be expected by chance. The formula for the **chi-square statistic** (χ^2) will make the logic of the tests clear.

$\chi^2 = \Sigma \left[(O - E)^2 / E \right]$ where
O represents the observed frequency in a category,
E represents the expected frequency in a category, and
Σ indicates the results of the operations in the brackets should be summed across all categories.

An Example
As an example of the chi-square test for goodness of fit, a group of psychologists conducting group therapy sessions for people suffering from posttraumatic stress disorders is interested in the effects of the disorder on sleep patterns. A review of the research on the topic indicates that the psychologists can expect 45% of the participants in their therapy sessions to experience insomnia, 15% to experience hypersomnia (excessive sleepiness), 10% to experience parasomnias (e.g., nightmares), and 30% to experience no sleep disorders. If the psychologists have 60 people attending therapy sessions, the expected frequencies would be 9 people experiencing hypersomnia, 27 experiencing insomnia, 6 experiencing a parasomnia, and 18 experiencing no sleep disorder. When surveyed, 6 people reported experiencing hypersomnia, 26 reported experiencing insomnia, 14 reported experiencing a parasomnia, and 14 reported experiencing no sleep disorder. The steps of hypothesis testing for conducting the chi-square test for goodness of fit would be as follows.

The next step is to determine if differences in the numbers sleep disorders reported by participants in the psychologists' therapy sessions are significantly different from the numbers that would be expected based on previous research, i.e., are the observed differences larger than the differences that would be expected if the differences are due to chance? As has been the case with other tests, a distribution called the **chi-square distribution** reflects the distribution of the chi-square statistic when the statistic is due to chance. The shape of a particular chi-square distribution depends on the number of degrees of freedom, which is one less than the number of categories. Thus, the formula for determining the number of degrees of freedom for a chi-square test of goodness of fit is $df = N_{Categories} - 1$. Remember that all chi-square distributions are skewed to the right because the chi-square statistic cannot be less than zero, but it can be very large. Once the chi-square statistic has been calculated and the number of degrees of freedom has been determined, a cutoff sample score on the comparison distribution can be determined by consulting a **chi-square table**, and the cutoff score can be used to make a decision about the null hypothesis.

Steps of Hypothesis Testing

Step 1: Restate the question as a research hypothesis and a null hypothesis about the populations.
Population 1: People experiencing posttraumatic stress disorder like those participating in group therapy.
Population 2: People experiencing posttraumatic stress disorder who are experiencing sleep disorders in proportion to the percentages of disorders reported in previous research.

Research hypothesis: The distributions of people over categories of sleep disorders in the two populations are different.
Null hypothesis: The distributions of people over categories of sleep disorders in the two populations are no different.

Step 2: Determine the characteristics of the comparison distribution.
Since the psychologists are interested in three types of sleep disorders and have includes a category of people who are not experiencing any disorder, the analysis includes four categories. Applying the formula $df = N_{categories} - 1$, the comparison distribution is a chi-square distribution with 3 degrees of freedom.

Step 3: Determine the cutoff sample score on the comparison distribution at which the null hypothesis should be rejected.
At the .05 level of significance, the cutoff sample chi-square with 3 degrees of freedom is 7.815.

Step 4: Determine the sample's score on the comparison distribution.
Applying the formula for chi-square yields
$$\chi^2 = \Sigma [(O - E)^2 / E]$$
$$= \Sigma [(6 - 9)^2 / 9] + [(26 - 27)^2 / 27] + [(14 - 6)^2 / 6] + [(14 - 18)^2 / 18]$$
$$= \Sigma [(-3)^2 / 9] + [(-1)^2 / 27] + [(8)^2 / 6] + [(-4)^2 / 18]$$
$$= \Sigma [(9 / 9) + (1 / 27) + (64 / 6) + (16 / 18)]$$
$$= \Sigma [1.00 + 0.04 + 10.67 + 0.22]$$
$$= 11.93$$

Step 5: Decide whether to reject the null hypothesis.
The chi-square statistic for the sample of 11.93 is more extreme than the cutoff sample chi-square of 7.815. Therefore, the psychologists will reject the null hypothesis, accept the research hypothesis, and conclude that the types of sleep disorders experienced by participants in their therapy sessions are different from those experienced by participants in previous studies.

Chi-square Tests for Independence
The most common use of chi-square involves two nominal variables, each having two or more categories. For example, suppose the psychologists expanded their study of sleep disorders by adding 20 participants and analyzed the types of disorders experienced based on whether a participant acquired posttraumatic stress disorder through exposure to combat or to a natural disaster. In this situation, a chi-square test for independence will be the appropriate analysis.

The table that follows is called a **contingency table**. These tables are used to show the distributions of two (or more) nominal variables and include the frequencies of the combinations of the variables in addition to the total frequencies. This table is a 2 x 4 contingency table.

Traumatic Event	Sleep Disorder Hypersomnia	Insomnia	Parasomnias	None	Total
Combat	4	11	17	8	40
Disaster	8	20	8	4	40
Total	12	31	25	12	80

The question to be answered by this analysis is whether there is any relation between the traumatic event that precipitated posttraumatic stress disorder and the type of sleep disorder experienced. If no relation is present, the proportion of people experiencing each type of sleep disorder will be the same, regardless of which type of traumatic event precipitated the posttraumatic stress disorder. The reverse statement, that sleep disorders experienced by people who experienced combat or a disaster will be the same, is also true. **Independence** is the term used to describe the situation in which there is no relation between the two variables.

In order to conduct a chi-square test for independence, the differences between the observed and expected frequencies for each combination of categories must be calculated. Each combination is reflected in one **cell** of the contingency table. Each expected frequency is based on the premise that the two variables are independent, i.e., that there is no relation between the variables. In the example, 50% of the people experienced combat and 50% experienced a disaster. Therefore, this same 50-50% division should be true for each of the four sleep disorders. To determine the expected frequency for any cell, compute each row's percentage of the total number of participants. Next, for each cell, multiply its row percentage by the total number of participants in its column. As a formula, $E = (R / N) (C)$ where
E = the expected frequency for a particular cell,
R = the number of participants in the row containing the cell,
N = the total number of participants in the analysis, and
C = the number of participants in the column containing the cell. [This formula is especially useful when the row percentages are not equal.]
The expected frequencies for the example analysis are shown in parentheses.

Traumatic Event	Sleep Disorder Hypersomnia	Insomnia	Parasomnias	None	Total
Combat	4 (6.0)	11 (15.5)	17 (12.5)	8 (6.0)	40 (50%)
Disaster	8 (6.0)	20 (15.5)	8 (12.5)	4 (6.0)	40 (50%)
Total	12	31	25	12	80

The chi-square statistic is then calculated as before. However, the number of degrees of freedom is equal to the number of rows minus 1 multiplied by the number of columns minus 1. As a formula,
$df = (N_{Rows} - 1) (N_{Columns} - 1)$.

The steps of hypothesis testing for conducting the chi-square test for independence would be as follows.

Steps of Hypothesis Testing
Step 1: Restate the question as a research hypothesis and a null hypothesis about the populations.
Population 1: People experiencing posttraumatic stress disorder like those participating in group therapy.
Population 2: People experiencing posttraumatic stress disorder for whom having experienced combat or a disaster is independent of the type of sleep disorder they are experiencing.

Research hypothesis: The types of sleep disorders reported by people who experienced combat are different from the disorders reported by people who experienced disasters.
Null hypothesis: The types of sleep disorders reported by people who experienced combat are the same as the disorders reported by people who experienced disasters.

Step 2: Determine the characteristics of the comparison distribution.

Since the psychologists have identified two groups of participants based on experiencing combat or a disaster and three types of sleep disorders and have includes a category of people who are not experiencing any disorder, the comparison distribution is a chi-square distribution with 3 degrees of freedom; $df = (N_{Rows} - 1)(N_{Columns} - 1) = (2 - 1)(4 - 1) = (1)(3) = 3$.

Step 3: Determine the cutoff sample score on the comparison distribution at which the null hypothesis should be rejected.

At the .05 level of significance, the cutoff sample chi-square with 3 degrees of freedom is 7.815.

Step 4: Determine the sample's score on the comparison distribution.

Applying the formula for chi-square yields

$\chi^2 = \Sigma [(O - E)^2 / E]$

$= \Sigma [(4 - 6)^2 / 6] + [(11 - 15.5)^2 / 15.5] + [(17 - 12.5)^2 / 12.5] + [(8 - 6)^2 / 6] + [(8 - 6)^2 / 6] + [(20 - 15.5)^2 / 15.5] + [(8 - 12.5)^2 / 12.5] + [(4 - 6)^2 / 6]$

$= \Sigma [(-2)^2 / 6] + [(-4.5)^2 / 15.5] + [(4.5)^2 / 12.5] + [(2)^2 / 6] + [(2)^2 / 6] + [(4.5)^2 / 15.5] + [(-4.5)^2 / 12.5] + [(-2)^2 / 6]$

$= \Sigma [(4 / 6) + (20.25 / 15.5) + (20.25 / 12.5) + (4 / 6) + (4 / 6) + (20.25 / 15.5) + (20.25 / 12.5) + (4 / 6)]$

$= \Sigma [0.67 + 1.31 + 1.62 + 0.67 + 0.67 + 1.31 + 1.62 + 0.67]$

$= 8.54$

Step 5: Decide whether to reject the null hypothesis.

The chi-square statistic for the sample of 8.54 is more extreme than the cutoff sample chi-square of 7.815. Therefore, the psychologists will reject the null hypothesis, accept the research hypothesis, and conclude that the types of sleep disorders experienced by participants whose posttraumatic stress disorder was precipitated by combat are different from the sleep disorders experienced by participants whose posttraumatic stress disorder was precipitated by a disaster.

Assumptions for Chi-square Tests

Chi-square tests are not restricted by the assumptions that variables be normally distributed in populations or that they have equal variances when comparisons are to be made. However, no score can be related to any other score, i.e., scores must be independent of all other cases. For example, chi-square would be inappropriate for comparing the proportions of sleep disorders experienced by the 80 people before and after some number of therapy sessions.

Effect Size and Power for Chi-Square Tests for Independence

When chi-square is calculated from a 2 X 2 contingency table, the measure of association is the **phi coefficient (Φ)**. The formula is

$\Phi = \sqrt{\chi^2 / N}$. Phi can have values from 0 to 1 and be interpreted like correlation coefficient. Cohen's conventions for Φ are the same as those for r,

- .10 indicates a small effect,
- .30 indicates a medium effect, and
- .50 indicates a large effect.

Suppose the psychologists identified 40 people experiencing posttraumatic stress disorder and obtained the data in the following table about the number who reported sleep disorders and who did not report a sleep disorder. Again, the expected frequencies are included in parentheses.

Traumatic Event	Sleep Disorder Yes	No	Total
Combat	14 (10.0)	6 (10.0)	20 (50%)
Disaster	6 (10.0)	14 (10.0)	20 (50%)
Total	20	20	40

$$\chi^2 = \Sigma \left[(O - E)^2 / E\right]$$
$$= \Sigma \left[(14 - 10)^2 / 10\right] + \left[(6 - 10)^2 / 10\right] + \left[(6 - 10)^2 / 10\right] + \left[(14 - 10)^2 / 10\right]$$
$$= \Sigma \left[(4)^2 / 10\right] + \left[(4)^2 / 10\right] + \left[(4)^2 / 10\right] + \left[(4)^2 / 10\right]$$
$$= \Sigma \left[(16 / 10) + (16 / 10) + (16 / 10) + (16 / 10)\right]$$
$$= \Sigma \left[1.60 + 1.60 + 1.60 + 1.60\right]$$
$$= 6.40$$

$\Phi = \sqrt{\chi^2 / N} = \sqrt{6.40 / 40} = \sqrt{0.16} = 0.40$, which is a medium to large effect size.

The extension of phi to larger contingency tables is **Cramer's Φ**. The only difference from phi is that the denominator involves multiplying N by the number of degrees of freedom for the variable with fewer categories. In the case of the analysis of the 2 x 4 table described earlier, $\chi^2 = 8.54$ and the traumatic event category had only $1 df$ (2 − 1). Therefore, Cramer's $\Phi = \sqrt{\chi^2 / [(N) * (df_{Smaller})]} = \sqrt{8.54 / [(80) * (1)]} = \sqrt{8.54 / 80} = \sqrt{.11} = .33$, which is a medium effect size. Remember that Cohen's effect size conventions for Cramer's Φ depend on the number of degrees of freedom for the variable with the fewest categories. When one variable has two categories, the effect size conventions are the same as the conventions for phi. When the smallest number of categories is 3 or more, a table like Table 13-8 in the text should be used.

Power and Sample Size for Chi-Square Tests for Independence
The power for a chi-square test for independence can be determined by referring to tables like Table 13.9 in the text. For example, with a medium effect size, 100 participants would be needed to obtain 85% power if the analysis involved a 2 x 2 contingency table at the .05 level of significance. If only 50 participants had been included in the study in which the association between the two types of traumatic events and the four types of sleep disorders was determined, the power would have would have been 40% to detect a medium effect size at the .05 level of significance. The power would have increased to 71% if 100 participants had been included.

Table 13.10 in the text can be used to determine the approximate number of subjects needed to achieve 80% power for small, medium, and large estimated effect sizes at the .05 level of significance. For example, if the psychologists had anticipated a medium effect size between the type of traumatic event and the presence or absence of a sleep disorder, they would have needed to plan to obtain responses from 107 participants to achieve 80% power. If the psychologists had anticipated a medium effect size when determining the association between the two types of traumatic events and the four types of sleep disorders, they would have needed to plan to obtain responses from 121 participants to obtain 80% power.

Chi-Square Tests in Research Articles
Experimenters generally report the observed frequencies for each category or cell, the degrees of freedom, the total number of participants, the chi-square statistic, and the level of significance. For example, the results of the chi-square test for goodness of fit between the proportions of people experiencing posttraumatic stress disorder in the psychologists' group therapy sessions and the proportions reported in previous research might be reported as $\chi^2 (3, N = 60) = 11.93, p < .05$. A report of the 2 x 4 chi-square test for independence described would begin with a description of the categories followed by the results of the chi-square test, e.g., $\chi^2 (3, N = 80) = 8.54, p < .05$. Reports may or may not include an estimate of effect size because these estimates can be calculated from the information given.

Chapter Self–Tests

The test items that follow are based on the following scenario. A group of psychologists conducting sessions for students to help them learn to deal with conflicts more effectively has administered an inventory that will indicate whether a student deals with conflict primarily by responding aggressively, manipulatively, passively, or assertively.

Understanding Key Terms in Chapter 13

Directions: Using the word bank that follows, complete each statement.

Word Bank: cell / chi-square distribution / chi-square statistic / chi-square table / chi-square test for goodness of fit / chi-square test for independence / chi-square tests / contingency table / Cramer's phi / expected frequency / independence / observed frequency / phi coefficient

If the psychologists are interested in determining whether the distribution of students across the four ways of dealing conflict agrees with the distribution the psychologists expect, the psychologists will conduct a (1) _____. If the psychologists are also interested in determining whether students who have been suspended from school use different methods of conflict resolution than students who have not been suspended, they will conduct a (2) _____. The general name for tests used when one or more variables are nominal is the (3) _____. When conducting these tests, the psychologists will first determine the number of students who use each of the four methods of dealing with conflict. This number is the (4) _____, and it will be compared to the number of students that would be expected to use each method of the null hypothesis is true. This latter number is the (5) _____. When the difference between these two types of numbers is weighted and summed across all the categories in a particular analysis, the result is a (6) _____. In order to determine whether their result could have occurred by chance, the psychologists will use a (7) _____. To identify the appropriate cutoff sample score, the psychologists will refer to a (8) _____.

In order to be sure that the numbers of students in any category, or combination of categories, as well as the total numbers of students across categories is clear, the psychologists will organize their data in a (9) _____. If the psychologists find that 10 of 40 students primarily respond to conflict aggressively, 10 manipulatively, 15 passively, and 5 assertively, each number will be shown in a (10) _____. If the psychologists conduct a test to see if there is any relationship between being suspended from school and method of conflict resolution, they will be conducting a test of (11) _____ between the two variables. If the psychologists have conducted an analysis to see of there is an association between being suspended from school and responding either assertively or passively to a particular type of conflict, they can estimate their effect size using the (12) _____. If the psychologists have conducted an analysis to see of there is an association between being suspended from school and all four ways of responding to a particular type of conflict, they can estimate their effect size using (13) _____.

Multiple Choice Items

1. Which pair of variables would the psychologists analyze using a chi-square test?
    A. Anxiety and self-esteem scores
    B. GPA and class rank
    C. Conflict resolution style and self-esteem
    D. Being suspended from school and conflict resolution style

2. In which of the following situations would the psychologists conduct a chi-square test for goodness of fit?
    A. If they want to determine whether there is an association between method of conflict resolution and having been suspended from school
    B. If they want to determine whether the same proportions of students use each method of conflict resolution
    C. If they want to determine whether of method of conflict resolution and academic success are independent
    D. If they have used Cramer's Φ to estimate the effect size of there chi-square test

3. If the psychologists find that there is no association between method of conflict resolution and academic success,
   A. the variables are said to be independent.
   B. the analysis will yield a chi-square statistic much larger than 1.00.
   C. the analysis will have a large effect size.
   D. the variables will be contingent on each other.

4. Chi-square distributions are
   A. rectangular.
   B. symmetrical.
   C. skewed to the left.
   D. skewed to the right.

5. Values of the chi-square statistic
   A. can be negative.
   B. are normally distributed.
   C. can be very large.
   D. are unweighted.

Items 6–12 are based on the following scenario and table.

The psychologists having surveyed a group of 20 students referred for causing behavior problems and obtained the following results.

Suspension from School	Conflict Resolution Assertive	Other	Total
Yes	1 (3.5)	9 (6.5)	10 (50%)
No	6 (3.5)	4 (6.5)	10 (50%)
Total	7	13	20

6. This type of table is called a
   A. frequency table.
   B. grouped frequency table.
   C. chi-square table.
   D. contingency table.

7. The square in the table indicating that one student who used assertive methods of conflict resolution had been suspended from school is an example of
   A. a cell.
   B. a contingency.
   C. an observed frequency.
   D. an expected frequency.

8. In the square in the table indicating that nine students who used other methods of conflict resolution had been suspended for school, 9 is the
   A. cell mean.
   B. expected frequency.
   C. observed frequency.
   D. partial chi-square.

9. In the same square, 6.5 is the
   A. cell mean.
   B. expected frequency.
   C. observed frequency.
   D. partial chi-square.

10. The value of 6.5 was obtained using
    A. $(R / C)(N)$.
    B. $(N / R)(C)$.
    C. $(R / C)(R)$.
    D. $(R / N)(C)$.

11. The effect size for this table should be estimated by calculating
    A. X.
    B. B.
    C. Φ.
    D. η.

12. If the category labeled "Other" is expanded to show the three methods of conflict resolution it includes, the effect size should be estimated by calculating
    A. Cramer's Φ.
    B. Cramer's X.
    C. Pearson's B.
    D. Pearson's X.

Problems

1. The table that follows includes the primary method of conflict resolution used by 20 students.

Method	Aggressive	Manipulative	Passive	Assertive
N of Students	8	2	2	8

(a) Following the five steps of hypothesis testing, conduct the appropriate chi-square test to determine whether the observed frequencies are significantly different from the frequencies expected by chance at the .05 level of significance. (b) Explain your response to someone who has never had a course in statistics.

2. Next, the psychologists categorized the students based on the primary method of conflict resolution used and whether the student had been suspended from school for misbehavior. These data are presented in the table that follows.

	Method				
Suspended	Aggressive	Manipulative	Passive	Assertive	Total
Yes	7	1	1	1	10
No	1	1	1	7	10
Total	8	2	2	8	20

(a) Following the five steps of hypothesis testing, conduct the appropriate chi-square test to determine whether the observed frequencies are significantly different from the frequencies expected by chance at the .05 level of significance. (b) Calculate the effect size. (c) Explain your response to someone who has never had a course in statistics.

3. Believing that assertiveness is the most effective method of conflict resolution, the psychologists categorized students so that the aggressive, manipulative, and passive categories were combined. These data are presented in the table that follows.

Suspension from School	Conflict Resolution Assertive	Other	Total
Yes	1	9	10
No	6	4	10
Total	7	13	20

(a) Following the five steps of hypothesis testing, conduct the appropriate chi-square test to determine whether the observed frequencies are significantly different from the frequencies expected by chance at the .05 level of significance. (b) Calculate the effect size.

4. A school psychologist interested in the attentiveness of kindergarten children asked teachers to place children in one of three categories: very attentive, normally attentive, and generally inattentive. The teacher ratings are shown in the following table.

Rating	Very Attentive	Normally Attentive	Generally Inattentive
N of Students	16	24	20

Following the five steps of hypothesis testing and using the .05 level of significance, conduct the chi-square test that would enable the psychologist to determine whether more children were placed in any one category than would be expected by chance.

5. The psychologist then divided the students categorized in Problem 4 into groups of older and younger students. (a) Following the five steps of hypothesis testing and using the .05 level of significance, conduct the chi-square test that would enable the psychologist to determine whether age and attentiveness are independent. (b) Calculate the effect size.

Age	Attentiveness Very Attentive	Normally Attentive	Generally Inattentive	Total
Younger	9	14	7	30
Older	7	10	13	30
Total	16	24	20	60

6. What is the effect size for the studies included in the table that follows?

Study	N	Chi-square	Design
(a)	60	12.00	2 x 2
(b)	80	12.00	2 x 4
(c)	60	12.00	3 x 3
(d)	80	12.00	2 x 2
(e)	120	12.00	2 x 2

7. What is the power of the planned studies listed in the table that follows at the .05 level of significance?

Study	Predicted Effect Size	Design	N
(a)	Medium	2 x 2	50
(b)	Large	2 x 4	50
(c)	Small	3 x 3	100
(d)	Medium	2 x 2	100
(e)	Large	2 x 2	200

8. Approximately how many participants would be needed for each of the studies in the table that follows to have 80% power at the .05 level of significance?

Study	Predicted Effect Size	Design
(a)	Medium	2 x 3
(b)	Large	2 x 4
(c)	Small	3 x 3
(d)	Large	2 x 5
(e)	Large	3 x 3

Additional Practice: Complete any Practice Problems in Set I that your instructor has not assigned and compare your responses to those provided by the authors. Pay particular attention to the problems that require you to explain your results to someone who has never taken a course in statistics.

SPSS Applications

Application 1: Chi-square Test for Goodness of Fit
Open SPSS.
The data for Problem 1 are shown in Figure 1. Remember that SPSS assumes that all the scores in a row are from the same participant. In this study, there are 20 students, some of whom have been suspended for misbehavior. The primary conflict resolution style used by each student is also entered. (Ignore the first variable in this analysis.) When you have entered the data for all 20 students, move to the Variable View window, change the first variable name to "suspend" and the second to "res_style," and set the number of decimals for both variables to zero if you wish.

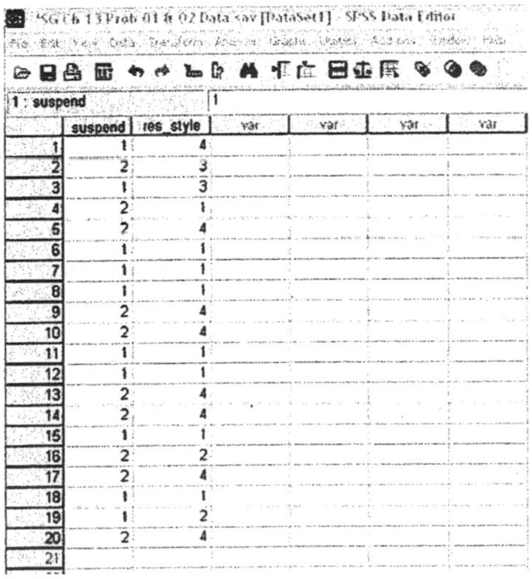

Figure 1
🖰 Analyze

$\sqrt[]{\theta}$ Non-Parametric Tests and $\sqrt[]{\theta}$ Chi-Square
$\sqrt[]{\theta}$ the variable "res_style" $\sqrt[]{\theta}$ the arrow next to the box labeled "Test Variable List" to indicate that the chi-square test for goodness of fit should be conducted on the conflict resolution style variable
The Chi-Square Test window should look like Figure 2.

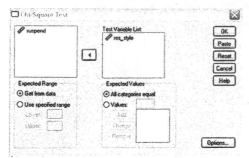

Figure 2
Note that "All categories equal" is the default selection in the "Expected Values" box, which means that SPSS will conduct the goodness of fit test using equal expected frequencies for each of the four styles, i.e., SPSS will assume that the proportions of students using each style are equal.
$\sqrt[]{\theta}$ OK

The two tables provided by SPSS follow.

res_style

	Observed N	Expected N	Residual
Aggressive	8	5.0	3.0
Manipulative	2	5.0	-3.0
Passive	2	5.0	-3.0
Assertive	8	5.0	3.0
Total	20		

Test Statistics

	res_style
Chi-Square[a]	7.200
df	3
Asymp. Sig.	.066

a. 0 cells (.0%) have expected frequencies less than 5. The minimum expected cell frequency is 5.0.

The first table includes the observed frequencies, the expected frequencies, and the column labeled "Residual," the difference between the observed and expected frequencies. The second table includes the chi-square statistic, the number of degrees of freedom and the exact significance level. The exact significance level of .066 is greater than .05, confirming the decision you made using the steps of hypothesis testing for Problem 1 that the null hypothesis that the conflict resolution styles are used equally by students cannot be rejected.

Application 2: Chi-square Test for Independence
Open SPSS.
Now you can use SPSS to analyze the data for Problem 2, adding the variable "suspend" to the analysis. Remember that in this problem, we were interested in whether there was an association between conflict resolution style and having been suspended from school for misbehavior. Since the analysis will involve two nominal variables, the appropriate test is a chi-square test for independence.

$\sqrt[]{\theta}$ Analyze
$\sqrt[]{\theta}$ Descriptive Statistics and $\sqrt[]{\theta}$ Crosstabs
$\sqrt[]{\theta}$ the variable "suspend" $\sqrt[]{\theta}$ the arrow next to the box labeled "Rows"
$\sqrt[]{\theta}$ the variable "res_style" $\sqrt[]{\theta}$ the arrow next to the box labeled "Columns"
$\sqrt[]{\theta}$ Statistics $\sqrt[]{\theta}$ the box labeled Chi-square
$\sqrt[]{\theta}$ Cells $\sqrt[]{\theta}$ the box labeled Expected

The Crosstabs window should look like Figure 3, the Crosstabs: Statistics window should look like Figure 4, and the Crosstabs: Cell Display window should look Figure 5.

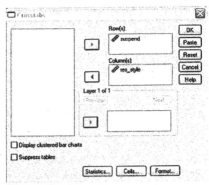

Figure 3
🖱 Continue

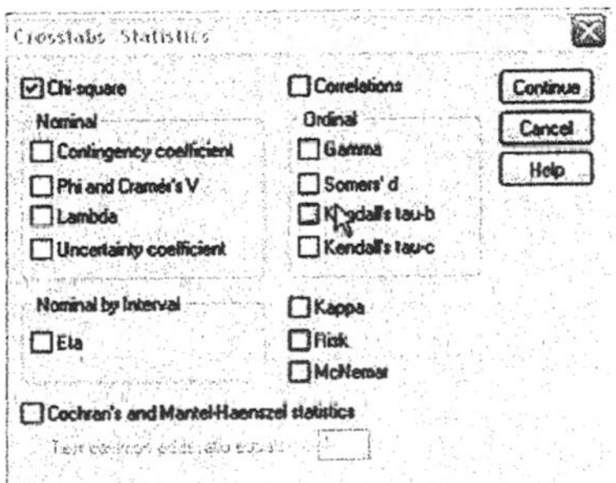

Figure 4
🖱 Continue

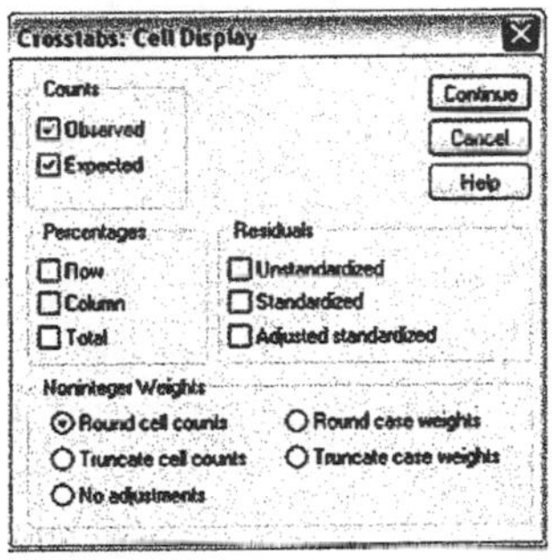

Figure 5
🖱 OK

The three tables provided by SPSS follow.

Case Processing Summary

	Cases					
	Valid		Missing		Total	
	N	Percent	N	Percent	N	Percent
suspend * res_style	20	100.0%	0	.0%	20	100.0%

suspend * res_style Crosstabulation

			res_style				
			Aggressive	Manipulative	Passive	Assertive	Total
suspend	Yes	Count	7	1	1	1	10
		Expected Count	4.0	1.0	1.0	4.0	10.0
	No	Count	1	1	1	7	10
		Expected Count	4.0	1.0	1.0	4.0	10.0
Total		Count	8	2	2	8	20
		Expected Count	8.0	2.0	2.0	8.0	20.0

Chi-Square Tests

	Value	df	Asymp. Sig. (2-sided)
Pearson Chi-Square	9.000a	3	.029
Likelihood Ratio	10.124	3	.018
Linear-by-Linear Association	8.319	1	.004
N of Valid Cases	20		

a. 8 cells (100.0%) have expected count less than 5. The minimum expected count is 1.00.

The first table indicates how many students have data for each of the two variables, and would indicate if any students were missing data for any variable. The second table is the contingency table for the two variables. Requesting "Expected" in the Crosstabs: Cell Display window caused SPSS to print both the observed and expected frequencies. The first line in the third table presents the same Pearson chi-square you calculated when you solved Problem 2, and the exact significance level of .029 confirms the decision to reject the null hypothesis and accept the research hypothesis that there is an association between primary conflict resolution style and suspension from school for misbehavior.

166

Chapter 14
Strategies When Population Distributions Are Not Normal: Data Transformations, Rank-Order Tests, and Computer-Intensive Methods

Learning Objectives
After studying this chapter, you should:
- Know when data transformations are appropriate.
- Know how to use the square-root and rank-order transformations.
- Know how rank-order tests are conducted.
- Be able to interpret the results of data transformations and rank-order tests as reported in research articles.

Assumptions in the Standard Hypothesis-Testing Procedures
As has been indicated, many standard hypothesis-testing procedures (e.g., t tests, analysis of variance, and the significance tests for correlation and regression) require that variables in populations
- Be normally distributed and
- Have equal variances.

The results of these tests are still reasonably accurate when violations of these assumptions are not serious. However, when distributions are clearly not normal or variances are clearly unequal, errors in interpreting the results of these tests are likely. Such situations may arise when a sample distribution has a floor or ceiling effect, or when one or more outliers are present.

Data Transformations
When characteristics of sample scores indicate that the population from which the sample was drawn may not be normally distributed, a **data transformation**, such as taking the square root of each score, may be performed to make the characteristics of the sample distribution more like those of a normal distribution. The advantage of these transformations is that they permit the use of familiar statistical tests. Transformations are justified when they are applied to all scores in a dataset because the order of the scores does not change.

Commonly used data transformations include:
- The **square-root transformation**, which is used to reduce the skew of a distribution that is skewed to the right, i.e., a distribution that is positively skewed.
- The *log transformation*, taking the logarithm of each score, which is also used to reduce the skew of a distribution that is skewed to the right, but its effect is stronger than the square-root transformation.
- The *inverse transformation*, dividing each score into 1, which provides a more powerful correction for distributions that are skewed to the right than a log transformation.

Datasets that are skewed to the right are the most commonly encountered deviations from the normal curve. However, when a dataset is skewed to the left, the scores may be *reflected*, i.e., subtracted from a larger number so that their order is reversed. After performing this transformation, the transformations mentioned previously will make the appropriate adjustment.

Rank-Order Methods
A **rank-order transformation** provides another way to deal with the potential problems caused by nonnormal distributions. Using this transformation involves changing the scores in a dataset to ranks, which yields a rectangular distribution instead of a normal distribution. Scores from any distribution can be transformed into ranks and analyzed using statistical methods called **rank-order tests**, also called **distribution-free tests**. Such tests are also called **nonparametric tests** because they do not require estimation of population values like the variance. Tests that do require estimation of population values; e.g., the t tests, analysis of variance, and the significance tests used with correlation and regression analyses, are called **parametric tests**. (Rank-order tests that correspond to the parametric tests presented in the text are presented in Table 14-4 in the text).

The basic logic of rank-order tests involves ranking all scores from lowest to highest, regardless of the group in which a score is found, adding the ranks in the group with the lower scores, and comparing the sum with a cutoff sample score from a table appropriate for the statistical test being used. The null hypothesis of a rank-order test is that the medians of the experimental populations are equal. Parametric tests like t tests or analyses of variance on ranked data may yield results similar to those of the rank-order tests, but the results of the parametric tests will not be as accurate as the ordinary parametric test or the rank-order test.

The advantage of data transformations is that they permit use of familiar parametric tests. However, not all datasets can be adequately modified by transformation. On the other hand, while rank-order methods can be applied to any dataset,

- Rank-order methods may not be familiar,
- Rank-order methods for complex analyses are not available,
- The logic of rank-order methods does not hold when large numbers of scores have tied ranks, and
- The original dataset is distorted, which results in loss of information.

With respect to Type I and Type II errors, parametric tests are as good as, or better than, any of the alternatives when the assumptions of the test are met. When the assumptions of parametric tests are not met, the comparative advantages of data transformations and rank-order tests are not clear.

Computer-Intensive Methods

The speed with which computers can do computations has led to the development of **computer-intensive methods**, of which **randomization tests** and *bootstrap tests* are the primary techniques. These techniques involve randomly assigning participants in a study to groups, regardless of the participant's original group, and comparing the differences observed in the experimental variables with the differences between the actual experimental groups. This process is repeated until all possible groupings have been compared or, in the *approximate randomization tests*, until a very large number of groupings, say 1,000, have been compared. While these methods are flexible and do not require that either the normality or equal variance assumptions be met, they are so new that the computational details are still under investigation, and they are not available in many statistical software packages.

Data Transformations and Rank-Order Tests in Research Articles

Data transformations are typically described just before the description of the statistical analysis in the Results section. Rank-order tests are described in the same way as the parametric tests presented earlier.

Chapter Self–Tests

The test items that follow are based on the following scenario. The psychologists studying depression have observed that some of their clients make very high scores on the inventory used to measure depression compared to the majority of their clients. Therefore, the psychologists are considering alternative methods for analyzing their data.

Understanding Key Terms in Chapter 14

Directions: Using the word bank that follows, complete each statement.

Word Bank: computer-intensive methods / data transformation / distribution-free tests / nonparametric tests / parametric tests / randomization tests / rank-order tests / rank-order transformation / square-root transformation

The previous analyses using the *t* tests, analysis of variance, and the significance tests for correlation and prediction studies all assumed that the variables being compared were normally distributed in the population and had equal variances. Therefore, these tests are called **(1)** _____. Since the outlying scores observed by the psychologists are high scores, the distributions of scores are skewed to the right. Due to the nature of their data, the psychologists decide to adjust the scores so that the distributions appear more like the normal distribution by making a **(2)** _____. With a dataset that is skewed to the right, an adjustment that often works well is a **(3)** _____. If the psychologists arrange the scores in order from lowest to highest, they will be making a **(4)** _____. One advantage of this adjustment is that the psychologists could use the familiar statistical tests used earlier. Alternatively, the adjustment would permit the use of different tests called **(5)** _____. Since the transformation results in a rectangular distribution, the psychologists do not need to estimate values like the population variance. Therefore, these tests are also called **(6)** _____. Since the shape of the score distribution does affect the results of the analysis, these tests are also called **(7)** _____. An additional alternative would be for the psychologists to use newer methods called **(8)** _____. These procedures involve combining scores into all possible groupings based on chance, so they are called **(9)** _____.

Multiple Choice Items

Items 1–5 are related.

1. The psychologists have examined a frequency distribution of their data and note that the distribution appears to be slightly skewed to the right. The general term for the adjustment they can make to reduce the skew so that the distribution is more like a normal distribution is called
   - A. an arcsine transformation.
   - B. a data transformation.
   - C. an inverse transformation.
   - D. a square-root transformation.

2. A more specific adjustment they can make to reduce the skew so that the distribution is more like a normal distribution is called
   - A. an arcsine transformation.
   - B. an inverse transformation.
   - C. a log transformation.
   - D. a square-root transformation.

3. If the distribution is more seriously skewed, the psychologists can
   - A. use an arcsine transformation.
   - B. reflect the data.
   - C. use a log transformation.
   - D. transform the outlying scores.

4. If the distribution is skewed to the left, the psychologists can
   - A. use an arcsine transformation.
   - B. reflect the data.
   - C. use a log transformation.
   - D. transform the outlying scores.

Items 5–8 are related.

5. Another alternative available to the psychologists is to arrange the scores in order from the lowest to the highest, in which case, they will be making
   - A. an arcsine transformation.
   - B. a rank-order transformation.
   - C. a log transformation.
   - D. an inverse transformation.

6. The assumptions of the tests the psychologists have used previously are not applicable because the resulting distribution is
   - A. only slightly skewed.
   - B. bimodal.
   - C. normal.
   - D. rectangular.

7. The hypothesis-testing procedures based on this type of adjustment are called
   A. reflective tests.
   B. parametric tests.
   C. nonparametric tests.
   D. error-free tests.

8. Another name for these hypothesis-testing procedures is
   A. parametric tests.
   B. distribution-free tests.
   C. inverse tests.
   D. error-free tests.

9. The hypothesis-testing procedures the psychologists have used previously depend on assumptions about the characteristics of the population distribution and are called
   A. reflective tests.
   B. nonparametric tests.
   C. error-free tests.
   D. parametric tests.

10. An advantage of rank order tests is that they
    A. can be applied regardless of the shape of the original distribution.
    B. are familiar to most readers of research articles in psychology.
    C. are rarely involved in controversies among statisticians.
    D. yield consistently fewer Type I errors than parametric procedures.

11. An important advantage of computer-intensive methods is that
    A. they can be found in most computer statistical packages.
    B. many examples of their use can be found in psychology journals.
    C. the details of their use have been clearly defined and described.
    D. problems caused by failure to meet parametric assumptions are overcome.

Problems

1. The variables used in the hypothetical studies described in previous chapters all could have encountered problems meeting the assumptions of normality and equal variances. Why does each of the following sample distributions suggest that the population distribution may not be normal and why?
(a) Stress scores: 30, 34, 71, 36, 62
(b) Self-esteem scores: 36, 34, 35, 39, 33
(c) Depression scores: 10, 12, 15, 8, 11, 12, 7, 14, 8
(d) Anxiety scores: 36, 58, 39, 41, 38
(e) Attentiveness ratings: 8, 10, 2, 9, 7

2. Calculate a square-root transformation, rounding each square root to one decimal place, on the scores in (a), (d), and (e) in Problem 1and explain the effect of the transformation on the scores.

3. Make a rank order transformation of each of the five datasets in Problem 1.

4. A psychologist divided a group of 12 students into two groups of six students each. One group underwent a training program designed to help them view their surroundings in more creative ways, while the second group heard a lecture about creative thinking. After the sessions, the students in the two groups made the following scores on a creativity test.
Training Group: 16, 14, 15, 17, 16, 24
Lecture Group: 10, 12, 14, 11, 13, 18

(a) What is the most likely reason that a data transformation may clarify analysis of this dataset? (b) Conduct a *t*-test for independent means on the actual creativity scores. (c) Transform the data using a square-root transformation and conduct a *t*-test for independent means on the transformed data. (d) Transform the data using a rank-transformation and conduct a *t*-test for independent means on the transformed data. (e) Compare the results of the three analyses. (f) Explain what you have done to someone who is familiar with the *t*-test for independent means but not with data transformations.

5. The school psychologist interested in attentiveness rated the attentiveness of 10 kindergartners divided into two groups of five children each. One group was observed one hour before recess and the other one hour after recess. The psychologist's ratings follow.
Before recess: 6, 4, 4, 5, 10
After recess: 2, 3, 3, 5, 2
(a) What is the most likely reason that a data transformation may clarify analysis of this dataset? (b) Conduct a *t*-test for independent means on the actual ratings. (c) Transform the data using a square-root transformation and conduct a *t*-test for independent means on the transformed data. (d) Transform the data using a rank-transformation and conduct a *t*-test for independent means on the transformed data. (e) Compare the results of the three analyses. (f) Explain what you have done to someone who is familiar with the *t*-test for independent means but not with data transformations.

6. A psychologist interested in the effects of three methods of treating test anxiety has created three groups of five randomly assigned students each. One group will receive counseling, a second group will be taught to use a relaxation technique, and the third group will be taught to use the relaxation technique in the rooms where they take tests. The test anxiety scores for the three groups at the conclusion of the study follow.
Counseling: 30, 29, 24, 26, 22
Relaxation: 27, 25, 28, 20, 16
Relaxation in setting: 23, 20, 21, 19, 12
(a) What is the most likely reason that a data transformation may clarify analysis of this dataset? (b) Conduct an analysis of variance using the actual scores. (c) Transform the data using a square-root transformation and conduct an analysis of variance on the transformed data. (d) Transform the data using a rank-transformation and conduct an analysis of variance on the transformed data. (e) Compare the results of the three analyses. (f) Explain what you have done to someone who is familiar with analysis of variance but not with data transformations.

Additional Practice: Complete any Practice Problems in Set I that your instructor has not assigned and compare your responses to those provided by the authors. Pay particular attention to the problems that require you to explain your results to someone who has never taken a course in statistics.

SPSS Applications

Application 1: Data Transformations and Rank-Order Tests
Open SPSS.
Analyze the data for Problem 4. Remember that SPSS assumes that all the scores in a row are from the same participant. In this study, there are 12 participants divided into two groups of six students, each having a score on a creativity test. Although the variable labeled "group" is not necessary for the data transformation, it will be used in the application, so enter these data, as well. When you have entered the data for all 12 students, move to the Variable View window, change the first variable name to "group" and the second to "creativity." and set the number of decimals for both variables to zero if you wish. The SPSS data editor window should look Figure 1.

group	creativity
1	16
1	14
1	15
1	17
1	16
1	24
2	10
2	12
2	14
2	11
2	13
2	18

Figure 1

To check the skewness of a distribution,
⤏ Data
⤏ Split File ⤏ the circle to *Organize output by group*
⤏ "group" and move the variable to the *Groups based on* box
⤏ OK

⤏ Data
⤏ Analyze ⤏ Descriptive statistics
In the Descriptives window, ⤏ "creativity" and move the variable to the *Variables* box
⤏ Options ⤏ Skewness ⤏ Continue
⤏ OK
The SPSS output should look like Figure 2.

Group = 0

Descriptive Statistics[a]

	N	Minimum	Maximum	Mean	Std.	Skewness	
	Statistic	Statistic	Statistic	Statistic	Statistic	Statistic	Std. Error
Creativity	6	10	18	13.00	2.828	1.193	.845
Valid N (listwise)	6						

a. Group = 0

Group = 1

Descriptive Statistics[a]

	N	Minimum	Maximum	Mean	Std.	Skewness	
	Statistic	Statistic	Statistic	Statistic	Statistic	Statistic	Std. Error
Creativity	6	14	24	17.00	3.578	2.005	.845
Valid N (listwise)	6						

a. Group = 1

Figure 2
⤏ Graphs ⤏ Legacy Dialogs ⤏ Histogram
⤏ "creativity" move the variable to the *Variables* box
⤏ the box beside *Display normal curve*
⤏ OK
The histograms should look like Figure 3 and Figure 4.

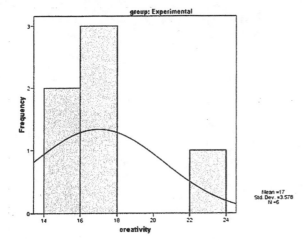

Figure 3

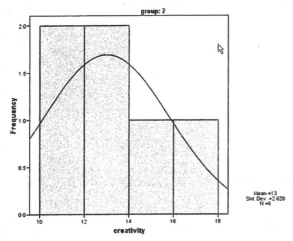

Figure 4

Before continuing, take the following steps to turn the "Split File" function off.
-ᗮ Data
-ᗮ Split File
-ᗮ The circle beside *Analyze all cases, do not create groups*
-ᗮ OK

To analyze the data after performing a square-root tansformation'
-ᗮ Transform
-ᗮ Compute, which will cause a "Compute Variable" window to be displayed
Type the name of the new variable "sqrtcvty" in the "Target Variable" box
Type "sqrt(creativity) in the "Numeric Expression" box to indicate that SPSS will compute the square root of each score and create a new variable called "sqrtcvty"
The compute variable window should look like Figure 5.

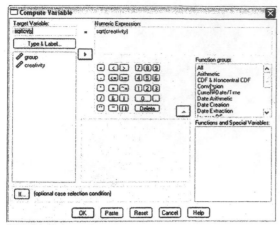

Figure 5

🖱 OK

Now the SPSS data editor window should look Figure 6.

group	creativity	sqrtcvty
1	16	4.00
1	14	3.74
1	15	3.87
1	17	4.12
1	16	4.00
1	24	4.90
2	10	3.16
2	12	3.46
2	14	3.74
2	11	3.32
2	13	3.61
2	18	4.24

Figure 6

The transformed variable can now be used in a *t* test for independent means, and the results should be consistent with those you obtained when you solved Problem 4.

To conduct a rank-order test on the creativity test scores for the two groups of students,

🖱 Analyze

🖱 Nonparametric tests

🖱 2 Independent Samples

🖱 Nonparametric tests

🖱 the variable "creativity" and 🖱 the arrow next to the box labeled "Test Variables" to indicate that the rank-order test should be conducted on the creativity variable.

🖱 the variable "group" and 🖱 the arrow next to the box labeled "Grouping Variable" to indicate the group to which each student belongs.

🖱 "Define Groups" and enter "1" in the box for Group 1 and "2" in the box for Group 2

🖱 Continue

The "Two-Independent-Samples Tests" window should look like Figure 7.

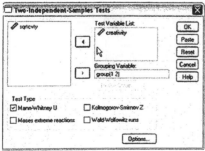

Figure 7

🖱 OK

The SPSS output should look like Figure 8.

Mann-Whitney Test

Ranks

	group	N	Mean Rank	Sum of Ranks
creativity	Experimental	6	8.58	51.50
	2	6	4.42	26.50
	Total	12		

Test Statistics[b]

	creativity
Mann-Whitney U	5.500
Wilcoxon W	26.500
Z	-2.009
Asymp. Sig. (2-tailed)	.045
Exact Sig. [2*(1-tailed Sig.)]	.041[a]

a. Not corrected for ties.

b. Grouping Variable: group

Figure 8

The output indicates that a NPar Test (nonparametric test) was conducted. If you remember, the box for the Mann-Whitney Test was checked in the "Two-Independent-Samples Tests" window. Notice that the Test Statistics box includes results for the Mann-Whitney U test and the Wilcoxon rank-sum test, which give mathematically equivalent results, s well as a value for Z. Note that the mean ranks presented in the Ranks table are the same as those you calculated when you solved Problem 4, and you would make the same decision to reject the null hypothesis that you made on the basis of the t test for independent means you conducted.

Application 2: Data Transformations and Rank-Order Tests
Open SPSS.
Analyze the data for Problem 5. Remember that in this study, there are 10 kindergartners divided into two groups of five, each having an attentiveness rating. When you have entered the data for all 10 kindergarteners, move to the Variable View window, change the first variable name to "group" and the second to "attentive" and set the number of decimals for both variables to zero if you wish. The SPSS data editor window should look Figure 9.

group	attentive
1	6
1	4
1	4
1	5
1	10
2	2
2	3
2	3
2	5
2	2

Figure 9

To check the skewness of a distribution,
🖱 Data
🖱 Split File 🖱 the circle to *Organize output by group*
🖱 "group" and move the variable to the *Groups based on* box
🖱 OK

🖱 Data
🖱 Analyze 🖱 Descriptive statistics 🖱 Descriptive statistics
In the Descriptive Statistics window, 🖱 "attentive" and move the variable to the *Variables* box
🖱 Options 🖱 Skewness 🖱 Continue
🖱 OK
The SPSS output should look like Figure 10.

group = 1

Descriptive Statistics

	N	Minimum	Maximum	Mean	Std.	Skewness	
	Statistic	Statistic	Statistic	Statistic	Statistic	Statistic	Std. Error
attentive	5	4	10	5.80	2.490	1.671	.913
Valid N (listwise)	5						

a. group = 1

group = 2

Descriptive Statistics

	N	Minimum	Maximum	Mean	Std.	Skewness	
	Statistic	Statistic	Statistic	Statistic	Statistic	Statistic	Std. Error
attentive	5	2	5	3.00	1.225	1.361	.913
Valid N (listwise)	5						

a. group = 2

Figure 10

🖱 Graphs 🖱 Legacy Dialogs 🖱 Histogram
🖱 "attentive" move the variable to the *Variables* box
🖱 the box beside *Display normal curve*
🖱 OK
The histograms should look like Figure 11 and Figure 12.

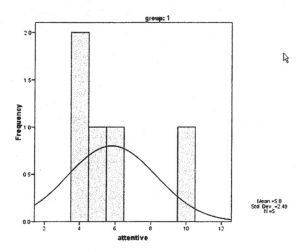

Figure 11

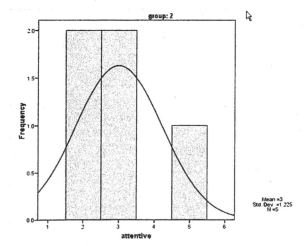

Figure 12

176

Before continuing, take the following steps to turn the "Split File" function off.
-ᐟᐤ Data
-ᐟᐤ Split File
-ᐟᐤ The circle beside *Analyze all cases, do not create groups*
-ᐟᐤ OK

To analyze the data after performing a square-root tansformation'
-ᐟᐤ Transform
-ᐟᐤ Compute, which will cause a "Compute Variable" window to be displayed
Type the name of the new variable "sqrtatt" in the "Target Variable" box
Type "sqrt(attentive) in the "Numeric Expression" box to indicate that SPSS will compute the square root of each score and create a new variable called "sqrtatt"
The compute variable window should look like Figure 13.

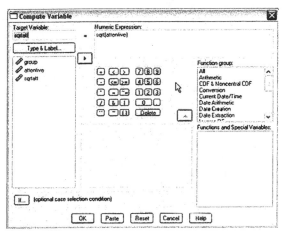

Figure 13
-ᐟᐤ OK
Now the SPSS data editor window should look Figure 14.

group	attentive	sqrtatt
1	6	2.45
1	4	2.00
1	4	2.00
1	5	2.24
1	10	3.16
2	2	1.41
2	3	1.73
2	3	1.73
2	5	2.24
2	2	1.41

Figure 14

The transformed variable can now be used in a *t* test for independent means, and the results should be consistent with those you obtained when you solved Problem 5.

To conduct a rank-order test on the creativity test scores for the two groups of students,
-ᐟᐤ Analyze
-ᐟᐤ Nonparametric tests
-ᐟᐤ 2 Independent Samples
-ᐟᐤ Nonparametric tests
-ᐟᐤ the variable "attentive" and -ᐟᐤ the arrow next to the box labeled "Test Variables" to indicate that the rank-order test should be conducted on the "attentive" variable.
-ᐟᐤ the variable "group" and -ᐟᐤ the arrow next to the box labeled "Grouping Variable" to indicate the group to which each student belongs.
-ᐟᐤ "Define Groups" and enter "1" in the box for Group 1 and "2" in the box for Group 2
-ᐟᐤ Continue

The "Two-Independent-Samples Tests" window should look like Figure 15.

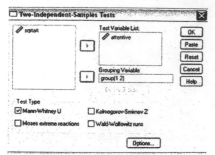

Figure 15

🖱 OK

The SPSS output should look like Figure 16.

Mann-Whitney Test

Ranks

	group	N	Mean Rank	Sum of Ranks
attentive	1	5	7.50	37.50
	2	5	3.50	17.50
	Total	10		

Test Statistics[b]

	attentive
Mann-Whitney U	2.500
Wilcoxon W	17.500
Z	-2.115
Asymp. Sig. (2-tailed)	.034
Exact Sig. [2*(1-tailed Sig.)]	.032[a]

a. Not corrected for ties.

b. Grouping Variable: group

Figure 16

Again, the output indicates that a NPar Test (nonparametric test) was conducted. If you remember, the box for the Mann-Whitney Test was checked in the "Two-Independent-Samples Tests" window. Notice that the Test Statistics box includes results for the Mann-Whitney U test and the Wilcoxon rank-sum test, which give mathematically equivalent results, s well as a value for Z. Note that the mean ranks presented in the Ranks table are the same as those you calculated when you solved Problem 5, and you would make the same decision to reject the null hypothesis that you made on the basis of the *t* test for independent means you conducted.

Chapter 15
The General Linear Model and Making Sense of Advanced Statistical Procedures in Research Articles

Learning Objectives
After studying this chapter, you should:

- Know how to interpret the results of advanced statistical procedures that explore relationships (partial correlation, factor analysis, multilevel modeling, and causal modeling) reported in research articles.
- Know how to interpret the information about the reliability of tests and measures reported in research articles.
- Know how to interpret the results of advanced statistical procedures that compare groups (analysis of covariance and multivariate analysis of variance and covariance) reported in research articles.
- Know how to read the results of unfamiliar statistical techniques reported in research articles.

The General Linear Model
The **general linear model** is a mathematical formula from which many statistical procedures presented previously can be derived. Multiple regression is the most general procedure based on this model. Special cases, i.e., procedures that can be derived from a more general model include:

- Bivariate correlation and prediction,
- Analysis of variance , and
- The t test.

The formula for the general liner model is $Y = a + (b_1) (X_1) + (b_2) (X_2) + (b_3) (X_3)+...+e$, where
Y is a person's score in the criterion variable,
a is a fixed influence that applies to all individuals,
b_1 is the degree of influence of the first predictor variable (the regression coefficient),
X_1 is the person's score on the first predictor variable, and so on for the remaining predictor variables, and
e is an error term reflecting the fact that not all the influences on a particular variable can be measured.

Bivariate regression is a special case of multiple regression with a single predictor, and because of the relationship between correlation and regression, bivariate correlation is a special case of multiple regression.
The t test is a special case of analysis of variance when there are only two groups, and both can be considered special cases of multiple regression if the grouping variable is used to predict a measured variable.

Partial Correlation
Partial correlation is used to determine the correlation between two variables while **partialing out**, *holding constant, controlling for*, or *adjusting for* the influence of one or more additional variables. (These four terms are used synonymously.) The result is a **partial correlation coefficient** that can have values between -1 and +1.

Reliability
Reliability refers to the consistency or stability of a measure like an achievement test or a personality inventory.

- **Test-retest reliability** is estimated by administering the same measure to the same group on two different occasions.
- **Split-half reliability** is estimated by correlating responses on one half of a test or inventory (e.g., the odd-numbered items) with responses on the other half of the test or inventory (e.g., the even-numbered items). If people are responding consistently, the correlation should be high.
- The way items are divided into halves can result in inaccurate correlation coefficients when using the split-half method. A more general method called **Cronbach's alpha (α)** is the equivalent of dividing a test or inventory into all possible split-halves, calculating the correlation for each split, and determining the average correlation of all splits. Since alpha provides a measure of how well items on a test or inventory assess a common characteristic, it provides an **internal consistency reliability** coefficient.
- **Interrater reliability** (also called *interjudge reliability, interrater agreement*, and *interjudge agreement*) is estimated when two or more raters observe behavior.

Multilevel Modeling
Multilevel modeling is an advanced type of regression analysis used in research situations in which people are grouped in ways that could affect the pattern of scores. The variables in the analysis that reflect the people in each grouping are called **lower-level variables**, and the variables that reflect the grouping as a whole are called **upper-level variables**. **Hierarchical linear modeling (HLM)** is the most common name for these methods.

Factor Analysis
When large numbers of variables have been measured in a group of people, **factor analysis** may be used to identify groups of these variables that have high correlations with each other, but low correlations with other variables. Each group of variables is called a **factor**, and the correlation between a variable and its factor is its **factor loading**. Variables have loadings on each factor, but high loadings on only one. While loadings can range from -1 to +1, only loadings of ±.30 or more are considered to be meaningful. While the calculations used in the several methods of factor analysis are objective, naming factors is subjective.

Causal Modeling
Causal modeling methods are used to determine whether a pattern of correlations among variables confirms a theory about which variables are causing which.

- The results of a **path analysis** are included in a diagram in an arrow indicates the **path**, or cause-and-effect relationship relationships between pairs of variables. The strength of the causal relationship, controlling for the influence of any other variables that may have arrows indicating paths to the same variable, is indicated by a **path coefficient**, which can be interpreted like a standardized regression coefficient.
- In **mediational analysis**, the purpose is to determine whether a third variable, the mediator variable, explains the causal relationship between two other variables.
- **Structural equation modeling** is an extension of path analysis with the advantage that a **fit index** can be calculated to indicate how well the observed correlations correspond to those hypothesized by the experimenter. While higher values indicate better fit for most indexes, for the **RMSEA** (the root mean square error of approximation), a smaller number indicates a better fit. A second advantage of structural equation modeling is that combinations of variables can be combined into a **latent variable** that, while not actually measured, can be used to approximate a construct of interest to the experimenter.

The results of causal modeling procedures are subject to the same limits on interpretation that are true for correlation.

Procedures that Compare Groups
Statistical tests used to compare groups involve two types of variables. An **independent variable** defines group membership, e.g., experimental and control groups, especially when the groups are created by random assignment. [Tests like factorial analysis include at least two independent variables.] A **dependent variable** reflects the effect of the experimental treatment.

- **Analysis of covariance (ANCOVA)** is an analysis of variance in which the effects of the experimental treatment on the dependent variable are adjusted to partial out the effects of one or more variables that may influence the effect of the treatment, but are of no interest in a particular study. Each of these unwanted variables is called a **covariate**. The results of ANCOVA are interpreted like an analysis of variance except that **adjusted means** are reported when the dependent variable is described.
- **Multivariate statistics** are procedures that involve more than one dependent variable, so **multivariate analysis of variance (MANOVA)** is an analysis of variance involving more one dependent variable. The result is still an F ratio, but it is calculated using one of several slightly different methods, perhaps the most frequently encountered being *Wilk's lambda*. If the multivariate F is statistically significant, separate *univariate analyses of variance* are conducted for each dependent variable to determine which of these variables are contributing to the significant multivariate result.
- **Multivariate analysis of covariance (MANCOVA)** is an analysis of covariance with more than one dependent variable.

The statistical techniques discussed in this chapter are summarized in Table 15-7 in the text.

How to Read Results Using Unfamiliar Statistical Techniques

Even experienced experimenters encounter unfamiliar statistical methods in research articles. In such cases, the basic intent of the analysis can usually be determined. First examine the p value(s), which should clarify the pattern of results that is being considered significant. Next, look for an indication of the degree of association or the size of the difference. If the purpose of the analysis and the interpretation of the results are still not clear, refer to a more advanced statistics text or consult someone who has taken an advanced course. New statistical methods are being developed constantly, e.g., computer-intensive methods, so the need to learn about new techniques should be expected.

Chapter Self–Tests

The test items that follow are based on the following scenario. The psychologists studying depression have measured a number of additional variables so that they can study a variety of influences on the depression they observe among their clients by conducting more complex analyses of the associations between and among variables and by making more detailed comparisons between and among groups.

Understanding Key Terms in Chapter 15

Directions: Using the word bank that follows, complete each statement.

Word Bank: adjusted means / adjusting for / analysis of covariance / controlling for / covariate / Cronbach's alpha / dependent variable / factor / factor analysis / factor loading / fit index / hierarchical linear modeling / holding constant / independent variable / internal consistency reliability /interrater reliability / latent variable / mediational analysis / multilevel modeling / multivariate analysis of variance / multivariate analysis of covariance / multivariate statistics / partial correlation / partial correlation coefficient / partialing out / path / path analysis / path coefficient / RMSEA / reliability / split-half reliability / structural equation modeling / test-retest reliability

The analyses conducted by the psychologists to date involving t tests, analysis of variance, correlation, and multiple regression are based on the **(1)** _____. Some of the first analyses the psychologists want to conduct involve determining variables that will help them predict depression. A review of their clients' files reveals that the psychologists have recorded information about or measured 20 variables for each client that may predict depression. As an initial step in their analyses, the psychologists want to examine the relationship between stress and depression over and above the influence anxiety. An appropriate analysis in this situation is **(2)** _____. In this analysis, the psychologists are said to be **(3)** _____, **(4)** _____, **(5)** _____, or **(6)** _____ anxiety, and the resulting statistic is called a **(7)** _____.

Having developed a 24-item inventory, the psychologists are now concerned about the consistency or stability of client scores, i.e., with the inventory's **(8)** _____. If the psychologists administer the inventory to a group of 50 people on two occasions separated by two weeks and calculate the correlation between the two sets of scores, they have calculated the **(9)** _____. If the psychologists divide the inventory by separating the odd-numbered and even-numbered items and correlate the scores resulting from this division of items, they have calculated the **(10)** _____. On the other hand, the psychologists might use a method that yields the average correlation of possible divisions of the inventory into two equal sets of items. This measure is called **(11)** _____, and is a measure of **(12)** _____. If the psychologists divide themselves into groups of three and make independent assessments of people's level of depression after watching videotaped interviews of each person, they will estimate the agreement among their assessments by calculating **(13)** _____.

In some of the situations in which the psychologists have collected data, the participants have been grouped in particular ways, e.g., whether the participants have been involved in group therapy with different therapists. Therefore, the psychologists decide to conduct a regression analysis across all the groups with therapist experience as the predictor variable and each group's average score on a depression inventory as the criterion variable. This type of analysis is called **(14)** _____, and the most common name for these methods is **(15)** _____.

Having reviewed the previous research on stress, the psychologists have for a relatively brief inventory that can be used to measure a person's functioning on any given day in terms of anxiety, stress, and depression. In their review of research articles, the psychologists identified 30 statements that described behaviors and emotions reflecting the three variables of interest. The statistical procedure that would permit reduction of these 90 statements to an inventory comprised of 24-30 items is **(16)** _____. After this reduction, the group of statements that the psychologists labeled as measuring one of the three variables of interest is called a **(17)** _____, and the correlation of a statement describing a characteristic associated with anxiety with the larger group of statements reflecting anxiety is called a **(18)** _____.

Having identified a set of variables that predict development of depression, the psychologists are interested in developing models that will enable them to test whether patterns of correlations among sets of variables can be predicted by a specific theory about which variables are causing other variables. If the psychologists present the results in a diagram in which variables are connected by arrows, they have conducted a **(19)** _____. Each arrow represents a **(20)** _____, and the correlation that summarizes the relationship between variables connected by arrows is a **(21)** _____. If the psychologists want to see if the relationship between stress and depression is due to an intervening variable like anxiety or perceived health status, they would us **(22)**_____. However, the psychologists are expanding their analysis to obtain an overall measure of how well their model agrees with their theory. In this case, they can use **(23)** _____. The number that summarizes the agreement between the model and the theory is a **(24)** _____, of which **(25)** _____ is one example. An additional advantage of this method is that it will allow the psychologists to combine variables like job and marital satisfaction to provide an overall estimate of general satisfaction with life without actually measuring such a broad variable. This overall estimate is called a **(26)** _____.

Having examined these associations, the psychologists are now interested in comparing groups. If they randomly assign one group of clients to participate in a program to teach them coping skills and a second group to receive traditional group therapy, measuring depression after six weeks, program type is the **(27)** _____ and depression is the **(28)** _____. If the psychologists decide to control for anxiety as part of their comparison of groups, they will use **(29)** _____. In this analysis, anxiety is a **(30)** _____, and the psychologists will report **(31)** _____. Due to the many correlations between and among variables the psychologists have observed, they decide to conduct some analyses involving two or more dependent variables. The procedures used in these analyses are called **(32)** _____. If the psychologists want to compare both stress and depression simultaneously for the two groups described above, the would conduct a **(33)** _____, and if they wanted to make the same comparison while controlling for anxiety, they would conduct a **(34)** _____.

Multiple Choice Items

1. The *t*-test, analysis of variance, product-moment correlation, and regression may be subsumed under the
    A. general linear model.
    B. nonlinear model.
    C. multivariable model.
    D. transformed model.

2. If the psychologists want to determine the association between anxiety and depression while adjusting for the level of stress, they would use
    A. multiple regression.
    B. partial correlation.
    C. bivariate correlation.
    D. stepwise regression.

3. Another term for the adjustment described in Item 2 is
   A. partialing out.
   B. internal consistency.
   C. factor loading.
   D. fit index.

Items 4–7 are related.

The psychologists are interested in the consistency and stability of the scores on the inventories they use to measure anxiety, stress, and depression.

4. The general term used to describe the consistency and stability of inventories like these is
   A. internal consistency.
   B. factor loading.
   C. reliability.
   D. partialing.

5. If the psychologists assess consistency by administering one of the inventories to the same people after a certain amount of time has elapsed and correlating the two sets of scores, they are estimating
   A. internal consistency reliability.
   B. interrater reliability.
   C. split-half reliability.
   D. test-retest reliability.

6. If the psychologists calculate Cronbach's alpha, they will obtain an estimate of
   A. internal consistency reliability.
   B. interrater reliability.
   C. split-half reliability.
   D. test-retest reliability.

7. If the psychologists ask two colleagues to read descriptions of their emotions written by their clients and give a diagnosis, they will want an estimate of
   A. internal consistency reliability.
   B. interrater reliability.
   C. split-half reliability.
   D. test-retest reliability.

Items 8–9 are related.

8. If the psychologists believe their clients are grouped in a way that could influence the results of their study, they could use an advanced type of regression called
   A. factor analysis.
   B. path analysis.
   C. multilevel modeling.
   D. latent modeling.

9. If the psychologists want to examine the effect of the number of years of experience therapists have conducting group therapy on client depression after three months of therapy across therapy groups, therapist experience would be
   A. an upper-level variable.
   B. a lower-level variable.
   C. an internal consistency variable.
   D. a mediated variable.

Items 10–14 are related.

Having measured a large number of variables, the psychologists are considering statistical procedures that will allow them to examine relationships among all these variables.

10. The method that involves examining correlations between pairs of variables to see which ones are correlated and which are not is called
    A. mediational analysis.
    B. partial correlation.
    C. factor analysis.
    D. path analysis.

11. If the psychologists apply this procedure and identify a group of variables that have high correlations with other and define the group "General Satisfaction," they are defining a
    A. path.
    B. constant.
    C. fit.
    D. factor.

12. If the psychologists examine patterns of correlations between variables to identify causal relationships, they are using
    A. mediational analysis.
    B. partial correlation.
    C. factor analysis.
    D. path analysis.

13. The cause-and-effect connections between variables are shown by arrows, which are called
    A. loadings.
    B. paths.
    C. steps.
    D. adjustments.

14. If the psychologists want to demonstrate that the relationship between anxiety and depression may be due to the influence of perceived stress, they can use
    A. mediational analysis.
    B. partial correlation.
    C. factor analysis.
    D. path analysis.

Items 15–17 are related.

15. If the psychologists want an overall measure of agreement between their theory about the causes of depression and the correlations they have observed, they can use
    A. mediational analysis.
    B. partial correlation.
    C. structural equation modeling.
    D. path analysis.

16. The measure of agreement in this analysis is called a
    A. factor loading.
    B. covariate.
    C. latent variable.
    D. fit index.

17. A variable that is not actually measured, but that is approximated by a combination of several variables in the analysis, is a
    A. factor loading.
    B. covariate.
    C. latent variable.
    D. fit index.

Items 18–19 are related.

18. If the psychologists compare the depression inventory scores of men and women in group therapy based on their marital status (married vs. unmarried), the dependent variable is
    A. depression.
    B. gender.
    C. therapy.
    D. marital status.

19. The independent variable is
    A. depression.
    B. gender.
    C. therapy.
    D. marital status.

Items 20–22 are related.

20. If the psychologists want to control for the anxiety level of these men and women, they would use
    A. structural equation modeling.
    B. analysis of variance.
    C. analysis of covariance.
    D. multivariate analysis of variance.

21. Anxiety level would be called a
    A. factor loading.
    B. covariate.
    C. latent variable.
    D. fit index.

22. The psychologists' results would include
    A. a fit index.
    B. RMSEA.
    C. factor loadings.
    D. adjusted means.

23. For any analysis including more than one dependent variable, the psychologists will need to use
    A. structural equation modeling.
    B. factor analysis.
    C. fit indexes.
    D. multivariate statistics.

24. If the psychologists want compare the depression inventory and stress inventory scores of men and women in group therapy based on their marital status (married vs. unmarried) in the same analysis, they will use
    A. multivariate analysis of variance.
    B. multivariate analysis of covariance.
    C. structural equation modeling.
    D. mediational analysis.

25. If the psychologists want compare the depression inventory and stress inventory scores of men and women in group therapy based on their marital status (married vs. unmarried) in the same analysis and while partialing out the effects of anxiety inventory scores, they will use
   A. multivariate analysis of variance.
   B. multivariate analysis of covariance.
   C. structural equation modeling.
   D. mediational analysis.

Problems

1. The psychologist studying attentiveness in kindergarten children has collected the following data from each child: age in months, sex, intelligence, achievement, and attentiveness ratings. (a) What statistical procedure would the psychologist use to determine the association between attentiveness and achievement while holding the effect of intelligence constant? (b) Explain the method to someone who is familiar with correlation and multiple regression, but not with this method. (c) What statistical procedure would the psychologist use to address the possibility that sex is an intervening variable in the hypothesized causal relationship between attentiveness and achievement? (d) Explain the method to someone who is familiar with correlation and prediction, but not with this method. (e) What statistical procedure would the psychologist use to test a prediction that age, sex, intelligence, and attentiveness cause achievement by examining the correlations between the variables? (f) Explain the method to someone who is familiar with multiple regression and partial correlation, but not with this method. (g) Finally, what statistical procedure would the psychologist use to obtain an overall measure of fit between the causal theory presented in (e) and the correlations among the scores? (h) Explain the method to someone who is familiar with multiple regression, but not with this method.

2. A psychologist has been hired to develop a brief (20 items of fewer) scale that employees of a large corporation can use to evaluate their supervisors. After reviewing published studies examining supervisory behavior, the psychologist has identified 60 statements that describe supervisory behavior. After administering a rating form including all 60 statements to a large number of employees in a variety of corporations and jobs, the psychologist is ready to begin reducing the number of statements. (a) What statistical procedure can the psychologist use to examine patterns of correlations between variables to see which variables are highly correlated and which are not correlated? (b) Explain the method to someone who is familiar with correlation, but not with this method. (c) After reducing the number of items to 20, what methods can the psychologist use to evaluate the consistency or stability of the rating scale? (d) Explain each method to someone who is familiar with correlation, but not with reliability.

3. A psychologist has conducted a study investigating the effects of four methods of teaching statistics on test anxiety of college students. Which variable is the (a) independent variable and which is the (b) dependent variable?

4. A psychologist has conducted a study to compare a computer-based course in introductory psychology with a traditional lecture course using the student scores on a comprehensive final examination as the dependent variable. Knowing that some students may have taken psychology courses in high school, the psychologist administered a pretest to determine the knowledge students brought to both courses. (a) What statistical procedure would the psychologist use to control for initial differences in knowledge of psychology identified by the pretest? (b) Explain the method to someone who is familiar with analysis of variance and partial correlation, but not with this method.

5. (a) What statistical procedure would a psychologist use to examine the effects of children's attentiveness in school (categorized as high, average, or low), teacher perceptions of a children's coping skills (categorized as adequate or inadequate), and the parenting style experienced by the children (categorized as liberal or strict) on measures of the children's self-esteem and self-efficacy simultaneously? (b) What statistical procedure would the psychologist use to examine the effects of attentiveness, coping skills, and parenting style on self-esteem and self-efficacy simultaneously , while partialing out each child's level of achievement? (c) Explain both methods to someone who is familiar with factorial analysis of variance, but not with either of these methods.

Additional Practice: Complete any Practice Problems in Set I that your instructor has not assigned and compare your responses to those provided by the authors. Pay particular attention to the problems that require you to explain your results to someone who has never taken a course in statistics.

SPSS Applications
There are no SPSS applications for this chapter.

Appendix

How to Use SPSS

SPSS stands for Statistical Package for the Social Sciences and is just that – a package of programs for conducting statistical procedures like the ones presented in the text. A good way to learn SPSS is to arrange a tutoring session with someone who knows how to use the package. If your instructor does not provide introductory sessions, you may want to see if the computing center at your institution offers such sessions. If you need to learn to use the package on your own, manuals provides by SPSS are available, and the help function available when you are using the package is useful. You may also go SPSS.com and register as a user, which will give you access to a compilation of frequently asked questions and their answers. Be aware that this manual will provide more information than you need to succeed in this course, so concentrate on learning the processes and procedures you need for this course and avoid getting bogged down with information you do not need. The purpose of this Appendix is to help you learn just what you need to open SPSS and begin using it.

The information presented in the text and in this Study Guide makes three assumptions, the first being that you are familiar with the fundamental operations of the computer system you will be using – how to turn it on, type in instructions, move between directories, and how to end a session. The second assumption is that you are familiar with basic computer terminology such as "file," "saving a file," and "cursor." The third assumption is that you worked with computers, at least a little, and understand the necessity to follow instructions exactly and to use commands precisely.

Opening SPSS

You should communicate with your instructor or the computing center at your university to determine how you are to access to SPSS. If a shortcut was installed on the computer you are using, ⌐⌐ the SPSS icon on the Desktop. (As in the text, ⌐ indicates a left mouse click.) The screen will look like the one shown in Figure 1 except that the files listed in the two windows will be different because they will be your files. Next, you should ⌐ *Type in data* and ⌐ *OK*. The screen will change so that it looks like the one in Figure 2.

Figure 1

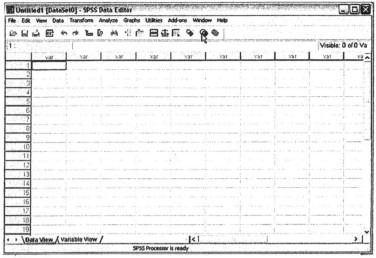

Figure 2

Entering Data

In behavioral science research, the data typically consist of scores on one or more variables measured for each individual enrolled in a study. For example, each of 10 students might have a score on a motivation inventory and on an examination. Thus, the dataset would contain two variables ("motivation" and "exam") with scores for each of the 10 students. To enter data in SPSS, begin by ✋ in the upper left cell and type the motivation inventory score for the first individual. Then press the Enter key. Then type the motivation score for the second individual, press Enter, and continue until the scores for all 10 students have been entered. Next, you should ✋ in the top cell of the second column. Type the examination score for the first individual. Then press the Enter key. Then type the examination score for the second individual, press Enter, and continue until the scores for all 10 students have been entered. The screen should look like the one in Figure 3.

	VAR00001	VAR00002
1	44.00	50.00
2	90.00	80.00
3	75.00	70.00
4	85.00	96.00
5	55.00	86.00
6	25.00	92.00
7	40.00	88.00
8	90.00	56.00
9	65.00	93.00
10	80.00	79.00

Figure 3

Naming Variables

✋ the Variable View tab at the bottom of the screen to obtain the screen shown in Figure 4.

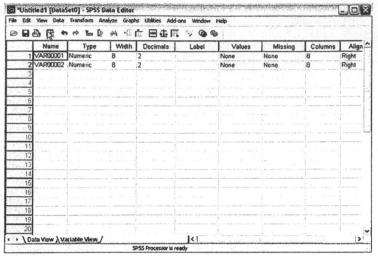

Figure 4

Place the cursor in front of the V in VAR0001 and 👆👆. This action highlights the cell and permits you to name the variable "motivation" as is done in Figure 5. This action was repeated for VAR0002, which was named "exam." In current versions of SPSS, variable names can be up to 64 characters long, but keeping variable names short, e.g., 8-12 characters, will make the data view window more manageable – you will not have to scroll so much to see the different variables. Remember that some characters cannot be used in variable names, and others cannot be used to begin or end variable names. Keep your variable names simple and consult the manual or help function if you have problems.

If you click in the cells labeled "Decimals," up and down arrows will appear. These arrows can be used to change the number of decimals that appear in cells in the Data View screen. The number of variables has been changed to zero for both variables as in Figure 5.

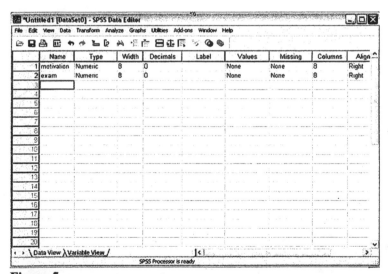

Figure 5

Thus, the rows represent data for students, and the columns represent the data for variables. You can select the data for both students and variables, e.g., if you want to copy the dataset or a portion of it, or you can use the mouse to select individual cells.

190

Using the Toolbar

Statistical analyses are conducted by selecting the desired analysis from the toolbar at the top of the screen. For example, to obtain the average motivation and examination scores
- ✐ Analyze
- ✐ Descriptive Statistics
- ✐ Frequencies

These commands will give the screen shown in Figure 6.

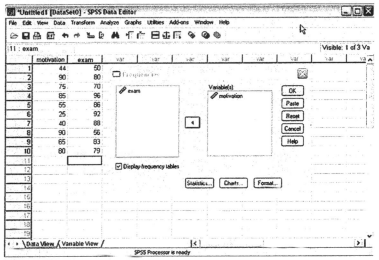

Figure 6

"motivation" has been highlighted and by clicking on the arrow, moved into the Variable(s) box. Repeating this process for "exam." will move it into the box, and when you ✐ OK, you will obtain output that includes the mean, or average, motivation and examination scores for the 10 students.

Creating New Variables

New variables can be created from existing variables. For example, suppose you wanted to weight the examination score so that its value is doubled.
- ✐ Transform
- ✐ Compute variable

Type the new variable name, e.g., "exam2" in the Target Variable box.

Type the computations using the name of any existing variables and the arithmetic symbols, in this case, exam*2. The screen will look like the one shown in Figure 7.

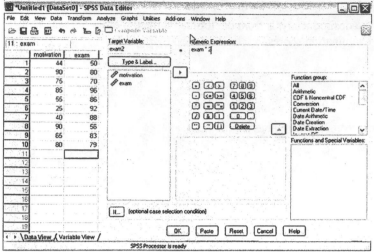

Figure 7

Note that many mathematical functions are listed in the lower right screen and that you can combine functions using parentheses to group computations following algebraic rules for operations like multiplication and division.
When you ⌐🖰 OK, the new variable will appear in the Data Window.

Saving the Data in Files

To save a dataset, on the toolbar
⌐🖰 File
⌐🖰 Save (or Save As)
Name your dataset, e.g., Appendix Data, and designate the drive to which you would like the data to be saved.
⌐🖰 OK

Ending an SPSS Session

After saving the dataset,
⌐🖰 The X in the box at the top right of the SPSS window or
⌐🖰 File
⌐🖰 Exit

Recalling a Dataset

If a dataset already exists, you do not need to reenter all the data. Simply open SPSS, but instead of choosing "Type in data," choose "Open an existing data source." Then choose one of the SPSS datasets listed, e.g., D:\Coups Big Book 5th\Appendix Data.sav in Figure 8.

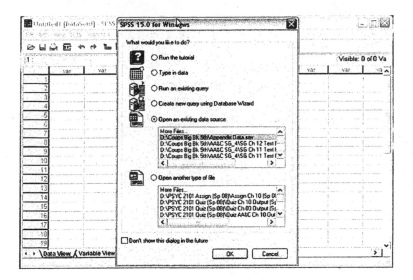

When you 🖱 OK, the SPSS dataset will open.

Answers to Chapter Self-Tests

<u>Chapter 1</u>

Completion Items:

1. statistics	11. continuous variable	21. bimodal distribution
2. inferential statistics	12. rank-order variable	22. multimodal distribution
3. descriptive statistics	13. nominal variable	23. rectangular distribution
4. variable	14. levels of measurement	24. symmetrical distribution
5. values	15. frequency table	25. skewed distribution
6. score	16. interval	26. floor effect
7. numeric variables	17. grouped frequency table	27. ceiling effect
8. equal-interval variable	18. histogram	28. normal distribution
9. ratio scale	19. frequency distribution	29. kurtosis
10. discrete variable	20. unimodal distribution	

Multiple Choice Items:

1. B	5. A	9. B	13. C	17. D
2. A	6. C	10. A	14. C	18. A
3. D	7. B	11. C	15. A	19. C
4. D	8. D	12. A	16. B	20. C

Problems:

1.
Frequency Distribution

Esteem

Score	Frequency	Percent
15	1	4.5
16	1	4.5
17	1	4.5
18	1	4.5
19	1	4.5
20	3	13.6
21	2	9.1
22	1	4.5
23	4	18.2
24	2	9.1
25	1	4.5
26	1	4.5
28	2	9.1
29	1	4.5
Total	22	100.0

Histogram

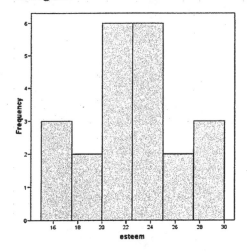

The distribution is beginning to assume the shape of a normal curve.
Note: This histogram was created using SPSS.

2.
Frequency distribution
Esteem

Score	Frequency	Percent
15	1	1.7
16	2	3.3
17	2	3.3
18	2	3.3
19	3	5.0
20	6	10.0
21	3	5.0
22	3	5.0
23	4	6.7
24	6	10.0
25	3	5.0
26	3	5.0
27	3	5.0
28	4	6.7
29	3	5.0
30	3	5.0
31	2	3.3
32	2	3.3
33	2	3.3
35	2	3.3
36	1	1.7
Total	60	100.0

A grouped frequency table would combine scores and make the distribution easier to visualize. Because there are so many scores obtained by two or three freshmen, this frequency table is not much easier to interpret than the ranked individual scores would be.

Grouped frequency table

Interval	Frequency	Percent
15-19	10	16.70
20-24	22	36.70
25-29	16	26.70
30-34	9	15.00
35-39	3	5.00
Total	60	100.1*

*Rounding Error

Histogram

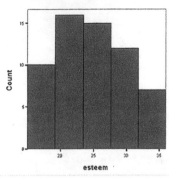

Note:This histogram was created using SPSS

3. A ceiling effect would exist if most of the scores on the self-esteem inventory were massed at the high end of the scoring scale, e.g., if most of the scores were 30 or higher. In this situation, students with very high self-esteem might not be able to express the full extent of their self-esteem. On the other hand, a floor effect would exist if most of the scores on the self-esteem inventory were massed at the low end of the scoring scale, e.g., if most of the scores were less than 10. In this case, students with very low self-esteem might not be able to describe their deficit fully.

Chapter 2

Completion Items:

1. central tendency	8. deviation score	15. computational formula
2. mean	9. squared deviation score	16. variance
3. $\sum$	10. sum of squared deviations	17. $\sum$
4. X	11. sum of squares	18. N
5. mode	12. variance	19. standard deviation
6. median	13. standard deviation	
7. outlier	14. definitional formula	

Multiple Choice Items:

1. C	3. A	5. A	7. B	9. C	11. A	13. B
2. C	4. D	6. B	8. A	10. C	12. A	14. A

Problems:

1. Stress scores

Mode	38
Median	36
Mean	33.68
Variance	125.42
Standard deviation	11.20

Compare your explanation to the "Outline for Writing Essays on Finding the Mean, Variance, and Standard Deviation" on p. 59 in the text and to the sample answers to Set I Practice Problems 4 and 5.

2. Self – esteem scores

Mode	23
Median	22.50
Mean	22.05
Variance	13.95
Standard deviation	3.73

Compare your explanation to the "Outline for Writing Essays on Finding the Mean, Variance, and Standard Deviation" on p. 59 in the text and to the sample answers to Set I Practice Problems 4 and 5.

Chapter 3

Completion Items:

1. sample	6. normal distribution	11. sample statistics	16. probability	21. addition rule
2. population	7. normal curve	12. population parameters	17. outcome	22. multiplication rule
3. raw score	8. normal curve table	13. μ	18. expected	23. conditional probabilities
4. Z score	9. haphazard selection	14. σ^2	19. long-run	
5. standard score	10. random selection	15. σ	20. subjective	

Multiple Choice Items:

1. B	5. C	9. C	13. C	17. D	21. B
2. D	6. A	10. B	14. B	18. B	
3. C	7. B	11. A	15. C	19. A	
4. A	8. C	12. D	16. D	20. C	

Problems:

1. -1.00	6. 96%	11. 45.12%	16. 24.83%	21(a). .4 or 40%
2. 2.00	7. 48%	12. 2.07%	17. 0.31%	21(b). .6 or 60%
3. 1.33	8. 48%	13. 84.11%	18. 9.18%	22.(a). .075 or 7.5%
4. -0.33	9. 9%	14. 28.27%	19. 90.825	22(b) .05 or 5%
5. 68%	10. 33%	15. 85.12%	20. 90.82%	

Chapter 4

Completion Items:

1. theory	6. one-tailed	11. cutoff sample
2. hypothesis	7. nondirectional	12. null
3. hypothesis testing	8. two-tailed	13. research
4. research	9. null	14. conventional
5. directional	10. comparison	15. statistically significant

Multiple Choice Items:

1. C	4. C	7. D	10. C	13. C
2. B	5. A	8. A	11. B	14. A
3. D	6. C	9. B	12. D	15. D

Problems:

1.
The null hypothesis states that there will be no difference between Population 1 and Population 2 after the experimental treatment, i.e., the experimental treatment will have no effect on behavior. The research hypothesis indicates the predicted relationship between Population 1 and Population 2 after the experimental treatment, i.e., the research hypothesis expresses the psychologists' expectation that the treatment will have some effect. A directional research hypothesis states that the behavior being measured will increase or decrease. In this case, the null hypothesis is that the behavior being measured will not change, or will change in the opposite direction. A nondirectional research hypothesis states that the behavior being measured will change, but no direction for the change is specified. The corresponding null hypothesis is that the behavior being measured will not change.

2.
Population 1: Bullied adolescents who participate in the 10-week self-defense training program.
Population 2: Bullied adolescents who do not participate in the 10-week self-defense training program.

Directional research hypothesis: The self-esteem of bullied adolescents who participate in a 10-week self-defense training program will be higher than the self-esteem of adolescents who do not participate in the program.
Directional null hypothesis: The self-esteem of bullied adolescents who participate in a 10-week self-defense training program will be the same as, or lower than, the self-esteem of adolescents who do not participate in the program.

Nondirectional research hypothesis: The self-esteem of bullied adolescents who participate in a 10-week self-defense training program will be different from the self-esteem of adolescents who do not participate in the program.
Nondirectional null hypothesis: The self-esteem of bullied adolescents who participate in a 10-week self-defense training program will be no different from the self-esteem of adolescents who do not participate in the program.

3.
Two-tailed .05 = ±1.96
Two-tailed .01 = ±2.58
One-tailed .05 = + 1.64 or -1.64
One-tailed .01 = + 2.33 or -2.33

4. Psychologists are reluctant to use directional hypotheses and their associated one-tailed tests because results in the opposite direction of the psychologists' prediction, which may be interesting, important, or both, must be treated as simple failures to reject the null hypothesis – as if the treatment had no effect.

5.

Student	Student Score	p	Tails of Test	Z Score	Cutoff Score	Decision
1	90	.05	2	2.00	+1.96	Reject
2	84	.05	1	1.50	+1.64	Fail to Reject
3	94	.01	2	2.33	+2.58	Fail to Reject
4	94	.01	1	2.33	+2.33	Reject

6.

Student	Student Score	p	Tails of Test	Z Score	Cutoff Score	Decision
1	20	.05	2	-1.50	-1.96	Fail to Reject
2	14	.05	1	-2.25	-1.64	Reject
3	10	.01	2	-2.75	-2.58	Reject
4	18	.01	1	-1.75	-2.33	Fail to Reject

7.

Step 1: Restate the question as a research hypothesis and a null hypothesis about the populations.
Population 1: People who participate in the 12-week exercise program.
Population 2: People who do not participate in the 12-week exercise program.

Directional research hypothesis: The life satisfaction of people who participate in a 12-week exercise program will be higher than the life satisfaction of people who do not participate in the program.
Directional null hypothesis: The life satisfaction of people who participate in a 12-week exercise program will be the same as, or lower than, the life satisfaction of people who do not participate in the program.

Nondirectional research hypothesis: The life satisfaction of people who participate in a 12-week exercise program will be different from the life satisfaction of people who do not participate in the program.
Nondirectional null hypothesis: The life satisfaction of people who participate in a 12-week exercise program will be no different from the life satisfaction of people who do not participate in the program.

Step 2: Determine the characteristics of the comparison distribution.
The comparison is a normal distribution with $\mu = 50$ and $\sigma = 10$.

Step 3: Determine the cutoff sample score on the comparison distribution at which the null hypothesis should be rejected.
The cutoff sample score for the one-tailed tests that would be used for the directional research hypothesis would be+1.64 at the .05 level of significance and +2.33 at the .01 level of significance.
The cutoff sample score for the two-tailed tests that would be used for the nondirectional research hypothesis would be+1.96 at the .05 level of significance and +2.58 at the .01 level of significance.
[Remember that if you were actually conducting this study, you would state either a directional or a nondirectional hypothesis, and you would select only one level of significance as your criterion for statistical significance.]

Step 4: Determine the sample's score on the comparison distribution.
The participant's Z score = (75-50) / 10 = +2.50.

Step 5: Decide whether to reject the null hypothesis.
Since +2.50 is more extreme than both +1.64 and +2.33, you would reject the null hypotheses for the directional research hypotheses at both .05 and .01 levels of significance and conclude that the exercise program did increase life satisfaction, i.e., the results are statistically significant. Also, +2.50 is more extreme than +1.96, so you would reject the null hypothesis for the nondirectional research hypothesis at the .05 level of significance and draw the same conclusion about the effects of exercise on life satisfaction. However, +2.50 is not more extreme than +2.58. Therefore, you would fail to reject the null hypothesis for the nondirectional research hypothesis at the .01 level and can only state that the results of your study are inconclusive.
Compare your explanation to the "Outline for Writing Essays for Hypothesis-Testing Problems Involving a Single Sample of One Participant and a Known Population" on pp. 130-131 in the text and to the sample answer to Set I Practice Problem 6.

8.

Step 1: Restate the question as a research hypothesis and a null hypothesis about the populations.
Population 1: People who participate in the 12-week exercise program.
Population 2: People who do not participate in the 12-week exercise program.

Directional research hypothesis: The depression of people who participate in a 12-week exercise program will be lower than the depression of people who do not participate in the program.

Directional null hypothesis: The depression of people who participate in a 12-week exercise program will be the same as, or higher than, the depression of people who do not participate in the program.

Nondirectional research hypothesis: The depression of people who participate in a 12-week exercise program will be different from the depression of people who do not participate in the program.
Nondirectional null hypothesis: The depression of people who participate in a 12-week exercise program will be no different from the depression of people who do not participate in the program.

Step 2: Determine the characteristics of the comparison distribution.
The comparison is a normal curve with $\mu = 15$ and $\sigma = 3$.

Step 3: Determine the cutoff sample score on the comparison distribution at which the null hypothesis should be rejected.
The cutoff sample score for the one-tailed tests that would be used for the directional research hypothesis would be -1.64 at the .05 level of significance and -2.33 at the .01 level of significance.
The cutoff sample score for the two-tailed tests that would be used for the nondirectional research hypothesis would be ±1.96 at the .05 level of significance and ±2.58 at the .01 level of significance.
[Remember that if you were actually conducting this study, you would state either a directional or a nondirectional hypothesis, and you would select only one level of significance as your criterion for statistical significance.]

Step 4: Determine the sample's score on the comparison distribution.
The participant's Z score = (9-15) / 3 = -2.00.

Step 5: Decide whether to reject the null hypothesis.
Since -2.00 is more extreme than -1.64, you would reject the null hypotheses for the directional research hypothesis at the .05 level of significance and conclude that the exercise program did reduce depression, i.e., the results are statistically significant. However, -2.00 is not more extreme than -2.58. Therefore, you would fail to reject the null hypothesis for the directional research hypothesis at the .01 level and state that the results of your study are inconclusive. Similarly, -2.00 is more extreme than -1.96, so you would reject the null hypothesis for the nondirectional research hypothesis at the .05 level of significance and conclude that the exercise program reduced depression. Again, -2.00 is not more extreme than -2.58. Therefore, you would fail to reject the null hypothesis for the nondirectional research hypothesis at the .01 level and state that the results of your study are inconclusive. Compare your explanation to the "Outline for Writing Essays for Hypothesis-Testing Problems Involving a Single Sample of One Participant and a Known Population" on pp. 130-131 in the text and to the sample answer to Set I Practice Problem 6.

Chapter 5

Completion Items:

1. means	6. standard deviation	11. confidence intervals
2. distribution of means	7. σ_M	12. confidence limits
3. $\mu_M /$	8. Z test	13. 95% confidence interval
4. variance	9. standard error of the mean	14. 99% confidence interval
5. σ_M^2	10. standard error	

Multiple Choice Items:

1. A	4. B	7. B	10. A	13. D
2. C	5. C	8. D	11. B	
3. D	6. A	9. C	12. C	

Problems:

1. Population $\sigma^2 = 8^2 = 64$ $[\sigma_M{}^2 = \sigma^2 / N$: Rule 2a]

$\quad \sigma^2{}_M = 64\ N$

$\quad \sigma_M = \sqrt{\sigma_M{}^2} = \sqrt{(\sigma^2/N)}$: Rule 2b

SEM Calculations

(a) $64 / 4 = 16 = \sqrt{16} = 4$	(b) $64 / 8 = 8 = \sqrt{8} = 2.83$
(c) $64 / 12 = 5.33 = \sqrt{5.33} = 2.31$	(d) $64 / 20 = 3.20 = \sqrt{3.20} = 1.79$

2.
Formula: 95% confidence interval $= (\pm 1.96)\ (SEM) + M$
(a) $20.16 - 35.84$
(b) $22.45 - 33.55$
(c) $23.47 - 32.53$
(d) $24.49 - 31.51$

Formula: 99% confidence interval $= (\pm 2.57)\ (SEM) + M$
(a) $17.72 - 38.28$
(b) $20.73 - 35.27$
(c) $22.06 - 33.94$
(d) $23.40 - 32.60$

3.
Step 1: Restate the question as a research hypothesis and a null hypothesis about the populations.
Population 1: Freshmen who participate in a self-help discussion group.
Population 2: Freshmen who do not participate in a self-help discussion group.

Research hypothesis: The perceived stress of freshmen who participate in a self-help discussion group will be different than the perceived stress of freshmen who do not participate in a self-help discussion group.
Null hypothesis: The perceived stress of freshmen who participate in a self-help discussion group will be no different than the perceived stress of freshmen who do not participate in a self-help discussion group.

Step 2: Determine the characteristics of the comparison distribution.
Distribution of means with
Mean = 56 [Population mean = 56: Rule 1]
Variance $= 8^2 / 25 = 64 / 25 = 2.56$ $[\sigma_M{}^2 = \sigma^2 / N$: Rule 2a]

Standard deviation $= 1.60$ $[\sigma_M = \sqrt{\sigma_M{}^2} = \sqrt{(\sigma^2/N)}$: Rule 2b]

Shape = normal [Population normally distributed: Rule 3]

Step 3: Determine the cutoff sample score on the comparison distribution at which the null hypothesis should be rejected.
Using the .05 level of significance for a two-tailed test, the cutoff sample score is ± 1.96 for a two-tailed test.

Step 4: Determine the sample's score on the comparison distribution.
$Z = (M - \mu) / \sigma_M = (33 - 36) / 1.60 = -1.88$

Step 5: Decide whether to reject the null hypothesis.
The psychologists would fail to reject the null hypothesis because a Z score of -1.88 is not as extreme as the cutoff sample score of -1.96 and state that their results are inconclusive.
Formula: 95% confidence interval $= M + (\pm 1.96)\ (SEM) = 29.86 - 36.14$.

4.

Step 1: Restate the question as a research hypothesis and a null hypothesis about the populations.
Population 1: Freshmen who participate in a self-help discussion group.
Population 2: Freshmen who do not participate in a self-help discussion group.

Research hypothesis: The perceived stress of freshmen who participate in a self-help discussion group will be lower than the perceived stress of freshmen who do not participate in a self-help discussion group.
Null hypothesis: The perceived stress of freshmen who participate in a self-help discussion group will be the same as, or higher than, the perceived stress of freshmen who do not participate in a self-help discussion group.

Step 2: Determine the characteristics of the comparison distribution.
Distribution of means with
Mean = 56 [Population mean = 56: Rule 1]
Variance = $8^2 / 25 = 64 / 25 = 2.56$ [$\sigma_M^2 = \sigma^2 / N$: Rule 2a]

Standard deviation = 1.60 [$\sigma_M = \sqrt{\sigma_M^2} = \sqrt{(\sigma^2/N)}$: Rule 2b]
Shape = normal [Population normally distributed: Rule 3]

Step 3: Determine the cutoff sample score on the comparison distribution at which the null hypothesis should be rejected.
Using the .01 level of significance for a one-tailed test, the cutoff sample score is -2.33 for a one-tailed test.

Step 4: Determine the sample's score on the comparison distribution.
$Z = (M - \mu) / \sigma_M = (30 - 36) / 1.60 = -3.75$

Step 5: Decide whether to reject the null hypothesis.
The psychologists would reject the null hypothesis because a Z score of -3.75 is more extreme than the cutoff sample score of -2.33 and conclude that the counseling sessions did reduce stress.
Formula: 99% confidence interval = $M + (\pm 2.57)$ $(SEM) = 25.89 - 34.11$.

5.

Step 1: Restate the question as a research hypothesis and a null hypothesis about the populations.
Population 1: Freshmen who participate in a self-help discussion group.
Population 2: Freshmen who do not participate in a self-help discussion group.

Research hypothesis: The self-esteem of freshmen who participate in a self-help discussion group will be different than the self-esteem of freshmen who do not participate in a self-help discussion group.
Null hypothesis: The self-esteem of freshmen who participate in a self-help discussion group will be no different than the perceived stress of freshmen who do not participate in a self-help discussion group.

Step 2: Determine the characteristics of the comparison distribution.
Distribution of means with
Mean = 65 [Population mean = 56: Rule 1]
Variance = $11^2 / 25 = 121 / 25 = 4.84$ [$\sigma_M^2 = \sigma^2 / N$: Rule 2a]

Standard deviation = 2.20 [$\sigma_M = \sqrt{\sigma_M^2} = \sqrt{(\sigma^2/N)}$: Rule 2b]
Shape = normal [Population normally distributed: Rule 3]

Step 3: Determine the cutoff sample score on the comparison distribution at which the null hypothesis should be rejected.
Using the .05 level of significance for a two-tailed test, the cutoff sample score is ± 1.96 for a two-tailed test.

Step 4: Determine the sample's score on the comparison distribution.
$Z = (M - \mu) / \sigma_M = (70 - 65) / 2.20 = +2.27$

Step 5: Decide whether to reject the null hypothesis.

The psychologists would reject the null hypothesis because a Z score of +2.27 is more extreme than the cutoff sample score of +1.96 and conclude that the counseling sessions did increase self-esteem.

Formula: 95% confidence interval = $M + (\pm 1.96)$ $(SEM) = 65.69 - 74.31$.

Compare your explanation to the "Outline for Writing Essays for Hypothesis-Testing Problems Involving a Single Sample of More Than One Participant and a Known Population (Z Test)" on pp. 166-167 in the text and to the sample answer to Set I Practice Problem 8(c).

6.

Step 1: Restate the question as a research hypothesis and a null hypothesis about the populations.

Population 1: Freshmen who participate in a self-help discussion group.

Population 2: Freshmen who do not participate in a self-help discussion group.

Research hypothesis: The coping skills scores of freshmen who participate in a self-help discussion group will be higher than the coping skills scores of freshmen who do not participate in a self-help discussion group.

Null hypothesis: The coping skills scores of freshmen who participate in a self-help discussion group will be the same as, or lower than, the coping skills scores of freshmen who do not participate in a self-help discussion group.

Step 2: Determine the characteristics of the comparison distribution.

Distribution of means with

Mean = 72 [Population mean = 56: Rule 1]

Variance = $14^2 / 25 = 196 / 25 = 7.84$ [$\sigma_M^2 = \sigma^2 / N$: Rule 2a]

Standard deviation = 2.80 [$\sigma_M = \sqrt{\sigma_M^2} = \sqrt{(\sigma^2/N)}$: Rule 2b]

Shape = normal [Population normally distributed: Rule 3]

Step 3: Determine the cutoff sample score on the comparison distribution at which the null hypothesis should be rejected.

Using the .05 level of significance for a one-tailed test, the cutoff sample score is +1.64 for a one-tailed test.

Step 4: Determine the sample's score on the comparison distribution.

$Z = (M - \mu) / \sigma_M = (76 - 72) / 2.80 = +1.43$

Step 5: Decide whether to reject the null hypothesis.

The psychologists would fail to reject the null hypothesis because a Z score of +1.43 is not as extreme as the cutoff sample score of +1.64 and state that the results are inconclusive regarding the effects of counseling on coping skills.

Formula: 95% confidence interval = $M + (\pm 1.96)$ $(SEM) = 70.51 - 81.49$.

Compare your explanation to the "Outline for Writing Essays for Hypothesis-Testing Problems Involving a Single Sample of More Than One Participant and a Known Population (Z Test)" on pp. 166-167 in the text and to the sample answer to Set I Practice Problem 8(c).

Chapter 6

Completion Items:

1. decision	6. meta-analysis	11. power tables	16. increasing
2. Type I	7. effect size	12. .20	17. stringent
3. Type II	8. statistical power	13. .50	18. one-tailed
4. alpha	9. effect size conventions	14. .80	19. statistically
5. beta	10. d	15. .80	20. practically

Multiple Choice Items:

1. D	6. C	11. C	16. C	21. B
2. A	7. C	12. A	17. B	22. D
3. D	8. D	13. D	18. D	23. C
4. C	9. A	14. B	19. A	24. A
5. B	10. A	15. D	20. A	25. D

Problems

1.

Problem	$(\mu_1-\mu_2) / \sigma$	Estimated effect size (d)	Effect size
(a)	$(54 - 63) / 12$	-0.75	large
(b)	$(57 - 63) / 12$	-0.50	medium
(c)	$(60 - 63) / 12$	-0.25	small
(d)	$(71 - 63) / 12$	0.67	medium / large
(e)	$(78 - 63) / 12$	1.25	large

2.

Problem	$(\mu_1-\mu_2) / \sigma$	Predicted effect size (d)	Effect size
(a)	$(35 - 44) / 8$	-1.13	large
(b)	$(42 - 44) / 8$	-0.25	small
(c)	$(50 - 44) / 8$	0.75	large
(d)	$(56 - 44) / 8$	1.50	large
(e)	$(60 - 44) / 8$	2.00	large

3.

Problem	$(\mu_1 - \mu_2) + (d)(\sigma)$	Predicted mean
(a)	$36 + (.20)(8)$	37.6
(b)	$36 + (-.50)(8)$	32.0
(c)	$36 + (-.80)(8)$	29.6
(d)	$36 + (.10)(8)$	36.8
(e)	$36 + (-1.25)(8)$	26.0

4

Study Version	μ	σ	Pred. μ	N	alpha	1- or 2-tailed test	Z for alpha	σ_M
(a)	75	5	76	50	.05	1	1.64	.71
(b)	75	10	77	50	.05	2	1.96	1.41
(c)	75	10	77	50	.05	1	1.64	1.41
(d)	75	10	76	100	.05	1	1.64	1.00
(e)	75	5	77	100	.01	2	2.58	.50

Score for Sign	Z for Sign on Pred. Pop.	Beta	Power	Effect Size
76.16	.23	.59	.41	.20
77.76	.54	.71	.29	.20
77.31	.22	.59	.41	.20
76.64	.64	.74	.26	.10
76.29	-1.42	.08	.42	.40

5.

The statistically significant difference between the treatment mean and the known population mean indicates that the psychologists have identified a real effect of the treatment. Due to the large sample size, the study should have high power. The question is whether the effect is large enough to be practically significant; i.e., to recommend that the teaching method be adopted in other courses.

6.

The statistically significant effect of the treatment is much more convincing in this replication because of the small sample size. Specifically, other factors being equal, the replication should have had lower power than the original study. If a study sample is small, the assumption that a statistically significant difference is also practically significant is safe.

7. Statistically significant results indicate a real effect, but not necessarily practical significance. Studies with high power attributable to factors like large sample size may reveal statistically significant differences despite small effect sizes. A nonsignificant difference from a study with low power is truly inconclusive. However, a nonsignificant difference from a study with high power suggests that either: a) the research hypothesis is false or b) the effect size is smaller than the effect size used to calculate power.

8. $\sigma_M = \sqrt{4^2/30} = \sqrt{16/30} = \sqrt{.53} = .73$
$X = 14 + (1.64)(.73) = 14 + 1.20 = 15.20$
$Z = 15.20 - 16 / .73 = -.80 / .73 = -1.10$
% Mean to Z = 36.43% (36%)
% above Z = 36% + 50% = 86% = Power

Chapter 7

Completion Items:

1. repeated-measures design	6. t test for a single sample	11. t table
2. unbiased estimate	7. t test for dependent means	12. degrees of freedom
3. degrees of freedom	8. difference scores	13. t distributions
4. biased estimate	9. change scores	14. assumption
5. t tests	10. t score	15. robustness

Multiple Choice Items:

1. A	6. A	11. C	16. C
2. B	7. B	12. D	17. D
3. D	8. D	13. D	18. A
4. C	9. A	14. B	19. A
5. C	10. B	15. A	20. C

Problems

1.

Step 1: Restate the question as a research hypothesis and a null hypothesis about the populations.
Population 1: Depressed people who participate in group therapy
Population 2: Depressed people whose number of activities of daily living is 14

Research hypothesis: The number of activities of daily living reported by depressed people after group therapy will not be equal to 14.
Null hypothesis: The number of activities of daily living reported by depressed people after group therapy will be equal to 14.

Step 2: Determine the characteristics of the comparison distribution.

$\mu = 14$

For *difference scores*

$M = 15.75$

$S^2 = 86.25 / 11 = 7.84$

$S^2_M = S^2 / N = 7.84 / 12 = 0.65$

$S_M = \sqrt{S^2_M} = \sqrt{0.65} = 0.81$

The comparison distribution will be a t distribution with 11 df.

Step 3: Determine the cutoff sample score on the comparison distribution at which the null hypothesis should be rejected.

The cutoff sample score for a t distribution with 11 df using a two-tailed test at the .05 level of significance will be ±2.201 for a two-tailed test.

The cutoff sample score for a t distribution with 11 df using a two-tailed test at the .01 level of significance will be ±3.106 for a two-tailed test.

Step 4: Determine the sample score on the comparison distribution.

$t = (M - \mu) / S_M$

$\quad = (15.75 - 14) / 0.81$

$\quad = 2.16$

Step 5: Decide whether to reject the null hypothesis.

Since 2.16 is not more extreme than +2.201, the psychologists will fail to reject the null hypothesis at the .05 level of significance and state that the results are inconclusive. Similarly, since 2.16 is not more extreme than +3.106, the psychologists will fail to reject the null hypothesis at the .01 level of significance and state that the results are inconclusive. Therefore, group therapy cannot be recommended as an effective technique for increasing the number of activities of daily living performed by depressed people using either level of significance.

The effect size for the study = $M - \mu / S = 15.75 - 14 / \sqrt{7.84} = 1.75 / 2.80 = 0.63$, which is a medium to large effect.

2.

Step 1: Restate the question as a research hypothesis and a null hypothesis about the populations.

Population 1: Depressed people who participate in group therapy

Population 2: Depressed people whose number of activities of daily living does not change

Research hypothesis: The number of activities of daily living reported by depressed people after group therapy will be different from the number of activities of daily living reported by depressed people before group therapy.

Null hypothesis: The number of activities of daily living reported by depressed people after group therapy will be no different from the number of activities of daily living reported by depressed people before group therapy.

Step 2: Determine the characteristics of the comparison distribution.

Pop $M = 0$

For *difference scores*

$M = 5$

$S^2 = 124 / 7 = 17.71$

$S^2_M = S^2 / N = 17.71 / 8 = 2.21$

$S_M = \sqrt{S^2_M} = \sqrt{2.21} = 1.49$

The comparison distribution will be a t distribution with 7 df.

Step 3: Determine the cutoff sample score on the comparison distribution at which the null hypothesis should be rejected.

The cutoff sample score for a t distribution with 7 df using a two-tailed test at the .05 level of significance will be ±2.365 for a two-tailed test.

The cutoff sample score for a t distribution with 7 df using a two-tailed test at the .01 level of significance will be ±3.500 for a two-tailed test.

Step 4: Determine the sample score on the comparison distribution.
$t = (M - \mu) / S_M$
$\quad = (5 - 0) / 1.49$
$\quad = 3.36$

Step 5: Decide whether to reject the null hypothesis.
Since 3.36 is more extreme than +2.365, the psychologists will reject the null hypothesis at the .05 level of significance and conclude that depressed clients performed significantly more activities of daily living following participation in group therapy than they performed before therapy. Since 3.36 is not more extreme than 3.500, the psychologists will fail to reject the null hypothesis at the .01 level of significance and state that the results are inconclusive. Therefore, if the psychologists use the .05 level, group therapy can be recommended as an effective technique for increasing the number of activities of daily living performed by depressed people. However, the same recommendation cannot be made if the psychologists use the .01 level of significance.

The effect size for the study = $M / S = 5 / \sqrt{17.71} = 5 / 4.21 = 1.19$, which is a large effect.

3.
Step 1: Restate the question as a research hypothesis and a null hypothesis about the populations.
Population 1: Students who participate in the anxiety reduction program
Population 2: Students whose anxiety score is 40

Research hypothesis: The anxiety scores of students after therapy will be less than 40.
Null hypothesis: The anxiety scores of students after group therapy will be equal to, or greater than, 40.

Step 2: Determine the characteristics of the comparison distribution.
$\mu = 40$
$M = 40.33$
$S^2 = 252 / 8 = 31.50$
$S^2_M = S^2 / N = 31.50 / 9 = 3.50$
$S_M = \sqrt{S^2_M} = \sqrt{3.50} = 1.87$

The comparison distribution will be a t distribution with 8 df.

Step 3: Determine the cutoff sample score on the comparison distribution at which the null hypothesis should be rejected.
The cutoff sample score for a t distribution with 8 df using a one-tailed test at the .05 level of significance will be -1.860 for a one-tailed test.
The cutoff sample score for a t distribution with 8 df using a one-tailed test at the .01 level of significance will be -2.897 for a one-tailed test.

Step 4: Determine the sample score on the comparison distribution.
$t = (M - \mu) / S_M$
$\quad = (40.33 - 40) / 1.87$
$\quad = 0.18$

Step 5: Decide whether to reject the null hypothesis.
In this case, the mean anxiety score is greater than the mean for the population and is in the opposite direction from the psychologist's prediction. Therefore, the psychologist cannot reject the null hypothesis, regardless of the level of significance chosen, and the psychologist cannot recommend the anxiety reduction program as an effective method for reducing test anxiety.

Compare your explanation to the "Outline for Writing Essays for a *t* test for a Single Sample on pp. 257-258 in the text and to the sample answer to Set I Practice Problem 5(c).

4.
Step 1: Restate the question as a research hypothesis and a null hypothesis about the populations.
Population 1: Students who participate in the anxiety reduction program
Population 2: Students whose test anxiety does not change

Research hypothesis: The anxiety scores of students after the anxiety reduction program will be different from their anxiety scores before the program.
Null hypothesis: The anxiety scores of students after the anxiety reduction program will be no different from their anxiety scores before the program.

Step 2: Determine the characteristics of the comparison distribution.
Pop $M = 0$
For *difference scores*
$M = -3.9$
$S^2 = 189.90 / 9 = 20.99$
$S^2_M = S^2 / N = 20.99 / 10 = 2.10$

$S_M = \sqrt{S^2_M} = \sqrt{2.10} = 1.45$
The comparison distribution will be a *t* distribution with 9 *df*.

Step 3: Determine the cutoff sample score on the comparison distribution at which the null hypothesis should be rejected.

The cutoff sample score for a *t* distribution with 9 *df* using a two-tailed test at the .05 level of significance = ±2.262 for a two-tailed test.
The cutoff sample score for a *t* distribution with 9 *df* using a two-tailed test at the .01 level of significance = ±3.250 for a two-tailed test.

Step 4: Determine the Sample Score on the Comparison Distribution
$t = (M - \mu) / S_M$
$= (-3.90 - 0) / 1.45$
$= -2.69$

Step 5: Decide Whether to Reject the Null Hypothesis
Since -2.69 is more extreme than -2.262, the psychologists will reject the null hypothesis at the .05 level of significance and conclude that the anxiety reduction program significantly reduced test anxiety. Since -2.69 is not more extreme than -3.250, the psychologists will fail to reject the null hypothesis at the .01 level of significance and state that the results are inconclusive. Therefore, if the psychologists use the .05 level, the anxiety reduction program can be recommended as an effective technique for decreasing the test anxiety experienced by students. However, the same recommendation cannot be made if the psychologists use the .01 level of significance. The

effect size for the study = $M / S = -3.90 / \sqrt{20.99} = -3.90 / 4.58 = -0.85$ – a large effect.

Compare your explanation to the "Outline for Writing Essays for a *t* test for Dependent Means on p. 258 in the text and to the sample answer to Set I Practice Problem 5(c).

5.

Study	Effect Size	N	Tails	Power
(a)	Small	50	One	.40
(b)	Medium	40	One	.93
(c)	Small	40	Two	.24
(d)	Small	100	Two	.55
(e)	Medium	40	Two	.88
(f)	Large	20	Two	.93

6.

Study	Predicted Effect Size	Tails	N
(a)	Medium	One	26
(b)	Small	Two	196
(c)	Large	Two	14

Chapter 8

Completion Items:

1. independent	5. pooled estimate	9. normal
2. dependent	6. weighted average	10. equal
3. single sample	7. $S^2_{Difference}$	11. harmonic mean
4. differences between means	8. $S_{Difference}$	

Multiple Choice Items:

1. A	4. D	7. C	10. B
2. D	5. C	8. A	11. A
3. C	6. B	9. C	12. D

Problems

1.
Step 1: Restate the question as a Research hypothesis and a null hypothesis about the populations.
Population 1: Depressed people who participate in group therapy
Population 2: Depressed people who participate in individual therapy

Research hypothesis: The number of activities of daily living reported by depressed people who undergo group therapy (Group 1) will be different from the number of activities of daily living reported by depressed people who undergo individual therapy (Group 2).
Null hypothesis: The number of activities of daily living reported by depressed people who undergo group therapy will be no different from the number of activities of daily living reported by depressed people who undergo individual therapy.

Step 2: Determine the characteristics of the comparison distribution.
$M_1 = 16.00$; $S^2_1 = 24.00 / 7 = 3.43$
$M_2 = 17.50$; $S^2_2 = 38.00 / 7 = 5.43$
$N_1 = 8$; $df_1 = N_1 - 1 = 8 - 1 = 7$
$N_2 = 8$; $df_2 = N_2 - 1 = 8 - 1 = 7$
$df_{Total} = df_1 + df_2 = 7 + 7 = 14$

$S^2_{Pooled} = df_1 / df_{Total} (S^2_1) + df_2 / df_{Total} (S^2_2)$
$= 7 / 14 (3.43) + 7 / 14 (5.43)$
$= 1.72 + 2.72 = 4.44$

$S^2_{M1} = S^2_{Pooled} / N_1 = 4.44 / 8 = 0.56$
$S^2_{M2} = S^2_{Pooled} / N_2 = 4.44 / 8 = 0.56$

$S^2_{Difference} = S^2_{M1} + S^2_{M2} = 0.56 + 0.56 = 1.12$
$S_{Difference} = \sqrt{S^2_{Difference}} = \sqrt{1.12} = 1.06$
The comparison distribution will be a t distribution with 14 df.

Step 3: Determine the cutoff sample score on the comparison distribution at which the null hypothesis should be rejected.

For a t distribution with 14 df, the cutoff sample score at the .05 level of significance will be ± 2.145 for a two-tailed test.

For a t distribution with 14 df, the cutoff sample score at the .01 level of significance will be ± 2.977 for a two-tailed test.

Step 4: Determine the sample score on the comparison distribution.
$t = (M_1 - M_2) / S_{\text{Difference}}$
$= (16.00 - 17.50) / 1.06$
$= -1.50 / 1.06$
$= -1.42$ (If you reverse the means, t will be positive.)

Step 5: Decide whether to reject the null hypothesis.
Since -1.42 is not more extreme than -2.145, the psychologists will fail to reject the null hypothesis at the .05 level of significance and state that the results are inconclusive. Similarly, -1.42 is not more extreme than -2.977, so the psychologists will fail to reject the null hypothesis at the .01 level of significance and state that the results are inconclusive. Based on these results, the psychologists cannot recommend either type of therapy to increase the number of activities of daily living performed by depressed people.

Estimated effect size $(M_1 - M_2) / S_{\text{Pooled}}$

$S^2_{\text{Pooled}} = 4.44$

$S_{\text{Pooled}} = \sqrt{4.44} = 2.11$

Effect size $= (16.00 - 17.50) / 2.11 = -1.50 / 2.11 = -0.71$ – a medium / large effect

Compare your explanation to the "Outline for Writing Essays for a t test for Independent Means on p. 298 in the text and to the sample answer to Set I Practice Problem 4(c).

2.
Step 1: Restate the question as a research hypothesis and a null hypothesis about the populations.
Population 1: Depressed people who participate in group therapy (Group 1)
Population 2: Depressed people who participate in individual therapy (Group 2)

Research hypothesis: The number of activities of daily living reported by depressed people who undergo individual therapy will be greater than the number of activities of daily living reported by depressed people who undergo group therapy.

Null hypothesis: The number of activities of daily living reported by depressed people who undergo individual therapy will be equal to, or lower than, the number of activities of daily living reported by depressed people who undergo group therapy.

Step 2: Determine the characteristics of the comparison distribution.
$M_1 = 15.87$; $S^2_1 = 131.73 / 14 = 9.41$
$M_2 = 18.35$; $S^2_2 = 147.88 / 16 = 9.24$
$N_1 = 15$; $df_1 = N_1 - 1 = 15 - 1 = 14$
$N_2 = 17$; $df_2 = N_2 - 1 = 17 - 1 = 16$
$df_{\text{Total}} = df_1 + df_2 = 14 + 16 = 30$

$S^2_{\text{Pooled}} = df_1 / df_{\text{Total}} (S^2_1) + df_2 / df_{\text{Total}} (S^2_2)$
$= 14 / 30 (9.41) + 16 / 30 (9.24)$
$= 4.39 + 4.93 = 9.32$

$S^2_{M1} = S^2_{\text{Pooled}} / N_1 = 9.32 / 15 = 0.62$
$S^2_{M2} = S^2_{\text{Pooled}} / N_2 = 9.32 / 17 = 0.55$

$S^2_{\text{Difference}} = S^2_{M1} + S^2_{M2} = 0.62 + 0.55 = 1.17$

$S_{\text{Difference}} = \sqrt{S^2_{\text{Difference}}} = \sqrt{1.17} = 1.08$

The comparison distribution will be a t distribution with 30 df.

Step 3: Determine the cutoff sample score on the comparison distribution at which the null hypothesis should be rejected.

For a t distribution with 30 df, the cutoff sample score at the .05 level of significance will be -1.698 for a one-tailed test.
For a t distribution with 30 df, the cutoff sample score at the .01 level of significance will be -2.458 for a one-tailed test.

Step 4: Determine the sample score on the comparison distribution.
$t = (M_1 - M_2) / S_{\text{Difference}}$
 $= (15.87 - 18.35) / 1.08$
 $= -2.48 / 1.08 = -2.30$ (If you reverse the means, t will be positive.)

Step 5: Decide whether to reject the null hypothesis.
Since -2.30 is more extreme than -1.698, the psychologists will reject the null hypothesis at the .05 level of significance and accept the research hypothesis that the number of activities of daily living reported by depressed people who undergo individual therapy (Group 1) will be greater than the number of activities of daily living reported by depressed people who undergo group therapy (Group 2). However, -2.30 is not more extreme than -2.458, so the psychologists will fail to reject the null hypothesis at the .01 level of significance and state that the results are inconclusive. Based on these results, the psychologists can recommend individual therapy to increase the number of activities of daily living performed by depressed people if they base their recommendation of the test of the null hypothesis at the .05 level. They cannot recommend either type of therapy to increase the number of activities of daily living performed by depressed people based on the test of the null hypothesis at the .01 level. (Remember that when a psychologist actually conducts a study, only one level of significance is used.)

Estimated effect size $(M_1 - M_2) / S_{\text{Pooled}}$
$S^2{}_{\text{Pooled}} = 9.32$
$S_{\text{Pooled}} = \sqrt{9.32} = 3.05$
Effect size = $(15.87-18.35) / 3.05 = -2.48 / 3.05 = -0.81$ – a large effect
Compare your explanation to the "Outline for Writing Essays for a t test for Independent Means on p. 298 in the text and to the sample answer to Set I Practice Problem 4(c).

3.
Step 1: Restate the question as a research hypothesis and a null hypothesis about the populations.
Population 1: Employees who participate in counseling (Group 1)
Population 2: Employees who do not participate in counseling (Group 2)

Research hypothesis: The job satisfaction of employees who participate in counseling will be higher than the job satisfaction of employees who do not participate in counseling.
Null hypothesis: The job satisfaction of employees who participate in counseling will be the same as, or lower than, the job satisfaction of employees who do not participate in counseling.

Step 2: Determine the characteristics of the comparison distribution.
$M_1 = 38.00$; $S^2{}_1 = 40.00 / 8 = 5.00$
$M_2 = 35.00$; $S^2{}_2 = 68.00 / 8 = 8.50$
$N_1 = 9$; $df_1 = N_1 - 1 = 9 - 1 = 8$
$N_2 = 9$; $df_2 = N_2 - 1 = 9 - 1 = 8$
$Df_{\text{Total}} = df_1 + df_2 = 8 + 8 = 16$

$S^2{}_{\text{Pooled}} = df_1 / df_{\text{Total}} (S^2{}_1) + df_2 / df_{\text{Total}} (S^2{}_2)$
 $= 8 / 16 (5.00) + 8 / 16 (8.50)$
 $= 2.50 + 4.25 = 6.75$

$S^2_{M1} = S^2_{Pooled} / N_1 = 6.75 / 9 = 0.75$
$S^2_{M2} = S^2_{Pooled} / N_2 = 6.75 / 9 = 0.75$

$S^2_{Difference} = S^2_{M1} + S^2_{M2} = 0.75 + 0.75 = 1.50$

$S_{Difference} = \sqrt{S^2_{Difference}} = \sqrt{1.50} = 1.22$

The comparison distribution will be a t distribution with 16 df.

Step 3: Determine the cutoff sample score on the comparison distribution at which the null hypothesis should be rejected.
For a t distribution with 16 df, the cutoff sample score at the .01 level of significance will be +2.584 for a one-tailed test.

Step 4: Determine the sample score on the comparison distribution.
$t = (M_1 - M_2) / S_{Difference}$
  $= (38.00-35.00) / 1.22$
  $= 3.00 / 1.22$
  $= 2.46$ (If the means are reversed, t will be positive.)

Step 5: Decide whether to reject the null hypothesis.
Since 2.46 is not more extreme than 2.584, the psychologists will fail to reject the null hypothesis at the .05 level of significance and state that the results are inconclusive. Based on these results, the psychologists cannot recommend counseling to increase the job satisfaction reported by employees after an industrial accident.

Estimated effect size $(M_1 - M_2) / S_{Pooled}$
$S^2_{Pooled} = 6.75$

$S_{Pooled} = \sqrt{6.75} = 2.60$
$= (38.00 - 35.00) / 2.60 = 3.00 / 2.60 = 1.15 -$ a large effect
Compare your explanation to the sample response to Practice Problem 4 in Set 1 in the text.
Compare your explanation to the "Outline for Writing Essays for a t test for Independent Means on p. 298 in the text and to the sample answer to Set I Practice Problem 4(c).

4.
The large effect size and high power indicate that the treatment did not have the desired effect at the level of significance specified. However, remember that the .01 level of significance is more conservative than the .05 level. At the .05 level, the cutoff sample score for a one-tailed test with 16 df is 1.746, and using this cutoff sample score, the results of the study would have been statistically significant.

5.
Step 1: Restate the question as a research hypothesis and a null hypothesis about the populations.
Population 1: Elderly people who walk and participate in flexibility exercises (Group 1)
Population 2: Elderly people who walk only (Group 2)

Research hypothesis: The perception of well-being reported by people who walk and participate in flexibility exercises will be different from the perception of well-being reported by people who walk only.
Null hypothesis: The perception of well-being reported by people who walk and participate in flexibility exercises will be no different from the perception of well-being reported by people who walk only.

Step 2: Determine the characteristics of the comparison distribution.
$M_1 = 6.67; S^2_1 = 49.33 / 14 = 3.52$
$M_2 = 5.00; S^2_2 = 34.00 / 10 = 3.40$
$N_1 = 15; df_1 = N_1 - 1 = 15 - -1 = 14$
$N_2 = 11; df_2 = N_2 - 1 = 11 - 1 = 10$
$df_{Total} = df_1 + df_2 = 14 + 10 = 24$

$S^2_{Pooled} = [(df_1 / df_{Total}) (S^2_1)] + [(df_2 / df_{Total}) (S^2_2)]$
$= [(14 / 24) (3.52)] + [(10 / 24) (3.40)]$
$= 2.05 + 1.42 = 3.47$

$S^2_{M1} = S^2_{Pooled} / N_1 = 3.47 / 15 = 0.23$
$S^2_{M2} = S^2_{Pooled} / N_2 = 3.47 / 11 = 0.32$

$S^2_{Difference} = S^2_{M1} + S^2_{M2} = 0.23 + 0.32 = 0.55$

$S_{Difference} = \sqrt{S^2_{Difference}} = \sqrt{0.55} = 0.74$

The comparison distribution will be a t distribution with 24 df.

Step 3: Determine the cutoff sample score on the comparison distribution at which the null hypothesis should be rejected.

For a t distribution with 24 df, the cutoff sample score at the .05 level of significance will be ± 2.064 for a two-tailed test.

Step 4: Determine the sample score on the comparison distribution.
$t = (M_1 - -M_2) / S_{Difference}$
$= (6.67 - 5.00) / 0.74$
$= 1.67 / 0.74$
$= 2.26$ (If the means are reversed, t will be negative.)

Step 5: Decide whether to reject the null hypothesis.

Since 2.26 is more extreme than 2.064, the psychologist will reject the null hypothesis at the .05 level of significance and accept the research hypothesis that the perception of well-being of elderly people who walk and participate in exercises to improve flexibility will be greater than the perception of well-being of elderly people who walk only. Based on these results, the psychologist can recommend the combination of walking and exercises to improve flexibility as a way to enhance perceptions of well-being in elderly populations.

Estimated effect size $(M_1 - -M_2) / S_{Pooled}$
$S^2_{Pooled} = 3.47$

$S_{Pooled} = \sqrt{3.47} = 1.86$
$= (6.67 - 5.00) / 1.86 = 1.67 / 1.86 = 0.90$, – a large effect.
Compare your explanation to the "Outline for Writing Essays for a t test for Independent Means on p. 298 in the text and to the sample answer to Set I Practice Problem 4(c).

6.

Study	Effect Size	N	Tails	Power
(a)	Small	50	One	.11
(b)	Medium	40	One	.61
(c)	Small	40	Two	.09
(d)	Small	100	Two	.29
(e)	Medium	40	Two	.60
(f)	Large	20	Two	.69

7.

Study	μ_1	μ_2	σ	Tails	Effect	Total N	Group N
(a)	36	58	44	2	-0.50	128	64
(b)	152	120	40	2	0.80	52	26
(c)	50	52	10	1	-0.20	620	310
(d)	12	9	6	1	0.50	100	50

8.

    A. *t* test for independent means
    B. *t* test for a single sample
    C. *t* test for a single sample
    D. *t* test for dependent means
    E. *t* test for dependent means
    F. *t* test for independent means

Chapter 9

Completion Items:

1. analysis of variance	7. S^2_{Within}	13. Bonferroni procedure	19. $SS_{Between}$
2. grand	8. F distribution	14. post hoc	20. SS_{Within}
3. $S^2_{Between}$	9. F table	15. Scheffé	21. SS_{Total}
4. S^2_{Within}	10. $df_{Between}$	16. R^2	22. analysis of variance table
5. F ratio	11. df_{Within}	17. η^2	
6. $S^2_{Between}$	12. planned comparisons	18. structural model	

Multiple Choice Items:

1. C	5. C	9. A	13. A	17. C
2. A	6. B	10. D	14. D	
3. C	7. A	11. D	15. B	
4. D	8. C	12. B	16. A	

Problems

1.

Subject	Group 1	Group 2	Group 3
1	16	21	24
2	15	20	21
3	18	17	25
4	21	23	20
5	19	19	22
$\sum X$	89	100	112
M	17.80	20.00	22.40
$\sum (X - M)^2$	22.80	20.00	17.20

Step 1: Restate the question as a research hypothesis and a null hypothesis about the populations.
Population 1: Depressed clients receiving 1 hour of individual therapy every 2 weeks
Population 2: Depressed clients receiving 1 hour of individual therapy every week
Population 3: Depressed clients receiving 2 hours of individual therapy every week

Research hypothesis: The mean number of activities of daily living performed by the three groups of clients will be different based on the type of therapy each group receives.
Null hypothesis: The mean number of activities of daily living performed by the three groups of clients will be no different based on the type of therapy each group receives.

Step 2: Determine the characteristics of the comparison distribution.
The study involves three groups of 5 clients each.
$df_{Between} = N_{Groups} - 1 = (3 - 1) = 2$
$df_{Within} = df_1 + df_2 + df_3 = (5 - 1) + (5 - 1) + (5 - 1) = 4 + 4 + 4 = 12$
The comparison distribution will be an F distribution with 2 and 12 df.

Step 3: Determine the cutoff sample score on the comparison distribution at which the null hypothesis should be rejected.

$F_{2,12}$ at the .05 level of significance = 3.89

Step 4: Determine the sample's score on the comparison distribution.

$M_1 = 17.80$

$M_2 = 20.00$

$M_3 = 22.40$

$GM = (17.80 + 20.00 + 22.40) / 3 = 60.20 / 3 = 20.07$

$S^2_M = \Sigma(M - GM)^2 / df_{Between} = [(17.80 - 20.07)^2 + (20.00 - 20.07)^2 + (22.40 - 20.07)^2] / 3 - 1 = [(-2.27)^2 + (-0.07)^2 + (2.33)^2] / 2 = (5.15 + 0.00 + 5.43) / 2 = 10.58 / 2 = 5.29$

$S^2_{Between} = (S^2_M)(n) = (5.29)(5) = 26.45$

$\Sigma(X - M)^2_1 = 17.20$

$S^2_1 = \Sigma(X - M)^2_1 / df_3 = 22.80 / 4 = 5.70$

$\Sigma(X - M)^2_2 = 20.00$

$S^2_2 = \Sigma(X - M)^2_2 / df_2 = 20.00 / 4 = 5.00$

$\Sigma(X - M)^2_3 = 22.80$

$S^2_3 = \Sigma(X - M)^2_3 / df_1 = 17.20 / 4 = 4.30$

$S^2_{Within} = (5.70 + 5.00 + 4.30) / 3 = 15 / 3 = 5.00$

$F = S^2_{Between} / S^2_{Within} = 26.45 / 5.00 = 5.29$

Step 5: Decide whether to reject the null hypothesis.

Since $F = 5.29$ is more extreme than 3.89, the psychologists will reject the null hypothesis at the .05 level of significance.

Effect size = $R^2 = (S^2_{Between})(df_{Between}) / (S^2_{Between})(df_{Between}) + (S^2_{Within})(df_{Within}) = (26.45)(2) / (26.45)(2) + (5.00)(12) = 52.90 / 52.90 + 60 = 52.90 / 112.90 = 0.47$, – a large effect.

<u>Planned Contrasts:</u>

Group 1 with Group 2:

$GM = (17.80 + 20.00) / 2 = 37.80 / 2 = 18.90$

$df = 2 - 1 = 1$

$S^2_M = \Sigma(M - GM)^2 / df_{Between} = [(17.80 - 18.90)^2 + (20.00 - 18.90)^2] / 2 - 1 = [(-1.10)^2 + (1.10)^2] / 1 = 1.21 + 1.21 / 1 = 2.42 / 1 = 2.42$

$S^2_{Between} = (S^2_M)(n) = (2.42)(5) = 12.10$

$S^2_{Within} = (5.70 + 5.00 + 4.30) / 3 = 15 / 3 = 5.00$

$F = S^2_{Between} / S^2_{Within} = 12.10 / 5.00 = 2.42$

Cutoff sample score for $F_{1,12}$ at the .05 level of significance = 4.75

Since $F = 2.42$ is not more extreme than 4.75, the difference between the means of Group 1 and Group 2 is not statistically significant.

Group 1 with Group 3

$GM = (17.80 + 22.40) / 2 = 40.20 / 2 = 20.10$

$df = 2 - 1 = 1$

$S^2_M = \Sigma(M - GM)^2 / df_{Between} = [(17.80 - 20.10)^2 + (22.40 - 20.10)^2] / 2 - 1 = [(-2.30)^2 + (2.30)^2] / 1 = 5.29 + 5.29 / 1 = 10.58 / 1 = 10.58$

$S^2_{Between} = (S^2_M)(n) = (10.58)(5) = 52.90$

$S^2_{Within} = (5.70 + 5.00 + 4.30) / 3 = 15 / 3 = 5.00$

$F = S^2_{Between} / S^2_{Within} = 52.90 / 5.00 = 10.58$

Cutoff sample score for $F_{1,12}$ at the .05 level of significance = 4.75

Since $F = 10.58$ is more extreme than 4.75, the difference between the means of Group 1 and Group 3 is statistically significant.

Group 2 with Group 3:

$GM = (20.00 + 22.40) / 2 = 42.40 / 2 = 21.20$

$df = 2 - 1 = 1$

$S^2_M = \Sigma(M-GM)^2 / df_{Between} = [(20.00 - 21.20)^2 + (22.40 - 21.20)^2] / 2 - 1 = [(-1.20)^2 + (1.20)^2] / 1 = 1.44 + 1.44 / 1 = 2.88 / 1 = 2.88$

$S^2_{Between} = (S^2_M)(n) = (2.88)(5) = 14.40$

$S^2_{Within} = (5.70 + 5.00 + 4.30) / 3 = 15 / 3 = 5.00$

$F = S^2_{Between} / S^2_{Within} = 14.40 / 5.00 = 2.88$

Cutoff sample score for $F_{1,12}$ at the .05 level of significance = 4.75

Since $F = 2.28$ is not more extreme than 4.75, the difference between the means of Group 2 and Group 3 is not statistically significant.

Scheffé test

The difference between the means of Group 1 and Group 3 was larger than for any other pair. The value of the F for the comparison (shown with the planned contrasts calculated previously) is 10.58, and $df_{Between} = N_{Groups} - 1 = (3 - 1) = 2$. Dividing 10.58 by 2 yields 5.29, which is more extreme than the cutoff sample $F_{2,12}$ at the .05 level of significance, which is 3.89. Therefore, the psychologists will reject the null hypothesis that the mean number of activities performed by Group 1 and Group 3 are not equal and conclude that Group 3 performed significantly more activities of daily living. This result confirms the result of the planned comparison between these two groups. Based on these results, depressed people who receive two hours of group therapy each week may be expected to perform more activities of daily living than depressed people receiving one hour of therapy every two weeks.

2.

Student	Group 1 (High)	Group 2 (Intermediate)	Group 3 (Low)
1	9.0	3.5	4.5
2	8.5	5.5	5.5
3	6.5	6.5	6.5
4	7.0	3.5	8.0
5	8.0	4.5	5.5
6	5.5	7.0	6.0
ΣX	44.50	30.50	36.00
M	7.42	5.08	6.00
$\Sigma (X - M)^2$	8.71	11.21	7.00

Step 1: Restate the question as a research hypothesis and a null hypothesis about the populations.
Population 1: Students who believe they have a high probability of succeeding in the statistics course
Population 2: Students who believe they have an intermediate probability of succeeding in the statistics course
Population 3: Students who believe they have a low probability of succeeding in the statistics course

Research hypothesis: There will be a difference in the mean motivation level of the three groups of students based on their perceived probability of succeeding in the statistics course.
Null hypothesis: There will be no difference in the mean motivation level of the three groups of students based on their perceived probability of succeeding in the statistics course.

Step 2: Determine the characteristics of the comparison distribution.
The study involves three groups of 6 students each.
$df_{Between} = N_{Groups} - 1 = (3 - 1) = 2$
$df_{Within} = df_1 + df_2 + df_3 = (6 - 1) + (6 - 1) + (6 - 1) = 5 + 5 + 5 = 15$
The comparison distribution will be an F distribution with 2 and 15 df.

Step 3: Determine the cutoff sample score on the comparison distribution at which the null hypothesis should be rejected.
$F_{2,15}$ at the .05 level of significance = 3.68

Step 4: Determine the sample's score on the comparison distribution.

$M_1 = 7.42$

$M_2 = 5.08$

$M_3 = 6.00$

$GM = (7.42 + 5.08 + 6.00) / 3 = 18.50 / 3 = 6.17$

$S^2_M = \Sigma(M - GM)^2 / df_{Between} = [(7.42 - 6.17)^2 + (5.08 - 6.17)^2 + (6.00 - 6.17)^2] / 3 - 1 = [(1.25)^2 + (-1.09)^2 + (-0.17)^2] / 2$

$= (1.56 + 1.19 + 0.03) / 2 = 2.78 / 2 = 1.39$

$S^2_{Between} = (S^2_M)(n) = (1.39)(6) = 8.34$

$\Sigma(X - M)^2_1 = 8.71$

$S^2_1 = \Sigma(X - M)^2_1 / df_1 = 8.71 / 5 = 1.74$

$\Sigma(X - M)^2_2 = 11.21$

$S^2_2 = \Sigma(X - M)^2_2 / df_2 = 11.21 / 5 = 2.24$

$\Sigma(X - M)^2_3 = 7.00$

$S^2_3 = \Sigma(X - M)^2_3 / df_3 = 7.00 / 5 = 1.40$

$S^2_{Within} = (1.74 + 2.24 + 1.40) / 3 = 5.38 / 3 = 1.79$

$F = S^2_{Between} / S^2_{Within} = 8.34 / 1.79 = 4.66$

Step 5: Decide whether to reject the null hypothesis.

Since $F = 4.66$ is more extreme than 3.68, the psychologist will reject the null hypothesis at the .05 level of significance.

Effect size $= R^2 = (S^2_{Between})(df_{Between}) / (S^2_{Between})(df_{Between}) + (S^2_{Within})(df_{Within}) = (8.34)(2) / (8.34)(2) + (1.79)(15)$

$= 16.68 / 16.68 + 26.85 = 16.68 / 43.53 = 0.38, -$ a large effect.

Planned Contrasts:

Group 1 with Group 2:

$GM = (7.42 + 5.08) / 2 = 12.50 / 2 = 6.25$

$df = 2 - 1 = 1$

$S^2_M = \Sigma(M - GM)^2 / df_{Between} = [(7.42 - 6.25)^2 + (5.08 - 6.25)^2] / 2 - 1 = [(1.17)^2 + (-1.17)^2] / 1 = 1.37 + 1.37 / 1 = 2.74 / 1 = 2.74$

$S^2_{Between} = (S^2_M)(n) = (2.74)(6) = 16.44$

$S^2_{Within} = (1.74 + 2.24 + 1.40) / 3 = 5.38 / 3 = 1.79$

$F = S^2_{Between} / S^2_{Within} = 16.64 / 1.79 = 9.18$

Cutoff sample score for $F_{1,15}$ at the .05 level of significance $= 4.54$

Since $F = 9.18$ is more extreme than 4.54, the difference between the means of Group 1 and Group 2 is statistically significant.

Group 1 with Group 3:

$GM = (7.42 + 6.00) / 2 = 13.42 / 2 = 6.71$

$df = 2 - 1 = 1$

$S^2_M = \Sigma(M - GM)^2 / df_{Between} = [(7.42 - 6.71)^2 + (6.00 - 6.71)^2] / 2 - 1 = [(0.71)^2 + (-0.71)^2] / 1 = 0.50 + 0.50 / 1 = 1.00 / 1 = 1.00$

$S^2_{Between} = (S^2_M)(n) = (1.00)(6) = 6.00$

$S^2_{Within} = (1.74 + 2.24 + 1.40) / 3 = 5.38 / 3 = 1.79$

$F = S^2_{Between} / S^2_{Within} = 6.00 / 1.79 = 3.35$

Cutoff sample score for $F_{1,15}$ at the .05 level of significance $= 4.54$

Since $F = 3.35$ is not more extreme than 4.54, the difference between the means of Group 1 and Group 3 is not statistically significant.

Group 2 with Group 3:

$GM = (5.08 + 6.00) / 2 = 11.08 / 2 = 5.54$

$df = 2 - 1 = 1$

$S^2_M = \Sigma(M - GM)^2 / df_{\text{Between}} = [(5.08 - 5.54)^2 + (6.00 - 5.54)^2] / 2 - 1 = [(-0.46)^2 + (0.46)^2] / 1 = 0.21 + 0.21 / 1 = 0.42 / 1 = 0.42$

$S^2_{\text{Between}} = (S^2_M)(n) = (0.42)(6) = 2.52$

$S^2_{\text{Within}} = (1.74 + 2.24 + 1.40) / 3 = 5.38 / 3 = 1.79$

$F = S^2_{\text{Between}} / S^2_{\text{Within}} = 2.52 / 1.79 = 1.41$

Cutoff sample score for $F_{1,15}$ at the .05 level of significance = 4.54

Since $F = 1.41$ is not more extreme than 4.54, the difference between the means of Group 2 and Group 3 is not statistically significant.

Scheffé test

The difference between the means of Group 1 and Group 2 was larger than for any other pair. The value of the F for the comparison (shown with the planned contrasts calculated previously) is 9.18, and $df_{\text{Between}} = N_{\text{Groups}} - 1 = (3 - 1) = 2$. Dividing 9.18 by 2 yields 4.59, which is more extreme than the cutoff sample $F_{2,15}$ at the .05 level of significance, which is 3.68. Therefore, the psychologists will reject the null hypothesis that the mean levels of motivation reported by Group 1 and Group 2 are equal conclude that Group 1 was significantly more motivated. This result confirms the result of the planned comparison between these two groups. Based on these results, students who believed they could be successful in the course reported higher levels of motivation

Compare your explanation to the "Outline for Writing Essays for a One-Way Analysis of Variance on p. 357 in the text and to the sample answer to Set I Practice Problem 3(d) and 3(g).

3.

Category	N	M	S^2
Judges	6	7.00	1.99
Attorneys	6	5.83	1.37
Jurors	6	7.83	1.37
Law Enforcement	6	3.00	3.61

Step 1: Restate the question as a research hypothesis and a null hypothesis about the populations.
Population 1: Judges
Population 2: Attorneys
Population 3: Jurors
Population 4: Law enforcement officials

Research hypothesis: There will be a difference in the mean evaluation of the effectiveness of testimony by psychologists by members of the four categories of court personnel.
Null hypothesis: There will be no difference in the mean evaluation of the effectiveness of testimony by psychologists by members of the four categories of court personnel.

Step 2: Determine the characteristics of the comparison distribution.
The study involves four groups of 6 members each.

$df_{\text{Between}} = N_{\text{Groups}} - 1 = (4 - 1) = 3$

$df_{\text{Within}} = df_1 + df_2 + df_3 + df_4 = (6-1) + (6-1) + (6-1) + (6-1) = 5 + 5 + 5 + 5 = 20$

The comparison distribution will be an F distribution with 3 and 20 df.

Step 3: Determine the cutoff sample score on the comparison distribution at which the null hypothesis should be rejected.

$F_{3,20}$ at the .01 level of significance = 4.94

Step 4: Determine the sample's score on the comparison distribution.

$M_1 = 7.00$

$M_2 = 5.83$

$M_3 = 7.83$

$M_4 = 3.00$

$GM = (7.00 + 5.83 + 7.83 + 3.00) / 4 = 23.66 / 4 = 5.92$

$S^2_M = \Sigma(M - GM)^2 / df_{Between} = [(7.00 - 5.92)^2 + (5.83 - 5.92)^2 + (7.83 - 5.92)^2 + (3.00 - 5.92)^2] / 4 - 1 = [(1.08)^2 + (-0.09)^2 + (1.91)^2 + (-2.92)^2] / 2 = (1.17 + 0.01 + 3.65 + 8.53) / 2 = 13.36 / 3 = 4.45$

$S^2_{Between} = (S^2_M)(n) = (4.45)(6) = 26.70$

$\Sigma(X - M)^2_1 = 10.00$

$S^2_1 = \Sigma(X - M)^2_1 / df_1 = 10.00 / 5 = 2.00$

$\Sigma(X - M)^2_2 = 6.83$

$S^2_2 = \Sigma(X - M)^2_2 / df_2 = 6.83 / 5 = 1.37$

$\Sigma(X - M)^2_3 = 6.83$

$S^2_3 = \Sigma(X - M)^2_3 / df_3 = 6.83 / 5 = 1.37$

$\Sigma(X - M)^2_4 = 18.00$

$S^2_4 = \Sigma(X - M)^2_4 / df_4 = 187.00 / 5 = 3.60$

$S^2_{Within} = (2.00 + 1.37 + 1.37 + 3.60) / 4 = 8.34 / 4 = 2.09$

$F = S^2_{Between} / S^2_{Within} = 26.70 / 2.09 = 12.78$

Step 5: Decide whether to reject the null hypothesis.

Since $F = 12.78$ is more extreme than 4.94, the organization will reject the null hypothesis at the .05 level of significance.

Effect size $= R^2 = [(S^2_{Between})(df_{Between})] / [(S^2_{Between})(df_{Between})] + [(S^2_{Within})(df_{Within})] =$
$[(26.70)(3)] / [(26.70)(3)] + [(12.78)(20)] = 80.10 / (80.10 + 255.60) = 80.10 / 335.70 = 0.24, -$ a large effect.

Planned Contrasts:

Judges with Attorneys:

$GM = (7.00 + 5.83) / 2 = 12.83 / 2 = 6.42$

$df = 2 - 1 = 1$

$S^2_M = \Sigma(M - GM)^2 / df_{Between} = [(7.00 - 6.42)^2 + (5.83 - 6.42)^2] / 2 - 1 = [(0.58)^2 + (-0.58)^2] / 1 = 0.34 + 0.34 / 1 = 0.68 / 1 = 0.68$

$S^2_{Between} = (S^2_M)(n) = (0.68)(6) = 4.08$

$S^2_{Within} = (2.00 + 1.37 + 1.37 + 3.60) / 4 = 8.34 / 4 = 2.09$

$F = S^2_{Between} / S^2_{Within} = 4.08 / 2.09 = 1.95$

Cutoff sample score for $F_{1,20}$ at the .01 level of significance $= 8.10$

Since $F = 1.95$ is not more extreme than 8.10, the difference between the means of Judges and Attorneys is not statistically significant.

Judges with Law Enforcement:

$GM = (7.00 + 3.00) / 2 = 10.00 / 2 = 5.00$

$df = 2 - 1 = 1$

$S^2_M = \Sigma(M - GM)^2 / df_{Between} = [(7.00 - 5.00)^2 + (3.00 - 5.00)^2] / 2 - 1 = [(2.00)^2 + (-2.00)^2] / 1 = 4.00 + 4.00 / 1 = 8.00 / 1 = 8.00$

$S^2_{Between} = (S^2_M)(n) = (8.00)(6) = 48.00$

$S^2_{Within} = (2.00 + 1.37 + 1.37 + 3.60) / 4 = 8.34 / 4 = 2.09$

$F = S^2_{Between} / S^2_{Within} = 48.00 / 2.09 = 22.97$

Cutoff sample score for $F_{1,20}$ at the .01 level of significance $= 8.10$

Since $F = 22.97$ is more extreme than 8.10, the difference between the means of Judges and Law Enforcement is statistically significant.

Attorneys with Jurors:

$GM = (5.83 + 7.83) / 2 = 13.66 / 2 = 6.83$

$df = 2 - 1 = 1$

$S^2_M = \Sigma(M - GM)^2 / df_{Between} = [(5.83 - 6.83)^2 + (7.83 - 6.83)^2] / 2 - 1 = [(-1.00)^2 + (1.00)^2] / 1 = 1.00 + 1.00 / 1 = 2.00 / 1 = 2.00$

$S^2_{Between} = (S^2_M)(n) = (2.00)(6) = 12.00$

$S^2_{Within} = (2.00 + 1.37 + 1.37 + 3.60) / 4 = 8.34 / 4 = 2.09$

$F = S^2_{Between} / S^2_{Within} = 12.00 / 2.09 = 5.74$

Cutoff sample score for $F_{1,20}$ at the .01 level of significance = 8.10

Since $F = 5.74$ is not more extreme than 8.10, the difference between the means of Attorneys and Jurors is not statistically significant.

Attorneys with Law Enforcement:

$GM = (5.83 + 3.00) / 2 = 8.83 / 2 = 4.42$

$df = 2 - 1 = 1$

$S^2_M = \Sigma(M - GM)^2 / df_{Between} = [(5.83 - 4.42)^2 + (3.00 - 4.42)^2] / 2 - 1 = [(1.41)^2 + (-1.42)^2] / 1 = 1.99 + 2.02 / 1 = 4.01 / 1 = 4.01$ [Note slight rounding differences.]

$S^2_{Between} = (S^2_M)(n) = (4.01)(6) = 24.06$

$S^2_{Within} = (2.00 + 1.37 + 1.37 + 3.60) / 4 = 8.34 / 4 = 2.09$

$F = S^2_{Between} / S^2_{Within} = 24.06 / 2.09 = 11.51$

Cutoff sample score for $F_{1,20}$ at the .01 level of significance = 8.10

Since $F = 11.51$ is more extreme than 8.10, the difference between the means of Attorneys and Law Enforcement is statistically significant.

Jurors with Law Enforcement:

$GM = (7.83 + 3.00) / 2 = 10.83 / 2 = 5.42$

$df = 2 - 1 = 1$

$S^2_M = \Sigma(M - GM)^2 / df_{Between} = [(7.83 - 5.42)^2 + (3.00 - 5.42)^2] / 2 - 1 = [(2.41)^2 + (-2.42)^2] / 1 = (5.81 + 5.86) / 1 = 11.67 / 1 = 11.67$ [Note slight rounding differences.]

$S^2_{Between} = (S^2_M)(n) = (11.67)(6) = 70.02$

$S^2_{Within} = (2.00 + 1.37 + 1.37 + 3.60) / 4 = 8.34 / 4 = 2.09$

$F = S^2_{Between} / S^2_{Within} = 70.02 / 2.09 = 33.50$

Cutoff sample score for $F_{1,20}$ at the .01 level of significance = 8.10

Since $F = 33.50$ is more extreme than 8.10, the difference between the means of Jurors and Law Enforcement is statistically significant.

Since the overall level of significance for the planned contrasts was set at .05, the Bonferroni procedure resulted in a .01 level of significance (.05 / 5 = .01). This procedure was applied to maintain the overall significance level at .05 while making multiple comparisons. Thus, the purpose of the procedure is to maintain the probability of Type I errors at the stated level of significance. The results show that Law Enforcement personnel gave significantly lower evaluations of the effectiveness of the testimony of psychologists than the other three groups, and that the evaluations of Judges and Attorneys and Attorneys and Jurors did not differ.

4.

One hour of therapy every two weeks

X	X – GM		X – M		M – GM	
	Deviation	Deviation^2	Deviation	Deviation^2	Deviation	Deviation^2
16	-4.07	16.56	-1.80	3.24	-2.27	5.15
15	-5.07	25.70	-2.80	7.84	-2.27	5.15
18	-2.07	4.28	0.20	0.04	-2.27	5.15
21	0.93	0.86	3.20	10.24	-2.27	5.15
19	-1.07	1.14	1.20	1.44	-2.27	5.15
$\Sigma = 89$		$\Sigma = 48.56$		$\Sigma = 22.80$		$\Sigma = 25.76$
$M = 17.80$						

[Note slight rounding differences in all tables.]

One hour of therapy every week

X	X – GM		X – M		M – GM	
	Deviation	Deviation^2	Deviation	Deviation^2	Deviation	Deviation^2
21	0.93	0.86	1.00	1.00	-0.07	0.0049
20	-0.07	0.00	0.00	0.00	-0.07	0.0049
17	-3.07	9.42	-3.00	9.00	-0.07	0.0049
23	2.93	8.58	3.00	9.00	-0.07	0.0049
19	-1.07	1.14	-1.00	1.00	-0.07	0.0049
Σ= 100		Σ = 20.02		Σ = 20.00		Σ = 0.02
M = 20.00						

Two hours of therapy every week

X	X – GM		X – M		M – GM	
	Deviation	Deviation^2	Deviation	Deviation^2	Deviation	Deviation^2
24	3.93	15.44	1.60	2.56	2.33	5.43
21	0.93	0.86	-1.40	1.96	2.33	5.43
25	4.93	24.30	2.60	6.76	2.33	5.43
20	-0.07	0.00	-2.40	5.76	2.33	5.43
22	1.93	3.72	-0.40	0.16	2.33	5.43
Σ = 112		Σ = 44.34		Σ = 17.20		Σ = 27.14
M = 22.40						

$GM = (17.80 + 20.00 + 22.40) / 3 = 60.20 / 3 = 20.07$

Sums of squared deviations:
$\Sigma (X - GM)^2$ or $SS_{Total} = 48.56 + 20.02 + 44.34 = 112.92$
$\Sigma (X - M)^2$ or $SS_{Within} = 22.80 + 20.00 + 17.20 = 60.00$
$\Sigma (M - GM)^2$ or $SS_{Between} = 25.76 + 0.02 + 27.14 = 52.92$
Check ($SS_{Total} = SS_{Within} + SS_{Between}$); $SS_{Total} = 112.92$ and $60.00 + 52.92 = 112.92$

Degrees of freedom:
$df_{Total} = N - 1 = 15 - 1 = 14$
$df_{Within} = df_1 = df_2 = df_3 = (5 - 1) + (5 - 1) + (5 - 1) = 4 + 4 + 4 = 12$
$df_{Between} = N_{Groups} - 1 = 3 - 1 = 2$
Check ($df_{Total} = df_{Within} + df_{Between}$) $14 = 12 + 2$

Population variance estimates:
S^2_{Within} or $MS_{Within} = SS_{Within} / df_{Within} = 60.00 / 12 = 5.00$
$S^2_{Between}$ or $MS_{Between} = SS_{Between} / df_{Between} = 52.92 / 2 = 26.46$

$F = S^2_{Between} / S^2_{Within}$ or $MS_{Between} / MS_{Within} = 26.46 / 5.00 = 5.29$

The F ratios for Problem 1 and Problem 4 are identical.

5.

Situation	(a)	(b)	(c)	(d)	(e)
Overall Significance Level	.05	.05	.01	.01	.01
# of Planned Comparisons	3	6	2	4	6
Adjusted level of significance	.0167	.0083	.005	.0025	.0017

6.

Study	Groups	$df_{Between}$	# per Group	df_{Within}	Significance	Cutoff F	Scheffé	Significant?
(a)	3	2	9	24	.05	3.40	4.83	Yes
(b)	4	3	8	28	.05	2.95	3.22	Yes
(c)	4	3	11	40	.01	4.31	3.22	No
(d)	5	4	10	45	.01	3.77	2.42	No
(e)	6	5	11	60	.05	2.37	1.93	No

7.

Predicted Effect Size	# of Groups	# of Participants in Each Group	Power
Small	5	30	.13
Medium	4	20	.43
Medium	5	30	.67
Large	3	30	.93
Large	4	20	.85

8.

Predicted Effect Size	# of Groups	# per Group
Small	5	240
Medium	4	45
Medium	5	39
Large	4	18
Large	5	16

Chapter 10

Completion Items:

1. one-way	5. interaction efect	9. cell mean
2. factorial	6. two-way factorial	10. marginal
3. factorial	7. two-way	11. repeated measures
4. main	8. cell	12. dichotomizing

Multiple Choice Items:

1. C	6. D	11. A
2. D	7. A	12. A
3. B	8. C	13. D
4. C	9. B	14. C
5. A	10. D	

Problems

1.

		Student Age		Marginal Means
		Younger	Older	
Course Format	Lecture-based	$M = 38$	$M = 28$	$M = 33$
	Computer-based	$M = 28$	$M = 38$	$M = 33$
Marginal Means		$M = 33$	$M = 33$	

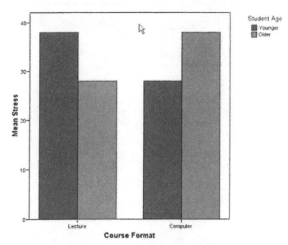

(The graph with age on the horizontal axis would simply reverse the order of the bars for method.)
Since all marginal means are identical, no main effects are present. However, as the cell means and bar graphs indicate, an interaction effect indicating that younger students report lower levels of stress in computer-based courses, while older students report lower levels of stress in lecture-based courses.

2.

		Method		Marginal Means
		Phonics	Whole-word	
Gender	Girls	$M = 19$	$M = 15$	$M = 17$
	Boys	$M = 16$	$M = 12$	$M = 14$
Marginal Means		$M = 17.5$	$M = 13.5$	

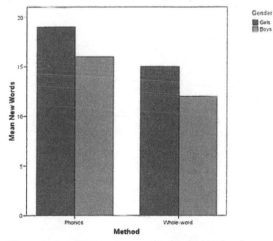

(The graph with gender on the horizontal axis would simply reverse the order of the bars for method.)
Since all marginal means are different, main effects for both format and age are present. However, as the differences between cell means and bar graphs indicate, no interaction effect is present. Each combination learns the number of new words expected by knowing the level of each variable separately, i.e., the difference between the cell means for each row and each column is three.

3.

		Orientation		Marginal Means
		Yes	No	
High school	Large	$M = 15$	$M = 30$	$M = 22.5$
	Small	$M = 20$	$M = 60$	$M = 40.0$
Marginal Means		$M = 17.5$	$M = 45.0$	

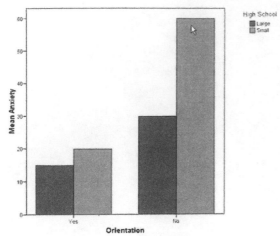

(The graph with high school on the horizontal axis would simply reverse the order of the bars for orientation.)

Since all marginal means are different, main effects for both format and age are present, as is an interaction effect. The level of anxiety is higher for students who did not attend the orientation program and for students from small high schools, but the combination of being unable to attend the orientation program and being from a small high school is greater than would be expected from the effect of either variable alone.

4.

		Student Age		Marginal Means
		Younger	Older	
Course Format	Lecture-based	$M = 36$	$M = 30$	$M = 33$
	Mixed	$M = 30$	$M = 36$	$M = 33$
	Computer-based	$M = 24$	$M = 42$	$M = 33$
Marginal Means		$M = 30$	$M = 36$	

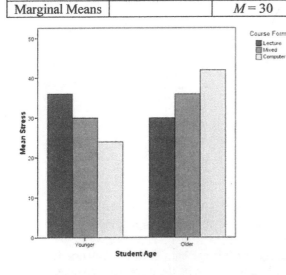

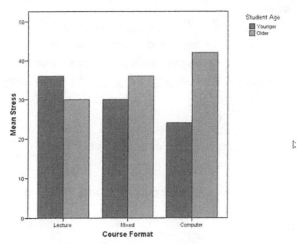

The marginal means indicate a main effect for age with older students reporting more stress than younger students. On the other hand, the marginal means do not indicate a main effect for format. However, a clear interaction effect is present stress for younger students being highest in the lecture-based format and lowest in the computer-based format, with the stress levels being reversed for older students. Connecting the midpoints of the bars in the second graph provides a very clear picture of the effect.

5. Advanced Topic:

Steps of Hypothesis Testing
Step 1: Restate the question as a research hypothesis and a null hypothesis about the populations.
Population 1,1: Depressed women whose therapist is a woman
Population 1,2: Depressed women whose therapist is a man
Population 2,1: Depressed men whose therapist is a woman
Population 2,2: Depressed men whose therapist is a man

Research hypothesis 1: The number of activities of daily living performed by the combined populations of depressed women who undergo individual therapy will be different from the number performed by the combined populations of depressed men who undergo individual therapy.
Null hypothesis 1: The number of activities of daily living performed by the combined populations of depressed women who undergo individual therapy will be the same as the number performed by the combined populations of depressed men who undergo individual therapy.

Research hypothesis 2: The number of activities of daily living performed by the combined populations of depressed clients who undergo individual therapy conducted by a female therapist will be different from the number performed by the combined populations of depressed clients who undergo individual therapy conducted by a male therapist.
Null hypothesis 2: The number of activities of daily living performed by the combined populations of depressed clients who undergo individual therapy conducted by a female therapist will be the same as the number performed by the combined populations of depressed clients who undergo individual therapy conducted by a male therapist.

Research hypothesis 3: The difference between the mean number of activities performed by the two populations of depressed clients whose therapy is conducted by a therapist of the same gender will be different from the difference between the mean number of activities performed by the two populations of depressed clients whose therapy is conducted by a therapist of the opposite gender.
Null hypothesis 3: The difference between the mean number of activities performed by the two populations of depressed clients whose therapy is conducted by a therapist of the same gender will be the same as the difference between the mean number of activities performed by the two populations of depressed clients whose therapy is conducted by a therapist of the opposite gender.

Step 2: Determine the characteristics of the comparison distribution.

The three comparison distributions will be F distributions. Since $df_{Within} = df_1 + df_2 + \ldots df_{Last}$, $df_{Within} = (5-1) + (5-1) + (5-1) + (5-1) = 4 + 4 + 4 + 4 = 16$. Since there are two rows, the numerator for the comparison distribution for the orientation main effect $= df_{Rows} = Nf_{Rows} - 1 = 1$. Likewise, since there are two columns, the numerator for the comparison distribution for the previous full-time employment main effect $= df_{Columns} = N_{Columnss} - 1 = 1$. Finally, since $df_{Interaction} = N_{Cells} - df_{Rows} - df_{Columns} - 1$, $df_{Interaction} = 4 - 1 - 1 - 1 = 1$.

As a check, the sum of the between-groups, within groups, and interaction degrees of freedom is $1 + 1 + 1 + 16 = 19$, which is equal to the total number of degrees of freedom computed as the number of participants minus 1, or $20 - 1 = 19$.

Step 3: Determine the cutoff sample score on the comparison distribution at which the null hypothesis should be rejected.

Using numerator degrees of freedom $= 1$ and denominator degrees of freedom $= 16$ and the .05 level of significance, the cutoff sample score for both main effects and the interaction effect is an $F = 4.49$.

Step 4: Determine the sample's score on the comparison distribution.

Follow the steps for calculating a two-way analysis of variance listed previously.

1. Compute each cell mean, row mean, column mean, and the grand mean.

		Therapist		Marginal means
		Woman	Man	
Client	Woman	$M = 19.00$	$M = 16.00$	17.50
	Man	$M = 14.00$	$M = 14.50$	14.50
Marginal means		16.50	15.50	$GM = 16.00$

2. Compute the deviation scores for each mean in Step 1. **Note that all values are rounded, so some discrepancies may be present.**

Client: Woman &

Therapist: Woman	$(X - GM)$	$(X - M)$	$(M_{Row} - GM)$	$(M_{Column} - GM)$	Intercept
19	3.00	0.00	1.50	0.50	1.00
17	1.00	-2.00	1.50	0.50	1.00
18	2.00	-1.00	1.50	0.50	1.00
20	4.00	1.00	1.50	0.50	1.00
21	5.00	2.00	1.50	0.50	1.00

Client: Woman &

Therapist: Man	$(X - GM)$	$(X - M)$	$(M_{Row} - GM)$	$(M_{Column} - GM)$	Intercept
16	0.00	0.00	1.50	-0.50	-1.00
16	0.00	0.00	1.50	-0.50	-1.00
17	1.00	1.00	1.50	-0.50	-1.00
15	-1.00	-1.00	1.50	-0.50	-1.00
16	0.00	0.00	1.50	-0.50	-1.00

Client: Man &

Therapist: Woman	$(X - GM)$	$(X - M)$	$(M_{Row} - GM)$	$(M_{Column} - GM)$	Intercept
15	-1.00	1.00	-1.50	0.50	-1.00
14	-2.00	0.00	-1.50	0.50	-1.00
13	-3.00	-1.00	-1.50	0.50	-1.00
14	-2.00	0.00	-1.50	0.50	-1.00
14	-2.00	0.00	-1.50	0.50	-1.00

Client: Man & Therapist: Man	$(X-GM)$	$(X-M)$	$(M_{\text{Row}}-GM)$	$(M_{\text{Column}}-GM)$	Intercept
16	0.00	1.00	-1.50	-0.50	1.00
15	-1.00	0.00	-1.50	-0.50	1.00
15	-1.00	0.00	-1.50	-0.50	1.00
15	-1.00	0.00	-1.50	-0.50	1.00
14	-2.00	-1.00	-1.50	-0.50	1.00

3. Square each deviation score in Step 2.

Client: Woman & Therapist: Woman	$(X-GM)^2$	$(X-M)^2$	$(M_{\text{Row}}-GM)^2$	$(M_{\text{Column}}-GM)^2$	$(Intercept)^2$
19	9.00	0.00	2.25	0.25	1.00
17	1.00	4.00	2.25	0.25	1.00
18	4.00	1.00	2.25	0.25	1.00
20	16.00	1.00	2.25	0.25	1.00
21	25.00	4.00	2.25	0.25	1.00
$\Sigma = 95$	55.00	10.00	11.25	1.25	5.00
$M = 19.00$					

Client: Woman & Therapist: Man	$(X-GM)^2$	$(X-M)^2$	$(M_{\text{Row}}-GM)^2$	$(M_{\text{Column}}-GM)^2$	$(Intercept)^2$
16	0.00	0.00	2.25	0.25	1.00
16	0.00	0.00	2.25	0.25	1.00
17	1.00	1.00	2.25	0.25	1.00
15	1.00	1.00	2.25	0.25	1.00
16	0.00	0.00	2.25	0.25	1.00
$\Sigma = 80$	2.00	2.00	11.25	1.25	5.00
$M = 16.00$					

Client: Man & Therapist: Woman	$(X-GM)^2$	$(X-M)^2$	$(M_{\text{Row}}-GM)^2$	$(M_{\text{Column}}-GM)^2$	$(Intercept)^2$
15	1.00	1.00	2.25	0.25	1.00
14	4.00	0.00	2.25	0.25	1.00
13	9.00	1.00	2.25	0.25	1.00
14	4.00	0.00	2.25	0.25	1.00
14	4.00	1.00	2.25	0.25	1.00
$\Sigma = 70$	22.00	2.00	11.25	1.25	5.00
$M = 14.00$					

Client: Man & Therapist: Man	$(X-GM)^2$	$(X-M)^2$	$(M_{\text{Row}}-GM)^2$	$(M_{\text{Column}}-GM)^2$	$(Intercept)^2$
16	0.00	1.00	2.25	0.25	1.00
15	1.00	0.00	2.25	0.25	1.00
15	1.00	0.00	2.25	0.25	1.00
15	1.00	0.00	2.25	0.25	1.00
14	4.00	1.00	2.25	0.25	1.00
$\Sigma = 75$	7.00	2.00	11.25	1.25	5.00
$M = 15.00$					

4. Add the squared deviation scores in Step 3.

$SS_{Rows} = \Sigma(M_{Row} - GM)^2 = 11.25 + 11.25 + 11.25 + 11.25 = 45.00$

$SS_{Columns} = \Sigma(M_{Column} - GM)^2 = 1.25 + 1.25 + 1.25 + 1.25 = 5.00$

$SS_{Interaction} = \Sigma[(X - GM) - (X - M) - (M_{Row} - GM) - (M_{Column} - GM)]^2 = 5.00 + 5.00 + 5.00 + 5.00 = 20.00$

$SS_{Within} = \Sigma(X - M)^2 = 10.00 + 2.00 + 2.00 + 2.00 = 16.00$

$SS_{Total} = \Sigma(X - GM)^2 = 55.00 + 2.00 + 22.00 + 7.00 = 86.00$, or

$SS_{Total} = SS_{Rows} + SS_{Columns} + SS_{Interaction} + SS_{Within} = 45.00 + 5.00 + 20.00 + 16.00 = 86.00$

5. Obtain the variance estimates by dividing each sum of squared deviations in Step 4 by the appropriate number of degrees of freedom.

S^2_{Rows} or $MS_{Rows} = SS_{Rows} / df_{Rows} = 45.00 / 1 = 45.00$

$S^2_{Columns}$ or $MS_{Columns} = SS_{Columns} / df_{Columns} = 5.00 / 1 = 5.00$

$S^2_{Interaction}$ or $MS_{Interaction} = SS_{Interaction} / df_{Interaction} = 20.00 / 1 = 20.00$

S^2_{Within} or $MS_{Within} = SS_{Within} / df_{Within} = 16 / 16 = 1.00$

6. Divide the between-groups variance estimates by the within-groups variance estimate.

$F_{Rows} = S^2_{Rows} / S^2_{Within}$ or $MS_{Rows} / MS_{Within} = 45.00 / 1.00 = 45.00$

$F_{Columns} = S^2_{Columns} / S^2_{Within}$ or $MS_{Columns} / MS_{Within} = 5.00 / 1.00 = 5.00$

$F_{Interaction} = S^2_{Interaction} / S^2_{Within}$ or $MS_{Interaction} / MS_{Within} = 20.00 / 1.00 = 20.00$

Step 5: Decide whether to reject the null hypothesis.

Analysis of Variance Table

Source	SS	df	MS	F
Between:				
Rows	45.00	1	45.00	45.00
Columns	5.00	1	5.00	5.00
Interaction	20.00	1	20.00	20.00
Within	16.00	16	1.00	
Total	86.00	19		

Since all three F ratios are more extreme than the cutoff sample score of 4.49, the psychologists will reject all three null hypotheses and accept the research hypotheses. As inspection of the means in the table presented in **Step 4** indicates, depressed women performed more activities than depressed men, and depressed clients whose therapist was a woman performed more activities than clients whose therapist was a man. The interaction effect is due to higher number of activities performed by women whose therapist was also a woman and the lower number of activities performed by men whose therapist was a woman.

The plot of the interaction effect should look something like the one below.

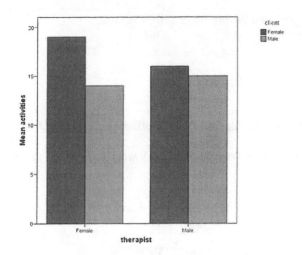

Calculating the sizes of the effects in the orientation study yields the following partial R^2 values.

Effect of client gender:

$R^2 = (S^2_{Rows}) (df_{Rows}) / (S^2_{Rows}) (df_{Rows}) + (S^2_{Within}) (df_{Within})$
   $= (45.00) (1) / (45.00) (1) + (1.00) (16)$
   $= 45.00 / 45.00 + 16.00$
   $= 45.00 / 61.00$
   $= 0.74$

Effect of therapist gender:

$R^2 = (S^2_{Columns}) (df_{Columns}) / (S^2_{Columns}) (df_{Columns}) + (S^2_{Within}) (df_{Within})$
   $= (5.00) (1) / (5.00) (1) + (1.00) (16)$
   $= 5.00 / 5.00 + 16.00$
   $= 5.00 / 21.00$
   $= 0.24$

Effect of the interaction between attending the orientation program and having had a full-time job:

$R^2 = (S^2_{Interaction}) (df_{Interaction}) / (S^2_{Interaction}) (df_{Interaction}) + (S^2_{Within}) (df_{Within})$
   $= (20.00) (1) / (20.00) (1) + (1.00) (16)$
   $= 20.00 / 20.00 + 16.00$
   $= 20.00 / 36.00$
   $= 0.56$

Based on Cohen's conventions for interpreting R^2 following analysis of variance, all three effect sizes are large.

Calculating effect sizes using F ratios and degrees of freedom yields the following partial R^2 values.

Effect of client gender:

$R^2 = (F_{Rows}) (df_{Rows}) / (F_{Rows}) (df_{Rows}) + (df_{Within})$
   $= (45.00) (1) / (45.00) (1) + (1.00) (16)$
   $= 45.00 / 45.00 + 16.00$
   $= 45.00 / 61.00$
   $= 0.74$

Effect of having had a full-time job:

$R^2 = (F_{Columns}) (df_{Columns}) / (F_{Columns}) (df_{Columns}) + (df_{Within})$
   $= (5.00) (1) / (5.00) (1) + (1.00) (16)$
   $= 5.00 / 5.00 + 16.00$
   $= 5.00 / 21.00$
   $= 0.24$

Effect of the interaction between attending the orientation program and having had a full-time job:

$R^2 = (F_{Interaction}) (df_{Interaction}) / (F_{Interaction}) (df_{Interaction}) + (df_{Within})$

$= (20.00) (1) / (20.00) (1) + (1.00) (16)$

$= 20.00 / 20.00 + 16.00$

$= 20.00 / 36.00$

$= 0.56$

[Note that because of the scores obtained in this study, the values used in the both sets of effect size calculations are identical. This will not always be the case.]

Compare your explanation to the "Outline for Writing Essays for a Two-Way Analysis of Variance on p. 415 in the text and to the sample answer to Set I Practice Problem 8(d).

6. Advanced Topic:

Steps of Hypothesis Testing
Step 1: Restate the question as a research hypothesis and a null hypothesis about the populations.
Population 1,1: Full-term babies whose mothers were present
Population 1,2: Full-term babies whose mothers were absent
Population 2,1: Pre-term babies whose mothers were present
Population 2,2: Pre-term babies whose mothers were absent

Research hypothesis 1: The number of toys handled by the combined populations of full-term babies will be different from the number handled by the combined populations of pre-term babies.
Null hypothesis 1: The number of toys handled by the combined populations of full-term babies will be the same as the number handled by the combined populations of pre-term babies.

Research hypothesis 2: The number of toys handled by the combined populations of babies whose mothers are present will be different from the number handled by the combined populations of babies whose mothers are absent.
Null hypothesis 2: The number of toys handled by the combined populations of babies whose mothers are present will be the same as the number handled by the combined populations of babies whose mothers are absent.

Research hypothesis 3: The difference between the mean number of toys handled by the two populations of full-term and pre-term babies whose mothers are present will be different from the difference between the mean number of toys handled by the two populations of full-term and pre-term babies whose mothers are absent.
Null hypothesis 3: The difference between the mean number of toys handled by the two populations of full-term and pre-term babies whose mothers are present will be the same as the difference between the mean number of toys handled by the two populations of full-term and pre-term babies whose mothers are absent.

Step 2: Determine the characteristics of the comparison distribution.
The three comparison distributions will be F distributions. Since $df_{Within} = df_1 + df_2 + ... df_{Last}$, $df_{Within} = (4-1) + (4-1) + (4-1) + (4-1) = 3 + 3 + 3 + 3 = 12$. Since there are two rows, the numerator for the comparison distribution for the orientation main effect $= df_{Rows} = Nf_{Rows} - 1 = 1$. Likewise, since there are two columns, the numerator for the comparison distribution for the previous full-time employment main effect $= df_{Columns} = N_{Columnss} - 1 = 1$. Finally, since $df_{Interaction} = N_{Cells} - df_{Rows} - df_{Columns} - 1$, $df_{Interaction} = 4 - 1 - 1 - 1 = 1$.

As a check, the sum of the between-groups, within groups, and interaction degrees of freedom is $1 + 1 + 1 + 12 = 15$, which is equal to the total number of degrees of freedom computed as the number of participants minus 1, or $16 - 1 = 15$.

Step 3: Determine the cutoff sample score on the comparison distribution at which the null hypothesis should be rejected.
Using numerator degrees of freedom = 1 and denominator degrees of freedom = 12 and the .05 level of significance, the cutoff sample score for both main effects and the interaction effect is an F ratio = 4.75.

Step 4: Determine the sample's score on the comparison distribution.

Follow the steps for calculating a two-way analysis of variance listed previously.

1. Compute each cell mean, row mean, column mean, and the grand mean.

		Mother		Marginal means
		Present	Absent	
Baby	Full-term	$M = 6.50$	$M = 4.75$	5.63
	Pre-term	$M = 5.50$	$M = 3.25$	4.38
Marginal means		6.00	4.00	$GM = 5.00$

2. Compute the deviation scores for each mean in Step 1. **Note that all values are rounded, so some discrepancies may be present.**

Baby: Full-term

Mother: Present	$(X - GM)$	$(X - M)$	$(M_{Row} - GM)$	$(M_{Column} - GM)$	Intercept
7	2.00	0.50	0.63	1.00	-0.13
6	1.00	-0.50	0.63	1.00	-0.13
5	0.00	-1.50	0.63	1.00	-0.13
8	3.00	1.50	0.63	1.00	-0.13

Baby: Full-term

Mother: Absent	$(X - GM)$	$(X - M)$	$(M_{Row} - GM)$	$(M_{Column} - GM)$	Intercept
6	1.00	1.25	0.63	-1.00	0.12
4	-1.00	-0.75	0.63	-1.00	0.12
5	0.00	0.25	0.63	-1.00	0.12
4	-1.00	-0.75	0.63	-1.00	0.12

Baby: Pre-term

Mother: Present	$(X - GM)$	$(X - M)$	$(M_{Row} - GM)$	$(M_{Column} - GM)$	Intercept
6	1.00	0.50	-0.62	1.00	0.12
7	2.00	1.50	-0.62	1.00	0.12
5	0.00	-0.50	-0.62	1.00	0.12
4	-1.00	-1.50	-0.62	1.00	0.12

Baby: Pre-term

Mother: Absent	$(X - GM)$	$(X - M)$	$(M_{Row} - GM)$	$(M_{Column} - GM)$	Intercept
3	-2.00	-0.25	-0.62	-1.00	-0.13
4	-1.00	0.75	-0.62	-1.00	-0.13
4	-1.00	0.75	-0.62	-1.00	-0.13
2	-3.00	-1.25	-0.62	-1.00	-0.13

3. Square each deviation score in Step 2.

Baby: Full-term

Mother: Present	$(X - GM)^2$	$(X - M)^2$	$(M_{Row} - GM)^2$	$(M_{Column} - GM)^2$	$(Intercept)^2$
7	4.00	0.25	0.40	1.00	0.02
6	1.00	0.25	0.40	1.00	0.02
5	0.00	2.25	0.40	1.00	0.02
8	9.00	2.25	0.40	1.00	0.02
$\Sigma = 26$	14.00	5.00	1.59	4.00	0.07
$M = 6.50$					

Baby: Full-term

Mother: Absent	$(X-GM)^2$	$(X-M)^2$	$(M_{Row}-GM)^2$	$(M_{Column}-GM)^2$	$(Intercept)^2$
6	1.00	1.56	0.40	1.00	0.01
4	1.00	0.56	0.40	1.00	0.01
5	0.00	0.63	0.40	1.00	0.01
4	1.00	0.56	0.40	1.00	0.01
$\Sigma = 19$	3.00	2.75	1.59	4.00	0.06
$M = 4.75$					

Baby: Pre-term

Mother: Present	$(X-GM)^2$	$(X-M)^2$	$(M_{Row}-GM)^2$	$(M_{Column}-GM)^2$	$(Intercept)^2$
6	1.00	0.25	0.38	1.00	0.01
7	4.00	2.25	0.38	1.00	0.01
5	0.00	0.25	0.38	1.00	0.01
4	1.00	2.25	0.38	1.00	0.01
$\Sigma = 22$	6.00	5.00	1.54	4.00	0.06
$M = 5.50$					

Baby: Pre-term

Mother: Absent	$(X-GM)^2$	$(X-M)^2$	$(M_{Row}-GM)^2$	$(M_{Column}-GM)^2$	$(Intercept)^2$
3	4.00	0.06	0.38	1.00	0.02
4	1.00	0.56	0.38	1.00	0.02
4	1.00	0.56	0.38	1.00	0.02
2	9.00	1.56	0.38	1.00	0.02
$\Sigma = 13$	15.00	2.75	1.54	4.00	0.07
$M = 3.25$					

4. Add the squared deviation scores in Step 3.

$SS_{Rows} = \Sigma(M_{Row} - GM)^2 = 1.59 + 1.59 + 1.54 + 1.54 = 6.26$

$SS_{Columns} = \Sigma(M_{Column} - GM)^2 = 4.00 + 4.00 + 4.00 + 4.00 = 16.00$

$SS_{Interaction} = \Sigma[(X - GM) - (X - M) - (M_{Row} - GM) - (M_{Column} - GM)]^2 = 0.07 + 0.06 + 0.06 + 0.07 = 0.26$

$SS_{Within} = \Sigma(X - M)^2 = 5.00 + 2.75 + 5.00 + 2.75 = 15.50$

$SS_{Total} = \Sigma(X - GM)^2 = 14.00 + 3.00 + 6.00 + 15.00 = 38.00$, or

$SS_{Total} = SS_{Rows} + SS_{Columns} + SS_{Interaction} + SS_{Within} = 6.26 + 16.00 + 0.26 + 15.50 = 38.02$

5. Obtain the variance estimates by dividing each sum of squared deviations in Step 4 by the appropriate number of degrees of freedom.

S^2_{Rows} or $MS_{Rows} = SS_{Rows} / df_{Rows} = 6.26 / 1 = 6.26$

$S^2_{Columns}$ or $MS_{Columns} = SS_{Columns} / df_{Columns} = 16.00 / 1 = 16.00$

$S^2_{Interaction}$ or $MS_{Interaction} = SS_{Interaction} / df_{Interaction} = 0.26 / 1 = 0.26$

S^2_{Within} or $MS_{Within} = SS_{Within} / df_{Within} = 15.5 / 12 = 1.29$

6. Divide the between-groups variance estimates by the within-groups variance estimate.

$F_{Rows} = S^2_{Rows} / S^2_{Within}$ or $MS_{Rows} / MS_{Within} = 6.26 / 1.29 = 4.85$

$F_{Columns} = S^2_{Columns} / S^2_{Within}$ or $MS_{Columns} / MS_{Within} = 16.00 / 1.29 = 12.40$

$F_{Interaction} = S^2_{Interaction} / S^2_{Within}$ or $MS_{Interaction} / MS_{Within} = 0.26 / 1.29 = 0.20$

Step 5: Decide whether to reject the null hypothesis.

Analysis of Variance Table

Source	SS	df	MS	F
Between:				
Rows	6.26	1	6.26	4.85
Columns	16.00	1	16.00	12.40
Interaction	0.26	1	0.26	0.20
Within	15.50	12	1.29	
Total	38.02	15		

The F ratios for the comparisons of full-term and pre-term babies and for the presence or absence of mothers are more extreme than the cutoff sample score of 4.75, so the psychologist will reject these two null hypotheses and accept the research hypotheses. As inspection of the means in the table presented in **Step 4** indicates, full-term babies handled more toys than pre-term babies, and babies whose mothers were present handled more toys than babies whose mothers were absent. The interaction effect was not statistically significant, so no plot is required.

Calculating the sizes of the effects in the orientation study yields the following partial R^2 values.
Effect of client gender:
$R^2 = (S^2_{Rows}) (df_{Rows}) / (S^2_{Rows}) (df_{Rows}) + (S^2_{Within}) (df_{Within})$
  $= (6.26) (1) / (6.26) (1) + (1.29) (12)$
  $= 6.26 / 6.26 + 15.48$
  $= 6.26 / 21.74$
  $= 0.29$

Effect of therapist gender:
$R^2 = (S^2_{Columns}) (df_{Columns}) / (S^2_{Columns}) (df_{Columns}) + (S^2_{Within}) (df_{Within})$
  $= (16.00) (1) / (16.00) (1) + (1.29) (12)$
  $= 16.00 / 16.00 + 15.48$
  $= 16.00 / 31.48$
  $= 0.51$

Effect of the interaction between attending the orientation program and having had a full-time job:
$R^2 = (S^2_{Interaction}) (df_{Interaction}) / (S^2_{Interaction}) (df_{Interaction}) + (S^2_{Within}) (df_{Within})$
  $= (0.26) (1) / (0.260) (1) + (1.29) (12)$
  $= 0.26 / 0.26 + 15.48$
  $= 0.26 / 15.74$
  $= 0.02$

Based on Cohen's conventions for interpreting R^2 following analysis of variance, the two effect sizes for the main effects are large, and the interaction effect size is small.

Calculating effect sizes using F ratios and degrees of freedom yields the following partial R^2 values.
Effect of client gender:
$R^2 = (F_{Rows}) (df_{Rows}) / (F_{Rows}) (df_{Rows}) + (df_{Within})$
  $= (4.85) (1) / (4.85) (1) + (12)$
  $= 4.85 / 4.85 + 12.00$
  $= 4.85 / 16.85$
  $= 0.29$

Effect of having had a full-time job:
$R^2 = (F_{Columns}) (df_{Columns}) / (F_{Columns}) (df_{Columns}) + (df_{Within})$
  $= (12.40) (1) / (12.40) (1) + (12)$
  $= 12.40 / 12.40 + 12.00$
  $= 12.40 / 24.40$
  $= 0.51$

Effect of the interaction between attending the orientation program and having had a full-time job:

$R^2 = (F_{\text{Interaction}}) (df_{\text{Interaction}}) / (F_{\text{Interaction}}) (df_{\text{Interaction}}) + (df_{\text{Within}})$

= (0.20) (1) / (0.20) (1) + (12)

= 0.20 / 0.20 + 12.00

= 0.20 / 12.20

= 0.02

7.

Study	Predicted Effect Size	Overall Design	#of Levels of the Effect	Participants per Cell	Power
(a)	Medium	2 X 2	2	20	.60
(b)	Medium	2 X 3	3	20	.67
(c)	Medium	2 X 2	2	40	.89
(d)	Large	2 X 2	2	10	.68
(e)	Large	2 X 3	3	20	.98

8.

Study	Predicted Effect Size	Design	Effect	Cell Size
(a)	Medium	2 X 2	Main	33
(b)	Large	2 X 2	Interaction	14
(c)	Medium	2 X 3	Two level main	22
(d)	Large	2 X 3	Two level main	9
(e)	Medium	2 X 3	Three level main	27
(f)	Large	2 X 3	Three level interaction	11

Chapter 11

Completion Items:

1. correlation	7. no	13. proportion of variance accounted for
2. scatter diagram	8. product of deviation scores	14. restriction in range
3. positive	9. correlation coefficient	15. reliable
4. negative	10. direction of causality	16. outliers
5. linear	11. correlational	17. Spearman's rho
6. curvilinear	12. proportionate reduction in error	18. correlation matrix

Multiple Choice Items:

1. A	6. D	11. D	16. D
2. C	7. C	12. D	17. A
3. B	8. A	13. B	18. C
4. B	9. D	14. A	19. D
5. A	10. C	15. C	20. A

Problems

1.
Scatter diagram

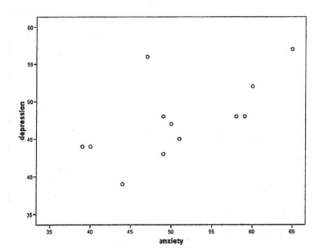

The general pattern of the scatter diagram indicates a positive correlation.

Calculation Table

$(X - M_X)$	$(X - M_X)^2$	$(Y - M_Y)$	$(Y - M_Y)^2$	$(X - M_X)(Y - M_Y)$
-3.58	12.82	-11.92	142.09	42.67
-0.58	0.34	-0.92	0.85	0.53
-8.58	73.62	-6.92	47.89	59.37
-4.58	20.98	-1.92	3.69	8.79
-2.58	6.66	0.08	0.01	-0.21
9.42	88.74	14.08	198.25	132.63
8.42	70.90	-3.92	15.37	-33.01
0.42	0.18	-1.92	3.69	-0.81
4.42	19.54	9.08	82.45	40.13
0.42	0.18	8.08	65.29	3.39
-3.58	12.82	-10.92	119.25	39.09
0.42	0.18	7.08	50.13	2.97
	$\Sigma = 306.92$		$\Sigma = 728.92$	$\Sigma = 295.58$

Depression = X and $M_X = 47.58$
Anxiety = Y and $M_Y = 50.92$

1. **Change the scores for each variable to deviation scores.** These scores are in the columns of the Calculation Table headed $(X - M_X)$ and $(Y - M_Y)$.
2. **Figure the product of the deviation scores for each pair of scores.** These products are in the column of the Calculation Table headed $(X - M_X)(Y - M_Y)$.
3. **Add up all the products of the deviation scores.** This sum is in the summation cell of the column in the Calculation Table headed $(X - M_X)(Y - M_Y)$. The sum is 295.58.
4. **For each variable, square each deviation score.** These squared deviation scores are in the columns of the Calculation Table headed $(X - M_X)^2$ and $(Y - M_Y)^2$.
5. **Add up the squared deviation scores for each variable.** These sums are in the summation cells of the columns in the Calculation Table headed $(X - M_X)^2$ and $(Y - M_Y)^2$. The sums are 306.92 and 728.92, respectively.

6. **Multiply the two sums of squared deviations and take the square root of the result.** The two sums of squared deviations are 306.92 and 728.92, and their product is 223,720.12. The square root of this product is 472.99.
7. **Divide the sum of the products of deviation scores from Step 3 by the correction number from Step 6.** 295.58 divided by 472.99 is .62.

Substituting these values into the formula yields

$$r = [\Sigma[(X - M_X)(Y - M_Y)] / \sqrt{(SS_X)*(SS_Y)}$$

$$r = 295.58 / \sqrt{(306.92)*(728.92)}$$

$$r = 295.58 / 472.99 = .62$$

Applying the formula for t using the correlation coefficient obtained in the example yields

$$t = r / \sqrt{(1-r^2)/(N-2)} = (.62) / \sqrt{(1-.62^2)/(12-2)} = (.62) / \sqrt{.62/10} = .62 / .25 = 2.48$$

Since the t value of 2.48 is more extreme than the cutoff sample t, which is 2.228 with 10 df at the .05 level of significance, the psychologists will reject the null hypothesis and accept the research hypothesis.
Compare your explanation to the "Outline for Writing Essays on the Logic and Figuring of a Correlation Coefficient on p. 474 in the text and to the sample answer to Set I Practice Problem 2(e).

The three possible directions of causality are
1. Depression causes anxiety,
2. Anxiety causes depression, or
3. Some third variable is causing both depression and anxiety.

2.
Scatter diagram

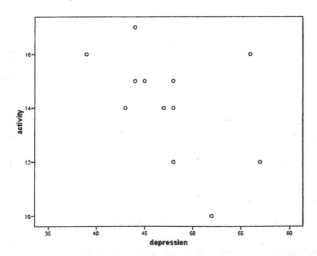

The general pattern of the scatter diagram indicates a negative correlation.

Calculation Table

$(X - M_X)$	$(X - M_X)^2$	$(Y - M_Y)$	$(Y - M_Y)^2$	$(X - M_X)(Y - M_Y)$
-3.58	12.82	2.83	8.01	-10.13
-0.58	0.34	-0.17	0.03	0.10
-8.58	73.62	1.83	3.35	-15.70
-4.58	20.98	-0.17	0.03	0.78
-2.58	6.66	0.83	0.69	-2.14
9.42	88.74	-2.17	4.71	-20.44
8.42	70.90	1.83	3.35	15.41
0.42	0.18	0.83	0.69	0.35
4.42	19.54	-4.17	17.39	-18.43
0.42	0.18	-2.17	4.71	-0.91
-3.58	12.82	0.83	0.69	-2.97
0.42	0.18	-0.17	0.03	-0.07
	$\Sigma = 306.92$		$\Sigma = 43.67$	$\Sigma = -54.17$

Depression $= X$ and $M_X = 47.58$
Activities $= Y$ and $M_Y = 14.17$

1. **Change the scores for each variable to deviation scores.** These scores are in the columns of the Calculation Table headed $(X - M_X)$ and $(Y - M_Y)$.
2. **Figure the product of the deviation scores for each pair of scores.** These products are in the column of the Calculation Table headed $(X - M_X)(Y - M_Y)$.
3. **Add up all the products of the deviation scores.** This sum is in the summation cell of the column in the Calculation Table headed $(X - M_X)(Y - M_Y)$. The sum is -54.17.
4. **For each variable, square each deviation score.** These squared deviation scores are in the columns of the Calculation Table headed $(X - M_X)^2$ and $(Y - M_Y)^2$.
5. **Add up the squared deviation scores for each variable.** These sums are in the summation cells of the columns in the Calculation Table headed $(X - M_X)^2$ and $(Y - M_Y)^2$. The sums are 306.92 and 43.67, respectively.
6. **Multiply the two sums of squared deviations and take the square root of the result.** The two sums of squared deviations are 306.92 and 43.67, and their product is 13403.20. The square root of this product is 115.77.
7. **Divide the sum of the products of deviation scores from Step 3 by the correction number from Step 6.** -54.17 divided by 115.77 is -.47.

Substituting these values into the formula yields

$$r = \Sigma[(X - M_X)(Y - M_Y)] / \sqrt{(SS_X) * (SS_Y)}$$

$$r = -54.17 / \sqrt{(306.62) * (43.67)}$$

$$r = -54.17 / 115.77 = -.47$$

Applying the formula for t using the correlation coefficient obtained in the example yields

$$t = r / \sqrt{(1 - r^2)/(N - 2)} = (-.47) / \sqrt{(1 - (-.47^2))/(12 - 2)} = (-.47) / \sqrt{.78/10} = (-.47) / .28 = -1.68$$

Since the t value of -1.68 is not more extreme than the cutoff sample t, which is -2.228 with 10 df at the .05 level of significance, the psychologists will fail to reject the null hypothesis and state that the results are inconclusive.

3.
A. This person would probably be an outlier.
B. The short rating scale makes this correlation subject to restriction in range.
C. Both of the scales will be less than perfectly reliable.

4.

Study	Effect Size	N	Power
(a)	Small	40	.09
(b)	Small	100	.17
(c)	Medium	40	.48
(d)	Medium	100	.86
(e)	Large	40	.92
(f)	Large	100	1.00

5.

Study	Effect Size	N
(a)	Medium	85
(b)	Large	28

Chapter 12

Completion Items:

1. predictor	6. regression line	11. standardized regression coefficient
2. criterion	7. intercept	12. bivariate prediction
3. regression coefficient	8. linear prediction rule	13. multiple correlation
4. regression constant	9. error	14. multiple regression
5. slope	10. sum of squared errors	15. multiple correlation coefficient

Multiple Choice Items:

1. D	6. D	11. D
2. C	7. C	12. A
3. A	8. B	13. C
4. B	9. A	14. A
5. C	10. B	15. C

Problems

1.

(a) Predicted Depression = 5.71 + (.45) (Stress Score)

(b) Predicted Depression = 5.71 + (.45) (18) = 13.81

(c) Predicted Depression = 5.71 + (.45) (26) = 17.41

(d) Predicted Depression = 5.71 + (.45) (32) = 20.11

(e) Predicted Depression = 5.71 + (.45) (39) = 23.26

(f) Predicted Depression = 5.71 + (.45) (45) = 25.96

(g) $(Y - \hat{Y})^2 = (22 - 13.81)^2 = 67.08$

(h) $(Y - \hat{Y})^2 = (15 - 17.41)^2 = 5.81$

(i) $(Y - \hat{Y})^2 = (18 - 20.11)^2 = 4.45$

(j) $(Y - \hat{Y})^2 = (26 - 23.26)^2 = 7.51$

(k) $(Y - \hat{Y})^2 = (23 - 25.96)^2 = 8.76$

2. The calculations for the example using anxiety to predict depression would be as follows.

Calculation table

$(X - M_X)$	$(X - M_X)^2$	$(Y - M_Y)$	$(Y - M_Y)^2$	$(X - M_X)(Y - M_Y)$
-11.92	142.09	-3.58	12.82	42.67
-0.92	0.85	-0.58	0.34	0.53
-6.92	47.89	-8.58	73.62	59.37
-1.92	3.69	-4.58	20.98	8.79
0.08	0.01	-2.58	6.66	-0.21
14.08	198.25	9.42	88.74	132.63
-3.92	15.37	8.42	70.90	-33.01
-1.92	3.69	0.42	0.18	-0.81
9.08	82.45	4.42	19.54	40.13
8.08	65.29	0.42	0.18	3.39
-10.92	119.25	-3.58	12.82	39.09
7.08	50.13	0.42	0.18	2.97
	$\Sigma = 728.92$		$\Sigma = 306.92$	$\Sigma = 295.58$

Anxiety = X and $M_X = 50.92$
Depression = Y and $M_Y = 47.58$

The steps for calculating b are:
1. **The scores for each variable are changed to deviation scores** in the 1st and 3rd columns of the calculation table.
2. **The products of the deviation scores for each pair of scores** are in the 5th column of the calculation table.
3. **The sum of the products of the deviation scores** is 295.58.
4. **The squared deviation scores for the predictor variable (X)** are in the 2nd column.
5. **The sum of the squared deviation scores for the predictor variable (X)** is 728.92.
6. **Dividing the sum of the deviation scores from Step 3 by the sum of the squared deviation for the predictor variable (X) from Step 5 yields b,** which is = 295.58 / 728.92 = .41.

The steps for calculating a are:
1. **Multiply the regression coefficient (b) by the mean of the X variable,** which is (.41) (50.92) = 20.88.
2. **Subtract the result of Step 1 from the mean of the Y variable** = 47.58 − 20.88 = 26.70.

(a)
Predicted Depression = 26.70 + (.41) (Anxiety Score)
The regression line should look like this line

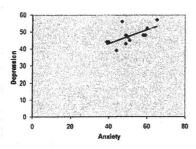

Depression on Anxiety

(b)
Predicted Depression = 26.70 + (.41) (40) = 43.10
Predicted Depression = 26.70 + (.41) (50) = 47.20
Predicted Depression = 26.70 + (.41) (60) = 51.30
Predicted Depression = 26.70 + (.41) (65) = 53.35

(c) $\beta = (b)\sqrt{SS_X} / \sqrt{SS_Y} = (.41) \sqrt{728.92} / \sqrt{306.92} = [(.41)(27.00)] / 17.52 = 11.07 / 17.52 = .63$

(d)
$(Y-\hat{Y})^2 = (40 - 43.10)^2 = 9.61$
$(Y-\hat{Y})^2 = (50 - 47.20)^2 = 7.84$
$(Y-\hat{Y})^2 = (60 - 51.30)^2 = 75.69$
$(Y-\hat{Y})^2 = (65 - 53.35)^2 = 135.72$

(e)
Predicted Depression = 31.70 + (.46) (40) = 50.10
Predicted Depression = 31.70 + (.46) (50) = 54.70
Predicted Depression = 31.70 + (.46) (60) = 59.30
Predicted Depression = 31.70 + (.46) (65) = 61.60
Original Rule: Sum of Squared Errors = 43.10 + 47.20 + 51.30 + 53.35 = 194.95
This Rule: Sum of Squared Errors = 50.10 + 54.70 + 59.30 + 61.60 = 225.70
The original rule is better because the sum of squared errors is smaller.

(f)

Anxiety	Depression	$\hat{Y}$ (Depression)	$Y - \hat{Y}$ (Depression)	$(Y - \hat{Y})^2$
39	44	42.69	1.31	1.72
50	47	47.20	-0.20	0.04
44	39	44.47	-5.74	32.95
49	43	46.79	-3.79	14.36
51	45	47.61	-2.61	6.81
65	57	53.35	3.65	13.32
47	56	45.97	10.03	100.60
49	48	46.79	1.21	1.46
60	52	51.30	0.70	0.49
59	48	50.89	-2.89	8.35
40	44	43.10	0.90	0.81
58	48	50.48	-2.48	6.15
				$\Sigma = 187.07$

$SS_{Total} = \Sigma(Y - M_Y)^2 = 306.92$
$R^2 = SS_{Total} - SS_{Error} / SS_{Total} = 306.92 - 187.07 / 306.92 = 119.85 / 306.92 = 0.39$

3. The calculations for the example using depression to predict days of work missed would be as follows.

Calculation table

$(X - M_X)$	$(X - M_X)^2$	$(Y - M_Y)$	$(Y - M_Y)^2$	$(X - M_X)(Y - M_Y)$
-3.58	12.82	2.17	4.71	-7.77
-0.58	0.34	-6.83	46.65	3.96
-8.58	73.62	-2.83	8.01	24.28
-4.58	20.98	0.17	0.03	-0.78
-2.58	6.66	1.17	1.37	-3.02
9.42	88.74	8.17	66.75	76.96
8.42	70.90	4.17	17.39	35.11
0.42	0.18	2.17	4.71	0.91
4.42	19.54	0.17	0.03	0.75
0.42	0.18	-2.83	8.01	-1.19
-3.58	12.82	-6.83	46.65	24.45
0.42	0.18	1.17	1.37	0.49
	$\Sigma = 306.92$		$\Sigma = 205.67$	$\Sigma = 154.17$

Depression = X and $M_X = 47.58$
Days Missed = Y and $M_Y = 16.83$

The steps for calculating b are:
1. The scores for each variable are changed to deviation scores in the 1st and 3rd columns of the calculation table.
2. The products of the deviation scores for each pair of scores are in the 5th column of the calculation table.
3. The sum of the products of the deviation scores is 154.17.
4. The squared deviation scores for the predictor variable (X) are in the 2nd column.
5. The sum of the squared deviation scores for the predictor variable (X) is 306.92.
6. Dividing the sum of the deviation scores from Step 3 by the sum of the squared deviation for the predictor variable (X) from Step 5 yields b, which is $= 154.17 / 306.92 = .50$.

The steps for calculating a are:
1. Multiply the regression coefficient (b) by the mean of the X variable, which is $(.50)(47.58) = 23.79$.
2. Subtract the result of Step 1 from the mean of the Y variable $= 16.83 - 23.79 = -6.96$

(a)
Predicted Days Missed $= (-6.96) + (.50)$ (Depression Score)
The regression should look like this line

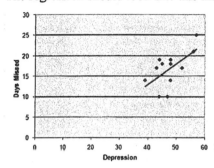

(b)
Predicted Days Missed $= (-6.96) + (.50)(39) = 12.54$
Predicted Days Missed $= (-6.96) + (.50)(45) = 15.54$
Predicted Days Missed $= (-6.96) + (.50)(52) = 19.04$
Predicted Days Missed $= (-6.96) + (.50)(57) = 21.54$

(c) $\beta = (b)\sqrt{SS_X} / \sqrt{SS_Y}$ $SS_Y = (.50)\sqrt{306.92} / \sqrt{205.67} = (.50)(17.52) / 14.34 = 8.76 / 14.34 = .61$

(d)
$(Y - \hat{Y})^2 = (14 - 12.54)^2 = 2.13$
$(Y - \hat{Y})^2 = (18 - 15.54)^2 = 6.05$
$(Y - \hat{Y})^2 = (17 - 19.04)^2 = 4.16$
$(Y - \hat{Y})^2 = (25 - 21.54)^2 = 11.97$

(e)
Predicted Days Missed $= (-5.75) + (.60)(39) = 17.65$
Predicted Days Missed $= (-5.75) + (.60)(45) = 21.25$
Predicted Days Missed $= (-5.75) + (.60)(52) = 25.45$
Predicted Days Missed $= (-5.75) + (.60)(57) = 28.45$
Original Rule: Sum of Squared Errors $= 12.54 + 15.54 + 19.04 + 21.54 = 68.66$
This Rule: Sum of Squared Errors $= 17.65 + 21.25 + 25.45 + 28.45 = 92.80$
The original rule is better because the sum of squared errors is smaller.

(f)

Depression	Days Missed	$\hat{Y}$ (Days Missed)	$Y - \hat{Y}$ (Days Missed)	$(Y - \hat{Y})^2$
44	19	15.04	3.96	15.68
47	10	16.54	-6.54	42.77
39	14	12.54	1.46	2.13
43	17	14.54	2.46	6.05
45	18	15.54	2.46	6.05
57	25	21.54	3.46	11.97
56	21	21.04	-0.04	0.00
48	19	17.04	1.96	3.84
52	17	19.04	-2.04	4.16
48	14	17.04	-3.04	9.24
44	10	15.04	-5.04	25.40
48	18	17.04	0.96	0.92
				$\Sigma = 128.23$

$SS_{Total} = \Sigma(Y - M_Y)^2 = 205.67$
$R^2 = SS_{Total} - SS_{Error} / SS_{Total} = 205.67 - 128.23 / 205.67 = 77.44 / 205.67 = 0.38$

Chapter 13

Completion Items:

1. chi-square test for goodness of fit	6. chi-square statistic	11. independence
2. chi-square test for independence	7. chi-square distribution	12. phi coefficient
3. chi-square tests	8. chi-square table	13. Cramer's phi
4. observed frequency	9. contingency table	
5. expected frequency	10. cell	

Multiple Choice Items:

1. D	5. C	9. B
2. B	6. D	10. D
3. A	7. A	11. C
4. D	8. C	12. A

Problems
1. The appropriate test would be a chi-square test for goodness of fit.
Steps of Hypothesis Testing
Step 1: Restate the question as a research hypothesis and a null hypothesis about the populations.
Population 1: Students using methods of conflict resolution like those observed by the psychologists.
Population 2: Students who use each method of conflict resolution equally.

Research hypothesis: The distributions of students using the methods of conflict resolution in the two populations are different.
Null hypothesis: The distributions of students using the methods of conflict resolution in the two populations are no different.

Step 2: Determine the characteristics of the comparison distribution.
Since the psychologists are interested in four methods of conflict resolution, the comparison distribution is a chi-square distribution with 3 degrees of freedom ($df = N_{categories} - 1 = 4-1 = 3$).

Step 3: Determine the cutoff sample score on the comparison distribution at which the null hypothesis should be rejected.
At the .05 level of significance, the cutoff sample chi-square with 3 degrees of freedom is 7.815.

Step 4: Determine the sample's score on the comparison distribution.
Applying the formula for chi-square yields
$\chi^2 = \Sigma\ [(O\text{-}E)^2\ /\ E]$
$= \Sigma\ [(8\text{-}5)^2\ /\ 5] + [(2\text{-}5)^2\ /\ 5] + [(2\text{-}5)^2\ /\ 5] + [(8\text{-}5)^2\ /\ 5]$
$= \Sigma\ [(3)^2\ /\ 5] + [(-3)^2\ /\ 5] + [(-3)^2\ /\ 5] + [(3)^2\ /\ 5]$
$= \Sigma\ [(9\ /\ 5) + (9\ /\ 5) + (9\ /\ 5) + (9\ /\ 5)]$
$= \Sigma\ [1.80 + 1.80 + 1.80 + 1.80]$
$= 7.20$

Step 5: Decide whether to reject the null hypothesis.
The chi-square statistic for the sample of 7.20 is not more extreme than the cutoff sample chi-square of 7.815. Therefore, the psychologists cannot reject the null hypothesis and must state that their results are inconclusive. Thus, despite the differences in observed frequencies, the psychologists cannot conclude that the distribution of methods of conflict resolution used by the students in their sample is different from the distribution of the population of students like those in the sample.
Compare your explanation to the "Outline for Writing Essays for a Chi-square Test for Goodness of Fit on pp. 564-565 in the text and to the sample answer to Set I Practice Problem 3(c).

2. The appropriate test would be a <u>chi-square test for independence</u>.
Steps of Hypothesis Testing
Step 1: Restate the question as a research hypothesis and a null hypothesis about the populations.
Population 1: Students for whom the primary method of conflict resolution is associated with being suspended from school for misbehavior or not being suspended.
Population 2: Students for whom the primary method of conflict resolution is independent of being suspended from school for misbehavior or not being suspended.

Research hypothesis: The primary methods of conflict resolution used by students who have been suspended from school are different from the methods of students who have not been suspended.
Null hypothesis: The primary methods of conflict resolution used by students who have been suspended from school are no different from the methods of students who have not been suspended.

Step 2: Determine the characteristics of the comparison distribution.
Since the psychologists have identified two groups of students based on whether or not students have been suspended from school for misbehavior and the students' use of one of four methods of conflict resolution, the comparison distribution is a chi-square distribution with 3 degrees of freedom; $df = (N_{Rows} - 1)\ (N_{Columns} - 1) = (2 - 1)\ (4 - 1) = (1)\ (3) = 3$.

Step 3: Determine the cutoff sample score on the comparison distribution at which the null hypothesis should be rejected.
At the .05 level of significance, the cutoff sample chi-square with 3 degrees of freedom is 7.815.

Step 4: Determine the sample's score on the comparison distribution.
Applying the formula for chi-square yields
$\chi^2 = \Sigma\ [(O - E)^2\ /\ E]$
$= \Sigma\ [(7 - 4)^2\ /\ 4] + [(1 - 1)^2\ /\ 1] + [(1 - 1)^2\ /\ 1] + [(1 - 4)^2\ /\ 4] + [(1 - 4)^2\ /\ 4] + [(1 - 1)^2\ /\ 1]$
$\quad + [(1 - 1)^2\ /\ 1] + [(7 - 4)^2\ /\ 4]$
$= \Sigma\ [(3)^2\ /\ 4] + [(0)^2\ /\ 1] + [(0)^2\ /\ 1] + [(-3)^2\ /\ 4] + [(-3)^2\ /\ 4] + [(0)^2\ /\ 1] + [(0)^2\ /\ 1]$
$\quad + [(3)^2\ /\ 4]$
$= \Sigma\ [(9\ /\ 4) + (0\ /\ 1) + (0\ /\ 1) + (9\ /\ 4) + (9\ /\ 4) + (0\ /\ 1) + (0\ /\ 1) + (9\ /\ 4)]$
$= \Sigma\ [2.25 + 0.00 + 0.00 + 2.25 + 2.25 + 0.00 + 0.00 + 2.25]$
$= 9.00$

Step 5: Decide whether to reject the null hypothesis.

The chi-square statistic for the sample of 9.00 is more extreme than the cutoff sample chi-square of 7.815. Therefore, the psychologists will reject the null hypothesis, accept the research hypothesis, and conclude that the primary methods of conflict resolution used by students who have been suspended from school for misbehavior are different from the primary methods used by students who have not been suspended.

(b) Cramer's $\Phi = \sqrt{\chi^2 /(N)*(df_{Smaller})} = \sqrt{9.00/(20)*(1)} = \sqrt{9.00/20} = \sqrt{.45} = .67$, a large effect size.

(c) Compare your explanation to the "Outline for Writing Essays for a Chi-square Test for Independence on p. 565 in the text and to the sample answer to Set I Practice Problem 6(d).

3. The appropriate test would be a <u>chi-square test for independence</u>.

Steps of Hypothesis Testing

Step 1: Restate the question as a research hypothesis and a null hypothesis about the populations.

Population 1: Students for whom the primary method of conflict resolution is associated with being suspended from school for misbehavior or not being suspended.

Population 2: Students for whom the primary method of conflict resolution is independent of being suspended from school for misbehavior or not being suspended.

Research hypothesis: The primary methods of conflict resolution used by students who have been suspended from school are different from the methods of students who have not been suspended.

Null hypothesis: The primary methods of conflict resolution used by students who have been suspended from school are no different from the methods of students who have not been suspended.

Step 2: Determine the characteristics of the comparison distribution.

Since the psychologists have identified two groups of students based on whether or not they have been suspended from school for misbehavior and their use of either assertiveness or one of the other three methods of conflict resolution, the comparison distribution is a chi-square distribution with 1 degree of freedom; $df = (N_{Rows} - 1)$ $(N_{Columns} - 1) = (2 - 1)(2 - 1) = (1)(1) = 1$.

Step 3: Determine the cutoff sample score on the comparison distribution at which the null hypothesis should be rejected.

At the .05 level of significance, the cutoff sample chi-square with 1 degree of freedom is 3.841.

Step 4: Determine the sample's score on the comparison distribution.

Applying the formula for chi-square yields

$\chi^2 = \Sigma [(O-E)^2 / E]$
$= \Sigma [(1-3.5)^2 / 3.5] + [(9-6.5)^2 / 6.5] + [(6-3.5)^2 / 3.5] + [(4-6.5)^2 / 6.5]$
$= \Sigma [(-2.5)^2 / 3.5] + [(2.5)^2 / 6.5] + [(2.5)^2 / 3.5] + [(-2.5)^2 / 6.5]$
$= \Sigma [(6.25 / 3.5) + (6.25 / 6.5) + (6.25 / 3.5) + (6.25 / 6.5)]$
$= \Sigma [1.79 + 0.96 + 1.79 + 0.96]$
$= 5.50$

Step 5: Decide whether to reject the null hypothesis.

The chi-square statistic for the sample of 5.50 is more extreme than the cutoff sample chi-square of 3.841. Therefore, the psychologists will reject the null hypothesis and conclude that there is an association between using assertiveness as the primary method of conflict resolution as opposed to using one of the other three methods.

(b) $\Phi = \sqrt{\chi^2 / N} = \sqrt{5.50/20} = \sqrt{0.28} = 0.52$, a large effect size.

4. The appropriate test would be a <u>chi-square test for goodness of fit</u>.
Steps of Hypothesis Testing
Step 1: Restate the question as a research hypothesis and a null hypothesis about the populations.
Population 1: The population of students whose attentiveness is like those rated by their teachers.
Population 2: The population of students whose attentiveness is equally distributed among the three categories.

Research hypothesis: The distributions of students across categories of attentiveness in the two populations are different.
Null hypothesis: The distributions of students across categories of attentiveness in the two populations are no different.

Step 2: Determine the characteristics of the comparison distribution.
Since the teachers placed students in three categories based on attentiveness, the comparison distribution is a chi-square distribution with 2 degrees of freedom ($df = N_{categories} - 1 = 3 - 1 = 2$).

Step 3: Determine the cutoff sample score on the comparison distribution at which the null hypothesis should be rejected.
At the .05 level of significance, the cutoff sample chi-square with 2 degrees of freedom is 5.992.

Step 4: Determine the sample's score on the comparison distribution.
Applying the formula for chi-square yields
$$\chi^2 = \Sigma [(O - E)^2 / E]$$
$$= \Sigma [(16 - 20)^2 / 20] + [(24 - 20)^2 / 20] + [(20 - 20)^2 / 20]$$
$$= \Sigma [(-4)^2 / 20] + [(4)^2 / 20] + [(0)^2 / 20]$$
$$= \Sigma [(16 / 20) + (16 / 20) + (0 / 20)$$
$$= \Sigma [0.80 + 0.80 + 0.00]$$
$$= 1.60$$

Step 5: Decide whether to reject the null hypothesis.
The chi-square statistic for the sample of 1.60 is not more extreme than the cutoff sample chi-square of 5.992. Therefore, the psychologists cannot reject the null hypothesis and must state that their results are inconclusive. The results do not indicate that the distribution of students across categories of attentiveness is different from the distribution that would be expected by chance.

5. The appropriate test would be a <u>chi-square test for independence</u>.
Steps of Hypothesis Testing
Step 1: Restate the question as a research hypothesis and a null hypothesis about the populations.
Population 1: Students whose attentiveness depends on age.
Population 2: Students for whom attentiveness is independent of age.

Research hypothesis: The attentiveness of older students is different from the attentiveness of younger students.
Null hypothesis: The attentiveness of older students is no different from the attentiveness of younger students.

Step 2: Determine the characteristics of the comparison distribution.
Since the psychologists have identified groups of older and younger students based on one of three levels of attentiveness, the comparison distribution is a chi-square distribution with 2 degrees of freedom; $df = (N_{Rows} - 1)(N_{Columns} - 1) = (2 - 1)(3 - 1) = (1)(2) = 2$.

Step 3: Determine the cutoff sample score on the comparison distribution at which the null hypothesis should be rejected.
At the .05 level of significance, the cutoff sample chi-square with 2 degrees of freedom is 5.992.

Step 4: Determine the sample's score on the comparison distribution.
Applying the formula for chi-square yields

$$\chi^2 = \Sigma\,[(O-E)^2 / E]$$
$$= \Sigma\,[(9-8)^2 / 8] + [(14-12)^2 / 12] + [(7-10)^2 / 10] + [(7-8)^2 / 8] + [(10-12)^2 / 12]$$
$$\quad + [(13-10)^2 / 10]$$
$$= \Sigma\,[(1)^2 / 8] + [(2)^2 / 12] + [(-3)^2 / 10] + [(-1)^2 / 8] + [(-2)^2 / 12] + [(3)^2 / 10]$$
$$= \Sigma\,[(1/8) + (4/12) + (9/10) + (1/8) + (4/12) + (9/10)]$$
$$= \Sigma\,[0.13 + 0.33 + 0.90 + 0.13 + 0.33 + 0.90]$$
$$= 2.72$$

Step 5: Decide whether to reject the null hypothesis.
The chi-square statistic for the sample of 2.72 is not more extreme than the cutoff sample chi-square of 5.992. Therefore, the psychologists cannot reject the null hypothesis and must state that the results are inconclusive regarding the association of age and attentiveness.

(b) Cramer's $\Phi = \sqrt{\chi^2 / (N) * (df_{Smaller})} = \sqrt{2.72/(60)*(1)} = \sqrt{2.72/60} = \sqrt{.05} = .21$, a small to medium effect size.

6.

Study	N	Chi-square	Design	Effect Size
(a)	60	12.00	2 x 2	0.45
(b)	80	12.00	2 x 4	0.39
(c)	60	12.00	3 x 3	0.32
(d)	80	12.00	2 x 2	0.39
(e)	120	12.00	2 x 2	0.32

7.

Study	Predicted Effect Size	Design	N	Power
(a)	Medium	2 x 2	50	.56
(b)	Large	2 x 4	50	.86
(c)	Small	3 x 3	100	.11
(d)	Medium	2 x 2	100	.85
(e)	Medium	2 x 4	200	.96

8.

Study	Predicted Effect Size	Design	N
(a)	Medium	2 x 3	107
(b)	Large	2 x 4	44
(c)	Small	3 x 3	1,194
(d)	Large	2 x 5	48
(e)	Large	3 x 3	48

Chapter 14

Completion Items:

1. parametric tests	6. nonparametric tests
2. data transformation	7. distribution-free tests
3. square-root transformation	8. computer-intensive methods
4. rank-order transformation	9. randomization tests
5. rank-order tests	

Multiple Choice Items:

1. B	5. B	9. D
2. D	6. D	10. A
3. C	7. C	11. D
4. B	8. B	

Problems

1.
(a) Skewed to the right
(b) Rectangular
(c) Bimodal
(d) Skewed to the right
(e) Skewed to the left

2.
Square roots

Study					
(a)	5.5	5.8	8.4	6.0	7.9
(d)	6.0	7.6	6.2	6.4	6.2
(e)	2.8	3.2	1.4	3.0	2.6

In each case, the distribution of scores appears more likely to have come from a normal distribution because the values of the outliers are more like the values of the other scores.

3.
The listing that follows includes the rank of score in the dataset followed by the raw score.
(a) 1-30, 2-34, 3-36, 4-62, 5-71
(b) 1-33, 2-34, 3-35, 4-36, 5-39
(c) 1-7, 2.5-8, 2.5-8, 4-10, 5-11, 6.5-12, 6.5-12, 8-14, 9-15
(d) 1-36, 2-38, 3-39, 4-41, 5-58
(e) 1-2, 2-7, 3-8, 4-9, 5-10

4.
(a) Both groups include potential outliers.
(b) Cutoff sample t, 10 df, $p < .05$, two-tailed = ±2.228. Training Group: $M = 17.00$, $S^2 = 12.80$; Lecture Group: $M = 13.00$, $S^2 = 8.00$; $S^2_{Pooled} = 10.40$; $S_{Difference} = 1.86$; $t = 2.15$; Do not reject the null hypothesis.
(c) Training Group: 3.32, 3.74, 3.87, 4.12, 4.00, 4.90; Lecture Group: 3.16, 4.00, 3.74, 3.46, 3.61, 4.24
Cutoff sample t, 10 df, $p < .05$, two-tailed = ±2.228. Training Group: $M = 3.99$, $S^2 = .27$; Lecture Group: $M = 3.70$, $S^2 = .15$; $S^2_{Pooled} = .21$; $S_{Difference} = .27$; $t = 1.09$; Do not reject the null hypothesis.
(d) Training Group: 8.5, 5.5, 7.0, 10.0, 8.5, 12.0; Lecture Group: 1.0, 3.0, 5.5, 2.0, 4.0, 11.0
Cutoff sample t, 10 df, $p < .05$, two-tailed = ±2.228. Training Group: $M = 8.58$, $S^2 = 5.14$; Lecture Group: $M = 4.42$, $S^2 = 12.84$; $S^2_{Pooled} = 8.99$; $S_{Difference} = 1.73$; $t = 2.41$; Reject the null hypothesis.
The rank-order transformation adjusted the potential outliers in each group so that the distributions more closely resembled normal distributions and the variances were more nearly equal.
Compare your explanation to the "sample answer to Set I Practice Problem 4(d).

5.
(a) The group rated before recess includes a potential outlier.
(b) Cutoff sample t, 8 df, $p < .05$, two-tailed = ±2.306. Before recess: $M = 5.80$, $S^2 = 6.20$; After recess: $M = 3.00$, $S^2 = 1.50$; $S^2_{Pooled} = 3.85$; $S_{Difference} = 1.24$; $t = 2.26$; Do not reject the null hypothesis.
(c) Before recess: 2.45, 2.00, 2.00, 2.24, 3.16; After recess: 1.41, 1.73, 1.73, 2.24, 1.41
Cutoff sample t, 8 df, $p < .05$, two-tailed = ±2.306. Before recess: $M = 2.37$, $S^2 = .23$; After recess: $M = 1.71$, $S^2 = .11$; $S^2_{Pooled} = .17$; $S_{Difference} = .26$; $t = 2.54$; Reject the null hypothesis.
(d) Before recess: 9.0, 5.5, 5.5, 7.5, 10.0; After recess: 1.5, 3.5, 3.5, 7.5, 1.5

Cutoff sample t, 8 df, $p < .05$, two-tailed $= \pm2.306$. Before recess: $M = 7.50$, $S^2 = 4.13$; After recess: $M = 3.50$, $S^2 = 6.00$; $S^2_{Pooled} = 5.06$; $S_{Difference} = 1.42$; $t = 2.81$; Reject the null hypothesis.

Both the square-root transformation and rank-order transformation adjusted the potential outliers in each group so that the distributions more closely resembled normal distributions and the variances were more nearly equal. Compare your explanation to the "sample answer to Set I Practice Problem 4(d).

6.

(a) The group learning the relaxation technique in the setting includes an outlier, and each of the other two groups includes one student with a relatively low score.

(b) Cutoff sample F 2, 12 df, $p < .05 = 3.89$. Counseling: $M = 26.20$, $S^2 = 11.20$; Relaxation: $M = 23.20$, $S^2 = 25.70$; Relaxation is setting: $M = 19.00$, $S^2 = 17.50$; $S^2_{Between} = 64.40$; $S^2_{Within} = 18.33$; $F = 3.07$; Do not reject the null hypothesis.

(c) Counseling: 5.48, 5.39, 4.90, 5.10, 4.69; Relaxation: 5.20, 5.00, 5.29, 4.47, 4.00; Relaxation in setting: 4.80, 4.47, 4.58, 4.36, 3.46. Cutoff sample F 2, 12 df, $p < .05 = 3.89$. Counseling: $M = 5.11$, $S^2 = .108$; Relaxation: $M = 4.79$, $S^2 = .296$; Relaxation is setting: $M = 4.33$, $S^2 = .263$; $S^2_{Between} = .760$; $S^2_{Within} = .222$; $F = 3.42$; Do not reject the null hypothesis.

(d) Counseling: 15.0, 14.0, 9.0, 11.0, 7.0; Relaxation: 12.0, 10.0, 13.0, 4.5, 2.0; Relaxation in setting: 8.0, 4.5, 6.0, 3.0, 1.0. Cutoff sample F 2, 12 df, $p < .05 = 3.89$. Counseling: $M = 11.20$, $S^2 = 11.20$; Relaxation: $M = 8.30$, $S^2 = 23.20$; Relaxation is setting: $M = 4.50$, $S^2 = 7.25$; $S^2_{Between} = 56.45$; $S^2_{Within} = 13.88$; $F = 4.07$; Reject the null hypothesis.

Inspection of the ranked data shows the influence of the two potential outliers in the dataset. Neither the analysis of the actual scores nor of the data following the square-root transformation was statistically significant. However, following the rank-order transformation, the distributions more closely resembled normal distributions and the analysis revealed the statistically significant difference indicated by the general consistency of the scores in the three groups. Compare your explanation to the "sample answer to Set I Practice Problem 6(d).

Chapter 15

Completion Items:

1. general linear model	8. reliability	15. hierarchical linear modeling	22. mediational analysis	29. analysis of covariance
2. partial correlation	9. test-retest reliability	16. factor analysis	23. structural equation modeling	30. covariate
3. holding constant*	10. split-half reliability	17. factor	24. fit index	31. adjusted means
4. partialing out*	11. Cronbach's alpha	18. factor loading	25. RMSEA	32. multivariate statistics
5. controlling for*	12. internal consistency reliability	19. path analysis	26. latent variable	33. multivariate analysis of variance
6. adjusting for*	13. interrater reliability	20. path	27. independent variable	34. multivariate analysis of covariance
7. partial correlation coefficient	14. multilevel modeling	21. path coefficient	28. dependent variable	

*In any order

Multiple Choice Items:

1. A	6. A	11. D	16. D	21. B
2. B	7. B	12. D	17. C	22. D
3. A	8. C	13. B	18. A	23. D
4. C	9. A	14. A	19. D	24. A
5. D	10. C	15. C	20. C	25. B

Problems:

1.
(a) Partial correlation
(b) Compare your explanation to the sample answer to Set I Practice Problem 1.
(c) Mediational analysis
(d) Compare your explanation to the sample answer to Set I Practice Problem 6.
(e) Path analysis
(f) Compare your explanation to the sample answer to Set I Practice Problem 5.
(g) Structural equation modeling
(h) Compare your explanation to the sample answer to Set I Practice Problem 7.

2.
(a) Factor analysis
(b) Compare your explanation to the sample answer to Set I Practice Problem 4.
(c) Test-retest, split-half, Cronbach's alpha
(d) Compare your explanation to the sample answer to Set I Practice Problem 2.

3.
(a) Teaching method
(b) Test anxiety

4.
(a) Analysis of covariance
(b) Compare your explanation to the sample answer to Set I Practice Problem 9.

5.
(a) Multivariate analysis of variance
(b) Multivariate analysis of covariance
(b) Compare your explanation to the sample answer to Set I Practice Problem 10.